Agriculture in New Jersey

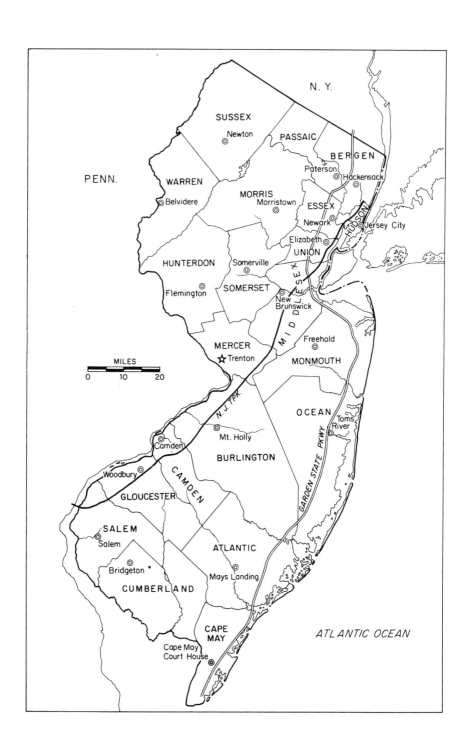

N. Y.

SUSSEX

Newton

PASSAIC

BERGEN

Paterson

Hackensack

PENN.

WARREN

Belvidere

MORRIS

Morristown

ESSEX

Newark

HUDSON

Jersey City

Elizabeth

UNION

HUNTERDON

Somerville

SOMERSET

MIDDLESEX

Flemington

New
Brunswick

MILES

0   10   20

Freehold

MERCER

Trenton

MONMOUTH

OCEAN

Toms
River

N. J. TPK.

Mt. Holly

GARDEN STATE PKWY

Camden

BURLINGTON

Woodbury

CAMDEN

GLOUCESTER

SALEM

Salem

ATLANTIC

Bridgeton

Mays Landing

CUMBERLAND

CAPE
MAY

ATLANTIC OCEAN

Cape May
Court House

Agriculture in New Jersey

A Three-Hundred-Year History

Hubert G. Schmidt

RUTGERS UNIVERSITY PRESS
New Brunswick, New Jersey

Other Books by Hubert G. Schmidt

Economic Assistance to West Berlin, 1949–1951
The First 250 Years of Hunterdon County (editor)
Food and Agriculture in West Germany, 1949–1951
George Washington's Map Maker: A Biography of Robert Erskine by
Albert H. Heusser (editor)
The Liberalization of West German Foreign Trade, 1949–1951
The Old Farm by Andrew D. Mellick, Jr. (editor)
Rural Hunterdon: An Agricultural History

Library of Congress Cataloging in Publication Data

Schmidt, Hubert Glasgow, 1905–
  Agriculture in New Jersey.

  Bibliography: p.
  1. Agriculture—New Jersey—History.
I. Title.
S451.N55S35   338.1'09749   73–5755
ISBN 0–8135–0756–1

To the memory of
HIRAM EDMUND DEATS
Farmer, scholar, philosopher, friend

Contents

List of Illustrations

Preface

Agriculture has been a dominant part of the economy of New Jersey during much of the three centuries since the first permanent settlements in the area, and has remained of some consequence even in the age of large-scale industry. As a province of the British Empire, New Jersey was known as one of the Bread Colonies, notable for its production and export of bread grains. In later times, someone called it the Garden State, a name which clings even today. Though agriculture in New Jersey has not been spectacularly different from that of the Northeast generally, and though it has been comparatively only a small sector of that of America as a whole, its development has been most interesting. Over a long period, succeeding generations of farmers have striven mightily to wrest a living from varied soils of New Jersey. In doing so, they have had the problems and frustrations, the compensations and rewards of farmers generally, besides some that were unique.

The predominance of agriculture in this area antedated the coming of the white man. For countless years Indian women and children grew in their tiny fields crops which in their economy were probably more important and, without a doubt, more certain than the game which their braves found in the surrounding forest. The European colonists who took over and enlarged the Indian fields were even more dependent on the soil. The Dutch and the Swedes who settled small areas in New Jersey prior to and immediately after the English conquest of 1664 became farmers after the failure of their fur trade. The New Englanders and the immigrants from the British Isles who together rapidly settled northeast New Jersey and the English and Irish Quakers who migrated slightly thereafter to their new haven in southwest New Jersey were farmers when they came or were forced to become farmers. This was likewise true of the Germans who followed up the Raritan into the interior or boiled over from the Pennsylvania settlements. As the two giant real estate ventures of East New Jersey and West New Jersey developed, Europeans scattered slowly throughout them. A century after the British arrival, pioneers were still carving farms from the scrub of Burlington County and the forests of Sussex.

The only occupation open to most New Jersey settlers was the exploitation of the soil. The owners of land had the highest mark of status and were veritable princes of their own possessions, be they large or small; and even tenants and squatters were freer of restrictions than the peasants of Europe. In general, land was easily acquired. A largely self-sufficient and almost invariably extensive and wasteful agriculture became the chief occupation of the great majority of the people. As an exporter of farm produce and a heavy purchaser of British manufactured goods, New Jersey fitted fairly well the mercantilist concepts regarding the proper place of a colony as a part of a self-sufficient empire.

After the Revolution, agriculture still dominated the economy of New Jersey. It was an agriculture so traditional and so static that adjustments to new conditions came only slowly and piecemeal. But in the early nineteenth century the pace of change accelerated. The same Industrial Revolution which gradually brought in the factory system provided farmers with horse-drawn laborsaving machinery and other equipment and with new markets in the growing industrial centers. But the competition of farmers farther west who had smaller investments and lower overhead costs made it necessary for those of New Jersey to revise their standards, to conserve and enrich their soils, to acquire and develop crops and livestock of merit, and to commercialize their production. In the latter part of the nineteenth century and the early part of the twentieth, agriculture seemingly reached a period of maturity, of nearly complete adjustment to new conditions.

But like the older pattern, this one also dissolved. In the period after World War I, New Jersey agriculture, in order to hold its own, was forced to adjust to many sweeping changes in technology, to a great increase in individual productivity made possible by new machines and by new sources of power, to the encroachment of other sectors of the economy of the area, and to regional competition more pervasive than ever before. Inevitably, the farmer became efficient, learned to specialize according to market demand, and became as commercial in viewpoint as a merchant or a manufacturer. Farming in New Jersey, during much of its history, had been a way of life. Now, willy-nilly, it had become a business. Unfortunately, in recent decades the farmers of New Jersey have found themselves in a plight for which no experience prepared them. The relentless push of urban and suburban development absorbed greater and greater areas of farmland. At the same time, one sector after another of New Jersey agriculture found itself in a relentless price squeeze. At present, it is clear that only very effective public policy can arrest further decline in farm population and farmland.

Though it seems rather obvious that knowledge of agricultural history in general benefits from the writing of regional studies, there are not many such studies. Why this is true is not clear. Certainly it is not because of a dearth of qualified scholars in the field of agricultural history. Nor is it because of the lack of an abundance of historical sources. It was my own continuing involvement with New Jersey history that eventually led to a resolve to provide a history of the state's agriculture. For much of its long history, the majority of the people of New Jersey were concerned directly or indirectly with agriculture. Yet viewers of the farming scene had always limited their observations as to time, breadth of coverage, or completeness of view. But the task of writing a complete and, I hope, definitive history of New Jersey agriculture soon proved a far greater task than I had expected. One cause has been the embarrassment of riches as to sources. Another has been the long sweep of history involved. But since one does not count costs in a labor of love, I have no regrets.

The story narrated in this book is that of New Jersey agriculture, but it is obvious that farming practices have been continuously conditioned by changes in other segments of the economy. Improvements in transportation through the years brought markets ever closer to the New Jersey farmer, while, on the other hand, railroad connections between this area's natural markets and the farms of the West created ruinous rivalry as regards one product after another. The scarcity and relative dearness of labor often placed bounds on productivity, for a long time made agricultural practices more extensive and wasteful than otherwise might have been the case, and eventually led to the development of laborsaving devices. Shortage of money capital hampered farmers on occasion and resulted in a high degree of financial mortality during hard times. These and other pertinent background factors will be kept in mind, but the focus of attention in this account will be on the farmer himself.

Many persons have given me scholarly aid and assistance. In particular, I wish to thank Phillip Alampi, Dr. John E. Brush, Dr. Paul W. Gates, Dr. Rodney C. Loehr, Dr. Wayne D. Rasmussen, Dr. Richard M. Huber, Van Wie Ingham, Dr. Wheaton J. Lane, Dr. John M. Hunter, Robert D. McMillen, Dr. William L. Park, Dr. Morris S. Fabian, Donald A. Sinclair, and Berthold A. Sorby. Any inadequacies in the final draft are, of course, my responsibility.

Agriculture in New Jersey

1

Genesis

1

Background Factors and Conditions

New Jersey contains within its boundaries a land area of approximately 7,500 square miles (4.8 million acres) and about 700 square miles of water, interior and coastal. In length it is some 166 miles, and in width it varies from a little over 33 miles to nearly twice that.[1] Though a relatively small area, considerable differences in climate, elevation, topography, and soils occur within its borders. These variations in the physical environment have been among the reasons for a degree of agricultural diversity during the more than three centuries since the white man came. In particular, they account for the kinds of crops that have been grown and the kinds of livestock that have been favored from region to region.

Climate ranks high among the factors that draw human beings to a region or discourage them from coming. The New Jersey climate is temperate in the usual understanding of the word, with, of course, considerable seasonal differences. It is controlled almost entirely by the continual influx of air masses from distant regions; the nearby ocean has much less effect than does the huge continent to the north and west. During the past three centuries there have been no drastic changes in the weather patterns. The belief that winters were somewhat more severe during the colonial period perhaps has some validity, but the contention that summers were hotter on the average is doubtful.

The climate, therefore, has been a favorable one for most Temperate Zone crops. The vegetative growing season ranges from 216 days in the far northwest to 255 days in the extreme southeast, and the farms of the greater part of the state enjoy at least 240 days. The frost-free period averages approximately 70 days less than the growing season in any part of the state. Two particular hazards to agriculture are the winterkill of crops and black frosts in spring and fall. The former is usually the result of the heaving of the soil around plants during alternate freezing and thawing, which tend to break their roots. A common cause of destructive frosts in some areas, spring and fall, is lack of air movement during

5

morning hours. In others, water-retentive soils freeze deeply in winter and are slow to thaw out in spring, with the result that farmers are plagued by heavy spring frosts.

Rainfall in New Jersey totals between 40 and 50 inches in most years. In general, the high elevations receive more than the low ones. Though droughts and rainy seasons are common enough as a result of changing wind patterns farther west, the average precipitation of the various months of the year is surprisingly uniform. Unfortunately, rainfall intensity is sometimes high and long in duration, and shock rains make erosion a serious problem. On the average from 30 to 35 thunderstorms a year are recorded at most of the weather stations of the state. New Jersey occasionally feels the effect of a tropical hurricane but seldom its full fury. Winter precipitation often comes in the form of snow, especially in the high areas. Probably the old-timers are right when they maintain that snowstorms are not what they used to be, but blizzards do occur on occasion.

It is understandable that the climate of New Jersey seemed severe to its first European settlers. For one thing, the summers are hotter and the winters are colder than those of most of Western Europe. The native-born to this day tell visitors that if they don't like the weather in New Jersey they have only to "wait five minutes." And it *is* changeable from day to day and hour to hour. On the whole, however, the climate is relatively mild, though invigorating, and quite favorable to man's economic activities.[2] The firstcomers here found that the Indians throve in this climate, and European immigrants generally learned to adjust to it. The first letters sent back to England by the Capner family and their friends, who settled in Hunterdon County during the two decades after the American Revolution, voice their complaints about the hot, clammy days of summer, frightening thunderstorms, soil-washing showers, severe cold, drifting snow, and freezing rivers. Later letters by the same persons hardly mention the weather at all.[3]

There was, of course, a time when man would not have found New Jersey habitable. Fairly late in its geological history, but nevertheless a long time ago, the northern part of present New Jersey was covered by glaciers at least three times. One of these ice sheets, perhaps the earliest, was halted just short of the narrow waist of the state, and another somewhat to the north. Erosion has removed most of the evidence, but the last glacier, known as the Wisconsin, has left its traces in many areas. Its terminal moraine crosses the state in a modified curve from Belvidere through Hackettstown, Dover, Morristown, and Plainfield, to Perth Amboy. A mile in width, and thickest in the valleys and thinnest on the ridges, it extends from the Delaware River, where it is 225 feet above sea level, to the area of Lake Hopatcong at 1,200 feet, and eventually down to sea level at its eastern end. The Delaware River on one end of the New Jersey portion and the Hudson on the other end eventually cut through the moraine, as did the Pequest River near Great Meadows, the Musconetcong below Lake Hopatcong, and the Passaic near Little Falls.

The moraine of the Wisconsin ice sheet, by obstructing valleys, created natural lakes in North Jersey and added to the size of others already there. One of the largest of these was in the valley of the upper Passaic. After the retreat of the ice, the water broke through the moraine and through the Watchung mountain barrier at Paterson. Today all that remains of Lake Passaic is the Great Swamp at Morristown. A somewhat similar development on a smaller scale occurred in the Hackensack Valley. At various times the glacier paused in its withdrawal, and on occasion it was pushed forward a bit, as attested by recessional moraines in a number of places.

The geological history of New Jersey, of which the Ice Age was only a late chapter, is a fascinating one. In the nature of the case, however, we are concerned with it here only as it helps to explain present-day topographical features and the distribution of soil types. It is an interesting but understandable fact that geological, physiographic, and soil maps of the state show at least some of the same district boundaries.

Elevations in New Jersey vary from sea level at the Atlantic shore to 1,803 feet at High Point in the extreme north. As to topography, the state shares in four physiographic areas or geographical provinces. Other designations have been applied on occasion to these natural divisions, but the accepted names among geographers and geologists at present are, from south to north, as follows: the Coastal Plain, the Piedmont Plain (or Triassic Lowlands), the Highlands (or Piedmont Upland), and the Appalachian Valley and Ridge Province. Within each of these belts there is considerable variation in relief.

The soils of these areas are as different as the topography. Intensive field studies show that New Jersey has within its rather small confines soil types running the gamut from sterile sands to stiff clays. Soil layers range from deep to shallow, from clear to extremely stony, from droughty to moisture-retentive, and from naturally sweet to naturally sour. Even within the major physical regions, variations are considerable. Natural forces have often so dispersed and mixed soil types that detailed description of their locations is difficult. Soil classifications early in the present century contained 172 types for the state. By the present classification there are 28 types, with numerous subtypes.

Except for the glacial moraines and recent flood plains, the Coastal Plain is, geologically speaking, the youngest part of New Jersey. Unlike the remainder of the state, it has no solid rock near the surface. During

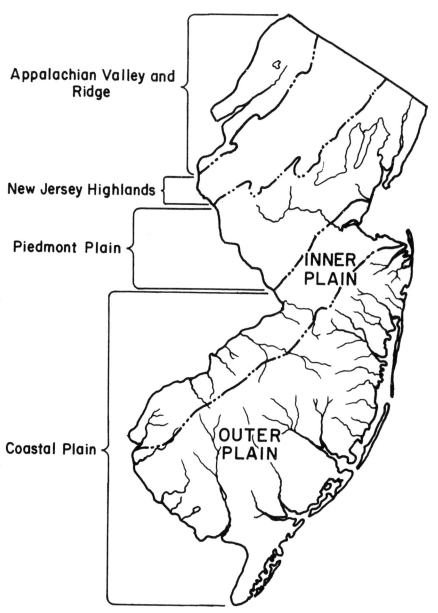

Appalachian Valley and
Ridge

New Jersey Highlands

Piedmont Plain

INNER
PLAIN

Coastal Plain

OUTER
PLAIN

Physiographic Provinces of New Jersey. Based upon a map by William
Goodwin of the Geography Department of Rutgers University.

periods of submergence under the ocean, bodies of such unconsolidated materials as sand, gravel, clay, and silt were deposited by stream action. Also, greensand marl or glauconite was laid down by tidal action during periods of greatest submergence. Since this last material is to be found only in the northwestern part of the Coastal Plain, it is presumed that the southeastern part was laid down at a later time when the water depth was much less. The present shoreline is not a permanent one. In fact, the Coastal Plain has been losing land to the sea in considerable amounts during recent millennia. This may be in part due to the sinking of the land, but the most important cause is the melting of the polar ice cap and the consequent rising of ocean levels.

The Coastal Plain contains approximately three-fifths of the land area of New Jersey, everything southeast of a line drawn across the narrow waist of the state from Trenton through New Brunswick and extending to include a narrow corridor north of Raritan Bay. The region contains the southern parts of Mercer and Middlesex counties and all of the nine counties lying south of them. More than half of the Coastal Plain in New Jersey is less than 100 feet in elevation, but the central portion rises to as much as 400 feet. This central ridge, unknown in other parts of the Atlantic Coastal Plain, extends down the full length of the New Jersey portion of that plain, dividing it into what are designated as the Outer and Inner coastal plains.

The Outer Coastal Plain, much the larger of the two sections, has more sand and less clay in its topmost formation than the Inner Coastal Plain. The former is drained by a series of tidal rivers and creeks emptying into Delaware Bay in the south and the Atlantic Ocean in the east. Best known of these and most important from the standpoint of acreage drained are the Maurice, the Great Egg Harbor, the Mullica, Toms, and the Navesink rivers. Behind the sandy coast of the Outer Coastal Plain and extending inland near the bays and the tidal portions of the rivers are extensive tidal marshes. Fresh-water marshes are found at slightly higher elevations where flat lands have an intricate drainage pattern. But there are also considerable areas of gently rolling land, usually of somewhat higher elevation. Many sections of low fertility here are covered with scrub pine and scrub oak and together constitute New Jersey's remarkable Pine Barrens. More than one-third of New Jersey's forested area today is found in the Outer Coastal Plain.

The Inner Coastal Plain is drained to the west by a series of streams from Salem Creek in the south to Assunpink Creek at the Trenton level, all flowing into the Delaware. The largest of these streams is the Rancocas. At the north, the Inner Coastal Plain is drained by South River, Lawrence Brook, and the Millstone River, all tributaries of the Raritan. The hilliest portion of this region is found where the ridge that divides it from the Outer Coastal Plain has been cut up by stream erosion. There were once sizable forests here of a type much superior to those of the Barrens, at least from the point of view of man's uses.

Soil researchers have bisected the Coastal Plain down its length into two zones on the basis of their origin, chemical composition, color, texture, drainage, and other characteristics. The dividing line, unfortunately, does not correspond closely with that between the Outer and Inner Coastal Plain. The eastern zone for soils, somewhat larger in area than the western, has roughly half of the width of the state at the south, two-thirds at a point halfway up the zone, and only an irregular strip following the coast at the north. This zone includes all of Cape May County, half of Cumberland, all of Atlantic, bits of Gloucester and nearly half of Camden, nearly two-thirds of Burlington, nearly all of Ocean, and a coastal belt in Monmouth. The soils of this zone are generally sandy, and because of the flatness of the land they are often poorly drained. On the other hand, where the land has better drainage the soils are quite droughty.

Least fertile of the soils in this eastern zone are the white sands of the Lakewood series. These prevail generally in the Pine Barrens. Soil subtypes designated as the Hammonton and Cape May phases of the Sassafras series are found in large areas of this zone, and especially in the north and the south. They are less fertile and sandier than the best Sassafras soils, but under natural conditions they grow far better timber than the Lakewood soils. Where cleared, they produce large vegetable crops when supplied with sufficient nutriments and moisture. A third soil series of the zone, much smaller in acreage but still important, is the Saint Johns. Though they have a sandy base, so much organic matter has been added that they are black in color and retentive of moisture. Where well drained by nature or by man, they are soils par excellence for cranberries and blueberries.

The soil zone to the west and north, constituting the remainder of the Coastal Plain, is quite in contrast with the one just described, particularly as to fertility. Its area includes nearly half of Cumberland County, all of Salem, most of Gloucester, over half of Camden, about one-third of Burlington, most of Monmouth, and the southern part of Middlesex. The soils here are sandy loams and loams, and are almost entirely free of stones and gravel. They respond well to heavy use of fertilizer and to irrigation; however, erosion has been a constant problem since early times, even though the land is relatively level.

The brown Sassafras soils of this zone have far more loam and less sand than those of the same general type nearer the coast. Found mainly on the level lands of the southern parts of Middlesex and Mercer counties, they are mellow and well drained. Considered one of the most fertile areas

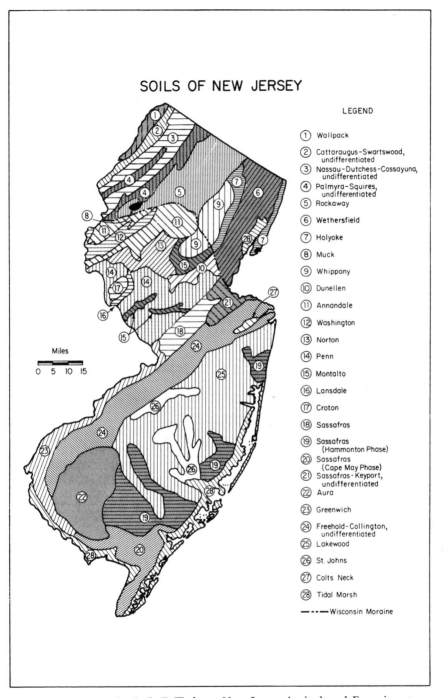

SOILS OF NEW JERSEY

LEGEND

① Wallpack
② Cattaraugus-Swartswood, undifferentiated
③ Nassau-Dutchess-Cossayuna, undifferentiated
④ Palmyra-Squires, undifferentiated
⑤ Rockaway
⑥ Wethersfield
⑦ Holyoke
⑧ Muck
⑨ Whippany
⑩ Dunellen
⑪ Annandale
⑫ Washington
⑬ Norton
⑭ Penn
⑮ Montalto
⑯ Lansdale
⑰ Croton
⑱ Sassafras
⑲ Sassafras (Hammonton Phase)
⑳ Sassafras (Cape May Phase)
㉑ Sassafras-Keyport, undifferentiated
㉒ Aura
㉓ Greenwich
㉔ Freehold-Collington, undifferentiated
㉕ Lakewood
㉖ St. Johns
㉗ Colts Neck
㉘ Tidal Marsh
– · · – Wisconsin Moraine

Miles
0 5 10 15

Based upon map by J. C. F. Tedrow, New Jersey Agricultural Experiment Station. (*Charlotte Carlson*.)

of the nation, this Sassafras soil belt gives large yields of grain, vegetables, fruit, potatoes, and hay crops. It has been one of the most productive sections of New Jersey since colonial times.

Akin to the Sassafras soils are those known as the Freehold Collington. The most extensive soils of the zone, they are found in a wide belt extending from near Delaware Bay to Raritan Bay. These are deep, mellow soils, basically of sand mixed with clay and silt. A universal characteristic is the presence of the mineral glauconite, generally known as greensand marl, sometimes prevalent enough to give the brown soils, especially the subsoils, a greenish cast. Except where there is considerable clay, the soils of this series are well drained. Most of them are nearly as productive as the best Sassafras soils. This area, too, has been well known as a rich agricultural section since frontier days. Some relatively small areas, however, are barren because of "poison soils" containing chemicals unfriendly to plant growth.

A soil type differentiated from the Freehold Collington is that known as the Aura, found for the most part in the southern part of the area, in Cumberland, Salem, and Gloucester counties. It has little or no greensand marl, and beneath a surface layer 2 or 3 feet in depth, consisting of silt and sand, there is a hardpan of red clay with a considerable admixture of sand. Though less productive than the soils of the two types last described, the Aura soils must still be classed as good lands for general farming, as well as for the growing of vegetables and fruit.

Soils classified under the name of Greenwich follow Delaware Bay and the Delaware River in a narrow belt the full length of this soil zone. The Greenwich soils are sandier than the Aura, but under modern methods give larger returns of vegetables and fruit. Peaches, in particular, thrive in these soils.

Another soil type, locally important but not extensive, is the Colts Neck series in Monmouth County. Basically of red sand, they vary in fertility and water-retentiveness with the degree of admixture of clay.

Contiguous to the Coastal Plain on its north and west, and extending in a belt just above the waist of the state, is the Piedmont Plain, often called the Triassic Lowland from the age of the underlying rocks. Containing about one-fifth of the state, this natural region occupies the northern parts of Mercer and Middlesex counties, large portions of Hunterdon, Somerset, Morris, and Passaic, and all of Union, Essex, Hudson, and Bergen. Though its soils are not as rich as those in some other areas, it early became agriculturally important, and today it has much of the population and industry of the state. Over most of its area it varies in elevation from sea level at Newark Bay to 400 feet, and its surface is for the most part one of gently rounded hills and wide, flat valleys. But rising above this general level are the Watchung Mountains, which attain a height of nearly 900 feet near Paterson, the famous Palisades, horseshoe-shaped Cushetunk Mountain, Round Mountain, and Sourland Mountain. These, and many smaller outcroppings, resulted from lava being forced through cracks and ruptures in the Triassic sedimentary series during three distinct episodes in geological history.

The Piedmont Plain in general is of sedimentary origin. Much of the area has thick underlying strata of sandstone and conglomerate. Once in flat layers, these strata now dip to the northwest. The higher areas, on the other hand, have very resistant igneous rocks as their foundation. The geological history of the region has resulted in a topography that is in no way very startling today; however, the various natural forces have left interesting evidence of many kinds. Semiarid conditions over a long period supposedly account for the predominant red color of the shales and of the soils which developed from them. A foreign traveler in 1783 wrote of "the red soil of New Jersey, known generally by that name in America." [4] The desert epoch was followed by one of great rainfall, during which shallow lakes and ponds were created, only to be filled eventually with silt. The heights resisted nature's leveling tendencies to a greater degree, but even there the soils that were created by alternating extremes of weather were eventually eroded and scattered to some extent.

The Piedmont Plain in New Jersey is part of the soil belt known as the Trap and Red Sandstone and Shale Belt, or simply as the Sandstone and Shale Belt. The sedimentary rocks of which this area was once entirely composed have decayed into soils in which clay and sand occur in various combinations, and which often have become loams through the admixture of decaying organic matter. The stony ridges of traprock, which are the heritage of volcanic action, have a soil covering entirely different in kind. The action of running water in both the glaciated northern section of this soil zone and in the southern unglaciated part has resulted in considerable transference of soils from some areas to others as silt. All of the soils of this zone are easily eroded, and there have been tremendous soil losses since the clearing of the forest cover.

The soils of the unglaciated southern part of the Piedmont Plain, except for the volcanic ridges, vary as greatly as the sedimentary rocks to which they owe their origin. Most extensive, and perhaps best known because of their Indian red color, are those of the Penn series, derived from red sandstone and shales. They cover large parts of Hunterdon and Somerset counties and the northern parts of Middlesex and Mercer, and include silt loams, gravelly loams, and shaley loams, in decreasing order of importance both as to extent and as to agricultural excellence. All are highly erodible by nature, and none stands dry seasons well. Nevertheless, the "red shell" lands, as they were known during most of their history, have been sturdy soils, with an ability to withstand a great deal of abuse, and they have been of considerable agricultural importance for three centuries.

A number of other Piedmont Plain soil types of local significance are found south of the Wisconsin glacial moraine. The Norton soils in the northern parts of Hunterdon and Somerset originated in part from drift deposited by earlier glaciers than the Wisconsin. Since this drift contained much red shale, the Norton series is akin to the Penn. The excellent Dunellen soils, largely silt from the Wisconsin moraine and found in the valleys southwest of it, are likewise similar to the Penn series. This is also true of the brownish Lansdale soils, which are found in narrow belts surrounding the Hunterdon Plateau in west Hunterdon and Sourland Mountain in the area in which Hunterdon, Somerset, and Mercer meet. Not very extensive in area, the Lansdale soils are nevertheless of historical interest because they were once considered superior to all others for the growing of peaches.

Atop the Hunterdon Plateau itself are the Croton soils, grayish silt loams underlain with compact clay. They have resulted from the decomposition of argillite, known locally as "blue jingler," a claystone that was used extensively by Indian artisans for making tools and weapons. The Croton is a very wet soil, and is not very productive even when drained by man's efforts. On Sourland Mountain, Round Mountain, Cushetunk Mountain, Rocky Hill, the Watchungs, the Palisades, and other formations resulting from lava flows, are the Montalto soils. Brownish, with a yellowish-red subsoil, they are composed of distintegrated traprock and humus. Any displacements of these soils have been the result of water erosion rather than glacial action. Except where they contain too large an amount of "mountain grit," they are used for general farming and fruit raising. The rough areas have natural forests of no great commercial value, and today private houses are often built among the trees.

The most common soils of the Piedmont Plain northeast of the Wisconsin moraine are those of the Wethersfield series, derived largely from the decomposition of red shale glacial drift. Less extensive and more scattered are the Holyoke soils found in the glaciated parts of the traprock areas. By nature, the latter are rather close to the Montalto soils on the ridges above them. A soil of local importance, found on the bottom of the ancient lake of the Passaic Valley, is the Whippany, which has resulted from the deposit of sediment. It is poorly drained and not very productive.

The drainage pattern of the New Jersey portion of the Piedmont Plain is a complicated one. Almost a plain when it was pushed above the sea the last time, its streams for a time were sluggish and meandering. But since the erodibility of the rocks, both sedimentary and igneous, varies considerably, stream channels have changed markedly over the millennia.

Glacial action and the continued uplift of the mountain area to the north also have had their effect. Except for some minor creeks flowing into the Delaware, the Piedmont drains east and south into Raritan Bay and New York Bay.

The Raritan River and its three important tributaries, the Millstone River, the South Branch, and the North Branch, take care of most of the Piedmont Plain. The Millstone flows nearly due north out of the upper portion of the Inner Coastal Plain to join the lower Raritan. In all probability, the Raritan at one time flowed across the upper part of the Coastal Plain and finally out to the ocean near Toms River. That the change to its present course has occurred attests to the general flatness of the terrain in the narrow waist of the state. The Piedmont portions of the South Branch and North Branch run almost counter to the Millstone. After breaking out of the Highlands to the north, they flow south and east and eventually join to form the Raritan.

The coastal parts of the New Jersey Piedmont Plain north of the Raritan are drained by small streams, including the Rahway and Elizabeth rivers. The Passaic, which even more than the Raritan is swollen by waters from Highland tributaries, is the main stream here. This river, blocked from earlier access to the sea, finally makes a spectacular break through the Watchung mountain barrier at Paterson. Old Lake Passaic was created or made larger by the damming of this passage by ice and sediment of the Wisconsin glacier, later being drained as the river cut through the obstruction. The Ramapo, a tributary of the Passaic, and the Hackensack, which parallels the Hudson, drain the most northerly portions of the Piedmont Plain and the adjacent Highlands.

Only 8 miles wide at the Delaware River end, and seldom more than 20 miles in width, the Highlands (formerly called the Piedmont Upland) constitute a physical belt somewhat narrower than the Piedmont Plain. Like the latter, it extends in a northeast-southwest direction, and contains about 900 square miles, or approximately one-eighth of the state. Sections of southern Warren and Sussex counties and of northern Hunterdon, Morris, and Passaic are included. This belt, of course, extends into New York on the north and into Pennsylvania beyond the Delaware.

The rock formations here are older than those of the Piedmont Plain. Originally laid down as sediment at the bottom of the large bodies of water that covered the whole area on several occasions, in time they became shales, slates, limestones, sandstones, and conglomerates. Some of them, subjected to great pressure and to the intense heat of invasive granites in the form of lava, were literally metamorphosed into much harder rocks, principally gneiss. A shifting of earth masses later contorted and folded the formations so that a series of deep faults separated by high ridges resulted. When the area was again under the ocean, sediments largely of limestone origin filled the faults and again leveled the surface. But again the ocean floor rose and became a plateau. During the next stage of development, flowing water cut savagely into the newer stones, eventually carving deep valleys down each of the former faults.

These valleys run in general from northeast to southwest. Between them are broad ridges with rounded or flat tops, rising in places to elevations of 800 to 1,400 feet. These are, of course, composed of older and harder rocks, formations that have resisted more successfully the onslaughts of the elements. The first ridge, in general a wide one, consists of the Ramapo Mountains at the New York state line and the less rugged Passaic Mountains farther south and west. The second, though it bears no single name, is remarkable in that it is continuous from beyond the New York state line to the Delaware River. Nearly 1,500 feet high at the New York line, it gradually declines to 800 at the Delaware. With only four convenient passes, all above 900 feet, this ridge was a barrier to early settlement from the south and east. The Longwood-German Valley separates it from the third ridge, which begins in the south with Schooley's Mountain. Beyond the Musconetcong Valley are shorter and more broken ridges.

The diversity of soils in the Highlands is a result of the considerable differences in the rocks from which they developed, and, to a somewhat lesser degree, of glacial action and erosion. Only the southwestern one-third lies south of the Wisconsin terminal moraine. The higher lands of this zone, both north and south of the moraine, are mostly covered with soils derived from their granite and gneiss. Universally brownish, they vary from loams to gravelly loams, and very often they are stony because water and wind have removed their finer elements.

Formerly the soils of the ridges were designated Chester soils and those of the uplands to the north Gloucester soils. Today, however, those to the south of the Wisconsin moraine are called the Annandale and those to the north, on both ridges and upland, the Rockaway. The Annandale soils have resulted mostly from earlier glaciations than the Wisconsin and from the long period of weathering since. The Rockaway soils have evolved from the glacial till left by the Wisconsin glacier. Both are well-drained, fairly strong soils, and support general farming in those sections where the terrain and the stoniness of the ground permit. Considerable areas are heavily forested.

The limestone soils of the valleys are considered the best in northern New Jersey. Originating from glacial drift which has had a long weathering process, they range from a mellow brown loam to a heavier silt loam, also brown. Soils of the former type are known as Washington soils, and those of the latter as Hagerstown. These are found in scattered areas at various heights, but usually near streams, most extensively along the

Delaware between Phillipsburg and Belvidere and in the valleys of the Musconetcong and other tributaries of the Delaware.

Had there been no Ice Age, the drainage of this physiographic area might have been simple, since each of the streams could have continued to follow the grain of the land, flowing either to the southwest or the northeast. This is still the pattern south of the Wisconsin terminal moraine, and to some extent north of it. The North Branch and the South Branch of the Raritan flow southward until they eventually come to the end of their barrier ridges and come out into the Piedmont Plain below. The Musconetcong, Pohatcong, and Pequest rivers follow their deep valleys until they reach the Delaware. Smaller streams, which flow northeastward, occupy the same geological troughs further north. But as a result of the damming effect of the glaciers at various times, the Whippany, the Rockaway, the Pequannock, and the Wanaque rivers have broken through the wide eastern mountain belt to join their waters with the Passaic. New Jersey's natural lakes are rock-basin lakes, often enlarged as a result of the damming of their Highland stream outlets by glacial drift. The two largest, Hopatcong and Greenwood, were made deeper and greater in area by the flowing and gouging effect of the ice sheet, and by man-made obstructions about 1830.

The fourth geographical region, the Appalachian Valley and Ridge Province, is aptly named. New Jersey's portion, in the extreme northwestern part of the state, contains about half of Warren County and nearly all of Sussex. It is bisected its complete length of nearly 40 miles by Kittatinny Mountain, a ridge of the Appalachians, which reaches to a height of 1,803 feet at High Point. Other hills and ridges, part of the same range, have elevations of up to 1,000 feet. Between Kittatinny and the geographical province of the Highlands is the Kittatinny Valley, which averages 10 miles in width and more than 600 feet above sea level. On the other side of the ridge lies the narrow Minisink Valley along the Delaware River. The Kittatinny and Delaware valleys are mostly underlain with slates and limestones and the ridge between with conglomerates, sandstones, and red shales. These rocks are younger than those of the Highlands, and although folded and faulted, have been disturbed far less by geological events.

The soils of the region are derived from its various sedimentary rocks, and tend to be somewhat heavy. The slate and shale soils of the Kittatinny and lesser valleys are brown and vary from rather shallow shale with considerable shale drift, to deep, well-drained loams with a large admixture of decomposed limestone and vegetable matter. Collectively, these soils are known as the Nassau-Dutchess-Cossayuna group. Occurring nearby are smaller belts of yellowish-brown, more purely limestone soils. Ranging from deep loams, with some gravel, to sandy loams, they are rich and mellow, the best soils of the region. Formerly called Dover soils, they are now known as the Palmyra-Squires group. Soils derived from sandstone and similar rocks, and known as Cattaraugus-Swartswood and Wallpack soils, are found near and on Kittatinny Mountain and other elevations. Because of their nature, and often because of gravelly subsoils, the soils of this zone are unable to withstand drought well. Nevertheless, where the terrain permits, general farm crops, vegetables, and fruit are successfully grown. In some poorly drained areas which have developed muck, large crops of vegetables are grown. Many of the high, rough areas are forested.

The grain of the land here is similar to that of the nearby Highlands, and the drainage pattern is much the same. Paulins Kill, named by early Dutch settlers, drains the greater part of the New Jersey portion of the Kittatinny Valley into the Delaware. An area near the state line drains northeastward. The Minisink Valley is drained into the Delaware by a number of small streams, largest of which is Flat Brook. Unless efforts of conservation groups are successful, much of this scenic and historic area will be inundated when the Army Engineer Corps constructs Tocks Island Dam just above the Delaware Water Gap, thus creating a reservoir of 12,100 acres. The projected plan will add nearly 60,000 acres to constitute, with the lake, the Delaware Water Gap National Recreation Area.[5]

The Europeans who first explored New Jersey found an almost unbroken forest, except for the stony ridges of North Jersey and areas of sand and swamp in South Jersey. John Coleman and his four companions, sent out from the *Half Moon* by Henry Hudson in early September 1609 to explore the lands along the Kill Van Kull, found "goodly trees, as ever they had seen." [6] David de Vries, a Dutch explorer of the lower Delaware Valley in 1633, reported that the land was "all beautifully level, full of groves of oak, hickory, ash, and chestnut trees, and also vines which grow upon the trees." [7]

Jasper Danckaerts, a Labadist missionary, wrote in 1679, after traveling the path across the waist of New Jersey: "The woods consist of reasonably straight oak and hickory, with some chestnut, but they are not very close." [8] Peter Kalm, the Swedish botanist who paid New Jersey a long visit in the middle years of the eighteenth century and took back with him a bride from what is now Swedesboro, left excellent descriptions of what he considered the unkempt native woods of New Jersey, which were as yet yielding only slowly to the American felling ax. Of the Penns Neck area, he wrote: "We find great forests here, but when the trees in them have stood a hundred fifty or a hundred eighty years, they are either rotting within or losing their crown. . . . Everywhere you find trees felled by the wind."

Trees varied as to kind with soils and altitude, and even more with moisture. The extensive Pine Barrens of the Outer Coastal Plain contained both pines and oaks, and occasional other trees, but there was little good timber. Kalm reported that the "Jersey pines," or rather their roots, yielded tar, but despite British bounties the production was never large. Of the lower Delaware Valley, he wrote, "The greater part of the country is covered with several kinds of deciduous trees," and went on to mention tulip poplar, chestnut, sassafras, and mulberry trees. The bark of the tulip poplar (canoe tree) and the dogwood, dried and powdered, had become the poor man's quinine for the cure of malaria, while tea made from sassafras roots was a specific for many diseases.

Elsewhere in his account of his New Jersey wanderings, which were for the most part in the Inner Coastal Plain and Piedmont Plain regions, Kalm reported seeing black walnut, red and white cedar, sweet bay (beaver tree), beech, water beech, fir, white, Spanish, and chestnut oak, maples, hickory, persimmon, laurel (spoon tree), ash, and elm trees.[9] In the poorly drained areas throughout the state, and commonly along streams, are still found willows, "water oaks," birches, ironwoods, sycamores, ashes, and poplars. Some indigenous evergreens, especially hemlocks, grow on the traprock heights of the Piedmont Plain, and particularly on the Watchungs. In the Highlands and the Appalachian Ridge and Valley sections, most of the hardwoods of the Coastal Plain and Piedmont Plain still prevail, with perhaps a greater preponderance of oaks of various kinds. In the northern part of the state, and to some degree on the heights everywhere, there were and still are areas of white pine, hemlock, and other evergreens.[10] As of 1971, two acres of every five of the surface of New Jersey is classed as woodland,[11] but only one or two small areas are virgin. The largest area of near-primeval forest in New Jersey is outside East Millstone in Somerset County. Fortunately for posterity, it has been saved from the real estate developers and is now owned by Rutgers University.

A tree mentioned by all early travelers, and especially common in the Piedmont Plain and Highlands, was the American chestnut. Used often by the pioneers for log cabins, it proved one of the most valuable trees of the region for such diverse uses as rail fences, frame buildings, and furniture. Unfortunately, the species was to become the victim of the Asiatic chestnut blight, which swept from one end of the Appalachians to the other, and beyond, in the years after 1910. Chestnut sprouts still occasionally reach bearing age, but invariably they are struck down by the scourge. In the past half century, the old chestnut areas, with many of the skeletons still standing, have been invaded by other trees of varying desirability and especially by the tulip poplar, ash, birch, and various oaks, hickories, and maples. Thus far no means of preventing or curing the chestnut blight has been found, and although crosses between American and Old World varieties have proved resistant to the blight, no cross has proved equal to the native chestnut in the quality of the timber or the palatability of the nut.

It seems probable that there were a few small prairies scattered through the forests of the Inner Coastal Plain and Piedmont Plain. Jasper Danckaerts mentions seeing small grassy plains among the woodlands along the path from the lower Raritan to the Falls of the Delaware.[12] Furthermore, local tradition has it that there was a treeless grassy plain of several hundred acres near Quakertown in Hunterdon County, and that the Indians burned it off each year in their game roundups.[13]

In addition, Indian fields of a few acres each, cleared or partially cleared, were to be found near the streams or on the leeward sides of ridges and hills. Fields abandoned in the not too distant past and small natural openings here and there in the forest were filled with such shrubs and bushes as crab apples, wild plums, red and black hawthorn, hazel, alder, sumac, huckleberries, leatherwood, bayberries ("tallow shrubs" or "candleberry bushes"), wild roses, witch hazel, blackberries and blackcap raspberries, many vines, including poison ivy, trumpet vines, wild grapevines, and wild honeysuckle, and innumerable weeds, among them pokeberry (pokeweed), jewelweed, giant ragweed (horseweed), wild asters, Spanish needles, wormseed, pennyroyal, goldenrod, thistles, dock, rues, sedges, rushes, ferns, mayapples, wood foxglove, golden club, bloodroot, wild hemp, wild hellebore, wild garlic, cattails, and skunk cabbage.[14]

The combination of growth in any given area depended on the amount of moisture and the nature of the soil. Some plants then known, such as those with edible roots noted by Kalm, have been eliminated by swine and cattle, but most are still to be found in untended and abandoned fields and along fences and roadways. The coming of the white man did, in fact, give a new lease on life to many plants by eliminating the forest trees that held them in check. A prime example is poison ivy, which might well be New Jersey's official flower. Regionally important native plants not already mentioned include the American holly and beach plum of the seashore area and the blueberry and cranberry of the boglands, all of which have been domesticated and developed in recent times. Quite inadvertently, the white men added to the New Jersey flora most European weeds, from dandelion to burdock, and such exotics as Japanese honeysuckle and Chinese mulberry.

The wildlife of the wilderness of New Jersey was not a serious hindrance to its settlement. The malaria-bearing anopheles was the most dangerous member of the animal kingdom, and the giant "Jersey mosquito" (*Aedes sollicitans*) the most talked about. Animals dangerous or disagreeable to man, if one may except the native lice, wasps, hornets, moths, crickets, and locusts, and the immigrant bedbugs and cockroaches, were almost unknown. The wolves often mentioned in pioneer accounts were for the most part coyotes, though timber wolves were sometimes seen. The former were eliminated in settled areas by the payment of bounties, and the latter soon migrated to safer regions. Bears were rare, and those lynxes and wildcats that escaped the bounty hunters moved off to the north and west, returning only for an occasional foray.

The small predatory animals, including the fox, raccoon, mink, skunk (polecat), and opossum, proved more adaptable to changing conditions, and long remained a hazard to poultry. The tradition that the opossum came across the frozen Delaware during the Revolution is apparently a myth, for Kalm and other early writers mention this remarkable beast. Several of the above animals were of value to the settlers for their furs or pelts, and some were used for food. Animals of the streams and swamps with economic value were the beaver, the otter, and the muskrat. The last was important for its skin, but even more for its musk, which was used as a moth repellent.

The American deer, prized for its meat and skin, was prolific, despite the fact that it had been constantly hunted by the Indians. The "American wild cows" mentioned by Kalm and others were apparently only strays or the descendants of strays. Other game animals were the native gray squirrel and the American rabbit, whose number increased as that of predators declined. Quite numerous in some areas were woodchucks (groundhogs), chipmunks, moles, meadow mice, and flying squirrels. Most of these animals are still to be found in the wilder parts of the state, and some have survived close to civilization, thanks to the game laws which protect them from hunters during most of the year. Many of the native animals, particularly deer, raccoons, opossums, and squirrels were often tamed in early days.

Snakes, once so numerous as to keep down the songbird population, fared less well. Neighborhood drives and constant hunting by the settlers cut down markedly on the population of rattlesnakes, copperheads, water moccasins, and occasional adders, the only poisonous varieties. Nonvenomous snakes, including useful ones, also suffered from man's prejudice against things that slither, and their numbers were drastically reduced. Four, the chicken snake, the hoop snake, the milk snake, and the pilot blacksnake, became the subjects of interesting folk beliefs. The name chicken snake was applied to the corn snake of South Jersey and was an alternative name for the milk snake in North Jersey. The hoop snake was probably the black racer of today.

Early observers marveled at the numbers and variety of wildfowl and other birds. Turkeys, woodcocks, grouse, quail, plover, snipe, and other game birds were found in abundance at all times. Geese and ducks in great numbers tarried for a while in spring and fall, and a few remained during the summer for nesting. The turkeys, geese, and ducks were often domesticated. Passenger pigeons, which darkened the sky several times during the year, were so easily killed that hunters sold their carcasses by the dozens or hundreds. Redbirds or cardinals, blackbirds, swallows, turtledoves or mourning doves, larks, jays, orioles, American robins, American cuckoos, brown thrashers, catbirds, native sparrows, and dozens of other varieties of small songbirds were numerous. Early writers listed seven kinds of woodpeckers.

The hummingbird was regarded as something of a marvel by Europeans, and unsuccessful attempts were made to domesticate it. Another much-admired bird of colonial times, the mockingbird, which tradition now erroneously states is a more recent arrival from the South, was, on the other hand, often caged, as were the cardinal and robin. Houses were provided for the purple martin, a very popular bird because its "anxious notes" were supposed to warn poultry of the proximity of hawks. The chimney swallow was also one of man's close associates. The whippoorwill, on the other hand, was considered a bird of ill omen by many, and not one to be encouraged. Immigrant birds then unknown, but which have done well since, include the English or house sparrow, the starling, and the Hungarian quail from Europe, the cattle egret from Africa, and the Oriental pheasant, released by the thousands each summer so that there will be enough in the fall for hunting purposes.

Some birds were liked and many were tolerated, but a number of them had a price on their heads in early days. The prejudice against woodpeckers, as being harmful to fruit trees, was probably mistaken, but the feeling against crows, grackles ("corn thieves"), redwing blackbirds, and cowbirds is understandable. These birds, which became far more numerous with the clearing of the forests, were such despoilers of sprouting grain that bounties were paid for killing them. The many varieties of hawks and owls, and several kinds of eagles, were indiscriminately disliked, and were killed at every opportunity, but the carrion-eating turkey buzzard was usually tolerated as a scavenger. Cranes, herons, and other water birds of the inland swamps were numerous in the early days, and were destined to remain relatively undisturbed until modern times, when pollution and the bulldozer and dredger finally caught up with them. The birds of the shore, once very numerous, declined in numbers from senseless killing, and at present many are in danger of becoming extinct. A few, notably the seagull and sandpiper, have continued to thrive.

Today the native gamebirds are either rare or extinct, but wild geese and ducks still lure the hunter, as do the Hungarian quail and Oriental pheasants. Many of the songbirds have adapted themselves to suburban backyards, though confronted by their worst modern enemy, the house cat, and by man's pesticides. The recent hobby of bird feeding has brought increasing numbers of birds to populous areas. Species less adjustable may yet be saved by the conservationists, who at long last command an audience.

The settlers in New Jersey found the bays, streams, lakes, and coastal waters of the new land literally teeming with fish. The most common varieties were the shad, pickerel, catfish, trout, perch, rockfish, bass, crappie, carp, pike, sunfish, flounder, and menhaden. Since mill dams interfered with the annual running of the shad, clashes between milling and fishing interests were common in colonial days. All these fish may still be found in New Jersey waters, although the pollution of the main streams has reduced their numbers and quality. Modern sportsmen have seen to it that the smaller streams of the state are stocked annually with game fish, particularly trout. Lobsters, oysters, and clams once drew the Indians to the shore every summer, and were to be prized by the people of New Jersey for more than two centuries. Unfortunately, in many places in recent times pollution or disease has either killed them off or made them unfit to eat. However, under modern scientific methods, oyster culture thrives today on the Maurice River in South Jersey. Frogs and crayfish, once very common, are still to be found, though it has been a long time since the succulent legs of the bullfrog were a common item of commerce.

As man's numbers multiply, the habitats of the lower animals are progressively destroyed. It is to be hoped, however, that the present belated drive to dedicate more parklands and to divert industrial wastes and sewage from our streams may save some of the wildlife of forest, stream, and shore.[15]

The Lenni-Lenape or Delaware Indians who once peopled this rich land were neither numerous nor warlike, and did not offer serious obstacles to settlement. Living in small, semipermanent villages in the forest, they were as much farmers as hunters. Their agricultural operations, though requiring much toil, were not very productive. Their fields were small, their methods of culture were primitive, and the depredations of animals were sometimes serious. Nevertheless, the Indian contribution to the agriculture of New Jersey was not small. The maize, beans, and squash that they grew were to become the principal crops of the white people during the pioneer stage and important ones thereafter. A fourth crop, a variety of tobacco too harsh for the white man's taste, was also preserved in wild patches and sometimes cultivated. The Indians made new fields periodically by girdling trees with their stone axes, then planting maize, beans, and squash together in hills under the dead trees. The hills were literally hills, for the mounds became higher year by year as soil was pulled around the plants during cultivation.

Maize was preserved for winter use and for next year's seed by storing it in leaf-lined pits. It was made edible in a number of ways. Immature ears were sometimes parched and roasted in the ashes. More commonly, mature grain was crushed in a stone or wooden mortar, and the meal was then boiled into mush, which might be cooked again as cakes. Hominy was made by soaking the grains in a solution of wood ashes and water, and then boiling them. Beans were stored in pots and were cooked by boiling. Squash slices might be boiled or roasted or might be preserved for the winter by drying. The Indian's fruits were wild ones, which were also dried for the winter. His only domestic animal was a small, vicious dog, useful as a watchdog and as a reserve food supply. Turkeys and other wildfowl were sometimes tamed and kept around the wigwams, but never on a large scale. Reserve supplies of fish were kept in spring wells. As agriculturists, the New Jersey Indians were greatly handicapped by lack of a variety of crops and even more by a lack of domesticated animals.[16]

2

The Europeans Arrive

The first European farmers in New Jersey were the Dutch and Walloons in New Netherland on the west bank of the Hudson, and the Swedes and Finns in the part of New Sweden east of Delaware River and Bay. The earliest Dutch settlement of any permanence was established at present-day Gloucester on the lower Delaware; however, it was never much more than a trading post. Of more significance were the continuing attempts to colonize the shores of the Hudson opposite New Amsterdam, which was itself settled in 1624. Had the Dutch West India Company, which held the whole area under charter from the Dutch government, been less narrowly commercial-minded, this fertile region might well have been colonized much faster.

In 1630 Michiel Reyniersz Pauw, a Dutch merchant-nobleman, was granted a patroonship on the peninsula that now constitutes lower Hudson County. Pavonia, as it was called after its proprietor, was strategically situated, for several Indian trails from the west terminated there; moreover, the fertility of the soil and the readiness with which European grains grew on Indian maize lands raised hopes that this area might provide foodstuffs for New Amsterdam. Pauw's agent, Cornelius van Vorst, probably New Jersey's first farmer, established the bouwerie of Ahismus within present Jersey City.

It proved difficult to coax many Dutchmen to settle in such an isolated place, and after a few years Pauw sold his patroonship back to the Dutch West India Company, which thereupon rented Ahismus to the van Vorst family. Grants were made for a number of bouweries or "plantations," where some desultory farming was practiced by owners or their employees, who commuted across the Hudson by boat; but it was only after a change in company policy in 1638 that other bouweries were established. Now that individuals might trade for furs, several entrepreneurs came to reside in what had been Pavonia. For most of them, agriculture was secondary, but in at least three places the equipment and cattle for permanent farming establishments were acquired. Aert Teunnison, the founder of Hoboken, imported servants to clear and fence the land and brought small herds of cattle, hogs, sheep, and goats. David de Vries, a noted ship-owner, who unlike most of the Dutch got on well with the Indians, also made a promising start at Vriesendale (Old Tappan). His plans included the growing of tobacco and the brewing of beer. The bouwerie of Achter Col (Ridgefield Park) had also made a good start by 1643.

Unfortunately for the new settlements, the stupid brutality of Governor William Kieft brought on the Indian war of 1643. With the exception of Ahismus, all of the bouweries west of the Hudson were wiped out. Ahismus was saved from fire by the simple fact that its roofs were made of plank rather than thatch. Because of his reputation for fairness, de Vries and his settlers were spared, as was Jacob Stoffelson, who had married the widow of Cornelius van Vorst in 1638. Only a few of the other pioneers escaped. The fact that a good number of cattle and some grain were saved by a privateer is some indication that a promising agricultural beginning had been all but ruined. The escape of de Vries was a fortunate one for historians, for his account is the best source of our knowledge of the period. The lack of company enthusiasm, understandable under the circumstances, prevented his return to his bouwerie, and he sailed away, first to Virginia and then to Holland. It was probably on his advice that the Dutch West India Company cashiered Kieft and sent over at last in 1647 a tough and experienced administrator, Peter Stuyvesant, as governor.

A reoccupation of the New Jersey bouweries began before the arrival of Stuyvesant and accelerated under his rule. Ahismus and Hoboken, still held by the original families, and new settlements at Communipaw and Paulus Hook, were the leading bouweries of this period. In all, about a dozen settlements were made. But in September 1655, when Stuyvesant and his little army, under company orders, were absent conquering the unresisting Swedish colony on the Delaware, the Indians struck the Dutch in force. There was no de Vries to soften the blow this time and no privateer to call on for aid. The savages took their time, burned every bouwerie west of the Hudson except Communipaw, killed all the adults they could find, and carried off the children for ransom. There are few records to guide us, but it is evident that the destruction was far greater than that of 1643. The acquisition of New Sweden had certainly been made at a heavy price.

Stuyvesant wasted no tears for the victims, but promulgated new rules for settlers west of the Hudson. Except for Jacob Stoffelson of Ahismus, who had survived two Indian wars, no settlers were allowed to return west of the Hudson until an Indian treaty was made in 1658. Refugees from the Communipaw area were then licensed to return. They were supposed to form a palisaded village, but apparently did not do so until 1663.

The next settlement was the carefully laid out village of Bergen in 1660. The thirty-two lots within the stockade and the twenty-seven without were soon sold. A few of the settlers were former residents of the area west of the Hudson, and some had been farmers on Long Island. Many, however, were recent arrivals from Europe, including a number of Huguenots and other refugees. The "village of Bergen in the new maize land," as the settlement was once called, soon became the metropolis of the area, and the bouweries, old and new, became dependent hamlets. Agriculture was no longer subsidiary to trade, and the residents of old Pavonia now hastened to clear the land and exploit the rich soil.

The English conquest in 1664 caused little more than a ripple of excitement. Stuyvesant alone had expected the British to come, and he alone was willing to fight. Once the surrender was made, even he retired to his own bouwerie on Manhattan and became a peaceable and respected citizen. James, Duke of York, who had sent the ships, gave away New Jersey, under that name, while they were still on the high seas. Richard Nicolls, the leader of the expedition and new governor of New York, protested in vain that this was the best part of his conquest. The new owners, Lord John Berkeley and Sir George Carteret, who were to share jointly in ownership and administration, accepted all Dutch land titles of the Bergen area and gave the Dutch settlers practical autonomy in government. In 1668 Bergen was recognized as one of the first seven "towns" of New Jersey. The agricultural prosperity of the last years of Dutch rule continued under the English. The reestablishment of Dutch rule from November 1673 to February 1675 had no lasting effects.

Emigration from Holland practically ceased in 1664, but the Dutch in America had been and continued to be a fecund group. As the rich lowlands along the Hackensack and Passaic rivers were thrown on the market, Dutch from the New York area, and particularly from Long Island, came in to create farms. Eventually, they went beyond the valleys and took up land in nearby parts of the Piedmont Plain and the Highlands. The migration up the Raritan River started a little later, but it was fully as important and eventually carried people of Dutch extraction as far west as Readington Township in Hunterdon County. The Minisink settlement of the Dutch on the upper Delaware, probably made during the period of Dutch rule, continued to flower in isolation. The settlers were tied to the Dutch village of Kingston, New York, by what became known as the Old Mine Road, which ran along one of the Highland valleys; and no one knew until about 1727 that the Minisink area was in New Jersey rather than New York. New Jersey, once avoided by most

Dutch as too isolated and too dangerous, became under the English the home of a great many people of Dutch extraction. The first Dutch in New Jersey had not taken up agriculture with any great enthusiasm, but soon their descendants were deservedly considered among the best farmers in the land.[1] During the Revolution, a captured British officer observed that Americans of Dutch extraction passed on to their children their "principles, industry, frugality, and an assiduous perseverance in the means of thriving." [2]

The story of the Swedes and Finns in New Jersey, like that of New Sweden generally, is an interesting one; however, it is clear that these two diverse groups, who had no great love for one another, did not play the important part in the settlement of the Delaware Valley sometimes ascribed to them, and that in regard to New Jersey in particular they were mostly latecomers. Their role has been somewhat magnified by Israel Acrelius, Peter Kalm, and Amandus Johnson, good storytellers all, and by those who have relied heavily on their accounts. Popular writings ever since that of Englishman Charles Joseph Latrobe, in 1835, have added to the myth, and the strong probability that the Scandinavian plank house was the progenitor of the American log cabin has increased the stature of the Swedes and Finns in popular thinking. Recent scholars recognize, however, that these groups were few in number, rather unhappy as colonists during the first generation, and rather unsuccessful as farmers until a late date. Ironically, New Sweden was originally conceived by a Netherlander, a Walloon named William Usselinx, and originally financed in part by Dutch capital. The first governors, Peter Minuit and Peter Hollander Ridder, were Dutch. Many of the first colonists were also Dutch, but these, even though the soldiers and traders at the Dutch fort at Gloucester were fellow countrymen, were soon drawn away to New Amsterdam.

The colonists who built and settled Fort Christina (Wilmington, Delaware) in 1638 were a motley lot of adventurers and as interested in the fur trade as the Dutch. Since they paid better prices in trade than the latter, and never provoked the Indians into a war, they were at first successful. Still, the virtual monopoly of local Indian trade by the New Sweden Company, which became entirely Swedish in 1641, left little room for individual enterprise. Furthermore, due to lack of support from their homeland, and to a certain extent to bad luck at sea, the Swedish lost their early commercial advantages to the Dutch and the English. The growing of tobacco proved unprofitable, although for a time it was pursued with energy. Through a process of elimination of possibilities, the Swedish settlers on both sides of the Delaware turned to the growing of grains, particularly maize and rye, and the raising of livestock. From necessity, individual farms became largely self-sustaining.

The Dutch conquest in 1655 changed the situation very little, and only a few of the Swedes returned to Sweden with Governor Johan Rising. Resisting the pressure of Stuyvesant to move to the Hudson, they took oaths of allegiance to the Dutch, probably with tongue in cheek, and remained where they were. They were to cause the Dutch administrators numerous headaches during the next nine years and would pointedly welcome the coming of the English in 1664. As for the New Jersey part of New Sweden, the Swedish were preceded by both Dutch and English settlers. The Dutch post at Fort Nassau (Gloucester) had been occupied most of the time since 1626; and when Governor Johan Printz and his Swedes established a fort at Elfsborg, near present Salem, in 1643, they found colonists from New Haven already living nearby. Printz promptly made them Swedish citizens, but apparently all or nearly all returned to New Haven before long. Swedes from the Wilmington area came over the river in increasing numbers during the remaining dozen years of Swedish rule and the nine years of Dutch rule. Some settled on Salem Creek, and others scattered from the Maurice River in the south to Raccoon Creek in the north. As with the Dutch, the greatest penetration of New Jersey by the Swedes was to come after the English takeover in 1664.

By this time a new generation had grown up. Indian trade, never important here, had declined rapidly, and agriculture had come into its own. When John Fenwick's English Quaker settlers arrived at Salem in 1675 they found prosperous Swedish farmers scattered along the lower courses of the rivers and creeks tributary to the Delaware. Two years later settlers sent by the West New Jersey Proprietors received substantial aid from the Swedes on Lower Raccoon Creek. In fact, it was a Swedish guide who suggested the site for the founding of Burlington. The Quakers who poured into Delaware and eastern Pennsylvania bought Swedish farms there and helped to accelerate the Swedish movement to New Jersey. The Swedish-Americans scattered widely through South Jersey, their chief centers during the next two decades being Salem and Port Elizabeth on the Maurice River, Pile's Grove, Helm's Cove, Penns Neck (Churchtown), Cohansie (Friesburg), Repaupo, and Raccoon (Swedesboro). Repaupo and Swedesboro, which flowered late, were the last of these outposts to drop the Swedish language. Unlike the Dutch, the Swedes made little effort to preserve their past.[3]

The story of the agricultural villages settled by New Englanders—Elizabethtown, Newark, Woodbridge, Piscataway, Middletown, and Shrewsbury—has been told many times, sometimes well and sometimes less well.

It is a long and tortuous tale, though withal a most interesting one; however, it is unnecessary to dwell here on the details of settlement or on
the long-continued strife between the village patentees on the one hand
and the East New Jersey Proprietors on the other. Our chief concern is
with the agricultural transformation brought about by these groups. With
patents or licenses to settle granted by Governor Nicolls, who was not
at first aware that the Duke of York had given New Jersey away, and
with arrangements for settlement already in motion before Governor
Philip Carteret arrived in August 1665 in behalf of new owners Lord
John Berkeley and Sir George Carteret, groups of Puritans, Baptists, and
Quakers proceeded with plans that might well have made a little New
England of the lower Passaic and Raritan valleys. Although the inrush
of other settlers prevented this, the New Englanders, who were themselves only a generation or two from Europe, were to prove a strong
element in New Jersey. They were the one group that had close ties with
an area where many of the adjustments necessary for life in America had
already been made. For them this section of New Jersey, like Long Island,
was only a frontier of New England.

The lodestone for the New Englanders, as for most early immigrants
to New Jersey, was farmland in plenty. To the last man, they wanted to
be landowners. The Indians, with no understanding of the white man's
concept of the individual ownership of land, gave up their titles almost
casually. The problem now became one of distribution. Two features of
the New England system, settlement by communities and private ownership of land in what amounted to fee simple by actual tillers of the soil,
were taken for granted. Also it was part of the intended pattern that the
farmers should reside on home lots within the village and receive most
of their land in outlying lots. The New England open field system of
cultivation and the accompanying rigid controls of crop and livestock
practices by the town meeting were not attempted. In Newark and Middletown the town meeting played a part in apportioning land. In the
other four villages the leaders or "associates" who put up the initial cash
investment divided the land as they saw fit. In all cases much of the land
was held for future apportionment to original settlers and for parceling
out, at a price, to newcomers.

The Elizabethtown patent was issued by Governor Nicolls on November 2, 1664. It granted to a Puritan group, most of whose members were
living on Long Island, a large tract of land between the Passaic and the
Raritan. The leaders thereby secured recognition of an already-made
Indian deed for the area, although the only signer, Mattano, had sold
the land at least once before. It is doubtful that some of the enterprisers
settled at Elizabethtown in the fall of 1664, as is often claimed, but certainly a number of families were resident when Governor Philip Carteret

arrived in August 1665. In the meantime, on April 8, Nicolls had given out in good faith another patent, this time to a Baptist and Quaker group from Long Island, but originally from Rhode Island. The land involved was south of Raritan Bay and the Raritan River, and became known as the Monmouth Patent. It was soon divided between the settlers of Middletown and those of Shrewsbury. On December 11, 1666, the south half of the Elizabethtown Patent was acquired by a small group from New England, who agreed to bring in more settlers. This was the genesis of Woodbridge Township, which in turn was soon divided to give roughly half of the tract to the Baptist settlers of Piscataway. Concurrently, a group of strict Puritans from Connecticut had set up a little theocracy at Newark, on lands bordering those of Elizabethtown on the north. Governor Philip Carteret welcomed some thirty families early in 1666, and granted them a patent; however, it was more than a year before Indian title was eliminated by purchase.

Though land seemed plentiful within these six rather extensive tracts, most grants to individuals were of moderate size, only a few over one hundred acres and even fewer over two hundred. Ownership of over five hundred acres, never very common, was usually the result of someone's purchase of acreage originally allotted to others. The farmers and planters of these villages, whether their holdings were large or small, before long ran headlong into the concept of Berkeley and Carteret that the province had been given to them so that they might make a profit. The real bone of contention was their demand for quitrents, which were periodic fees based on acreage. In other words, the settlers found themselves owning land, not under what we would call fee simple, but under "free and common socage." A half-penny or penny annually per acre was no great burden, and there was complete forgiveness until 1670. But such an impediment to ownership was practically unknown in New England, from which most of these settlers came. Furthermore, the original patents secured from Nicolls did not specifically require quitrents, as the patentees of three of the towns were quick to point out. In the case of Newark, no such argument could be used. In retrospect the reasoning of the settlers seems rather implausible. The fact that the documents given the Woodbridge and Piscataway groups specifically mentioned quitrents not only weakened the stand of the settlers of these two towns but cast doubt upon the arguments against quitrents urged so loudly at Elizabethtown. The position of the Monmouth patentees of Middletown and Shrewsbury was even weaker. Obviously, neither logic nor legality had much appeal where tradition and economic motives dictated the course of action.

Compliance with the requirements for payment of quitrents varied from town to town, with the settlers of Elizabethtown setting the example in avoiding compliance. The usual device at first was that of neglecting to complete the process for taking out a proprietary patent. Later, during the "rebellion of 1672" and the interlude of Dutch reoccupation from mid-1673 to the beginning of 1675, even those inscribed on the quitrent rolls allowed their quitrents to fall in arrears. Attempts to collect by Sir George Carteret, now sole Proprietor of East New Jersey, met with little success after 1676. When the Proprietors of East New Jersey took over from Carteret's widow by purchase in 1682, they had hopes of collecting substantial amounts in back quitrents. But despite a spate of lawsuits, in which most judges were proprietary in their sympathies but most jurymen were themselves patentees, the Proprietors were never able to collect much from the areas of the Nicolls patents, nor, for that matter, from the Newark region. A consequence of the controversy was that the New England settlers and their numerous descendants were sympathetic at a later time with all others who had problems as to land titles or who resented quitrents.

The East Jersey Proprietors were a numerous and fluctuating group. A council established in the new town of Perth Amboy supervised the parceling out of land to all shareholders, both resident and nonresident. Essentially speculators, the individual Proprietors gradually threw land on the market, usually subject to quitrents. The newcomers who carved out farms from these tracts were used to socage tenure in Britain or to even less satisfactory arrangements for landholding on the Continent, and raised no immediate protests. In time, however, as was generally true throughout the English colonies, these restrictions became onerous. In East Jersey the generally successful resistance of the Elizabethtown patentees encouraged others to try to avoid quitrents.

The situation was made worse by the activities of a group who called themselves the Elizabethtown Associates and who claimed to be the heirs to any vacant lands within the expanded boundaries of the Elizabethtown Patent. The Proprietors, who would have been wise to compromise with the Nicolls patentees in the beginning, found themselves competing, in the area between the Raritan and Passaic, with a group which sold land with no stipulation for quitrents. In the nature of the case, popular sympathy was on the side of those who held other than Proprietary titles, no matter how shaky. Evictions and attempted evictions led to the land riots of the 1730s and 1740s. The outcome was never a clear-cut one for either side, but a substantial number of the new landowners made good their titles. In an area of much vacant land, ownership subject to quitrents was never very acceptable. The American Revolution was to end such burdens in New Jersey, but in the meantime they were the cause of much resentment and some hardship.

The quitrent issue, and even more the holding of land by speculators for a rise in price, undoubtedly slowed to a degree the settlement and agricultural development of East New Jersey, commonly called East Jersey then and since. However, the area was advantageously situated and possessed good soils. It is little wonder that Europeans, and numerous residents of other colonies, responded to the promotional literature of the Proprietors as a group and as individuals. The policies adopted by the new group led to a change in the pattern of settlement. The Dutch and New Englanders had settled in fairly compact communities, and grants by Carteret outside their areas had been relatively few. Now, as other East Jersey lands were thrown on the market as the result of decisions of individual Proprietors, new settlements were dispersed and sometimes widely separated. Furthermore, there was a growing tendency on the part of landowners, and particularly of farmers, to live on their land. With few natural barriers, the settlers followed the stream courses or spread out on the lands in between them. Every settlement was a frontier and a melting pot. With such diverse national origins as England, Scotland, Germany, and France, sometimes by way of New England, Virginia, or Maryland, all settlers did not attack their agricultural problems in the same way in the beginning; however, they were forced by circumstances to be pragmatic and to adopt generally those methods and techniques that worked well for individuals. In the nature of the case, others drew most heavily on the experience of those who were already familiar with the American scene, particularly the New Englanders and the Dutch-Americans.[4]

Attempted settlements on the Delaware from New England and Maryland had come to naught during the periods of Swedish and Dutch rule. After the English conquest of 1664, it was obvious that the big gap in the line of English colonies would soon be filled, but for the time being Berkeley and Carteret concentrated on the parts of New Jersey nearest to the port of New York. Possibly they were deterred by the adverse report of Sir Robert Carr, the English conqueror of the Swedish and Dutch settlements on the Delaware, who underrated the agricultural possibilities of West New Jersey (already commonly called West Jersey) and overrated the strength of the Indians there. His account and that of George Fox, who traveled there in 1672 searching for a new homeland for the Quaker sect of which he was the founder, showed that West Jersey was almost an empty wilderness, despite the Swedish settlements. The reconquest of the Hudson and Delaware valleys by the Dutch in 1672 had only a temporary effect, but is supposed to have been the last straw for Lord John Berkeley, already discouraged by developments in East Jersey. He offered to sell his interest in New Jersey to a Quaker friend, Edward Byllinge, for one thousand pounds. Since Byllinge was on the verge of bankruptcy, the actual negotiations were carried out by John Fenwick, another Quaker who claimed half for his services and in the end was given one-tenth by Byllinge's trustees, one of whom was William Penn.

Unfortunately, this transaction had not been cleared with the Duke of York. After the Dutch again gave up New Netherland by the Treaty of Westminster in June 1674, the Duke willingly gave Sir George Carteret a patent to the eastern half of New Jersey in place of his former undivided half share of the whole. But he refused until 1680 to give title of the other half to Byllinge and Fenwick. In the meantime the trustees of Byllinge had devised a plan to rescue him from bankruptcy and at the same time make West Jersey a haven for the oppressed Quakers. A joint stock company was created with one hundred proprietaries or shares, ten of which would eventually go to Fenwick. The others were in part accepted by the creditors of Byllinge, all of whom were Quakers, and in part sold to investors, most of whom were also Quakers. Before long, shares and part shares were being bought and sold on the open market. Tracts of land in West Jersey were to be distributed periodically to shareholders of the moment as land dividends, and then could be sold to those who wished to farm. It was the intent of the founders that there should ultimately be no large landholding. In practice, land in West Jersey was put up for sale quite rapidly. Those owners who postponed sale were likely to have their lands denuded by woodcutters and taken over by squatters.

Long before the West Jersey proprietary scheme had been worked out in full, Quaker colonies had been founded. The impatient Fenwick brought one-hundred fifty settlers to Salem in the fall of 1675, and others who had purchased land rights from him followed rapidly. The settlement of Burlington in 1677 was the result of the pooling of interests by two groups of colonists sent over by separate proprietorial combinations. Guided by Swedish interpreters, the newcomers purchased Indian lands along the Delaware as far as Trenton Falls, and were soon passing out to themselves and to others, who came thick and fast, the land dividends for which they had left their homes in England. Most of the original Proprietors were prosperous townsmen, and only a part of them came to America. Those who did come seldom chose to be farmers themselves, but they were quite successful in enticing others to immigrate and become the actual tillers of the soil. Promotional activities made the settlement of West Jersey a rapid one, especially after 1680, when the trustees of Byllinge were able to announce that the right of the Proprietors to the land and to the government was now secure. Settlement was at first boosted by the harsh treatment of the Quakers in England. However, the new Quaker colonies of Pennsylvania and Delaware also soon drew many Quaker immigrants. Non-Quakers appeared in increasing numbers in West Jersey and constituted a sizable fraction of the population by 1700. A Council of Proprietors of West Jersey, which met periodically at

Burlington, looked after the interests of resident Proprietors and, to a degree, after those of nonresident ones.

Most of the settlements in West Jersey up to 1700 were situated within a narrow band along the east bank of the Delaware from Salem to Trenton Falls. Focal points of settlement were the numerous creeks, large and small, which broke out of the Barrens a dozen or so miles from the river. A few fertile areas in the coastal plain along Delaware Bay, as at Bridgeton, and a number of pockets of arable soil within the Barrens also drew settlers. The rapid settlement of Mercer and Hunterdon counties would come after 1700, and the somewhat slower settlement of Warren and Sussex after 1725. Settlers also gradually penetrated farther into the plain and Barrens areas. At Burlington and to some extent at Salem, there was an attempt to create a village-based agriculture whereby landowners possessed small home lots and outlying farms. Even less so than was the case with the New Englanders in East Jersey, this idea did not prove acceptable for very long.

In West Jersey the owners of proprietaries or part-proprietaries were usually willing to give what was in effect fee simple ownership to those who purchased land from them. Where quitrents were stipulated, the new owners after a time were usually able to avoid or postpone payment. The fact that quitrents were not usual here made it difficult for any landlords to maintain socage tenure. But in many instances, as was also true in East Jersey, owners of large tracts attempted to hold their lands for a rise in market prices. In such cases, and particularly if the owners were absentee, squatters pushed in and carved out farms for themselves. Some were evicted when the owners and the law caught up with them, but many others, probably a majority, were able to force a compromise in which they acquired title at a "reasonable" price. Tenancy was common in both Jerseys, but the arrangement was seldom to the advantage of either landlord or tenant. The family-owned farm, held in fee simple, was the ideal from the beginning, and in time it became the agricultural unit most commonly found. Furthermore, the farmer here, as in most of rural America, ultimately preferred living on his own farm, and as near the center of it as possible.[5]

The very nature of land distribution in New Jersey was such as to create a melting pot; however, one national group of considerable size was able to preserve its identity for a considerable time. These were the Germans. Known generally as Palatines, most of them came from the Rhine Valley and contiguous areas. A combination of religious persecution and long-time economic depression made many of these people receptive to the idea of emigrating. Among them were occasional persons from other parts of Germany. There were two waves of German settlement in New Jersey. The first Germans, for the most part, came by way of New York. In many instances, as at Hoboken, Hackensack, and New Brunswick, they were gradually absorbed into the more numerous Dutch-American group. An island of German settlement created near present Mahwah about 1714 by the promoters of the Ramapo tract lasted somewhat longer as an entity. The Germans who came in by way of the Raritan Valley did best. Beginning before 1730, and apparently lured by cheaper land in the interior, some but not all of the Germans of the lower Raritan and Millstone valleys sold their farms and migrated individually to new settlements at what became Pluckemin, Potterstown, Whitehouse, and Fox Hill.

These scattered settlements of Germans, distributed as they were among pioneers of other national origins, were held together by ties of language and religion. Yet their thin lines would soon have been broken had they not been reinforced in the 1730s and 1740s by large contingents of Germans who had come in by way of the port of Philadelphia. The newcomers were, of course, a part of the migration that created the misnamed Pennsylvania Dutch. In many cases they had resided for a while among fellow countrymen west of the Delaware before coming over the river. This influx, following the York Road from Philadelphia, had already founded new communities at Ringoes and Sand Hill by 1730, and before long Germans followed wilderness trails to reinforce the older German groups. At the same time, they created a settlement at New Germantown (Oldwick), which was to prove one of the most durably German. North and west of New Germantown the newcomers pushed on to start new settlements with Lutheran churches at present Glen Gardner and Long Valley and German Reformed churches at Lebanon and Mount Pleasant. Another point at which the Pennsylvania Germans overflowed into New Jersey was at present-day Phillipsburg, across the Delaware from Easton, Pennsylvania. Settlements were made near Greenwich in present Warren County and at Newton and Stillwater in present Sussex. Their ties with German communities across the Delaware enabled them to preserve the German language, customs, and names for a time before they were absorbed into the growing population about them. In general, the numerous Germans of northwestern New Jersey and the scattered ones of the rest of New Jersey were "Americanized," even as to their names, within a few generations.[6]

English, Scottish, and Irish immigration to New Jersey was a continuous stream during the whole of the colonial period. Some distinction should be made between the British immigrants coming to East Jersey and those coming to West Jersey, though their origins were the same. During the Carteret period in East Jersey, the number of immigrants straight from the British Isles was rather small. These newcomers either bought into one of the groups of "associates" which handled the land distribution of the various villages of the New Englanders or else received grants beyond the supposed limits of the village holdings. After the purchase of East Jersey by the East Jersey Proprietors in 1682, this group of promoters, operating from their new port of Perth Amboy, encouraged a considerable English and Scottish immigration. As individual proprietors threw new lands onto the market from their land dividends, these new groups became widely dispersed.

The West Jersey development came a little later than that of East Jersey, and, as already shown, was a result of the wish to find a homeland for the persecuted Quakers. An early plan to have a "Yorkshire tenth," and an "Irish tenth" created for a time small colonies of people with a common origin, but these groups were infiltrated from the start and rapidly lost their identities. As the owners of the proprietaries of West Jersey gave up their dream of a Quaker commonwealth, more and more of the settlers from Britain were other than Quaker. In the area above Trenton Falls, settled after 1700, British influence was still dominant, but there were enough non-British colonists to make the northern part of West Jersey as heterogeneous as much of East Jersey. British immigration, though not large after the initial stage, continued during the colonial period and resumed after the American Revolution.[7]

The Scotch-Irish immigration of the second half of the eighteenth century touched New Jersey lightly, but did not pass it by. A traveler from Newark to Easton in 1794 spoke of the immigrants, "especially Irish, poor, from among the poorest country people, and who had spent their first years in servitude (as is the custom of that class), and then became mechanics or carpenters, and had brought up their children in that way."[8] His reference is, of course, to the Scotch-Irish, who often became bond servants in order to defray the cost of their ship's passage to America. Presbyterians all, the Scotch-Irish tended to settle not too far from the Presbyterian churches established by earlier immigrants from Scotland. Not notably good farmers, and sometimes without agricultural experience even in northern Ireland, they nevertheless acquired the rudiments of New Jersey agriculture rather rapidly. Squatting was no longer popular, and often impossible, in New Jersey by the time they came, but those who wished to be farmers had no difficulty in becoming tenants or in purchasing cheap lands.

The above catalogue of European groups who settled here is, of course, not complete. One contingent that has almost always been slighted is the French-speaking one. There were certainly Huguenots among the Dutch and German settlers, and even more Walloons from what is now southern

Belgium. Few except genealogists have made an effort to distinguish between the two. At any rate, there were for a time a few small settlements
of French-speaking immigrants, such as that at Bergenfield. The French
language disappeared rapidly, and all reminders of the original groups
soon disappeared except for some of the French names. Later French
arrivals, like those at Frenchtown, merged into the native American
stream even more rapidly. In addition to the French, a few southern
Irish, a few Danes and Norwegians, and a number of adventurers of
other nationalities wandered into New Jersey during the colonial period
and remained here. Those who became farmers often did well enough,
but as far as is known they had little to contribute except their labor.[9]
A component of the population that will receive later attention was that
of the Negro slaves.

J. Hector St. John de Crèvecœur, writing before the Revolution from
his farm in southeastern New York, was probably the first commentator
to think of the mixing of nationalities in America as a "melting" process.
His answer to his own question, "What then is the American, this new
man?" would have applied well to New Jersey.[10] The mixing of men and
ideas he observed had been at work in both East and West Jersey almost
from the days of earliest settlement. By the time of the Revolution, the
amalgamation of the peoples of diverse origins who had settled in New
Jersey was well on its way. The use of the Swedish, Dutch, and German
languages had declined, even in the pulpit. Most though not all descendants of immigrants from the Continent had gradually Anglicized their
names. From the beginning the exchange of ideas and the development
of new practices and techniques had gradually obliterated many of the
original particularities of the various groups who had settled here. The
tendency toward standardization was especially noticeable in agriculture.

3

Taming the Wilderness

Although in a sense the frontier began at the water's edge, the pioneer period for the first immigrants to New Jersey was neither very long nor very severe. The earliest Dutch and Swedes, the migrating New Englanders in their six villages, the Quakers of Salem and Burlington, and the Scots and others of Perth Amboy either maintained close ties for a time with their earlier American homes or received considerable aid from Europe to soften the shock of wilderness life. Artisans and other nonfarmers relieved the tillers of the soil of many tasks that the self-sufficient, jack-of-all-trades pioneers of later frontiers must do for themselves. From the beginning there were merchants to supply vital needs and provide markets for agricultural surplus. It is understandable, therefore, that the various aspects of a settled civilization appeared rapidly in the first settlements. In many cases, even the houses were copies of those left behind.

Of the various groups, the New Englanders were best prepared to cope with New Jersey conditions. Even those European immigrants who had had agricultural experience (and there were a surprising number who had had none) found this such a surprising land that they must change their ways drastically. Although they brought with them their basic tools, skills, and ideas, they had to adjust and adapt at every turn. Settlers from Europe who followed them made a similar discovery, but for them it became more and more a matter of copying and applying lessons learned by earlier groups. At a time when European agriculture was still rather traditional and unbending, beginning farmers in the New World had to adapt to the new physical environment or give up agriculture entirely.

As more and more settlers intent on agriculture arrived, they fanned out in all directions from the older settlements. From necessity they must learn to cope with the wilderness without much help, and thus it was that a class of true pioneers was created. Yet it should be remembered that frontier families in New Jersey were never more than a few days travel from centers of economic and social life. In time new centers would be established even closer to them. Nonetheless, New Jersey did have a frontier, for a time, or rather several frontiers. By the period when the last one was reached, in the northwestern part, all the characteristics of what Frederick Jackson Turner called "the Old West" were to be found. As for New Jersey's frontier period, in general it should be kept in mind that the pioneer was seldom a pioneer for long; however, the more distant he was from established settlements, the longer frontier conditions persisted for him. Furthermore, the pace of settlement was not rapid. The wilderness was hardly gone by the outbreak of the Revolution; yet by that time the oldest communities had been settled for more than a century.

For a province so small, the pattern of settlement in New Jersey was a highly complicated one. Bypassed by the English until 1664, and touched only lightly by the numerically insignificant though scattered Dutch and Swedes before that time, it was New Jersey's bad luck to be carved up piecemeal as the result of two giant real estate ventures. Except for the holdings of the Dutch, Swedes, and New Englanders, lands received by Proprietors as dividends in both East and West Jersey were subjected to periodic subdivision as speculators bought and sold. In many cases, tracts were held off the market, sometimes briefly, sometimes for a long time. As a consequence, groups of farmers who held legal titles were often widely scattered. Illegal settlement by squatters helped fill in some of the vacant land between them, and a relaxation of policies by large landowners eventually brought most of the fertile lands of New Jersey into the hands of resident farmers. But the process was a slow one. The early centers of population in the Bergen-Newark-Elizabethtown-Perth Amboy area and the Salem-Burlington-Trenton area gradually grew toward each other to fill out what became known as the Progressive Belt across the waist of the province. But the regions to the north and south gained settlers much more slowly. In the south, naturally fertile areas were often surrounded or partially surrounded by less desirable tracts. In the north, deterring factors were the paucity of arable lands, the roughness of the terrain, and the fact that the ridges of land ran in a direction counter to the natural course of settlement.

In a discussion of frontier techniques and ways of life, there is always a danger of overstressing the distinctiveness of a particular area. No frontiersman worked hard and lived simply as a result of his own choice, nor did he invent new tools and devise new methods when the old would serve. On the other hand, he did not hesitate to adapt and improvise when real need arose. A willing ally was the local blacksmith, who was often an inventor at heart, and certainly a disseminator of ideas within the area he served. To a degree often not recognized, every frontier shared its findings with other frontiers, as witnessed by the rapid spread of the Scandinavian log house of the lower Delaware and the worm fence of Virginia. The frontier in New Jersey was only a part of a much larger American one, and not even an entirely detached segment. The first pioneers started out with European tools, or those already modified through practice in New England or Maryland or Virginia. Through the years, some of these were changed drastically, others were merely streamlined, and still others were changed very little, if at all. What was happening here was occurring elsewhere also, as common problems led to common practices.

The tools developed for the clearing of the forests and working with wood were simple, but adequate. Common items in the inventories of early estates were the felling ax, used for cutting down and trimming trees, and the broadax, used for squaring timbers. Less common was the two-man saw, used for cutting logs and laboriously sawing out boards at the saw pit. The felling ax, sometimes called the falling or pitching ax, had a thin blade, rather narrow, and a deep haft. The broadax had a thin but very wide blade. It was often called a "crooked ax" because its handle was offset somewhat to make it easier to give a timber a flat surface. Other indispensable tools were the beetle, often spelled bedel, and its accompanying wedges. The beetle was a large homemade wooden hammer or maul. Its driving surfaces were protected by iron collars, called beetle rings, which were made by local blacksmiths. Mattocks, usually called mathooks, were useful in grubbing roots and stones and brush hooks in clearing underbrush. Tools sometimes owned by pioneer farmers, and usually by the artisans who often helped them finish their log or frame houses, were the frow, used in making shingles, the splitting ax, the mortising ax, the hand augur, the adze, and the plane. The decided advantage of the log cabin over other types of houses was the fact that it could be built with less skill and fewer tools. In an emergency, a cabin of sorts could be built by one man using only a felling ax and a broadax. Since the log cabin was practically unknown in East Jersey until rather late, the main use for the broadax there was for the squaring of timbers for the skeletons of frame, stone, and brick buildings.[1]

By constant practice, early New Jersey farmers, like pioneers everywhere, became very proficient with their tools. In 1787, after the frontier had been pushed west, Thomas Capner, an English immigrant boy, wrote from Flemington:

I have sent Samuel two little wooden axes. They are all the kind that are used here. With the least they fell trees, cut wood, &c. If they want to square pieces of timber or trees, they cut them down and they line out the thickness they want. They then stand the tree out, notch two the line about a foot apart and split it off in small blocks. They then with the crooked ax stand on one side

of it and hew it so true that you would think it was planed . . . Brother John
says an American will cut a tree whilst an Englishman is looking where to begin.[2]

Early farmhouses in East Jersey were commonly of frame. The first
lumber for frame houses was made by manpower. In practice two men
labored on opposite ends of a long saw, one of them standing below the
log in a saw pit. A mark of progress in a community was the appearance
of a sawyer, who would build and operate a water-powered "up-and-down
saw." The frame building most usual in early days had a skeleton of
heavy squared timbers, fastened in place with wooden pegs. Heavy boards
were laid across the beams to make a floor for the second story or attic,
as the case might be. The outside walls were of thick sawed lumber or
weatherboarding, and the inside ones of uprights covered with laths and
plaster. Roofs were usually of oak shingles, made from trees near at hand.
Nails, which were used sparingly, were made by local blacksmiths.

The plank house of the Swedes and Finns, two of which are still preserved in New Jersey, after being considerably modified in practice became the log house or log cabin.[3] It was widely adopted in West Jersey
and in those parts of East Jersey that were settled fairly late. A pioneer
might use for a year or two a hastily constructed hut of unsquared logs,
with earth floor and roof of poles and bark. In the meantime he would
cut and prepare logs, usually of oak or chestnut, for a better cabin. The
green logs, cut to length, were laid on trestles for scoring and chipping
with a felling ax and dressing down with a broadax. They were then
stacked to one side to cure. The warping of the green timbers was cor-
rected at a later time, the "wind being taken out" by further dressing.
The timbers were by now ten or twelve inches square and carefully
notched at the ends for the corners of the cabin. In the construction, the
timbers were laid on top of one another, with mortar or mud between
them for chinking. A doorway was left in one of the longer sides. When
the walls were built to the required height, a roof was made of hewn
rafters covered with lath and riven shingles. The gabled ends might be
of logs, but were commonly of heavy weatherboarding held up by wooden
pegs. The "puncheon" floor was of split logs dressed on the smooth side.
The inside walls were sometimes, but not always, covered with laths and
plaster. Smith-made nails were used, if at all, only for shingles and lath,
and, sometimes, for weatherboards.[4]

One side of the cabin was dominated by the fireplace, made of stone
and topped with an oak mantel. A lug pole crossed the room just in front
of the fireplace for suspending pothooks and trammels. The walls were
pierced for one or two small windows. One or more room partitions were
often constructed, and the area between ceiling and roof was usually made
into a loft. Log houses varied considerably as to size. Whatever the case,

farm wives understandably did not like them and encouraged their husbands to build frame dwellings as soon as possible. When a farmer thus rose in the world, the log house became a stable or storage house.[5]

From the beginning not only the residences of the villages but the country houses varied in type of construction and pretentiousness. A house was a mark of status, and no local squire would be satisfied with the boxlike dwelling of most simple farmers. The better houses were usually of frame, but not uncommonly were made of field stones or bricks. The latter might be made on the spot from the local clay or might be carted from the nearest seaport or brickyard.[6]

The farmer in accomplishing his first task of providing shelter for his family made a start on his second and larger job, that of clearing land for crops and pasturage. The forest would furnish him also with materials for other buildings, for furniture, for fences, for fuel, and even for tools and utensils. Nevertheless, trees were generally considered obstacles to be disposed of as rapidly as possible. A traveler in New Jersey in the early 1780s was told of the young American who, when he saw the treeless expanse of Western Ireland, exclaimed, "What a wonderful country! What a lucky people with no woods to plague them!"[7] This attitude, which was to lead eventually to the destruction of most of our virgin forests, is widely censured today; but the pioneer's work with ax and fire, wasteful though it was, was necessary to his livelihood. The butchering of the forests on nonfarm and marginal land was largely the work of sawyers and of charcoal burners who supplied the early ironworks.

The process of changing timberland into cropland was a laborious one, and not to be completed quickly. A small beginning could be made easily by cutting off and burning the undergrowth and small trees. The next step was a matter of choice. Many pioneers adopted the Indian practice of girdling, that is of removing a band of bark around each tree. After the tree had died, branches which had fallen were burned at its base each winter. Under such practices, there were for many years protruding stumps and fire-scarred skeletons to handicap farming operations and excite adverse comment by visitors. As late as 1786 John Hall wrote from Flemington that immigrants from England must be prepared to suffer from "land sickness" for a time before becoming used to the American scene. Occasional farmers who had more "work in their bones," as he put it, preferred to clear the land completely before planting crops.[8]

The job of clearing land was spread over many years, interspersed among many other tasks, including that of keeping in cultivation areas already cleared. In the meantime, the farmer must of necessity provide shelter for his livestock and storage space for his crops. Logs and squared timbers from a nearby woodland were the usual construction materials at first, but with the appearance of sawmills rough lumber came into common use. The skeleton for a substantial building was usually made of white oak timbers, either squared by the use of axes or sawed out at the sawmill, whichever way was cheaper in time and effort. Shingles on heavy laths, supported by timber rafters, provided a roof for permanent structures, but a makeshift covering of boards or bark might be used on a temporary shelter. As a farmer's crops and livestock increased, he naturally found it necessary to build more commodious barns and sheds.

The Dutch and the Germans, in particular, liked to get as many operations as possible under one roof,[9] and many others followed their example. Auxiliary outbuildings were still necessary, however. Among them would be the smokehouse, corncribs, extra stables, perhaps a woodshed, shelters for hogs and poultry, and sometimes one or more barracks. The last, introduced from Holland, were frames with roofs which could be raised or lowered, and were used chiefly for the storage of hay. A root cellar under the house or in a nearby hillside was used for storage of fruits and vegetables, and for cider, dairy products, and meat. During the summer, perishables were often kept in a spring house, cooled by a spring or small stream.

The first season on the land was for every agriculturist a time of feverish activity. He must plant the acres he had cleared, be they many or few, and he must make more permanent provision for the feeding of his livestock. At this point it may be asked how he had provided himself with plants, seeds, and animals and how practices differed among the various early groups.

The meager records of Dutch agriculture in New Jersey merely indicate an emphasis on maize and cattle; however, it is likely that farm practices here were similar to those across the Hudson, for which there were fuller accounts, notably the one by Adriaen van der Donck, who resided in New Amsterdam from 1644 to 1653. The Dutch imported good draft horses from the Netherlands, particularly a breed from the province of Utrecht. They preferred these animals to oxen and lavished considerable care upon them, though some oxen, obtained in New England or brought in by New England colonists, were used for the roughest work. Horses for riding and driving were also brought in from New England, chiefly because they cost less than similar horses imported from Europe. Cattle were brought from Holland and did well, but more and more New England cattle were shipped in, since they were considered hardy enough not to require much winter shelter. They were small and gave little milk, but they were cheap and fattened fairly well for beef. Crossing of the Holland and New England cattle became an early practice.

Hogs were brought from both the Netherlands and New England. The Dutch hogs were larger and put on weight better, but hogs from New England were cheaper and hardier. Since swine were allowed to roam in the woods, intermixture of breeds was inevitable. The pork of hogs fed on maize was considered best, but, after all, the mast of the woodlands was free. Sheep likewise were acquired from the Netherlands and from New England, but they were easy prey for wild animals and their wool and mutton were not greatly in demand. Goats, which furnished both milk and meat, and which throve on a coarse diet, were more numerous than sheep in New Netherland. The Dutch brought from their home-land barnyard fowls, even pigeons, but apparently had more turkeys, geese, and ducks than chickens. Dogs, more useful for watching and hunting than for tending stock, abounded, and the common cat found New Netherland a land of opportunity.

In general as regards livestock, the debt of the Dutch-Americans to New England was greater than is commonly thought. It seems probable that this is especially true for those who settled in New Jersey, for many of them had lived near New Englanders on Long Island or settled in New Jersey areas contiguous to those which had been settled from New England. In any case, Dutch and British strains of livestock were eventually completely lost, both contributing to the makeup of the "common" horses, cattle, swine, sheep, and dogs of a later period. The story is much the same for barnyard fowls, though strains of fighting chickens were kept pure.

Vegetables grew prolifically, the Dutch found, but at the expense of quality. Van der Donck reported that all vegetables known in Holland were grown here, some more successfully than others. These included lettuce, cabbages, parsnips, turnips, carrots, beets, radishes, spinach, endive, onions, parsley, leeks, garden peas, and many herbs. Pumpkins, used in New England in pies and other ways, were grown by the Dutch in their cornfields, but were fed to livestock, a practice soon common in New Jersey. Muskmelons from their homeland, squash from the Indians, and watermelons from Portugal were much esteemed for human consumption, however. Cucumbers were particularly abundant in the new, humus-rich soils, as were calabash gourds, which were used when dried as dippers and containers. Indian beans were grown in the cornfields, particularly for dried beans, but "Turkish beans" were considered better to eat as green beans. Bean varieties from the Old World were slow in adapting to the climate here. The many flowers of Holland, already famous in that day, were all grown here. Roses of various kinds, European lilies, and tulips did especially well. The marigold was as common as today, though of a smaller variety. Native lilies and sunflowers were accepted into the Dutch flower gardens.

Fruit trees of many kinds were brought from the Netherlands, and those that grew well were used as grafting stock to some extent; however, the ease of raising apples, pears, peaches, and cherries from seeds and pits caused many to depend entirely on seedlings. This led to the development of some new varieties, for example, the Double Paradise apple of Bergen County and the special cider varieties in Essex and Bergen counties. Apples and pears were the most common fruits, but many kinds of cherries, peaches, and plums were also grown. Wine grapevines imported from southern Germany were not grown very successfully, and native varieties when domesticated proved to be more valuable. The quince apparently came by way of New England. Gooseberries and currants, both from Europe, were also common small fruits.

Van der Donck summarized the situation as follows: "In short, every kind of fruit which grows in the Netherlands is plenty already in New Netherland, which have been introduced by the lovers of agriculture, and the fruits thrive better here." In 1679 Jasper Danckaerts made a stop at the hamlet of Communipaw and later wrote, "We had nowhere, to my knowledge, seen or eaten finer apples. One kind was very large, fair, and of good taste, fifty-six of which only could be put in a heaped-up bushel." The Dutch bushel (Schepel) was equal to only three pecks English, but these were still giants among apples. In general, fruit trees, once planted, were left to fend for themselves.

Agricultural practices of the Dutch changed considerably in response to the conditions which were encountered. Canals and ditches kept farm animals in bounds in Holland, but here croplands were surrounded by post and rail fences made from the plentiful forest growth. Stock were permitted to wander, though this antagonized the Indians, prevented selective breeding, and permitted too early breeding of animals. Land was rich here and labor expensive, so it is not surprising that Van der Donck in nine years saw no manure hauled onto the fields. Land was kept continuously in crops, partly in order to keep down weed growth. Corn was often alternated with winter grains or tobacco, a rotation anything but restful to the soil.

The Dutch, like the later Germans, only reluctantly practiced girdling of trees to kill them. They preferred to cut off most or all of the growth, then continue to "subdue" the land by planting corn with a broad hoe in rows 6 feet apart, six grains to each hill. When the corn was 6 inches high, pole beans were planted near each hill, to climb up the stalks of corn. Pumpkins were then planted among the hills to cover and shade the ground. An Indian practice, which might well have been dropped at once but which was continued for some time, was that of burning off the forests. The huge fires which were started each year robbed the land of humus and on occasion resulted in the destruction of evergreen trees and of homesteads in their path.[10]

When Peter Kalm visited Raccoon (Swedesboro) in 1748 and 1749, he cast off for a time his role as a famous botanist and became an amateur historian. He visited and interviewed every old Swedish-American he could locate and carefully recorded his findings. One man in his nineties claimed to remember the period of Dutch rule of the Swedish settlers between 1655 and 1664, and stated that he was the son of a Swedish immigrant. He assured Kalm "that the Swedes brought their horses, cows and oxen, sheep, hogs, geese, and ducks with them." Some cattle, he knew, had also been bought in New York. During his boyhood the livestock had multiplied rapidly, and when the Quakers came from England to West Jersey and Pennsylvania, the Swedes had surplus animals to supply the newcomers. Also he had heard when he was young "that the Swedes had brought all kinds of grain and fruits and herbs or seeds with them." Wheat, rye, barley, and oats had been plentiful during his youth. Maize, acquired from the Indians, was already planted in large fields at that time. Among the vegetables he remembered were white cabbage, kale, carrots, and turnips, much loved by the Indians. Apple orchards were common, but the Swedes of that day preferred their own beer to cider. Another oldster related that his grandfather, when he came from Stockholm in 1642, "had brought apple seeds and several other tree and garden seeds with him in a box." This man remembered that Swedes of an earlier day had sheltered their cattle in winter, a practice by then long discontinued.

The accounts of these appealing old gentlemen, based largely on tradition, undoubtedly distorted the picture in several ways. The original expedition under Peter Minuit, which almost foundered in the North Sea, certainly brought no livestock from Sweden, and probably none from the Netherlands. Van der Donck tells how the newcomers alarmed the Dutch administrators in West Jersey by planting a little garden of "salads, pot herbs, and the like," thus showing intent of staying at least for a time. If they had had farm animals grazing near their camp, the fact would likely have been recorded. Minuit's records show that he had brought spades, hoes, and other tools, two barrels of seed wheat and two of barley, and some dogs. The emphasis was on trade goods for the fur trade, but since a colony was intended, he had undoubtedly carried over seeds of the most common vegetables and truck crops. In all likelihood, most seeds came from the Netherlands rather than Sweden.

Of the twelve expeditions sent from Sweden between 1638 and 1655, apparently only three or four brought livestock. A ship in 1641 had five horses, eight cows, five sheep, and two goats. But already the colony was purchasing cattle and horses from both Virginia and New Amsterdam, and very likely from New England. The new governor, Johan Printz, brought a few more cattle, sheep, horses, and perhaps chickens in 1643, but it is doubted that many more animals were introduced directly from Europe to New Sweden. The number of swine and sheep had apparently increased a great deal by 1655, but thefts by Indians had kept down the number of cattle. Since there were only ten Swedish cattle in the province in 1645, and few were brought over thereafter, it is certain that their blood line was eventually lost as completely as was that of their masters. As to swine, some of the animals imported were from Holland rather than Sweden, and this may have been true of horses.

The story was probably the same for grains, vegetables, and fruit. Governor Rising in 1654 wished to take along twenty or thirty barrels of good Swedish rye, but he was told to buy rye in New England instead. None of Kalm's informants had ever heard of rutabagas, which were a standard crop in Sweden. The Swedes had become the best winemakers in America, but, according to van der Donck, their vineyards were entirely of native American grapes.

Kalm came to the conclusion that the Swedes and Finns by 1675 had livestock in such numbers and grain in such quantity that they were able to fill most of the needs of the English colonists who came to the Delaware Valley. This supposition has been accepted by others, but mathematically it was an impossibility. At that time, there were not more than one thousand Swedes and Finns in the whole Delaware Valley, mostly west of the river. Undoubtedly, their presence cushioned the hardships of the newcomers, particularly at Salem and Burlington; but the colonization of the Delaware Valley, when it came, was rapid. Swedish farmers undoubtedly prospered as a result of the new demand, but it was a far greater market than they could supply.[11]

The most important contribution of the Swedish and Finnish colonists to the settlement of America was their introduction of the log cabin, a common structure at that time in the East Baltic area from which they came. Their records west of the Delaware mention one-room huts, "substantial" houses, "handsome mansions," bathhouses, mills, and forts, all built of logs.[12] When Jasper Danckaerts visited Burlington in 1679, he recorded staying overnight in a log cabin "made according to the Swedish mode." In this case, the logs were notched into one another to form the corners of the structure and allowed to protrude for a foot or so beyond.[13] The two Swedish houses still preserved in New Jersey are of snugly fitted squared timbers, and have had their carefully mortised corners squared with a saw. Peter Kalm in 1749 confined his description of early Swedish houses in the Raccoon (Swedesboro) area to windowless dwellings of one room. He found the descendants of the early Swedes and Finns in New Jersey building homes after the "English style," using clapboard, stone, or brick.[14]

The New Englanders who settled in New Jersey brought in with them farm animals descended from those originally shipped from England. Although already somewhat scrawny as the result of indiscriminate breeding and poor care, these animals were a tough lot. The seeds of grain, hay crops, and vegetables already acclimated in New England were found to grow readily in New Jersey. Apple, pear, and peach trees were transplanted at once by these drinkers of cider and brandy, and small fruits nearly as soon. Of all groups in early New Jersey, the New Englanders had the greatest advantages. Because they brought livestock and seed stock, tools and techniques, and pioneer experience, there was no hardship period for them in New Jersey. Their farms were self-sustaining, or nearly so, from the start, and soon were producing surplus wheat, livestock, and brandy for sale or exchange.[15]

Early records indicate that the immigrants who came straight to East Jersey and West Jersey from Great Britain seldom brought livestock and only occasionally seeds and nursery stock. It was well known that these things could be bought in the colonies. Not only did the Quakers of West Jersey buy from the Swedes on both sides of the Delaware, but also they purchased needed items from not-too-distant Maryland and Virginia and from New England. The practice of driving animals overland from New York, originated by the Swedes, was very probably expanded during the early years of shortage. It was not long before the first wave of farmers were producing a surplus of their own, which they were pleased to sell to newcomers, and within a relatively few years there was an overall surplus for export.[16]

The British contingents coming directly to East Jersey after 1682 found sources of supply close at hand in the settlements of the New Englanders and the Dutch-Americans. Due to ties by sea with older colonies and improved shipping with England at a later date there were some imports of animals, especially horses, and of seeds and plants. But most of the latecomers found that they could get the supplies they needed when they arrived. They discovered that the animals purchased in America were sturdier and stronger and that seeds and plants were more reliable than British stock. Generally speaking, the most serious difficulties of the colonists who came directly from Britain were the newness and rawness of conditions in the new land. Like other Europeans, they must learn to swing an ax, wield a broadax, and handle timber. They must withstand greater extremes of climate than in their homeland and diseases, particularly malaria, for which they had little resistance.[17]

As for the Germans, they received no aid from Europe in their enterprises, and brought very little with them except personal possessions. Furthermore, they were handicapped by language difficulties and lack of agricultural experience applicable to America. In the words of a later New Jersey observer, they came "late and poor." [18] A few brought sufficient money to buy farms, but most were forced to become tenants or squatters until they acquired by industry and frugality the money or credit to purchase land. The German contributions to agriculture in New Jersey were not great. In the main, the Germans purchased from the farming communities about them the livestock, poultry, fruit, and seed to get their start. They were willing and adaptable, and the indications are that they became as good farmers as their neighbors, but probably little better. German immigrants brought the practice of using land plaster to Pennsylvania,[19] and therefore probably to New Jersey. Vestiges of German agricultural practices were retained longest in the communities that were almost solidly German. The tradition of New Germantown (Oldwick) that long rows of Lombardy poplars were planted by the first Germans and remained until the third generation may well be true.[20] The many Germans who became "dispersed" among other groups, as John Rutherford phrased it in 1786, acquired somewhat sooner the agricultural techniques, good or bad, which marked New Jersey agriculture. Johann Schoepf, a Hessian physician who visited some of the Germans of New Jersey and Pennsylvania at the end of the Revolution, praised their "industry and economy" but was worried about their ignorance of politics and the higher things of life.[21]

One exception to the statement that the Germans brought little with them seems of sufficient interest to merit special mention. The Laurentz or Lorentz family of the Peapack Patent in Morris County, who had lived earlier in Pennsylvania, had in 1754 fields of spelt, a Central European grain intermediate between wheat and barley. Of this their landlord wrote:

> The Laurances have a graine they call Spelts, brought from Conestoga, which they recommend as very good swill for cows. It does not quit the chaff in threshing. They sow it as they do wheat, and two bus'ls to an acre, and if the land be very good, will yield from 40 to 60 bus'ls pr. acre; affords very good winter pasture for calves, and the straw makes much better fother than either wheat or ry. I have bespoak 2 bush. for seed.[22]

This interesting grain, still grown in parts of Europe, soon disappeared in New Jersey, along with whatever else the Germans may have imported. One can only wish he knew more about the German farmer, Fuchs, who lived near present-day Fairmount in Hunterdon County. Tradition says that he had a strain of wheat so superior that other farmers came for miles to obtain seed.[23]

A problem of first importance with the farmers of all the groups mentioned above was that of choosing what crops to grow. All alike owed a debt to the American Indian for that most versatile crop, maize, which was called "Turkish wheat" by the Dutch and Germans and Indian corn or simply corn by the English-speaking groups. Indian tradition had it that both corn and beans had come into the region from farther south

and west, which seems likely enough. In any case both were fully acclimated long before the whites came. As van der Donck succintly put it,
corn was "a hardy grain . . . fit for the sustenance of man and animals
. . . sufficient for the needs of the country." It is little wonder that it
became a prevailing crop.

Corn was often alternated with wheat, rye, oats, barley, or peas, all of
which had to be adapted to the new land. Seed from these crops had
been brought from Europe originally, though often by way of New England or New Netherland. A serious problem with newly cleared land for
each of these crops was the tendency for plant growth to be too luxuriant.
Van der Donck reported both rye and barley growing as tall as seven
feet, and reported that peas were seldom sowed because of their tendency
to grow more vines than peas. A simple remedy, however, was to grow
corn or tobacco for several years on new land before trying other crops.
Tobacco seed came from Virginia or Maryland, since the native Indian
variety in New Jersey was of very strong taste. A discouraging factor was
that the quality of tobacco grown in New Jersey was never equal to that
of Virginia. A crop that grew fairly well was buckwheat, but many farmers were discouraged with it because the birds stole it. Hemp grew well
enough, but was little superior to the plentiful wild hemp. Far more
important among all groups except the Dutch was flax, from which linen
and tow threads were obtained for the making of homespun clothing.

As was true of every frontier, the earliest settlers were forced to do
some experimenting with varieties of crops. In practice this meant eliminating strains that did not do well and saving seed from those strains
that did best. In the case of wheat, success was so marked that there was
soon surplus flour for export. Selected varieties of rye and barley with
less tendency to "go to straw" proved tougher and stronger on some lands
than wheat. In experimenting with oats, a crop regarded as indispensible
as feed for horses, farmers found types that produced grain abundantly
or that could be cut "in the milk" (while still immature) as a forage
crop. Unintentionally, British settlers brought in bluegrass and timothy
(herd's grass), probably in the bedding of imported animals. Both went
wild, and were commonly thought to be native American plants. In time
they were accepted as being far superior to most American grasses for
pasturage and hay. Common European vegetables and fruits adapted
themselves to American conditions fairly readily, for early accounts list
nearly every one. Cabbage, which was by far the most important vegetable, evidently flourished in New Jersey from the start. The versatile apple did especially well and became the fruit grown by everybody. The
experimentation was extended to native crops, and particularly to corn,
which through selection rapidly became a sturdy field crop and a mainstay for nearly every farmer.[24]

Tools and farm and household equipment were developed through a combination of inventiveness, imitation, and common-sense trial and error. In the brief frontier period, many items of equipment came directly from the forest. Makeshift brush harrows, drags made from logs, and forks from the branches of trees had their day, and the "gum" made from a cross section of a hollow sweet gum tree placed on a base of boards was so practical for storing grain, apples, and even brined pork that its use persisted long past the pioneer years. Other easily made devices, such as the gourd dipper and the lard lamp, lingered for decades. Meantime, farmers were never far from settled communities, and as these developed rapidly people throughout the province could acquire improved tools and equipment if and when they could afford it.

The pioneers of New Jersey were able to bring in more goods and gear than those on most other frontiers, and, though they had to improvise for a while, not many years elapsed before most could enjoy the goods and services of tanners, shoemakers, and harnessmakers, of blacksmiths, wheelwrights, and wagonmakers, of joiners, cabinetmakers, and coopers, of weavers and tailors, of distillers, and so on. Early farmers built simple vats and used bark from trees in nearby clearings and woodlots to tan the hides of animals they killed for meat, but sooner or later some individuals enlarged their operations, accepted custom work, and bought or traded raw hides from their neighbors. Since the average farmer was not skilled in the handling of leather, the appearance of a cordwainer (shoemaker) in a neighborhood was a welcome event. The shoemaker usually did part of his work in his home or shop, but often "whipped the cat" from farmhouse to farmhouse, making and repairing boots and shoes on the spot. The manufacture of harness and saddles was even more intricate and seldom attempted except by a trained artisan.

One of the first and most important of the artisans was the blacksmith, who not only shoed horses but made plows, harrow teeth, scythes, grindstones, hoes, spades, forks, spikes, and nails for the community. Iron was a scarce and expensive item and at first had to be imported by sea and then transported by wagon to the locality that required it. At a later time, local iron manufacturers would supply part of the need. Because of the cost of iron, wood was used as much as possible in making farm implements. For instance, the sturdy triangular harrow of the day was simply a frame of oak through which iron teeth had been inserted at intervals. Likewise, the plow had a point and share of iron, but a moldboard made mostly of wood, and of course a wooden frame. This utilization of native materials was a mark of the times. It was the result of the high cost of transportation and the acute shortage of buying power in the new farming areas.

The miller and sawyer, often the same man, were in a sense harbingers of the passing of the frontier, so necessary did they become in developing the economy. The blacksmith was often something of a wheelwright and a wagonmaker as well, but he became so much in demand for other tasks that he eventually found it necessary to take a partner or tolerate a rival for the supplementary trades. Frontier women were so busy with their wheels spinning flax and wool that they were quick to patronize a weaver when one made an appearance. Tailors were not numerous, but enough farmers needed good clothes for church services to support at least an occasional one whipping the cat through the neighborhood. There was always a need of carpenters of one kind or another, but lack of ability to pay caused the early farmer to do much of his own carpentry.

An immediate problem for the pioneer was fencing. Either every farmer of a neighborhood must restrain his livestock, or else growing crops must be so enclosed that wandering livestock would not eat and trample them. For several decades the latter choice was the usual one. In fact, early provincial laws in both East and West Jersey made it necessary for a farmer to enclose a crop with a "legal fence" 4 feet 3 inches in height to be eligible for the collection of damages caused by wandering livestock. Animals must, of course, bear the registered brand or earmark of the owner. Strays and animals caught within fenced areas were taken to the municipal pound. To redeem an animal the owner must pay a board bill and, in most cases, pay for damages done.[25] The first farmers on the frontier used makeshift fences of felled trees or stumps as supports for rails. No one is sure who invented the worm fence or snake fence, though another name, "Virginia fence," probably indicates its place of origin. In any case, such fences made of split rails from timber close at hand (usually, but not always, chestnut or oak), and laid in a zigzag pattern, were a natural answer to the problem of enclosing animals or protecting crops. A worm fence could be made high enough and strong enough to turn any stock.

The post and rail fence, which required less timber but more work both as to installation and as to upkeep, appeared more slowly, being used at first only by the few who were interested in appearances. At a later time, it came into its own, particularly in areas where timber was scarce. Another kind of fence, used for gardens and other small plots, was made of split palings. The fences of a farm represented a prodigious amount of labor, since every field must be enclosed. It may seem surprising that the white hawthorn or "quick," so common in the English Midlands, was not widely adopted here, though seriously introduced by English settlers in Hunterdon and elsewhere. Perhaps this was because of the large initial investment in labor or because of the time it took to grow a hedge formidable enough to turn a "breechy" cow or a roaming "wind splitter" hog. In a few areas, field stones for stockproof barriers were obtained as a side result of clearing the fields. Because of the high cost of labor, the stones were in most cases simply piled rather than carefully laid.

Pioneer farmers by their own accounts despised the forests, and deemed themselves lucky when they could acquire lands denuded of trees by the makers of charcoal for the iron furnaces. Nevertheless, it was from the forests that they obtained their building materials, their fences, and much of their equipment, as well as the fuel for the cavernous and voracious fireplaces of the day. There were limited markets for some timber products, and these increased as the country filled up. A by-product of the cutting of oak, hemlock, and to a lesser extent other trees was bark, which was sold to tanners. Good white and black oak timber might be sold for making staves and headings for barrels, and the best hickory could be marketed to makers of wagon frames and wheels and tool handles. Shell-bark hickory nuts, walnuts, butternuts, and chestnuts were too plentiful to have any regular sale value.

When large quantities of logs were burned in order to clear a field, it was sometimes worthwhile for a farm family to extract pearlash from the ashes for sale. At any rate, the ashes would furnish lye for making soap from waste fat. In his war on the forest, it was natural that the individual farmer should clear first the portions of his land best suited for crops and pasturage, leaving hilly, stony, or infertile areas as backwoods land. The good timber of these areas might tempt the pioneer or his immediate descendants, but it was only long after the frontier period that timberlands as such acquired much value. A time came, however, when those families that had done the best job of clearing their farms were forced to buy or lease woodlots, often at a distance, in order to have a supply of timber, rails, and cordwood.

The frontier in New Jersey changed constantly. It did not last for many years in most places, though it persisted longer the farther its remove from the first centers of settlement. Its various segments were pushed forward with uneven speed, bypassing for a time areas that would be developed later. The filling out of the farmland of New Jersey was, therefore, a slow process. Several generations lived and died between the time of the first pioneering of the Dutch and Swedes in the 1630s and the last frontier of consequence, that of northwestern New Jersey, which began in the 1760s.

To describe a typical or average new farm would be impossible, but there were features common to all. The pioneer was very busy with certain tasks, the completion of which would take his farm out of the frontier status. In the meantime, while enlarging year after year the area open to the sky, he must make a living for himself and those dependent on him. Among girdled trees or stumps, he must produce enough grain and other crops for his family and an increasing number of livestock. He must build barns and outbuildings to match his farming operations, and his dwelling very likely would have to be enlarged or replaced before he had cut the timber from his back fields. But as more and more acres were cleared he could gradually change from oxen to horses for power and could use lighter and more efficient tillage implements. A sure sign that a farmer was leaving the pioneer class was the increasing commercialization of his operations.

Although always a general purpose farmer, he had been, consciously or unconsciously, "in search of a staple," that is, a crop around which he could build most of his operations and of which he could have a surplus for sale. There eventually came a time when he had wheat, corn-fattened cattle or hogs, or cider above his own needs to put on the market. Some necessities he had had to buy from the beginning, and he had tried valiantly to pay for them with his by-products and small surpluses, but in addition there had always been other less vital needs and the small luxuries which he and his family craved but could not afford. Now he had the cash or, more likely, book credit at the local store to satisfy at least some of these desires. He left gladly enough, and without fanfare, the category of nearly self-sufficient pioneer for that of a true member of an agricultural economy.[26]

However, by the time this occurred there had been a notable change in the farmer's attitude. The first generation of immigrants had left behind them in Europe an agriculture which was on the whole static and traditional, though it is true that there were gentlemen farmers who were doing some experimenting. The very shock of leaving nearly everything behind perhaps made the newcomers to America more adjustable than would otherwise have been the case, and certainly sheer necessity made them adopt an experimental approach. But this was not true for long, for they were soon molded into a new pattern by the exigencies of their situation and the need of becoming nearly self-sufficient. The lessons of the frontier were so well learned that agriculture again became traditional. The emerging pattern soon became so firmly set that only necessity or very obvious advantage would change it.

Some examples of the hardening of custom will illustrate. The discovery that farm animals, or the toughest of them, could live through New Jersey winters without shelter led to poor treatment at a later time when giving them some protection might have paid off. Even the descendants of Dutch, Swedish, and German farmers eventually followed the usual custom in this matter. Again the pioneers had used woods and brushy land for pasturage, for lack of better. At a later time farmland that "wore out beyond bearing wheat" simply became "brushy pasture," no attempt being made to build it up despite obvious advantages from doing so. Apples grew so readily from the start that cider became the universal beverage, sweet or hard or in the form of applejack. After a time, not even the descendants of the beer-drinking Swedes and Germans, would have dreamed of changing the prevailing custom.

Sheer necessity sometimes did bring some later changes, such as the use of land plaster (calcined gypsum) to encourage the sprouting of grain on infertile land. Sometimes the lure of gain would cause a change in emphasis, as, for example, the expansion of the production of applejack, usually called apple whiskey and sometimes apple brandy, soon after the American Revolution. But in general the questioning mood of the average American farmer was gone. New traditions as binding as the old had been created. American agricultural methods and attitudes had slipped into a groove, and American agriculture had become fully as static and traditional as European agriculture. Ironically enough, when the Agricultural Revolution came, it began in Western Europe.

2

The Period of Static,
Traditional Agriculture

4

Agricultural Management

Those who like neat packaging are likely to be annoyed at this point, for the period to which we now turn has no beginning date that fits all of New Jersey. As each farming community slipped over from the stage of pioneer agriculture into that of settled agriculture, it can be said that it put on the mantle of conservatism. This happened early in northeastern and southwestern New Jersey, where agriculture was already mature by 1700, but only late in the colonial period for many others. Northwestern New Jersey, long a wilderness, ended its frontier stage only in the 1780s. As for a terminal point for the new period, none fits very exactly. Innovations of one kind or another had appeared in recent decades, but it was only about 1810 that they were marked enough to indicate real change. If we accept that date as the end point for the dominance of traditional agriculture, it must be with some trepidation because of a natural lag on the part of many farmers, but it does fit all regions about equally well, since by this time the areas settled last had nearly caught up with the earlier settlements. Thus it was that the period of static, traditional agriculture was very long for the earliest regions settled but a very short one for those last carved from the forests. Specifically, it lasted from about 1700 to 1810 in Middlesex and Salem counties, from about 1730 to 1810 in Monmouth and Hunterdon, from about 1775 to 1810 in Ocean and Warren, and only from about 1790 to 1810 in Sussex.

The European agriculture that the colonists left behind had been established through the centuries by trial and error. Farmers had worked out an agricultural pattern that fitted the time and place. Changes had come when necessity or obvious advantage dictated, but they had come slowly and had been adopted with reluctance by the mass of farmers. The emigrants did not at once forget their heritage or their habits. Some, perhaps, were more venturesome and open of mind than those who stayed at home, but one suspects that most were average people. Be this as it may, they had left a settled countryside for a wilderness. As we have

seen, this alone was enough to cause a terrific wrench in their lives and
to cause a reassessment of values and a change of emphasis. To survive,
they had improvised and had learned from their own experiences and
that of others. Once the forest had been tamed, however, the need for
innovation had declined, and a new pattern of agriculture had developed
with farming modes as rigid as those of Europe. During the ensuing period, when tradition ruled, most Americans looked askance at the new
devices and methods of the occasional innovators, and adopted them
reluctantly only if their superiority became obvious. The traditionalist
in agriculture fears anything except the known, the tried and true. Agriculture here for a surprisingly long time would be dominated by the dirt
farmer philosophy that *the* way to do a thing was that hallowed by time.

An outstanding characteristic of the farming of the period was its
extensive nature. Land there was in plenty, but capital and labor must
be sparingly applied because of their comparative high cost. Since land
was the cheapest factor in the economic formula, it received the least
respect. European travelers were very critical of this feature of New Jersey farming, as of farming elsewhere in America, without really understanding its cause. Kalm in 1749 considered New Jersey farm practices
hurried and careless, and the anonymous author of *American Husbandry,*
speaking of New Jersey farmers, stated in 1775 that "plenty of land ruins
their husbandry in every respect." [1] Théophile Cazenove, traveling in
Morris County in 1794, wrote, "They use their surplus not to improve
their places, but to buy more land." [2]

Since the typical farm family had from one to two hundred acres of
land, the simple mathematics of the situation shows that only part of
the land could have been fully utilized. Count Constantine Volney, a
French traveler journeying from Boston to Richmond in 1797, reported
that he was seldom out of sight of a forest.[3] In New Jersey he undoubtedly
saw more forest than cleared land in many areas. Travelers even decades
later mentioned repeatedly the large acreage of woods and brushy land,
both of which were used as indifferent pasture. The fact that the typical
farmer grazed more acreage than the number of his livestock would seem
to warrant indicates that the pasture was poor. As to the cropland, there
can be no doubt that the amount cultivated was high in proportion to
the return. Many observers thought that the farmer would have gained
by farming less land more intensively. Within limits, this may have been
true in the later part of the period, but the farmer until that time can
hardly be blamed for not applying principles that he did not know.

Land in America, in comparison with that of Europe, was cheap. But
both capital and labor were in short supply, and neither could normally
be used for conservation practices, particularly during the earlier part

of the period. The short view, often the only one the farmer could afford, prevented a rotation of crops, efficient use of natural fertilizers, and even attempts to slow the tendency of the soil "to go down the river" whenever it rained. By the time the pioneers had cleared a part of their land they had discarded such memories of soil care as they may have had. It is little wonder that their sons grew up without any inkling of its importance.

A farmer near Flemington in 1788 explained at some length that after a time land would wear out as a matter of course. Accused of spoiling his land, he huffily stated that this was the land of liberty and that a man could do as he pleased with what was his own.[4] The wastefulness of the day of the pioneer had thus been carried over into the period of settled agriculture. Economics had dictated an extensive agriculture in the beginning, and tradition had carried it forward. There was no recognized incentive for change, and sloth and ignorance undoubtedly played their part. It seems rather clear that a majority of New Jersey's farmers retained wasteful practices long after the economic reasons, even the short-term ones, had disappeared.

Perceptive foreign travelers and native observers noted this land butchery with concern. Peter Kalm gave a discouraging picture in which the typical farmer cropped a field with grain year after year until its fertility was gone, then fallowed it or used it for pasture, but without making any effort to keep down weed growth. "One can learn nothing on a large tract of land, neither of the English nor of the Swedes, Germans, Dutch, and French, except that, from their gross mistakes and carelessness for futurity, one finds opportunity every day for making all sorts of observations, and of growing wise at the expense of other people. In a word, the corn-fields, the meadows, the cattle, &c., are treated with equal carelessness."[5]

The writer of *American Husbandry* in 1775 was even more scathing in his remarks, though he found a number of experimenters already correcting the worst faults on their own land. He wrote,

There is no error of husbandry of worse consequence than not being sufficiently solicitous about manure; it is this error which makes the planters in New Jersey and our other colonies seem to have but one object, which is ploughing up fresh land. Whereas would they be properly attentive, raising as much manure as possible at the same time that they introduced their crops in a proper system so as to keep the land clean and in heart, in this case they would find no such necessity of changing the soil: and by the use of clovers in the manner they are shown in Britain, all of their lands would be in profit, and perhaps equally profitable; instead of which they have now only a part under the plow that pays them anything, and the rest are over-run with weeds and trumpery. One would imagine that the error of such conduct would soon be discovered and rectified of itself; but American planters are in general the greatest slovens in Christendom.[6]

The journal of Charles Read indicates that much of the original fertility had already been lost by the middle of the eighteenth century.[7] The Capner family of Hunterdon County in their letters to relatives in England in the 1780s and 1790s stated that in many fields the original fertility had been so depleted that neither grain nor bluegrass would grow and that considerable land once in cultivation was now on its way back to forest.

Most European immigrants had no experience with intense and sudden rains of the kind that occur frequently in New Jersey. This explains in part the fact that erosion became a serious, sometimes an insuperable, problem. Steep slopes were not cleared until a later date, but the soil losses from sheet erosion on comparatively level land and from gullying of hillsides and slopes were considerable in the early years, and unfortunately have continued to some degree to the present time. No remedy for the former was generally known, and the only cure known for the latter was to abandon the land to Nature's kinder care. Where erosion affected only part of a field, continuing farming operations eventually exposed the subsoil, thus creating discernible "red spots" in red shale areas. It has been calculated that New Jersey has lost more than half its soil since its first settlement. This calamity was perhaps inevitable, since the frame of mind that went with extensive agriculture was hardly one to cope with erosion losses.

The sad effects of neglect were so obvious that advocates of less wasteful farming methods were to be found from an early time. The usual farm leases during this period made pious mention of the duty of tenants to manure the fields and rotate crops. The landlords, many of whom lived in England or had come from England, doubtless hoped for at least some recognition of the terms of the agreement, but all available evidence is quite to the contrary. More important, an increasing number of gentlemen farmers adopted the soil-conserving practices already known and in time learned new techniques by trial and error. Charles Read in the 1740s was growing red clover, and possibly other legumes, in the crop rotations he practiced on his Burlington County farm. In the 1750s he expressed interest in rye grass ("Ray grass"), one of the best preventatives for erosion, but did not record any use of it by himself or his neighbors. He and others of his persuasion were especially interested in "mudding," the improvement of fields by hauling in and spreading various types of earth.

According to Read, a farmer near Mount Holly had added sand to mucky soil and was able to grow white clover. About 1754 the De Normandies of Northampton Township, Burlington County, plowed in fifty loads of "mudd" per acre on a 20-acre field. Half of it was "blew mudd out of an old ditch," the remainder somewhat sandy soil from "an inland swamp." Possibly the earth in one case or another was at least in part greensand marl, the rejuvenating qualities of which later led to its widespread use. In an experiment beginning in 1754, Joshua Fenimore of Willingsborough Township of the same county put a load of hassocks—that is, clumps or roots of bogland grass—on a plot of "dry, sandy land" and allowed them to rot for two years. In the spring of 1756 he "cut them in pieces" and plowed them under, later receiving a good crop of corn as a reward. Read wrote, "Hassocks if laid in a heap will rott tolerably in 2 yrs., if spread at once they roll about a field several years."

Read reported the use of numerous enriching agents. William Cooke of Crosswicks put shovelsful of "loose and fibrous" soil on his corn hills, and found the benefits equal to those of manure; however, he had "no noticeable service" from blue mud from an "adjoining bank." William Hugg on his "plantation" at Gloucester found "horse dung mudd ʸe best." A number of other farmers in Burlington County, and, by implication, elsewhere, were trying mudding operations, their success or lack of it depending on the type of earth they added. As Read pointed out, a weakness of the practice, which was laborious at best, was that soil could not profitably be transported very far. He mentioned two farmers on a local creek who had "extraordinary success" some years before in using silt from a stream. Since the fields they enriched were alongside the creek, the problem of carting was fairly simple.[8] The spreading of ashes on cropland probably originated as an answer to the problem of the disposal of ashes on recently cleared land. At any rate, many, including Read, were trying them out as an enriching agent. One criticism was that the benefits lasted for only a year or two.

Unfortunately, we can only guess how widespread were efforts to improve the soil, but there are indications that those favoring such measures were a growing number. It is significant that the men experimenting with "mudd," ashes, salt, and rotted vegetation were also careful to utilize all manure produced on their farms. These leaders in a movement for soil improvement were joined a few decades later by many whose land had become marginal from abuse. One of the earliest manifestations of the coming transformation of agriculture was the use of calcined lime and land plaster on the exhausted soils of the state.

The New Jersey farmer of this period knew from practice that crop land would produce more if it had an occasional rest. Sometimes he would fallow a field for a season, which meant in practice that he would allow a crop of weeds to grow. This growth he might or might not plow under. The laudable practice of plowing under green manure crops, such as clover, was strongly urged in a farmers' handbook in 1804,[9] but the practice as yet was far from universal. More commonly the farmer rested land from certain crops by planting others, in other words, by practicing a rotation. In any case, considerable diversification was forced upon him by the needs of his livestock and of his household. Furthermore, since different crops require work at different seasons, diversification enabled him to spread his work load and to farm a greater acreage. The working periods for corn and for the small grains scarcely encroached upon one another, and the oats and hay harvest came after corn was laid by and wheat and rye were in the shock. This balancing of operations sometimes led to a laudable rotation. For instance, since wheat and oats often were nurse crops for timothy and clover, which were needed for hay, the grain land had an occasional rest. Unless he had considerable untillable land, the farmer's needs for pasture might require him to encroach upon his arable land. Or he might deliberately convert into pasture land which had lost part of its fertility from overcropping. In either case, there would be some benefit from the manure of the grazing animals. On the other hand, the rooting of hogs and the making of hillside paths by other farm animals sometimes started gullies.

The farm unit during this period of static, traditional agriculture was seldom large. In consequence of land-jobbing operations of the proprietary groups, individuals often received considerable tracts of land. Many of them sat back waiting for a rise in land values, often attempting during the interim to rent out land on profitable terms. But the losses resulting from timber pilferage, farming by squatters, taxation, and lawsuits over land titles caused many estates to be broken up before very long. Furthermore, the seizure of Tory lands by the state and their sale to patriot farmers during the American Revolution accelerated this trend toward subdivision. Whether owner or tenant, the average individual farmer of the era ran a small establishment. He was seldom a specialist, though his diversification was not always from choice. Even in this period of slow change he would gladly have produced more staples in order to gain cash or credit; but with the tools at his command and the eternal shortage of labor, he could not profitably expand any operation beyond a certain point. To illustrate, it would have been nonsense for him to grow more wheat than he could reap during the short harvest season. Again he could not profitably raise cattle or hogs for meat, or sheep for wool, beyond the capacities of his farm for pasture, forage, and feed grains.

Since buying power was restricted, he must produce many necessities. These included nearly all foodstuffs, animal and vegetable, for his household, the flax and wool for making homespun cloth, and a multitude of homemade goods, ranging from goose-feather pillows to rye stalk ties for

fodder shocks. Under the circumstances, there were few regional variations of agriculture during this time. Such specialization as there was did
not loom large. Many farmers of northeastern New Jersey and quite a
few elsewhere produced cider and applejack ("Jersey lightning") to sell
to their neighbors and for eventual export to the South and abroad. But
in nearly every case this was a sideline to general farming. It must be
clear, however, that the self-sufficiency of the period was a relative thing.
Every farm had surpluses that were exchanged by book transactions with
the local storekeeper for articles needed or desired and which the farm
could not produce.[10]

It would be difficult, even in this period, to give a detailed description
of the operations of a typical or average farm. In his journey across the
state in 1794 Théophile Cazenove pictured farms ranging from those of
"the poorest country people" to the 1,650-acre "manor" of land-poor
Lucas van Beverhoudt of Morris County. The diversity within the state
as to surface and soil prevented the farms of one area from being entirely
like those of another. Again one farm might be within easy traveling
distance by wagon of a thriving village market for perishables, another
nearly cut off from contact with settled communities. Also one farmer
might be plagued by hillside erosion, another by the problem of draining
boggy fields. Nevertheless, there was a framework within which most
farmers of the period operated. Each must have enough pasture for his
livestock, which usually included his woodlot if it was an integral part
of the farm. (A farmer often had a woodlot at a distance, in land too
broken or boggy for agricultural use.) Nearly everyone produced bread
grains and meats, very often with a marketable surplus. A farmer's emphasis as to wheat or rye depended on his land, rye being considerably
the hardier of the two.

There was little advantage in producing extra corn, but the requirements of farm and family made it an essential and important crop, and
on most farms more acreage was devoted to it than any other grain. Oats
were relatively more important than at a later time, for the farmer required both the grain and the straw for his horses and cattle. Because of
the universal human liking for buckwheat cakes and because the grain
was an approved feed for hogs and poultry, nearly every farm had some
acres of this crop. The growing of barley was less prevalent, though it
was known in most neighborhoods. The perennial need for an adequate
supply of hay caused the farmer to mow native grasses on untilled and
unpastured meadows and to cultivate more and more hay crops of European origin, particularly timothy and clover. Though the acreage was
not large, flax was a crop of some consequence on most farms in that
day of home production of linen and tow cloth. The vegetable garden
was often disparaged, but it was an important adjunct of every farm. John

Rutherford estimated in 1788 that New Jersey farm women made such good gardens that they were "half the support of their families." [11]

In his livestock operations, as with his crops, the farmer of necessity practiced some diversification. Horses furnished most of the power and transportation. Cattle were needed for dairy products, meat, and leather, and oxen were used for heavy tasks throughout the period. Sheep were kept for wool, hogs furnished most of the winter meat supply, and poultry gave the farm family both eggs and meat. A Hunterdon County tax list of 1732 shows that almost every farmer of that area had horses, cattle, and hogs, and that nearly half had sheep. In 1734 Duncan Oliphant, a farmer slightly above average in the size of his operations, had 16 horses, 15 cattle, 16 sheep, and 16 hogs.[13] In 1788, rather late in the period, John Rutherford, describing the average New Jersey farm, wrote, "Each farm keeps from 20 to 40 sheep, from 3 to 10 Cows, besides young Stock, from 3 to 8 Horses, unfortunately few Oxen being used for Draught." His figure for sheep was too high, and he forgot to mention hogs until later in his account.[14]

The plentiful natural pasturage on vacant lands disappeared with the frontier, except for acorns and nuts in the woods in some sections. The practice of allowing animals to roam freely was progressively curtailed by local ordinances, which increased the pound charges assessed for boarding strays. Owners attempted to keep stock within bounds by building fences and by using hobbles, yokes, and other restraining devices. Yokes were used on horses, cattle, sheep, hogs, and even geese. Nevertheless, straying animals were a problem throughout the period, as evidenced by constant lawsuits for crop damages. Brands and other markings, registered with township authorities, were still used to make easier the recovery of lost animals, though to a lesser degree than formerly. Two stray ewes in 1742 in what is now Mercer County were thus described: "Marked as follows, one hath a Crop on each ear and a Half penny Under Side of ye Near Ear—the other hath a Crop on the Near Ear and a Half penny under the off Ear." [15] (A "half penny" was made with a type of nippers that cut an arc at the edge of the ear.)

Farming in this period was a most laborious business. In spring the farmer spent many weary days following a walking plow or harrow and planting fields of corn with a hoe, hill by hill; and week after week in the summer he swung a scythe, harvesting rye, wheat, oats, and hay in succession. At various times came backbreaking toil with ax and beetle, with hand rake and pitchfork, with corn knife and flail, and with the various devices for the broadcast sowing of seeds. Not only was farm work hard, but the rate of accomplishment was necessarily limited. With the best of intentions, the farmer, no matter how strong and efficient, could by himself farm only a small acreage. The farmer of consequence required help, and the economy was one in which the price of labor was high.

The farmer's own family was usually his greatest and most trustworthy source of labor. In fact, many a farmer had no other, except that he might trade labor in a rough and ready fashion with his neighbors through the institution of the "frolic" or "bee." Colonial records abound with references to men with three, four, five, or more sons. Daughters were considered lesser assets, but their household tasks were very essential. The injunction to multiply had a strong economic basis, generation after generation. Albert Opdyke, a farmer of Hopewell, had five sons and three daughters. John, his oldest son, had four sons and five daughters. Three of John's sons had ten, seven, and five children respectively, and four of his grandsons had seven, twelve, eight, and ten children. At least two of John's brothers were just as prolific. The nine 6-foot sons of Richard Opdyke of Kingwood Township, Hunterdon County, without doubt gave him as much of a labor force as he needed.[16]

The Rockefellers of that day were farmers. John Peter Rockefeller of Hunterdon County, an ancestor of John D. Rockefeller, had 2 sons who perpetuated his name by giving him 12 grandsons, who in turn passed on the name to 51 great-grandsons.[17] Mrs. Mary Capner, a midwife at Flemington in the 1790s, collected some interesting statistics from the farm people around her. In 1791 she wrote of a woman who at her death left 17 children, 130 grandchildren, 100 great-grandchildren, and 1 great-great-grandchild. A friend of one of her clients told Mrs. Capner apologetically that she herself had "but eight." Mrs. Capner, who was an English Midlands woman with a puckish sense of humor, wrote of a Yorkshireman who visited her family before going on to live in what is now Warren County:

He expects his wife and seven children in the spring. I tell him this is a fruitful country, so he may expect to be the father of Seventeen (Aew, Nae, he said) and that his daughter will be married and have children before her mother has done.[18]

Widows and widowers usually remarried, in many cases uniting two families.

Farmers could and did have productive tasks for their sons and daughters from an early age. Artisans and mechanics often put their whole families to work, and any son who did not respond well could be hired out to a farmer. Ministers, lawyers, doctors, and teachers did not have the same advantage, but their sons could find farm work and their daughters could spin and sew and cook to help earn their keep. The home labor force was without a doubt a large factor in the economy of the period.

Bond servitude was a device which in practice served a double function.

It brought in immigrants who would never have been able to raise money for ship's passage, and who helped to fill the acute labor shortage of the new land. Despite the common designation of "indentured servants," many such servants had no such indentures, or contracts, and became servants for four or five years under one or another of a series of colonial New Jersey laws. The probate papers of the period have many cases in which the "remaining time" of servants was itemized among the assets to be sold. Kalm reported that the number of servants in New Jersey in 1749 was large, and Cazenove in 1794 wrote that it was usual for poor Scottish and Irish (probably Scotch-Irish) and German immigrants to become servants. The number of such servants seems to have increased after 1740, but certainly it declined after the Revolution.[19]

Most servants were employed on farms or in houses, but occasionally an artist or professional man sold his services for a term in order to get passage to America. In 1757 Cornelius van Horn, a prosperous farmer near Whitehouse, "bought" Casper Berger, a German stonemason who had been shanghaied at a North German port. Instead of binding himself to a stated term of service, Berger agreed to build three stone houses for members of the family. That done, he settled down in the neighborhood and became a prosperous farmer. Eighteen years later he and four neighbors, including three of the van Horns, offered a reward for the return of a fugitive bond servant whom they had bought to teach their district school.[20] The Capners and their relatives brought over bond servants and in general preferred their labor to that of local hired helpers. They treated their servants kindly and gave them incentive pay, and, if possible, retained them as hired hands after their terms were up. However, many advertisements of runaways through the years indicate that personal relations between master and servant were not always good. When Richard M'Kane, the Irish servant of Bowton Shull of Salem County, departed abruptly in 1776, the latter characterized him as "a drunken, lying, deceitful fellow" who had stolen his beautiful "claret coloured coat." Just the same, he wanted him back.[21] Johann Karl Büttner, a German servant of a West Jersey Quaker in the early 1770s, complained to a justice of the peace that his master had struck him. On the advice of the magistrate, the master sold the boy's remaining time to a neighbor. Büttner later deserted from the American army to the Hessians. Back in Germany, he became a doctor and a prominent citizen. As an old man, it amused him to write that he had once been traded for a yoke of oxen.[22]

The farmers of this period sometimes acquired workers through the apprenticing of children. A parent or guardian made a contract which bound the child until he was of age or for a definite number of years. Poor children might be bound out by a township overseer of the poor with the consent of a local justice of the peace. The form of contract came by custom to include certain terms, and was later regulated by law. The master on his part must give the apprentice bed and board and must teach him a trade or business, in the case of a farmer that of farming or (for a girl) housewifery. The child must serve the master's interests, and of course must work for him. Under the best of conditions, the arrangement could be one to the advantage of both master and apprentice, but there were many examples of cruelty and ill-usage and others in which ungrateful brats took off over the hill with whatever they could steal.[23] The use of apprentices was an integral part of the economic system, and there were always advertisements for children "of good morals and industrious habits." Artisans, in particular, needed them, but farmers also could use a great many, of both sexes. Children of immigrants were often apprenticed, and sometimes parents in Europe sent children to America under a definite apprentice arrangement rather than ordinary indenture.[24] Probably the largest source of supply for apprentices was the pauper class. Orphans, in particular, were apprenticed in order to provide for them until they could make a living by their own efforts. Manumitted Negro children also were often apprenticed, and as a result of state legislation in 1804, children born henceforth of slave mothers became term apprentices rather than slaves of their masters.

An attempted answer to the labor shortage in early New Jersey was the acquisition of slaves. Only the Quakers were opposed in principle to slavery, and even they had some slaves. Among others the institution was widespread. The ratio of blacks to whites was never great, and the only true slave gangs were those at a few ironworks. The usual master had one or two, or at most three or four slaves. Sometimes a substantial part of the personal property of an estate consisted of one or two slaves. A provincial census of 1745 showed 4,600 slaves in a population of 61,383.[25] The first national census tin 1790 reported 11,423 slaves in New Jersey, which means that approximately one person in sixteen was a slave at that time. The number increased by a thousand by 1800, but declined after that time, especially after passage of the law of 1804 for gradual abolition. By 1830 only 2,246 persons were considered slaves, and by 1860 there were only a score or so left in the state, all of them old persons being cared for by their white patrons.[26]

The chief occupation of most male slaves in New Jersey was general farm work, and that of female slaves was housework. Records of stores and tanneries show numerous examples of slaves on farms, and doctors' records mention the bleeding of the slaves of their farmer neighbors and the administration of the emetics and cathartics that were the principal remedies of the times. The owners of runaway slaves who advertised in the newspapers were usually farmers. Negro farmhands were apparently allowed that freedom of action necessary to helpers on a general farm.

Account books of the period mention numerous instances in which slaves ran errands or made trips for their masters, the transaction often involving the exchange of money. The usual female slave was a maid of all work and a general helper in the household.[27] A vendue notice in a Trenton paper in 1781 read as follows:

A Negro Man and his wife, with two male Children. The man is a complete farmer. The wench is an exceedingly good dairy woman, and can wash, iron, and cook very well. They are honest and sober.[28]

A substantial number of the liberated slaves became hired hands, and a relatively few became farmers. Many became laborers in the growing villages and cities.

5

Working Equipment and Methods

In spite of the slowness of tempo, there were during this period some changes in the types of buildings, working equipment, and farming methods. It may seem something of an anomaly that, during the very time soil fertility was declining through land abuse, the devices for carrying out farming operations were being gradually improved. Soil chemistry was so far beyond the comprehension of the farmer of the period that even when he was faced with the obvious need of returning to the soil what he took out he did not know how to proceed. But when it came to techniques and equipment, he sometimes, almost in spite of himself, found or adopted something new. That changes came slowly and that innovations were only gradually adopted becomes apparent from a survey of the probate inventories through the period. The changes were always of a kind that the farmer could see and understand. Furthermore, it is clear enough that the degree of modification was never in any sense revolutionary. The farmer newly emerged from the pioneer stage would have felt quite at home at the end of the following period in the early nineteenth century.[1]

Specific problems led in some cases to the devising of entirely new tools or equipment or the adoption of new ones. The "tumbling Tom," a wooden device which helped beat out the grain as it was pulled over the threshing floor, was created in response to a need. The same can be said of the furrowing sled, used to mark the locations for the planting of corn hills. As for the grain cradle, a device invented in England before 1600 but brought here by gentlemen farmers only in the late colonial period, the advantages of using it were so obvious that it eventually came into general use. Windmills were also brought from England, and a number were in operation by 1750. Most of the new working tools and equipment of the New Jersey farmer, and of American farmers generally, in this static period were simply adaptations and variations of tools and devices known on both sides of the Atlantic. The constant stream of immigrants brought in European models, which might or might not be widely copied.

The slight variations between the tools and equipment of one area and those of another were due to differences in the original models, to the peculiarities and working habits of local blacksmiths, and to preferences of the farmers themselves, usually as a result of trial and comparison. John Hall, an opinionated Englishman who came to Flemington to live in 1786, endorsed some American devices and condemned others. For instance, he advised relatives against bringing over English metal containers for use in cheesemaking on the grounds that American cedar tubs were superior and cheaper. On the other hand, he suggested that they bring harrow teeth and either an English plow or the specifications for making one.[2]

Every family acquired in time a formidable array of tools, ranging in size and function from the shoemaker's awl to the long hooks used in harvesting ice for storage. Forks, rakes, spades, sickles, and scythes were made in various sizes and shapes. Axes and saws had already gone through a transformation during the frontier stage, and a multiplicity of augers, adzes, mauls, planes, drawknives, files, and other tools were added to the woodworking equipment.[3]

Wheelwrights who had had some training abroad before coming to America added to the number of vehicles in common use. A young lady traveling west from New Brunswick in 1793 wrote to her parents in England, "A light waggon that is what they travail in in America. I think they are much pleasanter than in coaches." [4] She probably referred to the Jersey wagon, a type of light farm wagon long peculiar to the area. Quite simple and made in various sizes, it seems likely that it was a New Jersey development adapted from English originals. For heavier hauling, the Conestoga wagon of the Pennsylvania Germans was freely copied in variations from the lightest farm type to the heaviest freighter. Vehicles for travel were even more varied. In the 1780s, the Capners reported two-wheeled carts, sulkies, chairs (pulled by one horse or two), chaises or "shays" with either two or four wheels, and occasional carriages. Other vehicles included phaetons and coaches.

Farming equipment for working the soil also went through something of a transformation. The heavy plows and harrows and log rollers, pulled by plodding oxen, gave way to lighter equipment drawn by horses. The plow was considerably improved, and the triangular harrow frame, useful among roots and stumps, was gradually replaced by a rectangular one of considerably larger size. But here too the changes were not fundamental ones. Methods of work were seldom altered very much, and any changes in the direction of efficiency and laborsaving were limited ones. In any case, there was always work in plenty to be done with hand tools, which of course could not be improved beyond a certain point.[5]

The problem of fencing had to a considerable degree been solved by the frontiersman. His temporary makeshifts by now had largely disappeared, though Thomas Capner in 1787 wrote that some farmers of northwestern New Jersey still used stumps to support their rails.[6] But for a farmer to have sufficient worm or snake fence was simply a matter of him finding enough manpower. Stands of oak, chestnut, cedar, walnut, or sassafras were close at hand or within hauling distance. In early parlance, all that was required was "a strong back and a weak mind." The legal height of a fence remained four feet three inches until 1714. In that year the Province of New Jersey, which had been created in 1702 by combining East and West Jersey, enacted a law setting a minimum of 4 feet 6 inches, which, as far as worm fences were concerned, remained the requirement into the national period.[7] Critics objected that this type of fence used a great deal of timber and that its zigzag path required a wide fence row which often encroached on arable land. Nevertheless it was much used. A typical West Jersey farm offered for sale in 1776 had "a strong new fence . . . round the lines, with convenient partition fences, and rails enough now to keep the fence in repair for many years." [8]

Some older areas had depleted their forests by this time, so that the farmers had to haul rails from a distance, often from woodlots that they owned in some partly cleared area. They, in particular, tended to make post and rail fences instead of worm fences. These were neater, required only a narrow fence row, and needed not nearly as many rails. Another advantage was that after 1730, as the result of new legislation, this type of fence need be only 4 feet 2 inches in height.[9] Unfortunately, the post and rail fence took more labor and time for construction. The posts were often squared, although this was not necessary, and holes had to be chiseled out for the ends of the rails, which must be dressed with a broadax so as to fit the holes. A vexing feature of this type of fence was that the posts were sometimes heaved out of line by the freezing of the ground in winter and had to be straightened in the spring. Since the post and rail fence made a better appearance than the worm fence, the rare farmer who cared for such things might put a post and rail fence along the public road and worm fences elsewhere. The paling fence was still used in this period, and stone fences in a greater degree than formerly where there was native field stone, particularly in North Jersey. Hedges were tried repeatedly by innovators, but they required too great an initial outlay of capital and labor to be widely used.[10] The use of wide ditches to restrain livestock in areas where salt meadows were pastured was recognized by the law in 1730.[11]

Log houses had by no means disappeared by the beginning of this period, and they were numerous in the newest areas, such as present Warren and Sussex counties, as late as the 1790s.[12] Some of the latter-day cabins of West Jersey were larger and more elaborate than ordinary cabins or huts and were often designated in farm advertisements as good log houses. One of them was later described as about 20 feet square, and another as 20 by 35, with windows on three sides. Still another had a partial second story.[13] But farmhouses of frame, brick, and stone were the order of the day, some of them architecturally nearly as good as those of England from which they were copied. A mark of status for a farmer was to have a house of two stories, and with the large families of the time one was likely to be needed. There were usually three or four rooms on a floor, and sometimes five or six. When additional space was needed, an ell of one or two stories might be added to the original building.

The wood frame house was still the most common. The materials were close at hand, and every stream with sufficient fall had a sawmill. The skeletons of the houses were often hand-hewn oak beams, but those sawed at a local sawmill became more and more common. The outside of the frame house was covered with rough sheathing, over which thin over-lapping clapboarding was nailed. The latter was usually pine, sometimes available locally but more usually transported by wagon from a seaport or from a sawmill on the Delaware which sawed up logs rafted down the river. Within the house, pine floors and pine trim were commonly used. Cedar and pine shingles (shakes) were often transported from a distance in preference to the more generally available oak shingles. Houses of brick became more common during this period, the bricks usually being made nearby with home equipment. The fine residence that John Reading the younger built at what is now Flemington Junction in 1760 is a good example. Sometimes half-timber houses, the walls of which were filled with homemade brick, were covered with clapboarding. The skeletons of brick and stone houses were similar to those of frame houses. Most farmhouses by this time had cellars. Cooking might be done there though this was more usually done except in winter in a separate build-ing with an outside brick or stone baking oven. The cellar in any case was used for storage, though some of its earlier functions might later be relegated to a milkhouse and others to a Dutch or root cellar. There was often attached to the house or near it a shop for weaving, mending tools, and doing odd jobs.[14]

New Jersey farmers of this period were often accused by travelers, and doubtless by their own wives, of attaching more importance to having good barns than to providing their families with substantial houses. The log barns of the pioneer day were rapidly replaced by more commodious frame buildings, generally modeled after or adapted from German, Dutch, Swiss, or English prototypes. Almost invariably, the skeleton was con-structed of white oak timbers, which were covered with boards placed perpendicularly or overlapping weatherboarding placed horizontally. Kalm described a "Dutch" barn of 1748 thus:

The roof was high, covered with wooden shingles, sloping on both sides, but not steep. The walls which supported it were not much higher than a grown man, but on the other hand the breadth of the building was all the greater. In the middle was the threshing floor and above it . . . they put the unthreshed grain, the straw, or anything else, according to the season. . . . In both ends of the building were large doors, so that one could drive in with a cart and horses through one of them and go out the other. Here under one roof were the threshing floor, the barn, the stables, the hay loft, the coach house, etc. This building is used chiefly by the Dutch and the Germans.[15]

Most barns were hardly this commodious, and the livestock were usually kept in separate barns and sheds, open to the weather. Other auxiliary buildings appeared on the typical farm from time to time, such as corncribs, smokehouses, milkhouses or springhouses, wagonhouses, icehouses, hog and poultry sheds, granaries, and hay sheds.[16] The hay barrack, copied from the Dutch during pioneer days, was often by now an elaborate affair. Sometimes a small cow shed was put at the bottom, and a haystack built on it. Barracks were more common in the northern part of New Jersey than in the south. A farm emphasizing livestock might well have several of these devices.[17]

The farming practices of this period were basically those of the pioneers, but many refinements had slowly developed, usually as the result of some change in conditions. As stumps rotted and stones were removed from the fields, horses could be used for tillage operations, and since horses walk nearly twice as fast as oxen, the farmer could tend more land. More thorough tillage was now possible, particularly in the plowing operation, though it is doubted that as yet very many farmers practiced crossing, that is, plowing the land a second time at right angles to the first plowing. The uneven surfaces left after plowing were now more effectively leveled and pulverized by the improved harrows, drags, and land rollers. The anonymous author of *American Husbandry* in 1775, who reported that American farmers were "the greatest slovens in Christendom," referred to tillage after rather than before planting.[18]

In general, this is borne out in the letters of the Capners and their friends, good English farmers all, who settled in West Jersey after the American Revolution.[19] With their cumbersome plows, usually constructed of wood with an iron point, New Jersey farmers could not cultivate deeply, but the indications are that they usually prepared a fair seed bed before planting, although on newly cleared lands, which were constantly being added to compensate for worn-out lands withdrawn from cultivation, the tillage was probably not much superior to that of the frontier. A practice probably introduced and abandoned again and again by English immigrants was that of "watering the meadows." This was the irrigating of hay land by damming a stream and letting the water spread over it. There are places where a trace of the operations can still be seen, but any technique as laborious as this one naturally had only a short life.[20] As a matter of fact, the practice slowly disappeared in England also, though it lasted much longer there than in America.

As in the earlier period, small grains and the seed of hay crops were sowed by the Old World method of broadcasting, either by hand or by using a throwing device of some type. The grains required one other tool, the harrow, but hayseeds were not harrowed in. By the 1770s, some farmers, probably from desperation rather than because of a progressive attitude, broadcast before the final harrowing a bushel or two per acre of land plaster (calcined and pulverized gypsum). This fertilizer encouraged the small plants after the seed had germinated. Since the gypsum was imported from the Hudson Valley or Nova Scotia, land plaster was expensive, and farmers were not very quick to take to its use.[21] Yet a well-known handbook for farmers in 1804 implied that it was often a necessity in order to get a stand of clover.[22] Hayseed was usually sowed with wheat or rye in early fall, but sometimes with the oats crop in early spring. Since buckwheat was not sowed until late June or July, it did not make a good nurse crop for clovers and grasses.

Once the small grains were in the ground, the farmer could forget about them until harvest. In the meantime, he could concentrate on his corn crop. Then in early July came a busy time, since he had only a few days for the harvest of rye and wheat before there was danger of the grain shattering. In the case of oats, speed was not quite so important, since the grain shattered less easily. Timothy and the clovers, which were usually not cut until their second year of growth, were next in line. The harvesting of buckwheat came last of all, often after the first frosts. The farmer, with all available hands, was obviously busy with his harvest during much of the summer. The long-bladed sickle used by many early settlers had been largely replaced by the crooked scythe from England in the early eighteenth century. Since the scythe was considerably faster, and in any case was much easier on the back, only true conservatives stuck with the sickle. By the 1760s, the cradle was sometimes attached to the scythe when reaping crops that were to be bound. This device did not speed up the mowing, but laid out the stalks evenly so as to make easier the next task of binding the crop into sheaves. Men who had learned the new technique were for some years designated in harvest records as "cradlers." Other specialized tools for the harvest were the clumsy three-pronged wooden "Dutch" fork and the flail, a simple beating device consisting of two sticks held together at one end by a deerskin or eelskin thong. The frontier practice of running horses over the scattered stalks to shatter the heads had fallen into disuse, and only a few farmers persisted very long in using the tumbling Tom or some other homemade device. The hand-operated "fan mill" or separator for winnowing the grain from the chaff was introduced from Europe toward the end of the period. The farm wagon, temporarily equipped with a flat frame instead of a bed, was essential for hauling in both the grain and the hay.

The most typically American of the farmer's crops was maize or Indian corn, in America usually called simply corn. The labor required for this crop was considerable, and the various operations must be interspersed among those for other crops. The techniques employed and some of the tools used in corn culture were unique. The hoe, preferably a heavy one, had been an essential frontier tool, and on occasion it was still used, although reluctantly, during a weedy season. The most necessary tools now were the sturdy plow, used not only in preparing the seedbed but also in cultivating the crop, and the heavy harrow. A peculiar implement for this crop was the furrowing sled. Its purpose was to check the cornfield, that is, to mark the hills in such a way that they lay in parallel rows each way of the field. The sled was dragged across the field by horse, first lengthwise and then crosswise. The points of intersection of the furrows made by the runners thus marked the location of the hills, which were planted by hand. Another special tool was the corn harrow, just wide enough to be pulled between the rows of corn. Tools used in the harvest were the simple husking peg for the right hand and the corn knife, the latter a rather deadly looking tool made by the local blacksmith. Corncribs were floored buildings with sides made of slats nailed horizontally to uprights, leaving air spaces between them so that the ears could continue to dry after cribbing.[23]

From farm to farm, buildings, equipment, and methods varied somewhat, though not significantly, with the origin of the settlers, with the amount of later immigration, and with the persuasiveness of gentlemen farmers in having their neighbors adopt the methods that they demonstrated. The majority of the New Jersey farmers of this period were hard-headed individuals who applied the lessons of the past as they saw them and who were chary about perilous new courses. Their chief sources of learning were to be found on the farms about them. They were, understandably, general farmers, with their eggs in many baskets. The variety of their operations caused them to acquire more tools and equipment than would have been necessary had their markets been more remunerative for particular products. The very spread of their operations kept them busy the year round, for there were always odd jobs, such as cutting wood, splitting rails, mending fences, and cleaning out barns, to occupy

them between more urgent daily or seasonal tasks concerned with livestock and crops. Their surplus products gave them a little money or a
little credit, but not very much. Most of their real income was consumed
on the spot by themselves and their families. If weather, insects, or disease
caused production to lag, they had, of necessity, to tighten their belts.
Their self-sufficiency was undoubtedly admirable; in any case they had
no choice.

6

Livestock Husbandry

The livestock of the pioneer period were a mixture of breeds, for it was not until relatively late that a few progressive farmers tried to raise the quality of their domestic animals by importing breeding stock from Europe. There had never been any attempt to keep various strains apart. Even had the farmer been so inclined, he would have found it difficult as long as there were open ranges. Through indiscriminate mixing, horses had truly become "jades" and cattle and sheep had become "common," to use the terms of the day. The various strains of swine, too, had been thoroughly mixed. The lean "wind-splitters" of the woods were now kept more closely confined, and before butchering were fattened on corn. But in many ways they were inferior animals still.

As the unoccupied lands of a neighborhood filled up with people, animals were increasingly kept behind fences or were discouraged from running at large. Nevertheless, the problem of straying animals was far from solution, as is well attested by township records and by the newspaper advertisements by owners of lost stock. Under such conditions, it is not surprising that the quality of livestock did not improve. Yet the enthusiasm over the selective breeding of race horses and fighting cocks showed that men of the day knew that livestock could be improved through selection. There were even laws against permitting male animals of inferior quality and size to run free. But in this matter, as in many others, the general apathy of the period prevailed. The attitude of the day was one of carelessness, and a man would only make himself a laughingstock if he were too fussy about breeding.[1]

During the frontier period, when hay and stabling were insufficient, many farmers had slipped into the habit of wintering most of their animals outside, often without any protection from driving winds and cold rains. Kalm in 1748 reported that some of the Dutch and Germans stabled their animals, but stated disapprovingly that the Swedes had fallen into the "English" way of handling animals in winter.[2] Johann Schoepf, a

German visitor during the Confederation period, wrote that the Pennsylvania Germans treated their livestock better than did others. In the light of present knowledge, it does not seem likely that the rugged outdoor life hurt the animals, and it is probable that their scrawniness was the result of poor feeding and indiscriminate breeding rather than the weather. Frontier practices were improved upon to some degree by provision of sheds and windbreaks, and some farmers pampered their milk cows and work horses by stabling them. When Joseph Capner settled at Flemington in the 1780s, he soon made good his boast that by better care and feeding he could double the milk production of the "poor little American cows." [3] There was little incentive for most farmers before the early nineteenth century to change their ways. They limited the size of their flocks and herds, fed them what they had, and always hoped for an early spring. This was the traditional way, and, in all fairness, it must be said that greater efforts would hardly have paid them. The care of sick and disabled animals was also traditional, a compound of near superstition and the results of trial and error. According to the Hankinson family commonplace book, probably from the Hopewell area, the cure for "dum stagers" in horses was asafetida or "devil's dung." This medicine was first soaked and boiled in vinegar. Pieces of cloth were then soaked with the solution and applied to the ears of the suffering animal. Breathing the smoke of burning leather or "any other stinking thing" was supposedly good for the Niagara horse disorder, but the alternate cure, that of feeding the horse boiled sweet fern, was at least kinder.

Crossbreeding of the English horses and the heavier draught horses of the Dutch, both inadvertent and intentional, gave a somewhat nondescript dual-purpose type which replaced oxen for general use after the fields were fairly clear. The Swedes, too, had practiced crossbreeding, since they had bought horses from both the Dutch colonists in New Netherland and the English colonists of New England and Virginia. The story is much the same for other colonizing groups. Thomas Budd reported in 1685 that the horses of West Jersey were "good serviceable Horses, fit for both draught and saddle," and that there were surplus animals for export to the West Indies.[4] A century later Charles Chesebrough reported that in northwestern New Jersey, an area only just past the frontier stage, horses had already replaced oxen for nearly all work.[5] Throughout the postfrontier period horses were allowed to graze freely in wooded areas. Owners branded and belled them, and sometimes hobbled or yoked them, so that they could not stray far. Nevertheless, many horses ran wild, and an unbranded one after a time became fair game for anyone who could catch it. Even after the countryside filled up to a considerable degree, farmers used vacant woodlands, sometimes at a distance from their homes, for pasturing horses that were not in use. The branding of horses continued after the branding and marking of other animals ceased, probably because of the occasional need of proving ownership of strayed or stolen horses far from home.

The usual punishment for stealing a horse was hanging. The severity of the penalty reflects the importance of the horse in rural living. A thief not only stole a piece of property but might seriously hurt its owner's mobility and livelihood. Nevertheless, the situation was a very inviting one for thieves, and thefts were common, particularly from woodland pastures. At least one gang operated for a time, rounding up horses in isolated New Jersey areas and driving them to the Maryland frontier for sale. Some of the gang had farms here and others in Maryland.[6] Thieves often appreciated good horse flesh, and waited for a good chance to rob a farm or village stable. Occasionally a fugitive or a ne'er-do-well, fortified by a dram of rum, would make off with the best horse tied to a rack at a tavern or church. On the morning of December 4, 1750, Samuel Taylor of Burlington opened his stable door and found his favorite saddle horse gone. He eventually advertised in the Philadelphia papers, offering a reward of thirty shillings and describing the animal thus: "A dark brown horse, about thirteen hands and a half high, branded on the near shoulder S T, and a small snip down the nose, small switch tail; he goes a fast travel, but goes short, and hand gallops well."[7] His advertisement brought results, and some months later the provincial high court, meeting at Burlington, sentenced two men to death for the theft. Governor Jonathan Belcher, noted for being soft-hearted, pardoned the culprits. One of them, John Crow, was already at the gallows when the news arrived. Crow was soon in jail again, but this time argued himself out of trouble by proving that he had only borrowed a horse. His luck eventually ran out, however, and he was hanged in 1754 for horse theft.[8]

When a man and a horse disappeared at the same time, no one believed it a coincidence. An advertisement of October 1753 reads:

Stolen from the Dutch Meeting House at Amwell, in Hunterdon County, a light coloured sorrel horse with a white mane, tail, and foretop, the mane trimmed with a comb, with a blaze along the forehead, is about thirteen hands high, branded on the near thigh A P. Had on him a good leather hunting saddle and snaffle bridle. The thief is supposed to have been seen at South Branch; he is of small stature, brown complexion, wore a cap, and light coloured coat in the newest fashion, a blue jacket, with a lapelled jacket under it and a large brimmed hat.[9]

Improved breeding practices came earlier for horses than for other livestock. It was customary to castrate most colts, and it was only natural that a farmer would keep only his best male animal, poor as it might be. A provincial law of 1710 required that unconfined stallions must be 14 hands or 56 inches in height, but it is probable that the law was not generally obeyed until after its reaffirmation in 1730.[10] Observers from Europe, for example Théophile Cazenove in 1794, did not rate very highly the stallions they saw here. Nevertheless, farmers who had comparatively good stud animals were paid high prices for their use. The owners of stallions Lofty and Herod at Freehold in 1782 charged a guinea or six bushels of wheat for each service.[11] Because of the interest in racing, stallions were selected more for their qualities as road horses than for their ability to pull heavy loads. The occasional stallion imported from Europe was light, and his progeny were seldom used as plow horses. When Robert Rutherford advertised in 1756 that he would "keep" at Trenton a stallion from Ireland named Young Tifter, he extolled its "descent from the best breed in England" rather than any work qualities.[12] The emphasis on fast horses in the advertising should not obscure the fact that farmers kept horses principally to do their hard work. They made a distinction between their road horses and plow horses, and cared not a whit about the pedigree of the latter. Probate records of the period invariably included riding equipment and "horse geer," and usually there were road vehicles of one kind or another as well as "farming utensils" which required horsepower.

The township pound records show something about the care of horses at that time. Many a horse was so poor in flesh that its ribs showed, and occasionally a horse had marks from a saddle or from harness. Winter coats were often so thick that brands could not be easily read. The average horse was not pampered, it seems, but there is evidence that an occasional owner curried his beast, trimmed its mane into a Dutch comb, and brushed its docked tail. The birth of a good colt was cause enough for elation. On the flyleaf of a miller's memorandum book is the entry, "The one Eyd. mare folded a valient Colt June 14th, 1774." [13]

Cattle were fully as important for the agricultural economy as were horses. In addition to their cows, even progressive farmers often had oxen for work that was too heavy for their horses.[14] In 1748 Kalm spoke of New Jersey cattle as "a small ill-favored breed." He reported that by European standards milk production was small and that the beef, milk, butter, and cheese were of inferior quality.[15] The stray cattle that were advertised as having been brought to the township pounds were certainly a nondescript lot. Those at Hopewell were described as red, red and white, black, black and white, brindle, and various combinations of the above, as well as "mouse colored," "flea bitten," and "blue." As to size, the strays were almost invariably "small" or "midling." [16]

The Capners in the 1780s and the Extons in the 1790s reported that American cows were smaller and much less productive than the cows they had owned in England. Nevertheless, they found that they responded fairly well to kind treatment. Furthermore, by using bulls imported from England, both families soon improved their herds, and yet retained in them the toughness of American cattle. The ordinary farmer had a few milk cows in various stages of production and some heifers of his own rearing for later replacements. Bulls were usually replaced with younger animals from time to time to avoid inbreeding and because of the tendency of older bulls to become dangerous. Nearly all of the cattle of the countryside were of so-called native or common stock. We would no doubt classify them today as scrubs. It is some indication of the smallness of cattle that a quarter of young veal bought by James Parker in 1778 weighed only twelve pounds.[17]

The earliest settlers had rejoiced that cattle feed grew wild everywhere, but they had soon found that the native pastures were not as palatable nor as nutritious as the ones they were used to in Europe. Fortunately European bluegrass spread rapidly through the countryside as native grasses were killed out, and the best bluegrass pastures generally proved quite satisfactory. However, many fields worn out by crops were not able to "bear sod," to use an expression of the period. As a rule, cattle received little feed except pasturage during much of the year, and only hay and corn fodder during the winter. An occasional farmer might feed his milkers a little grain in order to increase the family milk supply. Animals being prepared for butchering or market were often fattened for a time on corn.

The chief object of cattle raising on most farms was a milk supply from which cream, butter, and cheese could be made for home use. For some farmers near villages, there was a small market for butter and a smaller one for cheese. By the end of the eighteenth century, an increasing number of New Jersey farmers benefited from the growing demand for these products in New York and Philadelphia. The making of butter was one of the regular chores of every housewife, and milk pans, churns, and butter molds were to be found in nearly every household. Many women made cottage cheese from the skim milk, but only for family use. An unusual family, usually of German or English origin, retained its old skill in making hard cheese from whole milk. In general, Americans of the period, in New Jersey as elsewhere, did not eat as much cheese as their contemporaries in Europe. For this, European visitors had two explanations: the extremes of the climate, which made cheesemaking difficult, and the dislike of Americans for laborious tasks.[18]

The experiences of Joseph Capner of Flemington throw some light on practices and attitudes of the period. Capner had made cheese in the English Midlands and hoped to pursue the same occupation here. He looked over the Philadelphia tavern market, bought a farm at Flemington in 1786, brought over female relatives to act as dairymaids, and slowly built up a herd of milking cattle. Mrs. Mary Capner, Joseph's mother, was horrified at the taste of their first cheese and worked strenuously to improve it. The worst problem was that of the cheeses "going mad" in the press during hot weather. The family persisted, however, and soon built up a good market in Philadelphia. In 1791 they produced a ton and a half of cheese from nine cows. Soon they increased their herd to twenty, then twenty-five, milkers, and their output in proportion. On one occasion Mrs. Capner was inordinately proud that some of her cheeses were personally examined and purchased by Martha Washington.

The Capners eventually ran into the common American problem of labor supply. Joseph's sister and cousin found husbands, his mother's health failed, and his newly acquired American wife could not or would not take over the dairy. Joseph reluctantly sold most of his cows and bought more sheep. His experience and that of others of his group was such that they warned prospective immigrants in England that if they wanted "hard work to be done they must either bring it in their bones or bring somebody with them to do it." [19] In general, dairy farmers found in their own families their surest and most reliable labor supply. Despite the difficulties, there were New Jersey farmers whose chief products were cheese and butter for the growing market in the cities. A German bond servant in the area of present-day Camden just before the Revolution found the English Quaker families of his neighborhood producing cheeses weighing 30 or 40 pounds, and a traveler in northwestern New Jersey in 1794 reported that farmers there took cheeses to Easton for transportation downriver by Durham boat.[20] Dairy farmers were most numerous in present Mercer and Burlington counties, producing for the Philadelphia market, and in present Bergen and Essex for that of New York City. The New Jersey farmers had to compete both with the industrious Pennsylvania Germans and with farmers of German and Dutch descent in New York state.

The production of beef animals to be sold or slaughtered was in general a sideline during most of this period. There were always some surplus animals, but the market was small and mostly local. A farmer might occasionally butcher a calf, using some of the meat himself and selling the rest to his neighbors, the local storekeeper, and the artisans of the nearest hamlet or village. Some calves were castrated and raised as steers. A few might be trained for work, but the rest were to be butchered for home and local use or, more likely, sold to a drover who would drive them to the city for slaughtering. Poor milkers, and especially old cows, went the same route. A farmer sometimes pickled beef in brine for home use, or even sold barreled beef to the local storekeeper, who would cart it to the city. As city and foreign markets grew, the production of beef animals increased somewhat. Since they could be sold on the hoof and driven to market, distance was not a serious problem, except as it affected price. During the latter years of this period, production of beef animals for sale became more important than that of dairy products. Seldom, though, did a farm have more cattle than could be fed from its own fields.[21]

Early accounts note with enthusiasm the size of hogs fattened on native fare. There were many roots and fungus growths, and the mast from oaks and various nut trees was abundant in the autumn. A short feeding period with corn was not a necessity, but it would "sweeten" the pork before slaughter. To capture the half-wild creatures, the farmers of a neighborhood generally would get together and round up all the animals in the woods about and distribute them among their rightful owners. As far as could be ascertained, pigs and shoats were allocated to the owners of their dams. Frequent items in inventories and vendue lists of the period mention "hogs in the woods," and since the buyer bought them sight unseen it was up to him to locate and secure them. An occasional fleet razorback eluded capture and went wild to become lean, destructive, and sometimes dangerous, fair game for any hunter. A farmer could also lose hogs if they strayed outside the area in which their ear marks were known.[22]

As vacant lands diminished, farmers fenced their own woods and orchards for pasturage, put rings in the snouts of all their hogs, and attached yokes around the necks of the most obstreperous ones. The wise breeder also had a "tight" pen into which he could drive his hogs on occasion. The farmer could now, if he wished, practice selective breeding in an elementary way, and some farmers did, at least to the extent of castrating all but the best males. The hogs of the period, originally crosses of English and Dutch stocks, were as nondescript as the horses and cattle, but they had a quality much in demand at the time, the ability to put on fat. A hog from New Jersey caused a flurry in the market at Philadelphia in 1767 by tripping the scales at nearly 850 pounds. The reporter by implication disassociated himself from "the true lovers of fat pork." [23]

In a day when pork was the most important meat, the chief purpose of raising hogs was to ensure a family winter meat supply. Farmers killed and cured their own pork, usually with the help of neighbors, and killing time was one of the high points of the year. Every family had its butchering kettle for heating water and rendering lard, its scalding barrel, and an assortment of butcher knives, scrapers, ham hooks, and gambrels, as well as a smokehouse. Despite the enormous demand of home consumption, there was usually some extra pork, and there was always a demand for it in southern and foreign trade. As farmers became more numerous and roads were somewhat improved, it became possible to sell hogs on the hoof to local buyers or to drovers, to sell hams, shoulders, and bacon,

packed in brine, to local storekeepers, or to haul dressed carcasses to the
meat dealers of a seaport.[24] On a fine December day in 1787 Peter Case
of Flemington killed twenty-seven fat hogs on a butchering day. He sold
one carcass to a widow who lived nearby, stored sufficient pork for his
family during the year ahead, and sold the remainder, some three thousand pounds, in barrels to the proprietor of the local store, who sent it
by wagon to Philadelphia.[25]

Sheep had been a necessity in the frontier period to provide wool for
homespun. However, the pioneers had had to confine them more closely
than other animals because of the depredations of wild beasts and un-
controlled dogs. Consequently, their numbers did not increase very much
until the country was more settled. Then, despite the lack of care reported by Kalm, more and larger flocks developed, particularly in West
Jersey. In 1778 James Parker of Shipley farm in Somerset County owned
thirty-three animals, from which he sheared 104 pounds of wool. In addition, he had a stray ram, "small with crop in off ear," and a stray ewe
with lamb, the former marked by a "crop & half penny under near ear,
nick under off ear." [26] Though the Dutch and Swedes had brought in
sheep, it seems that the English types were dominant from an early time.
Furthermore, sheep did not deteriorate in quality from generation to
generation as much as horses, cattle, and swine. Since most sheep were
penned, the English breeds brought over directly or by way of New England were not subject to as much mixing of breeds as were other livestock. Nevertheless, sheep with no blood from recent importations were
known as common or native sheep. Their wool was somewhat coarser and
considerably shorter than that of the best European breeds.

There was, nevertheless, no lack of a market for the wool. Families with
no sheep bought wool from other farmers, or through the local stores.
Skeins of wool yarn made by industrious housewives were also a common
item of commerce. Wool, like pork, had a ready market abroad, and New
Jersey had much land fit only for sheep pasture. Just before the Revolution, New Jersey was reported to have more sheep than any other province. Some farmers disliked sheep because they ate the grass short and
sometimes pulled it up, but the prejudice against mutton apparently did
not come until later. During the Revolution, Parker made it a practice
to butcher a wether, or castrated male, from time to time and to distribute what he could spare among his neighbors on a barter basis. A
quarter carcass he sold to Robert Taylor in June 1778 weighed twenty
pounds.[27] In 1787 Mrs. Capner wrote that it was easy to sell mutton by
the quarter in the late summer in the Flemington area.[28]

The move to improve sheep began fairly late, and in its first stages was
largely contingent on importing English breeds. The stringent British
laws against the export of sheep after the Revolution was a deterrent for

a while, but ingenious sea captains managed to bring in a few animals, particularly Bakewell Improved Leicesters and Southdowns. A somewhat mysterious Captain Beans or Beanes appears in the records from time to time, and it may have been through him that Joseph Capner acquired his Bakewells, a breed he had owned in the English Midlands before coming to America.[29] A retired captain, George Farmer, who had a fine farm in Middlesex County where Highland Park now stands, built up, again with the help of Captain Beans, one of the finest pure-blooded Bakewell flocks in the country soon after 1800, and rams of his breeding improved many a New Jersey flock. At about the same time a gentleman farmer near Trenton owned Ancon sheep, and others in Burlington had those of Teeswater breed.[30] It was the Bakewells and Southdowns that persisted, and their blood strains most affected the sheep of the state. This interest in the improvement of sheep is one of the indications that the tradition-bound farmers of New Jersey were beginning to stir from their sleep. In fact, they were nearly ready to break radically with the past when economic conditions seemed to warrant it. The Merino craze, considered in this account as an event of the next period, was in a sense a manifestation of this change of attitude.

Poultry raising continued to be merely a sideline to more serious endeavors. Chickens were allowed to run around freely on most farms, feeding on what they could find and roosting at night in orchard and farm-yard trees or in outbuildings not intended for them. Geese were sometimes yoked and kept within rail fences. Ducks were common enough, but turkeys and guineas were rare and not much in demand. An indication of the lack of importance given poultry raising is the fact that poultry products were seldom mentioned in store or other accounts before 1800. The reasons are simple enough. Nearly every family kept enough poultry to supply eggs and meat, and the few village families who did not were able to get what they needed by barter or exchange. In 1804 the Capners occasionally sold a few eggs at the local store, and considered themselves lucky when they received a penny an egg.[31] Other accounts indicate that a fat goose was worth only half a dollar in 1811, and ducks sixty cents a pair. Chickens were worth less than ducks, and "guinea birds" still less.[32] By this time, however, the demands of the New York and Philadelphia markets were causing some farmers in nearby areas to increase their operations and improve their treatment of poultry.

Honeybees, which the Indians called "English flies," throve in their new home from the start. Probate records mention occasional hives of bees and even more empty hives, and indicate that some of the farmers of the day were daring enough to keep these industrious and generally feared insects. The usual beehives were made of spiral strands of rye straw fastened in place with thongs of hickory. Unfortunately, the bees of such a hive must be either dazed or suffocated with smoke from burning sulphur or wood punk in order to claim their honey. In practice, many hives were apparently exterminated in the fall or so weakened that they died over the winter. This was a wasteful method which prevented any rapid increase in beekeeping, despite the most assiduous efforts to catch every swarm in spring and summer from those hives that had been kept over winter.[33] Nevertheless, John Rutherford wrote in 1786, "Bees are also reared in great abundance, a tenant with Care sometimes pays his Rent with this Article."[34] Honey was more used as a sweetening agent then than today, and there was no lack of a market for it or for beeswax. In the 1780s, George Morgan, an experimenter at Princeton, had wooden beehives with frames, which made it unnecessary to kill the bees.[35] In 1788, English friends sent Thomas Capner at Flemington, at his request, the plan for a new type of wooden hive being used in England.[36] But in this matter, as in others, New Jersey farmers were slow to break with tradition.

7

The Growing of Crops

The field crops of the period ending about 1810 were the same as those of the pioneer stage, though there had been some change in emphasis. Descriptions in West Jersey by Thomas Budd in 1685 and Gabriel Thomas in 1698 mention Indian corn, wheat, rye, barley, oats, buckwheat, Indian beans, potatoes, melons, squash, pumpkins, flax, and hemp.[1] Probate records in West Jersey soon after 1720 mention "Indian Corne," fodder, "wheat in the barn," "woats in the stack," "bawley," rye, buckwheat, flax, and hemp.[2] East Jersey accounts repeatedly list the same crops. In fact, they were to remain New Jersey's most important field crops during much of its future.

The Indian crop of maize or corn remained the mainstay of New Jersey agriculture. Its advantages on newly cleared land were still as obvious as in frontier days; and since it was a clean culture crop—one in which an attempt was made to destroy all weeds—it was by far the best one to grow after fallowing. Furthermore, no other crop brought so large a return in relation to the amount of seed. The pioneers had eaten corn products from necessity, but by now corn on the cob, cornbread, and hominy were really liked. Cornmeal mush or hasty pudding was eaten with tolerance, if not liking. More important, no other crop was as good as corn for feeding livestock. Unlike wheat, corn could not be marketed in the city or abroad in any quantity; however, livestock fattened on corn could be driven with profit a greater distance than wheat could be hauled. Generally speaking, it was the rare farmer who did not put a substantial acreage into corn.

The tall maize plant grown among girdled trees by the Indians had undergone some changes through selection since the days of the first pioneers. The stalk was still rather tall and bore two or three ears of varying size, but its root system had become strong enough to support it in a plowed field under normal conditions. In areas settled by the New Englanders the rows at first seem to have been spaced about 6 feet apart.

89

Those of the Swedes stood just as far apart. After a time, however, 3 or 4 feet became the usual distance, and three or four or even five stalks were grown in each hill. The positions of the hills were usually located by use of the furrowing sled. Men with hoes and boys with pockets full of corn planted a hill at each furrow intersection. The yield depended in part on how well the weeds were kept down by cultivation or by hoeing. A yield of 25 bushels to the acre was considered fairly good, and 40 a large return.[3]

The cultivation of corn was seemingly an almost interminable task. The regular harrow was sometimes pulled across the field for a first cultivation, but this was a somewhat risky practice because of the danger of digging up the tiny corn plants along with the sprouting weeds. Many farmers preferred a slower way, that of pulling a narrow corn harrow down each "middle" between the rows. Cultivation began in earnest as soon as the corn plants had two or three blades. In cultivating or plowing, either the regular breaking plow or a smaller version was used. The soil was first plowed away from the row, then to it. In other words, for each cultivation of a row, the plowman and team would make two complete "rounds." The number of cultivations with the plow during the season was seldom more than three for the obvious reason that there was no time for more. The best farmers plowed crossways of the field the second time, and this seems to have become more usual as the period progressed. Travelers reported that under the best of conditions weeds were eliminated by this method without hoe work. But too often the fields in late summer seemed to be dominated by the weed-filled middles between the rows. Despite the problems, corn made a fair return if given half a chance.

Corn was usually planted in late April or May and laid by in July, after which the farmer could forget about it until harvest time. Harvesting of the ears must wait until they were fairly dry, and since corn ears have their own protection the job could be postponed until late in the fall if necessary. If they were husked from the standing stalks, they were thrown directly into a wagon to be hauled to the crib. Often, however, the farmer needed the stalks for feed and bedding. In that case, he would, after frost, cut off each stalk with a corn knife, a foot or so above the ground, leaving a stub. The cut stalks were stood together in shocks, which were circled with rye straw ties. The corn ears could be husked later in the field or at the barn at such time as the fodder was fed. In some areas, only the stalks above the ears were salvaged, and in this case the cutting could be done in early September.[4]

In 1778 James Parker planted in mid-May two varieties of corn, one white and the other yellow. On June 8 he recorded that he had men "plowing in the Indian corn." On June 12 he "began to harrow the Indian Corn with a heavy harrow." Because of the size of the stalks by this time, he must have been harrowing the middles with a short corn harrow, unless he was referring to a late planting of corn in "new ground," where he had men grubbing until at least June 8. On June 16 his earliest corn, by then four or five weeks old, had furrows plowed to the row, and the middles were plowed clean. The corn harrow was next drawn between the rows the other way of the field, thus partially pulling down the ridges and filling the furrows. The corn was now plowed in the same direction as the harrowing, and the middles were harrowed the opposite direction, that is, the same direction as the first cultivation. Men with hoes completed the job by going through the field freeing stalks of corn where necessary and cutting off weeds which were not covered up. Parker, a true gentleman farmer, admitted that the "great labor" was far more than his neighbors expended on their corn crops, but he thought that the extra work would pay off. He disapproved heartily of the usual practice of leaving the rows ridged after the last cultivation. On September 18 he began "topping corn," that is, cutting for fodder the stalks above the ears. In late November he husked the ears. He did not report his acreage, but his total crop was 532 bushels. Considering the number of days worked by his hired men, the return does not seem spectacular. He did not, however, voice any complaint. As he husked the corn, he sorted it into "good corn," "hog corn," and just "corn." [5] Parker, like many farmers, grew some field pumpkins at the edges of his cornfields. The pumpkins when ripe were broken or cut up for cattle feed.

Wheat, a successful crop in New Jersey from the beginning, was nearly equal to corn in importance during this period, and was by far the most important cash crop. There was always an export market for wheat, and a farmer could make a sale at any time simply by delivering the grain to the local merchant or by hauling it to a port. A new market was created as the older parts of New England abandoned wheat because of black stem rust, generally known as "the blast." This disease was never prevalent in the Middle Atlantic area, probably because the native barberry, a host plant for the disease, was not so common as in New England. Spring wheat had been brought in by both the Dutch and the New Englanders, and at least some of it was grown for several decades. Winter wheat, however, proved more productive and more resistant to rust, and gradually replaced spring wheat entirely. [6] Seed wheat came from many sources, but only those varieties were retained which adjusted well to climatic and soil conditions.

In the mid-1780s the Hessian fly made an appearance in New Jersey, apparently inadvertently introduced from straw bedding used on shipboard for horses brought in by German troops during the American Revolution. Farmers learned to cope with the fly, which fed on the stalks, by

choosing resistant varieties and by shifting their sowing time from late
August to early October, thus sacrificing considerable fall pasturage. An
even more serious problem was the lessening of fertility of the land. Because of its wheat exports, New Jersey was rated one of the Bread Colonies
in the colonial period. But already by the time of the Revolution some
farmers were giving up wheat, and others would soon do so. John Rutherford in 1786 reported, somewhat sadly, "Our whole attention seems to be
taken with raising Wheat, tho' it appears we are very little skilled in
it." [7] John Hall a decade later wrote that much land in West Jersey had
been reduced in fertility "below bearing wheat." [8]

The tillage of wheat was fairly simple. Sometimes, as in pioneer days,
seeds were dropped when the corn was given its last round of cultivation,
but this was undoubtedly a poor method. A better one was to harrow the
land vigorously after the fodder had been cut, and then broadcast the
seeds and harrow them in. One disadvantage here was that the grain had
to be sowed around the fodder shocks. If wheat followed wheat, or any
other crop except corn, the land had to be plowed before sowing. Since
the ground was often too hard for plowing in the fall, it was not unusual
to let it lie idle until the following spring, and then to plow it and leave
it fallow until sowing time in the fall. Sometimes it might be replowed
during the summer, in some cases plowing crosswise to the previous operation. An alternate method was to harrow it repeatedly during the summer. Unfortunately, weed growth often got ahead of the farmer, resulting
in an unwanted crop of weed seed. Various devices were used to broadcast the seed grain, but many farmers used only the bare hand. The degree to which the young crop was pastured depended on its growth and
on the amount of rainfall. The wise farmer did not pasture a muddy field.

Wheat harvest began in New Jersey in early July, perhaps a little later
than with the varieties of today.[9] The back-breaking sickle gave way to
the scythe early in the eighteenth century, and by 1750 the grain cradle
was fairly well known, as attested by probate and vendue lists. I believe
that the cradle came into widespread use, at least in the Middle Atlantic
area, earlier than is usually thought. Certainly James Parker had no difficulty in finding "cradlers" to harvest his grain in the 1770s. A sturdy
mower, with scythe and cradle, could mow from one to two acres in a
day. The cut grain was bound into sheaves, often called bundles, by men
who followed him, using a dozen or so stalks as a tie for each sheaf. The
sheaves were stood into shocks of several each. The shock was usually
capped by using one or two sheaves as a cover. After the hay harvest was
over and the corn was laid by, the farm crew would pick up the sheaves
by wagon and store them in the barn or under a barrack roof until
threshing time. The harvest of small grains was one of the most laborious
tasks of the year.

Although threshing was equally arduous, it could be spread over days or weeks of fall or winter. The process was simple, but tedious. The grain ends of the sheaves were beaten with a flail, and then the sheaves were broken open and the straw beaten again to thresh any stray heads. The straw was thrown aside, or else was rebound into "battons." The chief use for wheat straw, other than as bedding for animals, was as filling for bed ticks, which were the mattresses of that day, except for the few persons who preferred the more durable, but certainly more uncomfortable, corn husks. The last task of threshing was winnowing, that is, separating the grain from the chaff. This was accomplished by repeatedly throwing the grain into the air with a scoop shovel until all the chaff had been carried away by the wind blowing through the opened barn doors. James Parker in 1778 began threshing in August. Usually the task was postponed until cooler weather. In the 1790s some progressive farmers bought and used the new hand-driven grain separators for the winnowing operation.[10]

Many of the early immigrant groups had preferred rye to wheat as a bread grain, although wheat had a better world market. Rye was hardier than wheat, but not quite as productive under the best conditions. Probate and other records in this period, however, show that rye was almost universally grown in New Jersey.[11] The reasons were several. Rye bread was still a staple for many people, simply because they preferred its taste. Rye fields also gave better supplementary pasturage than wheat, and rye was just as useful as a nurse crop for timothy and clover. Still another reason for sowing at least a small acreage of rye was the farmer's need for the long, flexible rye stalks for such purposes as binding shocks of fodder. In some cases the farmer also used rye straw for thatching outbuildings and even, on occasion, barns.[12]

In some areas rye adjusted to the harsh winters and poor soils better than did wheat.[13] Its culture was the same as that for wheat, and both crops required a bushel or slightly more of seed per acre to bring a return of 10 to 15 bushels.[14] As land fertility declined, the differential in yield tended to disappear, and more farmers turned to rye as the surer crop of the two. The individual farmer preferred wheat because it fetched a higher price and had a ready market, but after wheat had failed him a few times he was often willing to turn to rye. On the basis of probate and vendue listings, it appears that perhaps half as much rye as wheat was grown during the early eighteenth century, and probably fully as much at the end.

A crop far more important in the agricultural economy than today was oats. The records show that it was a standard spring crop, useful as a nurse crop for clover and timothy, as a hay crop when cut "in the milk" (when the grain was immature), and as the grain considered best for horses, particularly road horses. Oats straw, too, was more palatable to cattle than either rye or wheat straw, and it made better bed ticks. Sowed in March or April, the crop was raised in much the same way as other small grains. If the field had been in corn the previous year, a seedbed could be prepared by a thorough harrowing. Otherwise, the ground must be plowed, then harrowed, before broadcasting the seed. If the crop was harvested when green, it was mowed with a grass scythe and harvested like any other hay. If the farmer wanted grain, he harvested the crop very much as he would rye or wheat, but two or three weeks later.[15]

In an emergency, if a farmer's hay or grain reserves ran short before spring, oats in the sheaf could be fed to his horses and cattle instead of being threshed. Oats were considered primarily horse feed, and were not used for human food except by a few Scots and Scotch-Irish.[16] In bushels per acre oats yielded considerably more than other small grains, but it must be remembered that the oat grain after threshing still has a hull and that the bushel is only slightly more than half as heavy as the bushel of wheat or rye. Oats do well in about the same kinds of soil as corn, but on freshly cleared ground have a tendency to "run to straw." As with corn, the return from oats declined rapidly as the soil was depleted.[17]

Buckwheat, a good grain for hogs and poultry, became increasingly popular as a human food. Buckwheat cakes, either leavened or unleavened in summer and always unleavened in winter, were a standard item of most New Jersey breakfasts for two centuries. The culture of buckwheat was as simple as that of oats. Peter Kalm reported in 1848 that buckwheat was commonly sowed during the first two weeks of July.[18] James Parker in 1778 waited until July 21, though the ground had been plowed in early June.[19] Since the crop was sowed so late in the year, it was not as good a nurse crop for grasses and clovers as the other small grains, though it was sometimes used for this purpose.[20] Buckwheat was fairly easy on the soil, and fitted well into crop rotations. Its flowers were much loved by the bees, and buckwheat honey could be sold at premium prices. The buckwheat yield on good ground was high, and there was a ready sale for any surplus.[21] Nevertheless, the average farm acreage of this crop in New Jersey was small. Probably this was because the straw was worthless as fodder and because harvesting and threshing buckwheat required considerable care.[22]

Another grain grown by a few farmers on a small scale was barley. Usually, but not always, sowed as a spring crop, it required a fairly good soil but gave a good return. It was excellent feed for swine and poultry, but was not used much as a food crop. The grain did not always have a ready market, at least in some areas. Apparently called "bawley" by most people, it was not a crop generally held in high regard. A possible explanation was that barley beards were even more agonizing to the harvesters than rye beards. Millet, grown by similar methods, was so little known

that Charles Read sowed it in his garden as an experiment.[23] Another
field crop, grown to some extent for cattle feed, was the pea or cowpea,
raised very much like buckwheat. It was such a minor crop that it was
seldom mentioned in the records. Broomcorn, said to have been introduced by Benjamin Franklin, was being grown by or for local broom-
makers by 1800. Its culture required the same practices as corn. Other
minor crops, grown chiefly in South Jersey, were hemp, for its fibers, and
the saffron crocus, from which a yellow dye was extracted.

Flax, brought in by the Dutch, Swedes, New Englanders, and English,
and above all by the Scotch-Irish, increased in importance only after the
frontier stage was fairly well over in most parts of New Jersey. Not
many acres were devoted to it; however, it was eventually almost universally grown, being one of the raw materials for homespun. Probate and
other records after 1700 increasingly listed flaxseed, flax in various stages
of manufacture, swingels, hatchels, brakes, and other tools used in extract-
ing the linen and tow fibers from the flax stalk, and the flax spinning
wheels, reels, and looms for making homespun. Both Kalm and Burnaby
indicate the importance of the crop in the period between 1750 and
1800.[24] In general, large ventures in flax growing did not prove successful, even during the period of British and provincial subsidies between
1764 and 1772.[25] The probable cause of this was the difficulty of finding
labor. But farmers certainly grew enough of the crop for household use,
and industrious wives occasionally made pin money by producing more
skeins of linen and tow thread than they would need and selling the
surplus either privately or through the local store. Another cash by-product was flaxseed, which was crushed in local mills to extract the oil. Linseed oil, as the product was called, had a ready market here and abroad.[26]

Flaxseed was broadcast on carefully prepared ground, preferably on
Saint Patrick's Day. An old superstition held that if the owner saw a tall,
well-dressed woman on Saint Valentine's Day his linen fibers would be
of good length. This probably proved an incentive for his wife or daughters to dress up on that day. In any case, the patches of tall green plants,
with their delicate blue flowers, were a thing of beauty often mentioned
in the letters of the period.[27] Harvesting was done before the seed was
fully ripe, the plants being pulled up by the roots in order to save the
full length of the fibers. The stalks were tied in small bundles ready for
the laborious series of operations required to extract the fibers and convert them into yarn for making the cloth for linen shirts and tow pants.[28]
When James Parker called in his neighbors for "pulling flax by frolick"
in the late summer of 1778,[29] he was following a common practice of the
countryside for more than a century.

Growing sufficient winter forage crops for his livestock was sometimes
a more serious problem for a farmer than that of producing grain. Fodder

and straw were always plentiful, but because of poor quality could be used only as supplementary or emergency feed. The bottom meadows of such lowland grasses as had survived years of pasturage and mowing were still important sources of hay,[30] the crop in some cases being encouraged by an occasional application of water. English plants of various kinds came into use, first timothy and red clover, then other clovers, redtop, burnet, sainfoin, and orchard grass. Timothy and red clover, though their times of maturity differ, were commonly sowed together, using wheat, rye, or oats as a nurse crop.[31] The sources seem to indicate an earlier widespread usage of various clovers than is usually thought.[32]

The following phrases, gleaned from farm sale advertisements for the year 1751, give some indication of the importance attached to meadows in this period: "15 acres of good Meadow, fit for the Scyth," "a tract of meadow and upland . . . at a place called Barnegat," "30 acres of meadow cleared, most of which is good grass, and a large quantity of rich swamp, capable of making considerable more," "natural meadow," "20 acres of drained meadows," "salt meadow," "English and fresh [that is, not salt] Hay," "Tide Swamp . . . in a good soard [sward] of grass and mowing order," "improved Meadow," "English meadow, a good part of which may be watered at pleasure," "Marsh and Meadow," "good English grass," "good clover Meadow ground," "very good mowing ground," "good Meadow ground . . . twice a year mowed," "50 acres of Low-Land, the chief of which is good English Meadow, great part of which may be overflow'd at proper seasons, from the Springs and Brooks that lie about it." [33]

Hay by the ton became a standard item of commerce, though the accounts seldom divulge the variety. Timothy hay, considered best for horses, was sometimes designated by name, and it seems probable that this adaptable plant was the most commonly grown of the cultivated grasses. It is of interest that its value, though it grew wild in England as meadow cat's-tail grass, was first discovered in America. In New England it was known as herd's grass, probably after a man named Herd or Heard. The name "timothy," which eventually became general, even in England, came from Timothy Hanson, who brought it from New England to the New York area.[34] Timothy seed became a common item of commerce before any of the clovers. As a matter of fact, many early farmers scattered unwinnowed chaff from haymows or from around haystacks or barracks as a method of getting a sward of timothy on a new field. The resulting crop would contain other plants, including Old World weeds. It is little wonder that the latter spread rapidly across the continent. A better method of obtaining timothy seed was that of beating it from well-ripened hay on the threshing floor.

Red clover was nearly as important a crop as timothy, and since it is a biennial, whereas timothy is a perennial, more clover seed was required in the farmer's operations than timothy. He must, therefore, harvest enough of the second crop of the second year as a seed crop to supply his needs. As was the case with timothy, the hay was cut with a grass scythe when dead ripe but damp with dew, and was hauled to the threshing floor while still damp. In 1778 James Parker cut the ripe clover from among the fruit trees of his young orchard, then hauled it home for hulling or threshing. Impatient with its toughness in handling, he stacked it in a nearby barrack for later attention.[35] Red clover seed could be purchased at a shilling per pound by 1790.[36] In 1793 John Hall wrote from Flemington that farmers in his area commonly grew several kinds of clover. Too often their seed was anything but clean, and Hall and his friends and relatives, all recent immigrants, imported English seed until they were able to produce their own.[37]

The cultivated hay crops varied considerably as to keeping qualities. Timothy hay would keep in stacks or ricks without much loss, particularly if they were topped out with long native grass hay or with rye straw. The barrack provided protection for tall stacks, inasmuch as the height of the roof of this shelter was adjustable. Since clover hay spoils easily, the wise farmer stored it in haymows or sheds. As late as 1750 it was thought necessary by many farmers that they have some acres of natural meadow; but the wide adoption of the English hay crops made this less important in later years.

The harvesting of hay was simpler than that of small grains, but nearly as laborious. Some of the hay crops, including green oats cut for hay and the various clovers, were mowed in June ahead of the grain harvest, whereas others, particularly timothy and timothy mixed with red clover, were postponed until the grain crops were in the shock. Haying required good judgment in more ways than one. The crop must not be mowed when wet with dew or rain, and it must be raked immediately after the right amount of curing, lest it "burn." A rain after the rakers had pulled the hay into piles, swath by swath, could ruin the hay unless it was quickly scattered and allowed to dry again. Even after the piles had been consolidated into shocks or cocks, danger from rain and wind was not over, and as soon as practicable the hay must be hauled by wagon to the hay barn or barrack. The European practice of piling hay on wooden frames while it cured, thus making haycocks, was not adopted widely in New Jersey, if at all, partly because the climate was less humid than Europe's and partly because labor costs were higher. As a result, generation after generation of New Jersey youngsters were to be puzzled about Little Boy Blue's taking a nap *under* a haycock. In some areas, at least in West

Jersey, haystacks were built in the hayfield itself and thatched with marsh or swamp grass. In such cases, the hay might be hauled later by wagon to the stockyard. A variation was to have the haystack fenced, then to feed the cattle daily in the field outside the fence.[38]

Garden and truck crops were not deemed very important by most farmers of this period. The typical farmer fenced off a small kitchen garden and saw to it that this was plowed or dug annually. Otherwise, the garden was a project for the overburdened women of his household. Observers do not agree as to how good they were as gardeners. John Rutherford in 1786 said that many New Jersey gardens were "half the support of their families," yet Cazenove in 1794 spoke disparagingly about the "lack of gardens" in the belt between Newark and Easton.[39] Probably the truth lay somewhere between their viewpoints. Garden crops there were in considerable variety. In addition to the standard European vegetables, the squash and beans of the Indians had now become common. To support the bean vines, poles took the place of the stalks of corn, hence the new name "pole beans."

The white potato was known in early days, but was seldom grown except as a garden vegetable and at that only by an occasional family. It seems to have been the Scotch-Irish who really brought the potato back to America,[40] which of course explains the designation Irish potato. Kalm in 1749 and Acrelius a decade later mention the potato as a garden crop grown only in small quantities.[41] But the taste for potatoes grew rapidly, and a market for them developed. In 1791, Mrs. Capner on her calls in the Flemington area as a midwife, found potatoes commonly served with roast meat and gravy.[42] The potato before long moved from the garden to the truck patch, on its way to becoming a minor field crop. In 1778 James Parker recorded that he had planted forty bushels of potatoes on three and one half acres.[43] The place of the potato in the garden was taken by the sweet potato, mentioned by Kalm as the Bermudian potato.[44]

The vegetables of Old World origin had adjusted readily to the new climate. Commonly grown after frontier conditions had passed were cabbage, turnips, onions, beets, peas, parsnips, and asparagus ("sparrow grass"), but lettuce, parsley, red peppers, carrots, endive, spinach, and leeks were also known. Favored crops were those most easily stored for the winter.[45] Watermelons and muskmelons, sometimes grown in the garden but usually in a patch of their own, were also very popular. Kalm feared that the eating of cold watermelons in the harvest field was a cause of malaria and other illnesses, but even his admirers paid no heed to his advice on this point. The author of *American Husbandry* reported that nearly every farm in New Jersey had a melon patch. Some commercial gardening developed near the cities and larger towns, particularly for white winter cabbage for sauerkraut and of turnips and onions, the latter braided or fastened together by the dried tops and sold in so-called ropes.[46]

Fruit trees and bushes had been imported from earliest days directly from Europe, and also from New England and Virginia, where new varieties had been developed. In 1698 Gabriel Thomas wrote that fruit trees, "befriended by the Sun's hot and glorious Beams," bore earlier and more abundantly in West Jersey than in England.[47] Various accounts show that by the year 1700 colonists in Burlington County were growing apples, peaches, apricots, plums, cherries, quinces, grapes, gooseberries, blackberries, raspberries, and currants. Kalm in his travels up and down the province in 1748 and 1749 wrote of "spacious" orchards of apples, peaches, and cherries.[48] The last, which he found in large orchards near Princeton, seem to have been mostly of the sour red or pie variety, which require no grafting or budding, but improved varieties of sweet cherries were also known by this time.

In 1787 Thomas Capner wrote from Flemington, "The planted fruits are apples, plums, cherries, currants, &c. Almost every person has an orchard, . . . [and] plants a number by the roadside, so that any person that may choose may gather what they want . . . and likewise peaches." [49] Three years earlier, Cazenove, in his coach trip across New Jersey from Hoboken to Phillipsburg, was told that many farmers at that time were planting additional orchards for cider.[50] Travelers during and after the Revolution wrote of orchards of mixed fruit at or near Belvidere, Hackettstown, and Morristown. One visitor in Essex County in 1799 was much impressed by the orchards of apples, peaches, and cherries, several varieties of which were unknown in Europe.[51]

Fruit was grown primarily for home use by most farmers, and since there was little market for fresh fruit, except to a limited degree for apples, much of it was wasted or eaten by hogs. In season, however, fruit was very much an article of diet. A teenage girl in 1793 wrote as follows:

Apple pye and sauce on the table three times a day constantly. they eat apple sauce to almost everything here. when the green apples are gone we have dried apples to serve until cherrys are ripe and then we shall have cherry pye till we are tired of it. Apples are so plentiful here that cousin Joseph says he has eat a waggon load this winter.[52]

Apple and cherry pie, apple dumplings, peach cobbler, cherry pudding, and other fruit dishes were standard desserts. Peaches were cooked long hours to make peach leather, and apple cider, with apple sections added, was boiled down to a butter of heavy consistency in the family butchering kettle. Both delicacies would keep for many months.[53] James Parker in late 1778 traded seed potatoes to a neighbor for a hogshead of sweet cider

to boil down to a sirup, presumably for use on buckwheat cakes.[54] Crèvecœur wrote of the almost universal custom of drying fruit for winter
use.[55] Apples, peaches, cherries, and grapes were all dried and stored, and
surpluses could be sold at the local store. In fact, dried apples were a considerable item of export.[56] Fresh apples were stored for winter in the root
cellars. There was, of course, a small local market for such storage apples.
The small fruits, particularly blackberries, gooseberries, currants, and
raspberries, were usually grown in the kitchen garden. They were of consequence to the family food supply, but had little market value.

Apple cider was the most useful and most versatile of fruit products.
In 1685 a colonist at the newly built capital of East Jersey, Perth Amboy,
wrote to England, "As I am certainly informed Fruit Trees advance at a
great rate in this place, for a Man may have an Orchard within a few
years after Planting, that may yield him great quantities of Cyder, which
is the chiefest of their drink in this Province, even among the meanest
of the Planters." [57] Obviously the New Englanders, the largest group of
settlers in East Jersey at this time, had brought their apple trees and
their taste for cider with them. Cider was drunk while sweet and for a
time after fermenting. The fermented cider was usually distilled to obtain
brandy. Another method, straight from Connecticut, was to partially
freeze the hard cider and then throw out the ice.[58] Another apple product,
cider vinegar, was required for cooking and preserving. Both brandy and
vinegar had an export market, which encouraged many farmers to grow
a surplus to process or sell.

Newark applejack, under that name, became something of a standard of
quality, and was known far and wide, particularly in the South. It is said
to have been made from two special varieties of apples, the Harrison and
the Campfield or Canfield. From Newark the making of brandy spread
in all directions and had a separate development in West Jersey, where
Burlington applejack was the standard and the usual cider apples were
the Vandevere and the Winesap. Northwestern New Jersey, too, made
brandy, which was shipped downriver from Easton by Durham boat in
barrels and hogsheads.[59] Kalm found that the cider of North Jersey was
reputed the best in America, and Cazenove forty some years later reported
that the new federal tax on spirits had not discouraged the growing of
orchards or the distilling of brandy.[60] According to travelers, distilled
cider was known variously as applejack, apple whiskey, apple brandy,
and Jersey lightning. Those who eulogized it were contemptuous of the
taste of those who drank other spirits, particularly rum.

The culture of fruit in that day was a rather simple matter. The home
orchard seldom had a particular pattern, and the different fruit trees
were often planted together. The ground was usually kept in sod of

some kind, so as to make a meadow or "mowing ground." Occasionally calves or sheep were allowed to graze in the orchard, sometimes with deleterious effect to the trees. Little work was done in the orchard, except for some pruning, the amount depending on the individual farmer's energy and knowledge of what was needed. At times an orchard pest, such as the canker worm, the peach borer, or the tent caterpillar, got a start in a neighborhood; but natural enemies were not far behind, and soon the insect was held in check again. The orchard of James Schureman near New Brunswick about 1800 can illustrate the home planting of the period. According to a drawing that has been preserved, there were about 260 trees, of various ages, with apples predominating. A high proportion were grafted or budded, but some were "natural," that is, seedlings, particularly in the case of the peach trees. In some of the rows peaches, plums, cherries, and pears were mixed, but there were also whole rows of peaches and cherries. At least seventeen varieties of apples were scattered about, including Newton Pippin and Early Harvest, two varieties long popular. A long apple season was assured by having varieties that matured at different times.[61]

In the orchards of apples grown for cider, however, a different philosophy obtained. Only good cider varieties were planted, and often there were only two or three kinds in the whole orchard. In 1787 Thomas Capner wrote, "The trees are planted in rows about 6 or 7 yards apart for the plowing of them." [62] Cazenove in 1794 recorded some figures probably given him by the tavernkeeper at Black River, present-day Chester: "An acre of land, planted with 65 or 70 apple trees, 20 feet apart, produces in good years 250 bushels of apples. . . . They calculate that 8 bushels of apples make one barrel of cider, . . . and these 32 gallons of cider make 4 gallons of spirits, which they sell for 6 s. or ¾ dollar a gallon." [63]

Since in this period nearly all farmers practiced diversification, it might be an interesting mental exercise to speculate on how their farms were divided up among the various crops. Actually, we know very little more about it than that the farmer's natural caution and his need to spread his operations during the season led him to grow many crops, and that the decline in the fertility of heavily cropped fields caused him to practice a rough kind of rotation. John Rutherford in 1786 described the farmer's operations thus:

These lands are in general laid out in Farms from fifty Acres to four hundred Acres, and of each Farm the arable Land is commonly laid out into four Fields, and the Course of Crop is 1st year Summer Crops of Indian Corn, Oats, Flax and Buckwheat, 2nd year fallowed, 3rd year in Winter Grain, and 4th year in

Grass, by this frequent tillage, and from the small stock of cattle having little help by manure, the Lands are very much exhausted . . . besides the arable each Farm has commonly an Orchard, a piece of natural meadow growing, and a proportion of one-fourth timber Land for fencing stuff, Buildings, Farming Utensils, and Firewood.[64]

The description is oversimplified, of course, but in a general way it portrays the situation during this long period when farmers seldom changed anything except under pressure.

3

Agriculture Comes of Age, 1810-1917

8

The Winds of Change

The selection of 1810 as a terminal date for the long period of traditional, relatively static agriculture in New Jersey is of course arbitrary. Some manifestations of a new era had been appearing gradually during previous decades, particularly on the lands of progressive farmers, whose numbers were increasing. On the other hand, many of the characteristics of the older period gave way slowly and some were retained throughout the new one, which for our purposes ends with our entry into the First World War. Farmers still relied on the timber of the nearby forests for many of their building materials. The horse continued to be the chief source of power. No new crops of importance and no new kinds of livestock were introduced, and all the old ones were retained. Agriculture, for the most part, remained diversified.

Nevertheless, different attitudes now prevailed, and new methods brought considerable changes in agriculture. The wisdom of returning to the soil the elements taken away from it was at last generally recognized. Crop varieties of greater productivity were sought after and grown, and efforts were made to improve livestock through selective breeding. New machines which either reduced labor or made it more productive were adopted, sometimes gradually, sometimes rapidly. The new age, unlike the old, was one of constant change, and each succeeding decade brought more innovations. Rejection was as much a part of the process as adoption. The fertilizers, plant varieties, breeds of livestock, and machines that were praised in one decade might be outmoded a decade or two later. Furthermore, the process of change was accelerated. A comparison of the agriculture of 1917 with that of a century earlier would show that many of the important differences were of fairly recent development.

The agriculture of New Jersey, and in general of the Middle Atlantic area of which it was a part, might well have remained becalmed for a much longer period, despite the achievements of a few innovators and the efforts of an agricultural press to disseminate widely the newest knowledge. The transformation that occurred was not self-generated. Jedidiah Morse in 1796 wrote that the clinging to old methods by New Jersey farmers was "almost an insurmountable obstacle to agriculture." [1] By 1819 he rated the Jerseyman somewhat higher as an agriculturist than previously and implied that increasing urban markets had something to do with the change.[2] In any case, it is clear that the New Jersey farmers did not break the bonds of tradition because they were ashamed of being called slovens, despoilers of the soil, or inefficient practitioners of their trade, but rather because new economic conditions made it obvious to an increasing number of farmers that changes in their methods would pay. On the one hand, demand was increasing and prices were improving; on the other, declining yields made it necessary for the average farmer to do something for his land or else move to the West to exploit new soils. Under the circumstances, changes did come when it was shown that they brought obvious advantages. Farmers in general became more receptive to new ideas. Almost in spite of himself, a farmer might become enough interested in a new idea to apply it. Then if he persisted stubbornly in a new practice, he might have the satisfaction of seeing the onetime detractors among his neighbors become his imitators.

In the political field Americans had recently shown a willingness to embark on great new ventures, but in agriculture the pace was a much slower one. In the early nineteenth century, the times were propitious for small changes, and especially for those made easily or at no great cost. The widespread adoption of more important ones must wait until necessity or an alteration in the intellectual climate favored their coming. At first the changes came piecemeal, for the typical farmer did not allow his enthusiasm to carry him very rapidly in any given direction. The various crazes that swept New Jersey in the early nineteenth century involved relatively few persons. The experimenter had always been distrusted and his ideas were accepted hesitatingly and only after their efficiency had been thoroughly demonstrated. The story of the adoption of the iron moldboard plow illustrates this point. Charles Newbold of Burlington County spent a small fortune trying to get his neighbors to buy and use his new iron plow in the 1790s, but to no avail. Their argument that the iron plow would poison the soil was perhaps only an excuse for their inertia and parsimony. Be that as it may, a similar plow made by David Peacock of the same county a decade later attracted many customers.[3] Other new plows appeared soon in many parts of the state, and after a decade or two nearly all farmers were ready to discard their old plows in favor of the new types.[4]

The earliest disseminators of knowledge concerning the great improvements in agriculture in England and Holland, and on the best American

farms, were the farm magazines. Gentlemen farmers received some attention already in the *New American Magazine,* published in Woodbridge
from 1758 to 1760, two decades before New Jersey had a regular newspaper. Several short-lived journals that were particularly concerned with
the amenities of country living but that also gave some attention to agricultural problems appeared in New Jersey by 1810. The first was the *New
Jersey Magazine and Monthly Advertiser,* published in New Brunswick
in 1786 and 1787. Others were the *Christian's, Scholar's, and Farmer's
Magazine,* Elizabethtown, 1789–90, the *Rural Magazine,* a four-page
weekly, Newark, 1798–99, the *United States Magazine,* which appeared
in Newark for a time beginning in 1794, and the *Rural Visitor,* also a
weekly, published in Burlington in 1810–11. Similar publications from
other states probably had New Jersey readers also. True farm magazines
began to appear about this time, but not at first within New Jersey's
borders.

The *American Farmer,* first published in Baltimore in 1819, and the
Ploughboy, which began in Albany the same year, gave respectability to
scribbling about new methods and even about agricultural experimentation in process. Both papers had subscribers and correspondents in New
Jersey. In the opening issue of the *Ploughboy,* a Salem County corre-
spondent reported that a progressive farmer there had grown 110 bushels
of corn per acre, an almost unbelievable yield for that day. Other papers
had their followers, too, but Jesse Buel's *Cultivator,* first published in Albany in 1834, became the one most widely read in New Jersey, perhaps
because Buel gave New Jersey agriculture considerable attention. He reported that he had 661 New Jersey subscribers in 1841, and the number
doubtless increased during the following decades. In the 1850s the *Cultivator* combined with another magazine, soon taking the name of *Country
Gentleman.* A rival was the *Farmer's Cabinet,* founded in Philadelphia
in 1836. Other farm papers much read in New Jersey were the *American
Agriculturist* of New York City and the *Horticulturist* of Philadelphia,
both long edited by natives of New Jersey.

From 1855 to 1861 New Jersey had its own farm magazine, the *New
Jersey Farmer,* a remarkably good one published at Freehold. Until it
was ruined financially by the Civil War, it had perhaps 2,000 subscribers.
A paper as newsworthy in its way was the *Working Farmer,* published in
New York City by James J. Mapes of Newark from 1849 to 1865. Mapes,
never one to underestimate, claimed 10,000 subscribers in 1856 and 30,000
in 1862.[5] After the war New Jersey farmers subscribed widely to agricultural magazines printed outside the state.

The effect of the farm press on New Jersey farmers must have been
considerable at a time when these magazines were one of the chief media
for transmitting agricultural knowledge. A fact often forgotten is that in

this era of long editorial shears a great many articles from farm magazines were borrowed with or without credit by county newspapers. Though
such plagiarism would not be commended today, its net effect was undoubtedly beneficial to agriculture at the time.

Agricultural societies were also instrumental in spreading agricultural
knowledge. The early ones had a membership of gentlemen farmers, who
were anxious to share with others the results of their own experiments
and their knowledge of improvements abroad. Unsuccessful attempts
were made to organize statewide agricultural societies in New Jersey in
1781, and later in 1818. An effort of 1790 to form a society about a nucleus
of gentlemen farmers in Morris County had no great success. However,
there was a considerable New Jersey membership in the prestigious Philadelphia Society for Promoting Agriculture, formed in 1795. An interest
in farming, not necessarily ownership of a farm, was the requirement for
membership. The slowness of the initial response of practical farmers
must have been frustrating to the dedicated members of the agricultural
societies. Only later would the more obviously usable of their findings
have some influence on general farming practices.[6]

Somewhat more effectual in eliciting immediate attention were the
societies copied after the Berkshire Agricultural Society, initiated in
Massachusetts by Elkanah Watson in 1810. The most important of their
activities were annual fairs for agricultural exhibits.[7] By 1820 several
groups of gentlemen farmers in New Jersey had started or were in the
process of starting local societies, usually on a county basis. Between 1818
and 1826 local fair-giving agricultural societies were organized, as follows:
New Brunswick, 1818; Morris County, 1820; Essex County, 1821; Sussex
County, 1821; Cumberland County, 1823; Salem County, 1826; and Monmouth County, 1838. In part because of the resistance of dirt farmers to
ideas promulgated by gentlemen farmers, all seven organizations failed
within a few years.[8] The New Jersey Agricultural Society, organized in
1840, was also a Berkshire-type organization. It held an agricultural exhi-
bition near Trenton in the year of its incorporation, and another, lasting
two days, at New Brunswick the following year. In both years most of
the prizes went to new breeds of livestock. The founders of this statewide
group bewailed the failure of the county fairs, and pleaded for their
revival. Unfortunately, they themselves were unable to give a third fair,
and after a few years of functioning as a discussion group for farm problems their organization failed.[9]

Thus ended the first wave of New Jersey fairs of the Berkshire type.
Their influence must have been greater than was apparent, for efforts
to revive them began almost at once. Of considerable importance was
the fact that the new groups now had a wider base of support among the
farmers. A revived Essex County Agricultural Society was organized in

1844, and a Morris County one in 1845. During the next decades nearly every county developed one or more fair associations.[10] In all, more than sixty societies were organized to sponsor fairs. Some were local and some involved more than one county, but most of them were on a single-county basis. The total number was swelled by the fact that associations often fell by the wayside only to be reorganized, usually with a slightly different name, and that many were absorbed through amalgamations.[11]

Unlike the earlier events, the fairs now drew large crowds. A typical farm diary entry is that by George W. Moore of Cumberland County on October 6, 1853, recording a large turnout at the agricultural fair at Salem on that day.[12] The coming of railroads undoubtedly helped to increase attendance. On October 4, 1855, John Ten Eyck near North Branch found it much easier to make the round trip to see the Somerset County Agricultural Fair at Raritan by taking "the cars" than by driving a team of horses.[13] However, Ralph Voorhees of Bernards Township, who had farther to go, did not flinch at driving to the same fair in 1860.[14] The fairs had appeal, but attendance was far from assured or regular. Some farmers went to a fair once or twice and considered that enough for a lifetime. This seems to have been the case with John Ten Eyck, who seldom went anywhere, and who clung persistently to the ways of the past. Others did not respond at all. The records of James Neilson, Jr., of New Brunswick, between 1862 and 1870, show that he was a true gentleman farmer with advanced ideas, but there is no indication that he took the time to attend even one of the nearby Mercer County fairs.[15] Perhaps he thought, with some justification, that he knew more about agriculture than the promoters of the fair. The reasons of William C. Lippincott were probably quite different. He was a progressive young farmer near Little Silver in Monmouth County in the 1860s, but he used all his spare time taking his girl to see New York, attending the circus and other diversions, and playing whist.[16]

On the other hand, there were many who appreciated the fairs and a somewhat smaller number who worked willingly to make them succeed. George W. Moore attended the fair at Salem quite regularly in the 1850s. He apparently did not exhibit, or at least not often, but he was genuinely interested.[17] David C. Voorhees of Blawenburg was a more serious supporter. A member of the Princeton Agricultural Association, he considered himself a progressive farmer with something of a mission. In 1875 he attended the state fair at Waverly, but nevertheless a week later gave several days of his time to the Somerset County fair. On October 5 he took a load of potatoes, sweet corn, squash, buckwheat, and so forth to exhibit. Two days later he and his wife drove to the fair and stayed overnight with friends. On the second day of the fair both served as judges of exhibits. On October 9 he sent a wagon to bring the exhibits home.[18]

Though men like Voorhees were in no sense important farm leaders, their enthusiasm and cooperation made the fairs of the period a success for reasons other than horse racing. It is understandable that many of the county fairs lasted far into the twentieth century, and a number to the present. The slow decline of some of them after 1880 and the fact that no new fair associations replaced those that failed are partly explained by the fact that the energies of men like Voorhees were channeled into the Grange movement and into new organizations concerned with farm specialties.

This second, successful wave of fairs of the Berkshire type met with considerable success on the state level also. In 1855 the New Jersey State Agricultural Society was formed. It had a distinguished membership from the start and its stated purpose was to spread the new agricultural knowledge through subsidized lectures, demonstrations, and publications, and by holding an annual fair. Helped by small state subsidies and larger local donations, the group held a fair and cattle show at Camden in 1855, at Trenton in 1856, at New Brunswick in 1857, at Trenton in 1858, at Elizabeth in 1859 and 1860, at Newton in 1861, and in Passaic County in 1862. After the Civil War the society acquired eighty acres at Waverly Station, Newark, a tract which is now Weequahic Park. The Waverly fairs, held there from 1867 to 1899, were in their heyday during the 1870s and 1880s. Hundreds of horticultural exhibits were shown each year, and after 1879 livestock exhibits were also accommodated. As with many of the county fairs, the exhibits and other educational features were financed by horse racing, which declined in importance after the 1897 antigambling amendment to the state constitution. The rise of the State Board of Agriculture, founded in 1872, and of the New Jersey Agricultural Experiment Station, founded in 1880, had left the Agricultural Society with no function except the holding of the fairs. Because of financial distress, the society sold its fairgrounds to the Essex County Park Commission after its fair in 1899, and terminated its activities as regards fairs.[19]

The large attendance at the Waverly fairs, and the attention given them by the county newspapers and agricultural press, attest to their importance to the farmers of at least the northern part of the state for three decades. A diary entry of David C. Voorhees in 1875 suggests how one farmer felt about the Waverly fairs. On September 24 he wrote as follows, "I went at 9 o'clock from Blawenburg Station to the state fair at Waverly. (Excursion ticket $2, admitting to the fair.) Found a pleasant show of Fruit-Vegetables, &c., &c." The decline and demise of the Waverly fairs was lamented by many.

The success of the later fairs is an indication that farmers by this time were considerably more receptive to new ideas. Just as indicative were the activities of the small local clubs, though most left no records. These groups met at members' homes, and the occasions were social as well as educational. We know of very active early farm clubs at Bowentown and Belvidere and in Burlington County in the 1850s, and there were undoubtedly many more.[20] At a later time numerous others entered the scene. The best known is the Princeton Agricultural Association, founded in 1867. Its fame rests partly on its elite membership, on the fact that it still exists, and partly on the fact that its records have been preserved. A listing of the subjects discussed at meetings has the appearance of an index for an agricultural encyclopedia.[21] A new member in 1875 described the talk at his first meeting as a "pleasant discussion." [22] Later, when the monthly meeting was held at his own home in Blawenburg, the subject was, "Will Commercial Fertilizers Pay?" [23] In December seven of the members attended a day meeting on apple culture in Brooklyn, and in the evening went to a concert in New York.[24]

Most local clubs were absorbed into the Grange movement after 1870. An example was the Union Farmers' Club of Delaware and West Amwell townships, Hunterdon County. Organized in 1870, this group met every two months for three years, with discussions of the various agricultural problems of the day.[25] Formation of the Ringoes Grange in 1873 apparently led to the club's downfall, as its members became "Patrons of Husbandry." The Grange first came to New Jersey with the organization of Pioneer Grange No. 1 at Dayton in Middlesex County on December 26, 1871. Eighty-three more groups were founded during the next two years, and by 1877 there were officially 103 local granges, of which 99 were active. A temporary decline was followed by a fairly rapid recovery. A State Grange had been organized in 1873, and though lack of success in cooperative buying gave it a bad start, it was by 1875 definitely at the head of the Grange movement in New Jersey. Pomona (county) granges, composed of some of the members of the subordinate granges, were also formed in most counties.[26] This hierarchy of organizations has been maintained to the present, except in counties now entirely urban.

In the later part of the nineteenth century, the farmer of New Jersey became a great joiner, and nowhere was this more apparent than in Grange statistics. The brief rise and fall of the Farmers' Alliance movement in the early 1890s, with its appeal first to cooperative buying and selling and then to political action, only strengthened the Grange, which was by this time long past its period of radicalism. In its heyday the Grange in New Jersey had a dozen or more county granges, over a hundred subordinate granges "in good standing," and approximately eleven thousand members. Officers of the Grange could point out with pride that their organization had taken over the educational functions of the farm clubs and at the same time had given farm families a social outlet. They could also claim a share in the lobbying at Washington which brought rural mail delivery, parcel post, free seed distribution, federal aid for road building, and so forth.[27]

The growing commercialization of agriculture after 1870 was accompanied by the formation of statewide organizations concerned with specialties. Actually, one group far antedated this time. The New Jersey State Horticultural Society began in 1836 as a discussion group, and in 1844 became a fair-giving group. Between that year and the demise of the organization in 1853, it sponsored nine exhibitions at various places, the first and last given at Princeton. The group was revived as a service organization for its members in 1875. A very active specialty group organized in 1873 was the New Jersey Cranberry Growers' Association, much concerned with better varieties, state legislation for uniform packaging, and other practical matters. The New Jersey Poultry Society was organized with a small membership in 1877, but nevertheless gave well-attended exhibits. It was this group that brought to a rapidly growing branch of New Jersey agriculture the latest news on incubators, brooders, and other laborsaving devices. These and other specialized groups had, in the very nature of the case, very little of the social appeal of the Grange, but they drew into their ranks the increasing number of farmers who were deserting general farming.

A sign of the times was the formation of the New Jersey State Board of Agriculture as the result of a state law of 1872. There had long been serious reasons for having an official central agency for agriculture in the state, not least of which was the need to coordinate the activities of agricultural groups and to supervise the drive against livestock diseases. Such a group would obviously cut into the intended educational and other functions of the New Jersey State Agricultural Society, the structure of which had proved too loose for efficiency except in holding fairs. The leadership of the movement did not, in the beginning, come from among the farmers themselves. George H. Cook, state geologist, professor of chemistry and natural sciences at Rutgers College, and more recently professor of agricultural theory and practice there as a result of putting into operation the Morrill Act, was the primary force in getting a state board started. He and others had attended an agricultural convention at Washington earlier in the year at which the states were urged to form boards of agriculture. The time was propitious, one of post–Civil War agricultural letdown, and the farmer societies and the Grange backed the idea. Nevertheless, their participation during the first decade was not noteworthy. After that time the formation of county boards of agriculture brought more local backing and more local participation. A move to abolish the state board by legislation in 1894 shows that not everyone believed in agriculture having a voice at the state level. Many of the most important programs of the board, such as the farmers' institutes and the support of the program to eradicate bovine tuberculosis, caused bitter opposition, even after 1900. The able leadership of Franklin Dye, secretary of the New Jersey State Board of Agriculture from 1888 to its reorganization along new lines in 1916, was a strong contributing factor in the increasingly greater success of the board.

During its forty-four years, the board had its fingers in many pies. It supervised preparation of agricultural exhibits for the national expositions at Philadelphia in 1876, New Orleans in 1885, Chicago in 1893, and Buffalo in 1901. From 1874 to 1880 it administered the state program for regulating the manufacture and sale of fertilizers. Through the years it backed legislation for the establishment of the New Jersey Agricultural Experiment Station and the New Jersey Weather Service, for the control of milk quality, for the eradication of livestock diseases, for the state inspection of plant nurseries, for the establishment of short courses in agriculture, and for state support of local road improvements. At all times it worked closely with the State Agricultural College and the State Experiment Station, and its reports and bulletins on various subjects were instructional to all who took the time to read them. It promoted agricultural exhibits through the allocation of state funds to state and county fair associations, and in other ways encouraged all agricultural groups.

Undoubtedly the most important function of the board was in the field of what became known as agricultural extension. Through providing speakers at county farmers' institutes, and by means of other meetings, field days, and displays, the board, through its elected officers, brought to progressive farmers of the state the latest agricultural knowledge. Between 1891 and 1916 approximately one thousand farmers' institutes were held, each with three sessions and an average of three talks per session. Secretary Franklin Dye scheduled all speakers at these sessions and attended most of them until 1912, when the new Agricultural Extension Service took over supervision of the farmers' institutes. It is clear that during the long existence of the board a legion of poorly paid, or unpaid, workers labored to help the farmers of the state to help themselves. Many a farmer grieved to see the "old board" replaced in 1916 by one quite different, with its chief function the supervision of the newly formed New Jersey State Department of Agriculture.[28]

The demand for formal education in agriculture led in the 1840s to a number of attempts, mostly by academies and none successful for long, to add courses in agriculture. More fruitful were the efforts at the State Normal School at Trenton, where half a dozen such courses were regularly offered to future teachers between 1860 and 1873. This development had the blessing of the State Agricultural Society.[29] But it was the legislative acceptance in 1863 of the terms of the federal Morrill Land-Grant College Act of the previous year which was to prove a milestone in agricultural education, though the results were anything but spectacular for a time. Since New Jersey, unlike New York, sold at once the western lands it received as a result of the act, it benefited only to the amount of $116,000. This sum was held in trust by the state, which must pay at least 5 percent per year on the principal.

In 1864, though Princeton University and the State Normal School at Trenton both applied, the Rutgers Scientific School was made the State College for the Benefit of Agriculture and the Mechanic Arts. Though often called the State Agricultural College, it was at first more important for the natural sciences and engineering than for agriculture. The Rutgers College trustees, as administrators under the act, had to lay out $15,000 to buy a college farm, which proved a financial liability. On the other hand, the annual income from the Land-Grant College money went to hire instructors who would only incidentally teach students of agriculture. Combining agricultural courses with those in the natural sciences made possible a three-year curriculum in agriculture in 1865 and a four-year curriculum in 1871. Graduate courses were added in 1876. Imposing as this was on paper, almost no students in agriculture appeared. The seemingly vital subject, Theory and Practice of Agriculture, had no classes for years.[30]

The slow pace of formal agricultural education in New Jersey, as in other eastern states, seems hardly in accord with other progress made by agriculture. But "book farming" was still distrusted, and for forty years farmers generally lined up with other vested interests in successfully opposing state appropriations that might have made a new start toward a true college of agriculture. And when additional federal funds came as a result of the so-called second Morrill Act in 1890, the results were more rewarding for the sciences than for agriculture. Cook's successor in many jobs, Edward B. Voorhees, made heroic efforts to create a distinct agricultural curriculum, but drew only a few students. A requirement, made in desperation, that all students in the Scientific School must take the course Elements of Agriculture did little to help the situation.

At the same time, short courses were initiated for farmers and their sons. But there were fewer takers of agricultural subjects than of a course on Indian and Persian literature. After a couple of years, short courses were given up for the time being. It seems certain that the annual lecture given in each county, a Morrill Act requirement to this day, brought more solid results for several decades than did the training given a few individual students of agriculture at New Brunswick. The Rutgers Scientific School, with its small contingent of agricultural students, at last secured its own home in 1891 in newly built New Jersey Hall on the Rutgers campus across Hamilton Street from Old Queens. Though other reasons were given, it was perhaps a sign of the state's parsimony as far as agricultural education was concerned that the building belonged to the Agricultural Experiment Station.[31]

About 1906 there was evidence of change for the better. A state appropriation in that year provided a new building for short courses at the college farm and financed a whole new venture in short courses in agriculture. As a result, forty students appeared in January 1907 for twelve weeks of study in general agriculture, horticulture, dairying, and animal husbandry. This time the idea caught on from the start, and short courses became an annual event. The short courses helped greatly in building up goodwill for agricultural education and in forming a vocal group of farm leaders who asked for the creation of a true College of Agriculture with partial or total autonomy. After 1908 the agricultural sector of Rutgers Scientific School also gained with respect to curriculum and number of faculty and students. The latter grew in numbers from five in that year to sixty-eight in 1914. Unknowingly and despite its handicaps, it was training the personnel for the great expansion of agricultural extension soon to come as the result of state and federal legislation. But for years it was a stepchild at Rutgers.[32]

Creation of the New Jersey Agricultural Experiment Station in 1880 has been justly considered a momentous victory for the progressive farmers of the state. It may seem surprising that the same agricultural groups that spurned formal education for nearly half a century should have been ardent adherents of the idea of state support for research. State agricultural leaders such as Cook, Voorhees, and Dye understood that both were needed, but were forced to settle for half a loaf. In fact, agricultural experimentation had begun earlier with the founding of the College Farm in 1864. Required to provide "an experimental farm" by the terms of the Morrill Act, the trustees of Rutgers College had purchased an impoverished farm of 98.4 acres at the southeasterly edge of New Brunswick. Luther B. Tucker, editor and owner of the *Country Gentleman*, was appointed professor of the theory and practice of agriculture, with no students, and given charge of the College Farm but soon became discouraged with both parts of his job. The versatile George H. Cook, who replaced him in 1867, could report seven years later, after considerable losses, that the whole farm was at last under profitable cultivation. His successful fight to turn a run-down farm into a model farm was a series of lessons to the many visitors. There were those who complained that taxpayers' money was being squandered. It was easily proved, however, that not a cent of state or federal money had gone into the farm. Both its purchase and improvement had been at the expense of Rutgers College. But by now it was obvious that if it were to be used as it should be for experimentation with crops and livestock, and for work with fertilizers and insecticides, it could not remain financially profitable.

Dr. Cook, after a visit to European agricultural experiment stations in 1874, suggested that the state give $3,000 dollars annually to establish a state agricultural experiment station at the College Farm. According to the officers of the New Jersey State Horticultural Society, who backed the plan, the legislature "fairly laughed at the idea." But the New Jersey State Board of Agriculture and other state organizations and the strong Burlington County Agricultural Society incessantly badgered the state politicians until it looked politic for them to give way. Forgetting their horror of "special legislation," the legislature in 1880 passed an act giving up to $5,000 per year for the maintenance of an agricultural experiment station, the third such state act in the nation. The new Board of Directors (Managers), the same men as the Board of Visitors of the Agricultural College plus three ex officio members, promptly located the station at the Rutgers College Farm and made Dr. Cook the first director. The new institution met with great enthusiasm, which probably explains the fact that the legislature almost immediately increased its appropriations and resisted a strong reactionary movement in 1883 to abolish it.[33]

During the first decade of the New Jersey State Agricultural Experiment Station the staff were very active in experiments with crops, including cotton, tobacco, and sorghum cane for sugar, in testing fertilizers, and in aiding the drive for federal aid that culminated in passage of the Hatch Act in early 1887. The Hatch Act, the terms of which were promptly accepted by the state of New Jersey, brought about at once both an improvement of science instruction at the Scientific School and a considerable expansion in agricultural research. By the terms of the legislation, a new federal experiment station was set up under Rutgers control. Dr. Cook was made director of the new institution, also, and spent the last year of his life merging the programs of the state and federal institutions. After his death in September 1889, there were acting directors and then separate directors for the two stations. Luckily, Dr. Edward B. Voorhees, a young chemist who had been bypassed so far in the search for a director and was only properly appreciated when he was offered the directorship of the New York State Experiment Station, took the helm in 1895. Between this time and his death in 1912 he merged the programs of the state and federal stations so completely that few people were aware of the separate origins and separate financing, or, for that matter, that the Experiment Station was in reality a combination of two stations.

Although quarters for both agricultural instruction and the Experiment Station had been provided with the construction of New Jersey Hall in 1891, this building after a decade proved inadequate to the needs for increased office space and laboratories. All the later buildings were erected at the College Farm beginning with the Short Course Building in 1906. State appropriations increased considerably, but much of the money went for new programs, such as the inspection of feedstuffs and insecticides, for investigation of mosquito control, for oyster studies, and for the maintenance of the New Jersey Weather Service.

Although administrators were handicapped by the need to make farm operations break even financially (largely through milk production), the record of experimentation was a respectable one. It was distinctly improved after 1906, when the passage of the Adams Act doubled the federal grants. Part of the additional funds went for instruction in the sciences, but most went into experimental research in plant breeding and soil chemistry and bacteriology. There was an improvement in methods of reaching the public, particularly through the publication of bulletins, the furnishing of lecturers at farmers' meetings, and, in later years, through field experiments and demonstrations on the farms of short course graduates.[34] The stage was being set for the great expansion in agricultural extension soon to be ushered in.

9

A Countryside in Transition

There were probably not many more acres under farmer ownership in New Jersey in 1850, when the first statistics on the subject were gathered, than there had been in 1790. A great deal of forest had been cut down and had been made into lumber by portable sawmills during this time, but most of the denuded land had long been within farm boundaries. In 1850 approximately 2.8 million acres of New Jersey's 4.8 million acres were in farms, and by 1860 the amount had risen to nearly 3 million. Nearly unchanged in 1870 and 1880, it fell back to 2.8 million by 1900, and to just over 2.6 million in 1910, by which time urbanization had precipitated the great decline. The fact that acreage changes for the state as a whole were small and only gradual during this period masks the fact that they were rapid in certain parts toward the end. In the northeast, in particular, many farms were quickly swallowed up by cities and suburbs. On the other hand, the success of commercial fertilizers had brought into cultivation some lands formerly considered waste, with a consequent noticeable increase in vegetable and fruit acreage in scattered areas of South Jersey. Changes in farm acreage in the general farming sections, on the other hand, were not of importance. A few figures will illustrate. Between 1890 and 1910 the percentage of the total land area of the state committed to farms declined from 54.4 percent to 53.5 percent. But for Bergen County it declined from 54.4 percent to 34.8 percent, and for Cumberland County it rose from 33.5 percent to 49.5 percent. In Hunterdon, which had the highest percentage of land in farms in 1890 and again in 1910, the change was only from 90.3 percent to 87.3 percent.

The changes in the number of farms and in farm size were more significant. The first statistics, not very detailed, were those of 1850. Because of slight variations as to the acreage and minimum product before a holding was considered a farm, comparisons thereafter are approximate, but still significant in showing trends. The number of farms in 1860 was 27,460, very probably a considerable increase since the turn of the century.

118

In 1870 the number was 30,652. By counties, the number of farms in 1860 ranged from 207 in Atlantic to 2,651 in Hunterdon. In 1880 there were 34,304 farms in the state, and the number had not changed greatly by 1910. In Atlantic County, with its development of vegetables and fruit, the number of farms had risen to over 1,500 by 1910. Hunterdon's figures had risen slightly to 2,900. The number of farms in urban Essex declined from 1,082 to 633 between 1860 and 1910.

The changes in the size of farms reflected changing agricultural patterns. Since poultry and vegetable farms were seldom large, there was a significant increase in the number of small farms. In 1860 there were approximately 10,500 farms under 50 acres in size; by 1910 the number had climbed to 20,000, the greater part of the increase being in very small farms. It was the medium-sized farms that had declined in numbers. For example, in 1860 there were 9,652 farms of between 50 and 100 acres each; in 1910 there were 8,194. The largest units did not decline in numbers, however. The 23 farms of over 500 acres each in 1860 had grown to 171 farms by 1910. The average farm of the state dropped from 85 to 77 acres between 1880 and 1910. In the counties known for fruit and vegetables, the decline was considerably greater. The drop in Atlantic County was from 92 to 46 acres, in Camden from 86 to 52, and in Ocean from 105 to 74. In the areas of general farming the story was quite different. During these thirty years the average farm in Burlington County rose from 107 to 120 acres and in Hunterdon from 78 to 84 acres.[1]

The farmsteads of New Jersey continued the slow transformation which had begun at an earlier time. The log house was still common in the northwest part of the state in the 1790s,[2] and did not disappear until surprisingly late. James Ten Eyck, Jr., of North Branch, Somerset County, still used thatch for roofing his house in 1809.[3] But the usual farmhouse was of frame, with a roof of cedar shakes or shingles. Houses were often larger than those built at an earlier time, and in any case became more habitable as domestic manufacturing declined and as more and more household occupations were moved to outbuildings. Persons advertising houses for sale stressed the number of rooms and made great use of the adjectives "comfortable," "substantial," and "commodious."[4] The use of lighter materials in construction of frame houses was coming in gradually by the middle of the nineteenth century. Old-timers were skeptical of the "balloon frame" and in general of the "modern method," which used lighter construction, particularly in the skeleton of buildings.[5] But because of increasing costs and because of the decline in timber supplies as woodlands were destroyed, the newer ways of building rapidly replaced the old. As the costs of frame houses increased relative to those of brick and stone, these building materials came into greater use.

Barns continued to be large and were still usually of frame, but the

uses to which they were put were changing to some extent. By the middle
of the nineteenth century, farmers who used threshing machines needed
no threshing floor, or a smaller one, and they stored their grain in the
sheaf for a shorter time than formerly. On the other hand, more stables
were required, especially for dairy cattle, and more storage space was
needed for hay and feed grains. Often new stables or storage buildings
were attached to the barn. If built separately, they were usually close
enough to the barn to be served by the same barnyard. A considerable
array of buildings was characteristic of the farms of the period, sheds for
farm machinery and equipment being among the new ones. A farm of
two hundred acres near Lambertville in 1828 had two barns, a cow stable
seventy feet long, corncribs, a smokehouse, a shop, and a cider house and
distillery.[6] A farm on the Old York Road in 1890 had a large barn with
an annex, a cow house, a hay barn, granaries, poultry houses, and wagon
houses.[7] Barracks were known throughout the state, but were commonest
in central New Jersey, where Dutch influence had been strongest. Some
barracks were still built after 1900.[8] But it was the addition of an upright
silo which most changed the appearance of many farms in the 1890s and
early 1900s.

For more than a century there were enough forests for all, but by the
end of the eighteenth century a shortage of wood was felt in some parts
of New Jersey. At Chatham in 1794 Cazenove recorded, "The wood has
most all been cut down in this district. You have to pay two dollars for a
cord of walnut for burning." He found that comparable firewood cost
less at Morristown.[9] At about the same time Isaac Passand wrote to England that there was a shortage of rail timber in the Flemington section.[10]
Even in areas where cropland values had greatly increased, most farm
families still had to maintain woodlots for their farms. Usually the woodlot was situated on the poorest or roughest of their land. Or else they
tried to purchase inferior land at a reasonable distance from their homesteads.[11] James Ten Eyck, Sr., in the 1790s, had a woodlot in Dutches
Swamp, from which he hauled wood for burning and rails for his worm
fences.[12] His son used the same area, now called Quick's Swamp.[13] His
grandson John Ten Eyck, still on the same farm in the 1850s, also brought
cordwood and rails from what he called the Swamp, but supplemented
his firewood supply by burning anthracite coal.[14] William C. Lippincott
of Monmouth County was still hauling firewood and chestnut rails from
the family woodlot in "the Pines" in 1868,[15] and the Voorhees family of
Blawenburg had a woodlot in "the mountains," that is, on Sourland
Mountain.[16]

In addition to supplying the farmer's own needs, a woodlot brought
other compensations. There were always markets for surplus logs, rails,
and cordwood, the price depending on scarcity and quality.[17] By-products

were oak bark, and occasionally other kinds, particularly hemlock, sold to local tanneries.[18] James Ten Eyck, Jr., had, according to his diary, a steady market for "Hoop poles to hoop Sider Barrels." Ralph Voorhees three decades later regularly sold hickory logs and poles from "the Flat" on his farm in north Somerset County to a wheelwright in Morristown, his hoop poles to a nearby cooper, and many loads of bark to someone who came by wagon to get it. Cherry and maple logs he cut into firewood.[19] A diary entry of James Ten Eyck, Jr., in 1809 reads, "pin oak log for axle trees."

The owners of large timber tracts often sold the privilege of cutting to farmers and villagers. One of them advertised in 1828 that his land would produce from two to three thousand chestnut rails per acre, and another in 1831 stated that his stand of timber had logs that would make six or eight rails per cut.[20] Hickory timber, important in making tools and vehicles, and walnut, needed by cabinetmakers, were often sold by the lessee of a woodlot instead of being used for firewood.[21] There were, of course, many areas with no timber shortage, and here cutting logs, posts, rails, and cordwood were regular winter work. There was many a "Brandy Road," so named because the favorite beverage of the woodcutters was applejack. But the inroads of the portable sawmill after about 1840 very rapidly reduced the amount of forest land.[22] Where the soil was poor, cutover timber was allowed to grow to sprouts, which in time became trees. In the meantime, such a tract was known as brushy land, and generally considered worthless.[23] Eventually, the shortage of timber was so acute in many places that farmers turned to imported lumber, barbed wire, and anthracite coal as answers to their needs for building materials, fencing, and fuel.

Farmers were reluctant to turn to new types of fencing materials, and usually did so only when forced by economic factors. The snake or worm fence was still common far into the nineteenth century, and in some areas continued to its end.[24] Such a fence, once made, did not require much timber for annual repairs. However, the time eventually came when it would no longer turn livestock. The owner must then face up to the problem of replacement. Cleaning up a fence row was a major task, for it entailed cutting brush and brambles between the fence sections, as well as tearing out the remaining rails and cutting up the better ones for oven wood.[25] If rails were not too expensive in money and effort it was wise for the farmer to make another worm fence. In such case, part of the clearing of brush could be avoided by laying the new fence exactly on the path of the old. But if timber was too costly or the land was too valuable to waste, he might put up a post and rider fence, despite the problem of its upkeep.[26] When David C. Voorhees of Blawenburg had this problem in 1875, he decided to tear out a considerable stretch of old fence along

the outside border of his farm and replace it with a "four-rail post fence."
The posts and rails had been cut in the family's rather distant woodlot
on Sourland Mountain and hauled home. On March 6, after the laborious
task of pointing the rails and boring holes through the posts was finished,
Voorhees put his labor force to work on the fence row. They "tore out
the zig-zag fence along the woods," piling the old rails for "summer wood"
and for use at the base of haystacks. On April 29 they attacked "the worm
fence along the meadow." When the men began setting posts for the new
line on May 24, his neighbor questioned their placement, offered to fight,
then brought in a surveyor, who agreed with Voorhees as to the location
of the line. By May 29 Voorhees could write, "I have a good line fence
on every side." [27]

By this time alternatives to rail fences were available, but none of them
were very satisfactory. Farmers in stony areas, with great expenditure of
labor, sometimes replaced the long piles of field stones along their boundaries with true stone walls.[28] An occasional farmer still tried to duplicate
the hawthorn or "quick" fences of the English Midlands, but with little
success.[29] A sturdy new hedge plant was the Osage orange, which rapidly
became popular in the second half of the nineteenth century. During this
time farmers set out miles of hedgerows, which were to be the despair of
later generations, because by shading and sapping crops they wasted far
more land than had the old worm fences.[30] One of David C. Voorhees's
fences between his own fields was an "Osage hedge." He recorded in his
diary that the labor required for annual pruning and hauling away of the
brush was a considerable item. William C. Lippincott of Little Silver had
already cut down one of his hedges in 1868.[31] In 1903 Dr. J. B. Thompson,
owner of Moriscot Farm near North Branch in Somerset County, perhaps
worried that his hired man had taken so long to prune his hedges, ordered
that one portion be chopped off.[32] Many farmers neglected the pruning,
with the result that a row of thorny trees grew up, so vigorous that they
must be eradicated by a bulldozer decades later.

Various kinds of wire fences were being tried as early as 1850.[33] John
Ten Eyck, not usually in the forefront of progress, had a wire fence of
some type, possibly woven wire, around his cattle pasture in 1870.[34] The
leading successor of the rail fence, however, was barbed wire, which appeared in the late 1870s. When the New Jersey Board of Agriculture
met at the Rutgers College Farm in June 1877 its members, "together
with various citizens," took an interested look at "the new barbed-wire
fence." [35] It seems likely that Dr. George H. Cook's advocacy of the new
device speeded up its introduction in New Jersey, but, once in use, barbed
wire sold itself. Popular opinion and early court decisions disapproved
of the "murderous contrivance," [36] but farmers turned to it with great
relief. Diary entries of Elmer Bonnell, a farmer near Clinton, will illus-

trate the point. After laboriously splitting rails in his woodlot for years, he gave barbed wire a trial in 1887. He was pleased with the results from the start, and became at once a confirmed user. He put up a six-strand fence in 1890 and found that it cost him "not quite 3¢ per foot counting posts and wire." [37] It is little wonder that fences of barbed wire rapidly replaced rail fences of both types. In time this innovation greatly changed the look of the countryside, in part because the weeds, bushes, and trees usually found in fence rows had less space in which to grow. Since cash outlays were involved, new arrangements about fences had to be worked out between landlords and tenants. In one case on record a mutually acceptable arrangement was for the landlord to furnish the wire and the renter to cut the posts and install the fence.[38] Dr. J. B. Thompson found that labor was a big element in the cost of installing barbed wire.[39]

Wood for heating and cooking was by this time only occasionally a by-product of the clearing of cropland. In many cases cordwood already was in nearly as short supply as rails. The capacious fireplaces inherited by the farmers of this era consumed enormous amounts of wood, but were given up only gradually. Yet during the late colonial period, largely through the influence of German immigrants, cast-iron stoves were to some extent adopted for supplemental heating and to an even greater degree for cooking.[40] These "ten-platers" were large and cumbersome, but used less wood than fireplaces and wasted less heat. With the invention of the Franklin, Rittenhouse, and other lighter stoves both farmers and nonfarmers gradually adopted stoves in partial replacement of fireplaces.[41] James Ten Eyck, Sr., paid $20 for a stove on March 3, 1809.[42] This was a lot of money in his day, but even though the winter was nearly over he apparently thought that it was time to be more comfortable or to save firewood. The trend toward stoves was accelerated two decades later by the invention of the "airtight" and other new wood-burning stoves.[43]

The farmer was a busy man, and he would gladly have dispensed entirely with the tasks of cutting and hauling wood. His opportunity came with the introduction of cheap anthracite coal following the construction of canals and railroads. In the end, so popular were the cookstove or kitchen range, the parlor stove, and other types of coal stoves that the fireplace and its Dutch oven fell into disuse. An advertisement in 1843 mentioned a "very handsome metal and Sheet Iron Stove." [44] One may well disagree with the adjective, for the illustrations in stove advertisements of that time show boxlike affairs mounted on stubby legs. In keeping with the tastes of the late Victorian period, however, stoves became very ornate, with nickel-plated fenders and isinglass peepholes. The family of David C. Voorhees in 1875 depended for heat entirely on anthracite coal, hauled from the not-distant depot on the Reading Railroad. Taking down and storing the many stoves of their commodious house was a spring ritual, as was putting them up and giving them a coat of blacking in the fall. Mr. Voorhees paid $16 for a new cookstove in June.[45] Before the turn of the century the well-to-do began installing central heating in their houses. Fuel for the new furnaces was almost invariably anthracite coal.

Among the indications of a new epoch was a willingness on the part of New Jersey farmers to add fertilizing elements to the soil. The ill effects of mistreatment of the land had long been obvious, but only an occasional farmer had attempted to combat the problem in the previous period. But now there was a general recognition that the fertility used up by crops must in some manner be returned to the land. The experimenters of the former period became the sages of this one, as farm magazines spread the gospel of the great need for soil enrichment. Although a full understanding of soil chemistry must wait until the second half of the nineteenth century, considerable progress was made earlier through trial and error. While experimenters and farmers groped for precise answers, the one generally recognized natural fertilizer, barnyard manure, commanded more respect. Farmers now had more livestock, and they made a greater effort to save the manure. The more advanced farmers industriously mixed manure with the other ingredients of their compost piles, which would eventually be spread on the land. Others applied the manure directly to the land, but unfortunately most of them allowed the manure to collect too long before spreading it.[46] For most farmers, "drawing dung" was an annual or semiannual event,[47] and the greater part of the manure was therefore exposed to the weather for months before reaching the land, with consequent dissipation of fertilizing elements.[48] When George W. Moore of Cumberland County finished "carting out manure" for the year with his 160th wagon load in September 1862, and when David C. Voorhees of Somerset finished "hauling" with his 215th load in the same month of 1875, both probably drew sighs of relief. These men were progressive farmers, but it seems likely that neither was conscious of how much fertility had been lost through weathering.[49]

Other farm-produced fertilizers, which had been burned or thrown away in the past, such as stubble, chaff, surplus straw, and waste fodder, were now more commonly spread on the land and plowed under. Some farmers, following instructions printed in farm magazines, composted these waste products along with manure, hay, swamp mud, and other materials rich in humus before spreading.[50] In the 1860s James Neilson, Jr., of near New Brunswick bought "night soil" from New York to mix with muck from a nearby swamp.[51] Ashes resulting from the burning of brush and tree limbs were now considered to have value, particularly if spread on grain land at sowing time, in the same fashion as land plaster. In fact,

wood ashes had become a regular item of commerce, retailing for a shilling a bushel in 1800.[52] In the 1850s both James H. Blackwell and John
Ten Eyck dropped a handful of ashes in each hill of corn at planting
time.[53] A farmers' handbook printed in Philadelphia in 1804 particularly
advised the use of ashes on clay soil, and farm magazines of the 1850s
recommended them as a top dressing for fallow ground.[54] When ashes
became scarce locally, they were brought in by rail from areas that still
had forests to cut. Canadian unleached ashes were being advertised as
late as 1888.[55] The considerable increase in the growing of clovers must
also be recognized as an early effort at soil enrichment.

Three land improvers already favored by some farmers in the later
years of the previous period were land plaster, calcined lime, and greensand marl. Increasingly widespread use of these materials was characteristic of the new period after 1810 though all were to be out of favor by
1890. Land plaster, or plaster of Paris, was calcined gypsum. No one knew
why at the time, but it was obvious that if land plaster was broadcast
thinly, a bushel or two per acre, at sowing time, the sprouting grain
would be off to a better start. This fertilizing element had to be imported
from Nova Scotia or the Hudson Valley, where it had been quarried and
calcined. Since it caked en route, it had to be pulverized with a "plaster
breaker" at a local mill before it could be used.[56] Its cost, therefore, was
not negligible. The practice of using plaster evidently came from Germany, and its virtues were generally known by 1770.[57] But at first only
dire need would induce most farmers to spend the money for it. By 1800,
however, it had come into fairly general use, and was particularly important when a farmer wished to sow clover seed with his small grain.[58]
In 1804 Job Roberts's handbook for farmers spoke of the "general use"
of land plaster.[59] A decade earlier Cazenove reported that farmers in
nearby Pennsylvania had found that too heavy or too frequent applications of plaster injured the soil.[60] It seems probable that this was because
of imperfect slaking after calcining.

Farmers in West Jersey who brought plaster hauled from New Brunswick by wagon paid 10 shillings ($1.25) per bushel in 1810 and 6½
shillings (81 cents) in 1816.[61] Yet a general store at Mount Airy was charging only 50 cents in 1824, probably because the plaster had been brought
by water to a point on the Delaware River only a few miles away.[62] With
the coming of canals and railroads, the price of plaster declined sharply.
Blackwell paid only $7 per ton in 1848, and used it freely for wheat and
corn, putting a handful in each hill in the case of the latter crop.[63] John
Ten Eyck followed a similar pattern in the 1860s, but Ralph Voorhees
of the same county, Somerset, broadcast plaster before using the furrowing sled to mark the corn rows. The winner of a potato yield contest in
1875 attributed his prize to plentiful use of land plaster,[64] and Elmer

Bonnell was a firm believer in its effectiveness as late as the 1880s.[65] Farm records seem to indicate that plaster had gradually fallen into disuse by the 1870s. In most cases farmers at first apparently substituted calcined lime, but soon turned to newer fertilizers. Field studies by the new Agricultural Experiment Station on the farms of cooperating farmers in 1881 and 1882 indicated that plaster did not compare well with the new commercial fertilizers as to return on investment.[66] Whatever the reason, the use of plaster dropped to zero during the next two decades.

Decline in the productivity of land was often as much the result of sourness as of the depletion of the basic elements. A sure sign that land was becoming acid was the appearance of the meadow weed horse sorrel, known locally as sourweed.[67] Charles Read of Burlington County wrote in the 1760s of various experiments with lime, but the idea did not catch on at the time.[68] In June 1778 James Parker made a contract with a lime burner, very probably someone from the German settlements not far away in Pennsylvania, where the calcining of lime was already a common practice. For calcining a kilnful of lime he paid $26, part of it in seed wheat.[69] However, since the anonymous author of *American Husbandry* in 1775 mentioned neither land plaster nor calcined lime in New Jersey, both were probably quite new at that time. John Rutherford wrote in 1786, "Limestone is good and plenty, and if not so dear calcining might be used to great advantage as manure." [70] Visitors reported in the 1790s that some West Jersey farmers were using small quantities of "burnt" (calcined) lime rather than land plaster at wheat-sowing time.[71] High labor and capital costs were evidently factors in discouraging the use of very much calcined lime, but habit and inertia were undoubtedly also causes. When a landlord near Flemington offered to buy lime for a field on his farm in 1793, he found that his tenant was unwilling to take on the job of hauling the lime and spreading it on the land.[72]

There were lime deposits in plenty in the New Jersey Highlands and across the Delaware River in Pennsylvania. Farmers who owned deposits had a great advantage over others. It is understandable that at a time earlier than most James Parker of north Hunterdon was applying per acre as much as forty bushels of lime that had been quarried and calcined on his own farm, and that he used it freely as a side dressing for corn.[73] Eventually the evident results of the new practice impelled farmers who had no limestone on their farms to invest time and money in obtaining either the calcined lime or the raw limestone. In the latter case they built kilns and themselves did the calcining. As the custom of using lime spread, parties of farmers, often organized as "lime frolics," would haul lime as far as horses and wagons could travel in a long day.[74] The owner of a farm near Quakertown in 1831 advertised that most of his farm of two hundred acres had been limed in recent years, and that he had a lime kiln on his farm.[75] If there were no deposits or kilns within hauling distance, the farmer had to wait until canals and railroads made transportation practicable.

Much of the calcined lime used in New Jersey had its origin in eastern Pennsylvania. Toll bridges on the Delaware River granted special rates to lime wagons in the 1830s,[76] and probably earlier. Pennsylvania kiln owners advertised constantly in West Jersey papers, advising farmers as to the best routes of travel.[77] On occasion they offered to accept farm produce for calcined lime. The ratio in 1843 was two and a half bushels of lime for one of oats, four for a bushel of corn, nine for a bushel of wheat, and five for a bushel of buckwheat.[78] The cash price for lime during several decades was about ten cents per bushel at the kiln. The supply after 1830 was increased as anthracite coal for firing the kilns became available over a larger area. The opening of the Lehigh Canal along the Lehigh River in 1829 and of the Delaware Division Canal along the Pennsylvania bank of the Delaware River in 1832 brought coal to the Pennsylvania limestone country.[79] At about the same time, the two canals of New Jersey were completed, the Morris-Essex in 1831 and the Delaware and Raritan in 1834. Both carried great quantities of calcined lime, thus making this product available to a much larger agricultural area. Canal boats loaded with coal or lime were shunted by cable across the Delaware River at Phillipsburg and Lambertville. To accommodate the large boats of the Lehigh Canal, the Morris Canal was widened and deepened in 1844.[80]

Lime was also carried down the lower Delaware in Durham boats. In September 1855 Dr. George H. Cook reported from Salem County, "Lime is the principal fertilizer used. It is brought from Pa. in boats and sold—slaked—for $7\frac{1}{2}$ cts. a bushel, on the shore." [81] With the coming of railroads, calcined lime became available to nearly all the farmers of New Jersey. The price of freighting, however, was considerably more than that of canal or river boats. In 1860 calcined lime by the carload sold for $12\frac{1}{2}$ cents per bushel delivered in Flemington.[82] The farmers of New Jersey, once they accepted calcined lime, used enormous quantities over a century, as attested by such observers as Jesse Buel in 1839 and Dr. George H. Cook in 1868.[83] Only toward the end of the nineteenth century was it gradually replaced by pulverized limestone.

The reign of calcined lime as a soil improver was thus a long one. There was, unfortunately, a sad chapter in the story, one which has seldom been recited, perhaps for understandable reasons. Unless the calcined lime was thoroughly slaked before application, its net long-term effect on the soil was malign rather than benign. Many farmers who were more interested in immediate yield increases than in the welfare of their soil did their fields permanent harm by applying lime which had been "air-slaked" or to which not enough water had been added. The diary of James Parker, which gives the earliest known account of the application of calcined lime in New Jersey, illustrates the error into which many farmers later fell. In 1778 Parker's hired men hauled the calcined lime from his kiln and piled it in large heaps in the field. Water was then taken out to the field in hogsheads, and the lime was slaked on the ground before spreading. In the case of the well-meaning Parker, who was better versed in the ways of politics and finance than in those of agriculture, this method, apparently already traditional in eastern Pennsylvania, probably stemmed from ignorance. But in both England and Germany, where lime had long been used, it was well known that the caustic effects of improperly slaked calcined lime were invariably deleterious to the soil. Charles Read, an experimenter in Burlington County a decade earlier, certainly had been cognizant of this fact.[84]

By their own accounts, many progressive farmers took great care to slake the lime with abundant water before hauling it to the fields for spreading.[85] John Ten Eyck, evidently one of the careful ones, entered the following remark in his diary in 1857, "I got a load of lime & slaked it up by the spring." Generally the farmers in southwestern New Jersey seem to have done the job properly, slaking their lime with river or creek water before hauling it to the fields if they had not bought it already slaked. Some mixed the calcined and slaked lime with greensand marl before application.[86] But many farmers elsewhere were too impatient or too lazy or too greedy to do the job of slaking correctly. Traditions of the countryside tell of spots that gave amazing yields in the recently limed fields, the spots, of course, being the sites where lime had been piled before slaking and spreading. After a few years the same spots could be located, not by their fertility, but by their complete barrenness. Farmers who spread large amounts had tremendous yields for a time. Jesse Buel in 1849 reported that the first crop often paid all of the costs of applying the lime.[87] But the decline in fertility after a few years was very marked, and future applications had less and less effect. George H. Cook wrote in the 1860s that farmers were trying to avoid the bad effects of large applications by putting on smaller amounts at shorter intervals.[88] They would have been better advised to have seen to it that the lime they used was always completely slaked beforehand. The considered opinion of experts today is that the soil of many farms was badly harmed by the improper application of the very agent that was supposed to cure its ills. It was Professor Frank Helyar, in 1938, who first mentioned to me that the calcined lime story needed amendment. H. E. Deats, to whose memory this book is dedicated and whose own father had always seen to it that all lime applied on his land was carefully slaked, agreed fully with the above thesis.

The story of the third of the soil improvers, greensand marl, is in some ways the most interesting. One of the many geological formations laid down when the Coastal Plain was deeply submerged in the ocean was that known as Hornerstone marl. Of sedimentary origin, it consists essentially of greensand marl (glauconite), clay, and sand, with a plentiful admixture of marine fossils. Sometimes thirty feet in thickness, this deposit comes near the surface in a belt from six to thirteen miles in width from the Atlantic coast below Sandy Hook through Freehold, Mullica Hill, Woodstown, and Salem to the lower Delaware.[89] Thus there are substantial deposits in the counties of Monmouth, Burlington, Camden, Gloucester, and Salem. The early agricultural experimenters in this area hauled many kinds of earth to improve depleted lands, and sometimes had particularly good results from "blue mud," which undoubtedly contained at least some greensand marl. Since the benefits of marl were known in England, one can only wonder that it was not used sooner in New Jersey.

Signs of the changing times were the opening up of pits in many localities of the marl belt, beginning just before 1820, and a rapid adoption of the practice of spreading marl on fields within carting distance of the pits. Farmers of the whole marl area were busy during the late fall and winter hauling and piling the marl, and again in the early spring spreading it on the soil.[90] By 1834 it was reported that marl had "already saved some districts from depopulation and increased the inhabitants of others." The writer optimistically suggested that the use of marl might "convert the sandy and pine deserts into regions of agricultural wealth." [91] Dr. George H. Cook in 1868 went even further with his praise, pointing out that marl had rebuilt the worn-out soil of the farms of the section near where it was found and had made areas of "bare sand" productive.[92] Applications were so heavy that marling was a costly business. The results were phenomenal, however, and land values rose considerably as the result of increased productivity.

The diary of George W. Moore of Cumberland County in the 1860s and 1870s and that of William C. Lippincott of Monmouth County in 1868 illustrate the practice of marling. Moore, the less industrious of the two, started carting marl in early January each year. Apparently he purchased it already dug, for there is no account of his doing any digging. With his one team and wagon, he would haul six or seven loads to his fields each day. Spreading was done just before planting time. He was not especially enamored of his task, for he began as early as 1862 to experiment with other fertilizing agents. Lippincott lived near .pits where the marl was sold undug. He alternated between "grubbing in the marl pitts" and hauling home the marl. When the weather was foul or the roads were icy, he would pile up marl for days ahead. He was able to haul ten loads to his fields in a long day. On February 20, 1868, he hauled his last load for the winter. However, he was back at the task again in December. During that month he dug for ten days and hauled for several more. Undeterred by cold and snow and ice, the man was almost too busy with his marling to take his girl to the Christmas fair at Navesink, an event which cost him $8.[93]

Naturally the railroads made it possible to expand the use of marl, and commercial companies were formed to dig and sell it. Many sandy areas became good cropland after a heavy application of marl, and the productivity of thin soils was often increased more than fivefold.[94] The products of the Squankum and Freehold Marl Company and other entrepreneurs were to be found in agricultural supply stores as far from the pits as Hunterdon County in the 1850s. In 1855 James H. Blackwell bought twenty-five bushels for an experiment on a measured piece of ground.[95] Marl was selling for $3.10 per ton at Lambertville in 1870.[96] David C. Voorhees of Blawenburg in Somerset County bought his marl by the carload in 1875,[97] something that was probably a common practice for larger farmers near railroads. Voorhees, who lived near the Delaware and Raritan Canal, very probably could have brought in calcined lime at smaller transportation cost. He evidently preferred the marl.

George H. Cook, in his extensive study of the marl areas in 1855 and succeeding years, found the farmers there using not only the green marl, with its "beautiful green color," but the clays and sands that separated and covered the relatively thin layers of pure greensand. Local usage applied to these other elements, which were mixed with greensand in varying degrees, such terms as blue marl, gray marl, yellow or shell marl, black marl, white marl, reddish marl, blue shell marl, chocolate marl, marly clay, clayey marl, gunpowder marl, ash marl, wet bank marl, and dry bank marl. Practices varied as to these various mixtures. So-called poison marls, made astringent or acid by admixture of bog iron, were avoided in some cases, applied only on grassland in others, and mixed with calcined lime in still others. Sometimes it was thought advisable to put guano or barnyard manure on recently marled land. Applications of marl varied from a few loads per acre ahead of a grain crop to as many as four hundred loads on land that was being completely rehabilitated. When pure greensand, which everybody agreed was "quick and durable," was used the applications were lighter.[98] A typical notation made by Cook, this time at Spottswood, reads as follows: "In farming here the common rotation is clover, marl for potatoes, & barnyard manure for wheat." [99]

By the time of publication of his giant report, *Geology of New Jersey*, in 1868, Cook had visited dozens of marl pits and hundreds of farms. He concluded that it would be "possible to increase the number [of pits] until they actually join each other, and the whole distance from Sandy-

Hook Bay to the Delaware River has become one great marl-pit." [100] In some areas, of course, this fantasy would have required removal of considerable overburden. His reportage was less complete, and somewhat disappointing to himself, as regards the southwestern part of the marl belt. In this area fewer pits had been opened, and marl was not generally "so highly prized as a fertilizer," possibly because farmers were able to purchase calcined lime cheaply. Farmers in New Jersey, and the world over, have nearly always made decisions on short-term factors; however, the best farmers of the state used one or the other of the soil improvers, or a judicious mixture of the two, as their soil requirements seemed to dictate, and grew clover in their rotation to add nitrogen to the soil. [101]

The decline in the use of marl was a direct result of the appearance of reasonably priced commercial fertilizers, which required much less labor in application and which were sold with a guaranteed chemical analysis. The first areas to change over were those at a distance from the marl belt. The local papers in northwestern New Jersey, which had carried extensive advertisements for the Squankum and Freehold Marl Company and other commercial producers of marl, carried not one by 1880. Gradually the contagion spread to the marl belt itself. Farmers there were faced individually with a choice, and, at some time during the back-breaking tasks of digging and applying marl, one after another decided in favor of commercial fertilizers. This was not necessarily because of laziness. Cook in 1868 concluded, after analyzing samples from numerous pits, that marl, once applied to a field was worth from $6 to $10 per ton. [102] A few years later he wrote, "Considering the phosphoric acid and potash as the only parts of the marl worth transportation, their value ranges from $3.50 to $8.50 a ton." [103] These calculations seemed to show that marlers were not receiving much, in money equivalent, for their hard labor. The experience of John H. Demise, a Freehold farmer, is indicative of what was happening. He had been hauling marl from a nearby pit, and during a rest period one day decided to have it chemically analyzed. After some calculation he concluded that commercial fertilizers, everything considered, were more economical than marl. He experimented with mixing various elements to make a balanced fertilizer, and during the following years gradually became a dealer in commercial fertilizers with a large local trade. [104] Some farmers stayed with marl for a while, perhaps longest for use as a side dressing for potatoes. [105] But marl as a fertilizer was merely a memory in most areas by 1890, and attempts at a revival in the twentieth century did not get far. [106] Marl is still dug in small quantities, but its chief use is as a water softener.

The story of commercial fertilizers had begun long before the decline of marl. Strictly speaking, one of the first commercial fertilizers was guano, made from the excrement of sea birds of Peruvian islands. The heyday of its use in New Jersey was from 1845 to 1865. Widely advertised in this period,[107] it was seldom mentioned thereafter. Guano was a very rich fertilizer, but costly. John Ten Eyck, wedded to the idea that guano was the best fertilizer to put with corn on sod ground, paid nearly $6 per hundredweight for it in 1854.[108] George W. Moore paid twice that amount in 1868,[109] the rise in price being largely a result of the inflation of the period. Even before the Civil War, guano was gradually being replaced by fertilizers made from the night soil of New York and other large cities and sold under such trade names as Poudrette, Pablette, and chemical compost.[110] But such fertilizers were also rather too costly for widespread agricultural use.

The mineral theory of soil composition, advanced by a German scientist, Justus von Liebig, became known to Americans as a result of an American edition of his book in 1841, and the knowledge was soon popularized by the agricultural press.[111] Numerous promoters appeared who were willing to make fertilizers containing the various elements that Liebig had found in the soil. An interesting person who rushed into the commercial fertilizer field was James J. Mapes of Newark, who patented and placed on the market in 1852 a "superphosphate of lime," a product which competed successfully with guano and Poudrette. The new fertilizer, composed of bone dust dissolved in sulphuric acid and mixed with sulphate of ammonia,[112] grew in popularity, along with various rivals that appeared almost at once. George W. Moore of Cumberland County was purchasing "bone dust" at $35 per ton in 1862 and 1863 to apply with marl. After that time he called his purchases simply "phosphate." [113]

Dr. George H. Cook became tremendously interested in the new fertilizers, and for many years he and his helpers and successors gave lectures on the subject, "Commercial Fertilizers." At Cook's urging the state legislature passed a law in 1874 requiring that fertilizers be accompanied by a printed analysis. At first, formulas were tested by a chemist of the State Board of Agriculture, later by the New Jersey Agricultural Experiment Station.[114] As knowledge of soil chemistry increased, fertilizers were improved accordingly. The farmers of New Jersey turned very rapidly to "mineral fertilizers" as the answer to the long-time problem of compensating the soil for the elements taken from it by growing crops. The names of fertilizers of another day sound strange in our ears. In 1903 Dr. J. B. Thompson of Moriscot Farm in Somerset County was using, among other fertilizers, "acid phosphate," "potato manure," and "Universal Fertilizer of the Packers' Union." [115] One of his problems was "poisoning" or burning the roots of the growing grain, a problem that troubled many farmers until they learned how to apply the new fertilizers.

10

The New Machinery

Farm labor outside the family circle had always been in short supply, especially during the critical times of the crop year. With the general decline of bond servitude, apprenticeship, and slavery, the farmer had to depend more and more on free labor. The family labor force, always the most stable and usually the most reliable, fortunately remained large. Youthful marriages were the rule, and children came often. One West Jersey woman, aged thirty-six in 1850, had at that time eight children in elementary school and three below school age.[1] This was a bit unusual, even then, but the records show that the average family was large and spanned a considerable age range. Though huge families became somewhat less common toward the end of the nineteenth century, the average farm family began to decrease noticeably in size only toward the end of the period to 1917. The diaries of childless farmers such as James H. Blackwell of Hunterdon County and John Ten Eyck of Somerset show that they were constantly short of farm help, though Blackwell had a brother as his partner and Ten Eyck persuaded a brother to return from Illinois after his own health failed. The diary of David C. Voorhees of Blawenburg in 1875 shows repeatedly how lucky he was to have one or two sons still at home and two living on nearby farms.

Hired labor fell into two categories, "hands" employed by the month or the year and day laborers. The latter were sometimes farm or village boys who made a little pocket money dropping corn or doing odd farm tasks for a neighbor. Or they might be village laborers, who were coaxed into coming to the country when farmers were behind in their work. Most important of the day laborers were villagers or city men who left their regular employment briefly to share the bonuses that farmers unwillingly paid at harvest time. The long-term hired man, who might live with the family or, if married, in his own home nearby, was in most cases the farmer's alter ego in keeping the farm running efficiently. The wise farmer, if he could afford it, made great efforts to keep such an employee

133

satisfied. The diary of James Ten Eyck, Sr., in the 1790s shows that he gave various presents to his hired man, including large amounts of apple brandy. Also he supplied Cuff, a black and possibly a slave, with good clothes and even "bespoke" his shoes to give him a good fit. James, Jr., relied heavily on a Negro couple, who apparently considered the farm their home. John, a son of James, Jr., had Black Tige Van Nest as a regular helper, but tried a dozen German and Irish hands before Dutch Peter hired on regularly at $10 a month in 1853. It seems that the farmer showed great restraint in order to keep this rather rough jewel.

Other farm diaries show how important a good regular hand could be. James H. Blackwell in the 1840s and 1850s offered steady work to various German and Irish hands. He was very pleased with one German couple, but they left him after a year. An Irishman who became "a pretty good hand" stayed even longer, but then left hurriedly when it became apparent that he had seduced the Blackwells' maid. In the 1850s George W. Moore of Cumberland County had a good man at $8 a month. Later, unable to find a satisfactory replacement or unwilling to pay the cost, he curtailed his farming operations during the Civil War and for a time thereafter. In 1871 he was glad to find a hand at $10 a month or $140 for a full year. In the spring of 1903 Dr. J. B. Thompson of Somerset nearly had to give up farming for the year because of difficulty in finding a second hired man after sacking the first.

Day work took many forms. In 1795 James Ten Eyck, Sr., hired a boy for five days and paid him with "a pair of shoes for Winter." In 1797 he paid a harvest hand the high price of ten shillings a day for "a cradling." James, Jr., who took over the farm in 1802, hired men during the next two decades to split rails, hoe corn, rake and bind wheat, and perform many other farm chores. Like his father, he hired a neighbor woman on occasion to come in to spin linen or wool. In the 1850s John Ten Eyck, like some other New Jersey farmers, was hiring immigrant labor through a labor office in Brooklyn by the day, week, or month. His various experiences with such labor, often frustrating, were duplicated in the same period by James H. Blackwell of Hunterdon. Some of the workers for the latter drank heavily, others "sloaped," and still others "fooled away their time." But on one occasion he was quite pleased that by persistence he had taught an Irishman to mow with an American crooked scythe.

In the period after the Civil War, labor costs rose modestly, and satisfactory hands were in very short supply. At Readington in 1876 a man was paid a dollar a day for general farm work and more at harvest time. A woman, if lucky, could earn fifty cents a day.[2] A day laborer in 1883 could expect $1.50 a day.[3] In 1891 Elmer Bonnell of near Clinton paid peach hands during the summer $15 a month and keep.[4] In the late 1890s Thomas Lauderdale of southern Hunterdon County paid 75 cents for regular hands in winter and $1.50 during the crop season.[5] By their own accounts, many farmers bought laborsaving devices and machines because of the expense and trouble of finding satisfactory laborers. For example, it was Blackwell's difficulties in finding harvest hands, even at wages which he sarcastically called "modest," which caused him to buy a reaper.

The adoption of laborsaving machinery constituted one of the most revolutionary breaks with the past, and certainly the most spectacular. But even here the change was less sudden than one might suppose, and did not affect all farm processes at the same time. Some simple machines, for that matter, had come into use earlier. The separator or fanning mill, introduced before 1775, had eliminated for many farmers their dependence on the wind when threshing grain.[6] Like the various devices for chopping straw and root crops,[7] it was operated laboriously by manpower, but nevertheless it increased both efficiency and speed. In a sense the fanning mill was the progenitor of the power thresher, but the gap in time before the acceptance of the latter was a long one. In this case, the advances in design were made in Europe rather than in America. Manpowered threshers from Scotland were introduced as early as 1802, but another generation passed before any except gentleman farmers purchased the new contraptions.[8]

Similar halting progress marked the evolution of laborsaving devices of all kinds. With each new machine representing another stage in the process of development, the new implement of one decade might well be made obsolete by improvements in the next. Actually, the process of change was considerably accelerated as time passed. It would be simple to explain all this by the old saw, "Necessity is the mother of invention." Certainly both the shortage of labor and the ineffectiveness of the labor that was available put a high premium on inventiveness. But there was more to it than that. Ingenuity is in a sense catching, and the appearance of one invention often inspires a new crop of inventions. The intellectual climate of this time was exactly right for tinkering and experimentation. The prizes to be won were substantial if the inventor took the trouble to patent his device or technique. Quite often he did not bother, but had the satisfaction of seeing others copy his ideas.

Before 1800 equipment and techniques for preparing the soil for seeding used by most farmers had not been very superior to those of medieval Europe. The mental block to progress in this case was very serious and quite persistent. Some stubborn farmers were still using wooden plows with simple iron points far into the nineteenth century.[9] The fate of the Newbold plow in Burlington County in the 1790s has already been mentioned. But after the invention and successful demonstration of the David Peacock plow in the same county in 1806, the Jethro Wood plow at Scipio, New York, in 1819, and the Edwin A. Stevens plow at Hoboken in 1821, most farmers turned rather quickly to plows with iron moldboards.[10] Many blacksmiths tried their hand at making plows, generally copying the Wood principle of interchangeability of parts. Any one of them stumbling on a superior design was soon honored by having his ideas imitated. The best shop-made plows had a considerable local market, and apparently gave satisfaction to their purchasers. When John Ten Eyck of North Branch decided in 1854 that he needed two new plows, he went unhesitatingly to his regular blacksmith.[11]

A number of smith-made plows were patented, and a few went into larger production. The most famous New Jersey one, the Deats plow, was the product of John Deats, a blacksmith at Stockton. The letters of patent issued in 1828 stated that it had a moldboard "better calculated to scour than any other hitherto made." [12] A similar claim had been made for the Stevens plow, patented in 1821.[13] The Peacock, Stevens, and Deats plows were made in New Jersey, as was the Mapes subsoil plow.[14] All had their proponents, but before long they had to share the market with others made outside the state. The riding plow was used here and there during the later decades of the nineteenth century. If it had only one share it was known as a sulky; if it had two or more it was called a gang plow. A sulky was shown as early as 1856 at the Cumberland County Fair,[15] but apparently attracted little attention. Riding plows were never numerous, largely because of their high cost, but their numbers increased after 1900. A touch of the old conservatism showed in the argument that only a lazy man would avoid walking behind a plow.

Plows were soon made in various models, some with interchangeable moldboards so as to be adaptable for such purposes as cultivating corn and potatoes.[16] James H. Blackwell in 1858 had two No. 5 Deats plows and one each of No. 8 and No. 9.[17] By this time newspaper advertisements showed that special types of plows, as the subsoil plow, the double plow or double shovel, and the corn plow were made by nearly every manufacturer. The increasing use of steel in place of iron after 1870 permitted the making of plows which scoured better, pulled more easily, and were lighter and easier to handle.[18] By this time, of course, the plow was almost entirely a factory product. But farm diaries and accounts show that the farmer was still as dependent on the local blacksmith for sharpening his plowshares and making plow repairs as he was for shoeing his horses.

The harrow, the most important pulverizing implement, underwent a complete metamorphosis during this period. The old "A" harrow and the original rectangular harrow had wooden frames into which iron teeth were inserted. Usually a farmer did not attempt to make his own harrow. In 1795 James Ten Eyck, Sr., wanted a one-horse harrow or corn harrow for use between the rows of corn. His diary shows that he purchased the spike teeth, furnished timber from his own woodlot, and hired the

local blacksmith to make the implement. By 1800 the "A" harrow had
fallen into almost complete disuse, and the rectangular harrow had
been redesigned so that it had two sections, sometimes hinged together.
This sectional harrow was built of lighter wood, and it was possible to
adjust the angle of the teeth in accordance with soil conditions.[19] After
1850 sectional harrows with frames of iron appeared, and when steel
became cheap as a result of the Bessemer process, that metal was used for
both teeth and frames.[20] About 1880 the spring-tooth harrow was invented.[21] The older type of harrow was now designated by the name
spike harrow. In 1903, when Dr. J. B. Thompson's hired man at Moriscot
Farm found the clods too much for a spike harrow, he borrowed a new
Acme spring-tooth harrow from his father on an adjoining farm.[22]

The harrow had always been supplemented by other pieces of equipment, and particularly by the drag, made of squared timbers, and the
land roller, made of a carefully selected log attached to a frame. The
drag continued to be a homemade device, but blacksmiths and farm
implement manufacturers took over the roller early in the nineteenth
century. Logs were still sometimes used, but the manufactured plank
land roller became the more usual type.[23] Later in the century various
new pulverizing implements were developed. The disc harrow, not really
a harrow at all, was known before 1870,[24] but it was regarded as a "horse-
killer," and furthermore was rather expensive. As a consequence, it did
not come fully into its own until the day of the tractor. Much the same
was true of the "pulverator" and the "cultipacker." The corrugated roller,
made by stringing metal discs on an axle, was highly esteemed by farmers who had soils that clodded easily.[25] If some of the sections were removed, the implement could be used for row cultivation of young corn.[26]

The methods of seeding corn and the small grains were badly in need
of improvement, but various mechanical difficulties caused a considerable delay. The corn drills mentioned in county newspapers in the 1820s
were machines to push by hand. They did not perform very well, nor did
they save enough labor to sell well.[27] But in the 1840s one-row and two-
row corn planters, pulled by horses, began to appear. One type that was
much advertised in 1857 was pulled by a single horse. The one-row type
cost $16, the two-row type $18. One man guided the horse and another
man or boy operated a lever so that the seed was dropped in checked
hills along with fertilizer. Pumpkins could be planted at the same time.[28]
An illustration in the *Lambertville Press* on November 11, 1858, showed
two simple wheel planters fastened side by side, both apparently controlled by the same operator. Despite the saving of labor, New Jersey
farmers were slower than those farther west to adopt the new machines.
John Ten Eyck's diary shows that he used the old method of planting
until his death in 1877. His brother Tunis had spent the middle years

of his life in corn country in Illinois. He introduced a hand corn planter that was lifted from hill to hill, but continued until his death in 1893 to use his brother's furrowing sled to mark the location of the hills of corn.[29]

The Deats factory at Pittstown was still making furrowing sleds as late as 1895, and one farmer, at least, used the ancient method as late as 1909.[30] It seems probable that the reason for the tardiness in adopting mechanical planters was that the old way, which used child labor plentifully, was cheap and not unreasonably slow. An objection of many farmers was that a corn planter dribbled the corn in the rows, making it impossible to cultivate both ways of the field. David C. Voorhees, who had a corn planter in 1875, found also that the crop had to be thinned in those rows that were planted by machine. For most of his crop that year he "planted with two hoes as usual," employing neighbor boys to drop the grains in the holes.[31] But before 1900 the new improved wheel corn planters, pulled by a team and operated by a single man, were gaining general approval.[32] These machines had supplemental equipment which enabled the farmer to plant checked hills if he wished.

The grain drill or seed drill for small grains came into use at about the same time as the horse-drawn corn planter. The first drill other than homemade devices came to the state about 1840. The Pennock drill, made in Pennsylvania, sowed seven rows 9 inches apart and placed the seed about 3 inches in the ground. It thus sowed a width of over 10 feet each "round" in the field, and a man and a team during a long day could sow fifteen acres.[33] James H. Blackwell left among his papers a broadside dated June 19, 1856, which advertised Lee's Patent Premium Grain Drills. Many other makes were soon on the market, but sales resistance for a long time proved very strong. The method of sowing recorded by Ralph Voorhees in his diary in 1860 apparently persisted on many farms. In the spring he sowed his oats and clover by broadcasting and harrowing in the seeds, and in the fall used the same procedure for wheat and timothy. With improvement of the grass-sowing attachment of the grain drill and the introduction in the 1870s of devices for spreading commercial fertilizers, many farmers began to change their minds. According to their diaries, John Ten Eyck, never easy to persuade, stayed with the old methods, but David C. Voorhees bought a new drill early in 1875. On April 7 the dealer assembled the various drill parts at the farm. Voorhees tried out the machine until May 25, then "settled" for it. On September 13, when he first used it for sowing wheat, he wrote, "The new drill works like a charm." In the next few days one of his sons "drilled in" the whole crop without incident. Not every progressive farmer used the grass seed attachment on his grain drill, however. In 1903 Dr. J. B. Thompson, a man who prided himself on his modernity, used his drill for oats and fertilizer, but sowed clover seed on the same field with a hand seeder which broad-cast the seed.[34]

The first improvement in the cultivating of corn was made possible by the introduction of lighter corn plows. Plowing corn was still a tedious process, but persisted for many decades.[35] The old corn harrow was also retained by some farmers until late in the nineteenth century. Progressive farmers, however, discarded the corn plow and corn harrow as soon as efficient substitutes were available. The corn cultivator was introduced into New Jersey about 1820, and was considerably improved during the next decades. The cultivator was of such simple construction that a black-smith could easily make one, or even a farmer who was handy with tools. Local implement dealers soon elbowed in, however, selling factory-made cultivators at from $15 to $20 apiece.[36] The cultivator was essentially a wooden frame, beneath which short-necked shovels were attached. Pulled between the rows of corn by a horse, it dug up most of the weeds and loosened the soil. A pair of handles like those of a wheelbarrow gave some control over the clumsy device. The cultivator was a true laborsaver, requiring only half the time of a corn plow and doing a much more ef-ficient job than the corn harrow. After a field had been cultivated length-wise and crosswise very little hoe work was necessary in most years. By the 1850s the cultivator had been considerably improved. Now pulled by a team, it cultivated both sides of a row, rather than a whole middle be-tween two rows. This "straddle-row" cultivator was no faster than the old one-horse cultivator, but it did a better job. The designers and adapt-ers of the new device were legion. Among New Jersey inventors or im-provers of the cultivator were David Petit of Salem County and William S. Riggs of Hightstown.[37]

The next step in the development of the cultivator was to mount it on skids or runners, and then on wheels. Pulled by a team of horses, the skid cultivator plowed the corn on each side of the row with a number of small shovels. Its chief advantage over the old cultivator was its sta-bility. A skid cultivator which had a considerable New Jersey following for two or three decades was the one patented by Oliver Kugler of Three Bridges in 1873. Cultivators patented by Hubert D. Ganse of Freehold in 1856, John Smalley of Bound Brook in 1859, and Reuben K. Neice of Frenchtown in 1878 also had many local users. As was often done in this period, the inventors sold their patent rights to blacksmiths and others, each purchaser being allotted a definite territory.[38] Sales franchises for the Kugler cultivator, like those of the Deats plow earlier, were sold in the Middle West,[39] but how successfully is not known. Wheel cultivators eventually replaced all others, but not as rapidly as might have been ex-pected. Produced in both walking and riding types, they eventually be-came a monopoly of the big farm implement manufacturers. The combination of some firms and the elimination of others eventually removed all manufacture of farm implements from New Jersey.

For all these inventions, no method of cultivating corn was always satisfactory. Particularly in wet years, weeds would keep pace with the corn. This probably explains why some farmers occasionally used their lightweight corn plows and corn harrows until late in the period. But most of them preferred the much faster new cultivators. If a field was weedy, a farmer could do as William C. Lippincott of Little Silver did on the Fourth of July of 1868: he could take a sharp hoe and cut out the weeds in the areas that were worst infested.[40] David C. Voorhees, who used "wheel plows, six shovels each," to cultivate his corn in 1875, was satisfied with his results.[41] This type of implement was to be in common use for the next four decades.

As plowing and seeding operations were improved, farmers increased their acreage of small grains and hay. In consequence, the worst bottleneck of the crop year was harvest time, when grain and forage crops had to be gathered in close sequence. Homemade and experimental mowing machines, called reapers or harvesters, began to appear soon after 1800, but the first few farmers who bought them had so many troubles with them that they resumed the old methods. In time, however, persistent inventors evolved workable equipment. The machine of William Manning of Plainfield, patented in 1831, probably influenced both Hussey and McCormick.[42] By the time the McCormick reaper had local sales representatives in New Jersey in the early 1850s, several locally invented reapers had a following, particularly that of Andrew Dietz and J. P. Dunham of Raritan. Most early reapers could be changed into mowers by removing the grain platform and making a change of sickle bars.

George W. Moore of Cumberland County, after seeing various reapers demonstrated at county fairs, purchased the one of his choice soon after 1850. In 1853, according to his diary but for reasons not clear, he harvested his grain by hand but used the machine as a mower for his hay crop. On September 20 of that year he had an experience not unusual for the early users of the new machinery. He had just started to mow a seed crop of red clover, and all seemed well. But suddenly something snapped, and he had to drive to Shiloh and pay the blacksmith there 37½ cents for welding before he could proceed with his work. One of his 1861 diary entries reads, "July 4, Worked on the mowing machine in the morning and mowed in the afternoon." In 1854 James H. Blackwell had ordered a "reaper and mower" from Dietz and Dunham in Raritan, paying them $140. Though progressive in his inclinations, Blackwell did not relish spending so much money. But harvest hands were being paid from $2.50 to $3.00 a day, and they were scarce at that price. Apparently he was the first purchaser of a reaper in his neighborhood, for all the nearby farmers stopped their harvest and gathered at the Blackwell farm on the day of its tryout. The new machine performed perfectly, and Blackwell had his wheat crop cut and in the shock within two days. He then transformed the reaper into a mower, and made short work of putting up his crops of oats and hay. During the years following, the machine often needed repairs, but Blackwell evidently considered it a good investment.[43] In 1860 Ralph Voorhees of Somerset County cut part of his wheat "with a machine," but also had men working with scythes and cradles, probably in parts of the fields where the grain had been blown down. In the oats harvest, his men cut a swath around the field by hand, preparatory to using the reaper. However, in the end, because of "down oats," they also cut a part of the field itself. Like many farmers, Ralph Voorhees found the machine most useful for hay.[44]

Competition among different makers of reapers led to constant improvements. The self-rake was added by one maker after another in the 1850s. There had been several patented inventions for this device, including a number by New Jersey men.[45] The self-rake saved the labor of the man who had sat on the platform of the reaper to rake off the mowed grain in bunches to be bound by hand. In a reaping and mowing contest near Flemington in 1858, the machines of seven manufacturers competed. All did well at reaping, but some not so well at cutting tangled clover hay.[46] Mowing and reaping contests and demonstrations became a part of the county fairs of the period. Often a farmer who had purchased a reaper made back part of his outlay by doing custom work for his neighbors. According to his diary, John Ten Eyck until 1854 still cut his "grass" with a naked scythe and his wheat with a scythe and cradle, despite the fact that his father, James Ten Eyck, Jr., had been one of the inventors who patented a harvesting machine three decades earlier.[47] But in that year he hired a neighbor to mow his clover by machine, and eventually he came round to having his grain cut by reaper when it was standing well. In 1857 he himself purchased a reaper, but had a hired man operate it for him. Like others, he still fell back on the scythe and cradle whenever the grain had been beaten to the ground by the wind.

By 1870 most manufacturers were making separate machines for reaping grain and for mowing hay crops. In 1875 David C. Voorhees had two mowers cutting at the same time in the hay harvest. One was a straight mower, the other the old type. The latter he converted into a reaper when the wheat was ready for harvest. His sons and hired men bound the grain into sheaves behind the reaper and put them into "Dutch shooks." The reaper was then converted back into a mower for another field of hay. The oats harvest came next. The platform was put on the machine again, but Voorhees decided that the oats crop was down too badly to cut with the reaper. He therefore decided to cut it with scythes and not bind it into sheaves. His sons pleaded with him to use the reaper, but Voorhees recorded, "I would not listen to it." However, the machine was used to mow a patch of seed timothy before being put away for the winter. On August 6 he wrote, "All done at last." [48]

In the 1880s the reaper gave way gradually to the twine binder, an implement which saved the work of the men who followed the reaper to bind the grain. Some farmers derided the "lazy man's contraption," and at first there were complaints as to performance, particularly of the knotting device. Nevertheless, the binder was purchased rapidly by many farmers with sufficient wheat and rye acreage to justify the money outlay. In 1883 a farmer at Readington claimed that he cut twenty-three acres of wheat between noon one day and noon the next with his new binder.[49] The following year Elmer Bonnell, disgusted at the cost and quality of harvest hands, bought a binder and was soon sorry that he had waited so long.[50] The owners of binders, like those of reapers earlier, often did custom harvesting for smaller farmers. As time went on, the binder and mower were perfected mechanically and were made with longer cutting bars. It should be made clear that many farmers did not buy the new harvesting machines precipitately. John Ten Eyck, ever one to drag his feet a bit, did not have a mower separate from his reaper until 1875.[51] His brother Tunis, who succeeded him in 1877, was more used to machines as a result of his Illinois experience. He soon purchased a twine binder, which he pulled with three mules.[52] Often the old ways disappeared only with old men, but by 1894 a farmer harvesting a field with scythe and cradle was considered worth a news story by a newspaper, as was also the one who was still using an old reaper in 1899.[53]

Equipment for handling hay also received the attention of inventors. The first horse rake to be developed was the whoa-back rake, a device which raked the hay into windrows but which required that the horse be stopped and backed each time the rake was emptied. This simple piece of equipment appeared about 1820 and was still in use in 1840, although gradually being replaced by the revolving rake. The latter, also called the flip-flop rake or tumbler, was much faster because the horse did not have to be stopped.[54] David C. Voorhees still used two rakes of this type in his hay harvest in 1875. After raking, the hay was put in "heaps" by hand. The flip-flop had its users until about 1880,[55] even though the sulky or dump rake, mounted on wheels, had appeared much earlier. Equipped at first with a hand dump, then with a self-dump, the sulky rake eventually replaced all other types.[56] The tedder, an implement used to stir up mown hay, in order to speed up its drying, appeared before 1870.[57] James Neilson, Jr., of near New Brunswick paid $98 for one in 1869.[58] David C. Voorhees found this device a most useful one in scattering heaps of hay which had been wetted by rain.[59]

Side delivery rakes and hay loaders were in use in the 1890s.[60] These machines were accepted slowly by most farmers because of their cost. A device which was not expensive, but which saved much labor after about 1850, was the hay fork on a track for carrying hay back into the interior of a hayloft.[61] Stationary hay presses were in use before 1840, but the farmer must usually haul his hay to a custom press if he wanted it baled, as did Neilson in 1863.[62] The portable, horse-powered baler, usually moved from farm to farm for custom work, came in about 1890. An innovation by the turn of the century was replacement of the horses with a gasoline engine.[63] Corn harvesting machinery appeared slowly, perhaps because the need was less pressing. Sled corn harvesters were manufactured by 1885, and a harvester mounted on four wheels by 1895.[64] The corn binder was invented soon after, but did not sell well in New Jersey until much later. Eventually its greatest use was at silo-filling time.

Machines for threshing grain were in use before 1800. With one such "threshing mill," introduced into New York in 1788, a man and boy could supposedly thresh seventy bushels of wheat in a day.[65] But few of such machines, either imported or produced in America, were used on this side of the Atlantic before 1825.[66] Demand improved briefly about that time, but horse-powered threshers soon captured the market. Demonstrations of newly patented "lever power" threshers were being held in agricultural communities by 1830, and one of the new machines in that year was described thus: "It may be worked by hand, or by horse power, and is applicable to the threshing of wheat, rye, oats, and flax, etc., which it performs very expeditiously, and takes the grain clear from the straw." [67] The usual power was that of a single horse or a team attached to a long sweep or shaft. During following years, the various inventors and developers, a number of them New Jersey citizens, found many customers.[68] The lever power machines, though not light, could be carried about in a farm wagon, thus making it possible to do custom threshing. The charges were one-tenth or one-eighth of the grain threshed.[69]

The tread power or treadmill thresher began to replace the lever power before 1850. Made in several places in the state and also imported from outside, it came into use very rapidly. After the harvest in 1853 George W. Moore recorded using his horse power thresher for threshing wheat, oats, buckwheat, and clover. On one occasion twenty-eight of his neighbors came in to thresh a stack of oats "by frolic," and, no doubt, to see the machine in action.[70] On December 22 of the same year James H. Blackwell wrote in his diary, "George T. Gray brought home and set up our thrashing machine. We put on Old Mike and run through one run of oats and it appears to run well. Price of machine and power $100." He had some trouble getting Old Mike to "keep up a steady motion," but the new machine proved a success. The tread power thresher was even more easily transported than the lever power. John Cox, a neighbor, did custom work for John Ten Eyck, and probably for other neighbors, between 1854 and 1860. Ten Eyck, who in 1853 still used a "frail" (flail) or else chased his horses around the threshing floor, on which had been placed a "flooring" of wheat or rye or barley, was not a man who parted lightly with his money. But he had become convinced that he would get a larger return of grain by using a machine. He had had his own separator or fanning mill for cleaning up the grain, and in 1857 borrowed that of Cox, perhaps a better one than his own. In 1860 he bought of Dunham and Staats of Raritan, who made threshers as well as reapers, a fine new threshing machine, for which he paid $104.41.[71] His thinking had evidently gone through quite a transformation by this time.

Before very long, inventive mechanics combined the threshing machine and separator, and through the years various refinements and new features were repeatedly added. For one thing, the tempo of threshing was greatly increased. In December 1888 Elmer Bonnell traded in his old thresher on a new "thresher and cleaner," which he bought of the Deats firm at Pittstown. On the first day of work, he recorded, "The machine gained speed all the time. Thrashed 100 sheaves of oats in 14 minutes, almost one bu. of oats to the minute."[72] A decade earlier James Neilson, Jr., had recorded a much slower rate with his old-type thresher and cleaner.[73] In the 1880s the addition of conveyors made it so that the operators did not have to work so close to the beaters of the machine. In 1875 David C. Voorhees had written, "Decidedly the meanest work on the farm is threshing, at least such is my opinion."[74] He probably changed his mind as the thresher was improved. By about 1890 large portable threshers, often called grain separators, were being pulled from farm to farm after harvest by steam tractors, which also supplied the necessary power for threshing by use of belts.[75] Threshing was now performed out-of-doors. A decade later many threshers were powered by large gasoline engines, and from here it was only a step to the gasoline tractor, which came into its own during World War I.[76]

Though machine succeeded machine with increasing tempo during these decades, it is interesting that use of the flail persisted for one particular farm task until fairly late. The use of rye straw as ties, especially for fodder shocks, was an old practice, and there had been markets for battens of "long straw" since pioneer days. Ralph Voorhees of Bernards Township, Somerset County, in 1860 spent two days threshing rye with a flail, then threshed the rest of his rye crop with his tread power machine.[77] Presumably he had saved enough of the long straw for his own purposes during the year ahead and was not tempted to produce for the market. His distant kinsman, David C. Voorhees of Blawenburg, on the other hand, in 1875 produced several tons of rye straw, for which he was paid $10 per ton. He himself, however, used tarred strings for tying purposes,[78] a practice fairly new at the time, but one which would eventually entirely supplant the use of rye straw ties.

Another effect of technical progress was the appearance of a special machine for threshing clover and grass seed. In the old days, flails and other beating devices were used, or horses were driven over succeeding layers of ripe hay on the threshing floor. Some farmers who needed only a few bushels of seed for themselves continued to employ such inefficient methods. Others turned to the lever power and later to the tread power threshers. Whether the farmer used an older or newer method of detaching the seed, he still had to put in laborious hours with his fanning mill to get rid of the chaff. The clover hullers which were operated by some millers on a custom basis, did an effective job, but only nearby farmers could afford to haul their crop to a mill. The appearance of the portable huller operated by tread power in the 1850s was a considerable advance. In 1860 John Ten Eyck borrowed such a machine from a neighbor rather than use his new thresher for his seed clover crop.[79] He was able to hook up his own tread power on the borrowed machine. The following half century saw a gradual improvement of the huller and its adaptation to the new kinds of power.

In the early 1800s there appeared homemade and smith-made devices for shelling corn, for slicing stock beets, carrots, and pumpkins, and for cutting up fodder and straw. The power in most cases was that of a man turning a crank. With the appearance of the horse power or treadmill about 1840, these machines were changed so as to use a horse instead of a man. Usually the farmer could use the same treadmill for these devices as for his threshing machine. In the 1850s shelling corn by tread power was sometimes called threshing it or thrashing it, at least by John Ten Eyck of Somerset County.[80] The corn sheller was eventually modified so that a steam engine, gasoline engine, or electric motor could run it by belt. Tread power machines for slicing root crops and pumpkins were exhibited at county fairs and other public places in the 1840s and 1850s,[81] but with the decline in the growing of these crops soon thereafter slicing machines were discontinued. A similar device for grinding grain into grist was in use in the 1850s,[82] but was never very common.

The straw and fodder cutter, a machine used for the most part in the preparation of bedding,[83] eventually evolved into the shredder or corn shredder, which was operated by a belt. The addition of a husking device made this machine an important laborsaver. Larger machines, transported and powered by steam tractors, did custom work, often on more or less regular routes, each fall in the 1890s and early 1900s.[84] Many farmers, on the other hand, had smaller machines, powered by gasoline engines or electric motors. As farmers turned to other feeds and other bedding, the

shredder declined in importance. It was gradually replaced by the ensilage cutter, which came in with the upright silo in the 1890s.[85] Operated
at great speed by use of a belt, this machine chopped green corn, ears and
all, into small bits and blew them up to the top of the silo, from which
they fell into the silo itself. As silos became taller, the ensilage cutters
became larger and more efficient.

Although no attempt is made to list here all the laborsaving devices
employed on New Jersey farms during the period from 1810 to 1917, a
few others besides those already mentioned have special interest or importance. By 1810 hollow wood pumps, often called cucumber pumps,
were replacing well sweeps, windlasses, and simple ropes and pulleys for
drawing water from the shallow wells of the time.[86] By 1830 cast iron lift
pumps were in fairly common use, if advertisements in local papers are
an indication. In 1838 Dr. John Bowne of southern Hunterdon, always
progressive, signed a testimonial saying that he had been one of the first
to try Maxwell's Cast Iron Double Lifting Pump and that he found it an
excellent pump.[87] In the early 1850s John Ten Eyck employed a windmill to pump water, as was the case with many farmers. When a gudgeon
broke or wore out, the local blacksmith was capable of making a new
one.[88] Some machinery saw gradual improvement without radical changes.
Examples were the cider press and the lime spreader, but the new models
were considered important enough to be on prize lists at county fairs.[89]

Manure spreaders appeared in the 1880s but were few in numbers before 1900.[90] At a farmers' picnic in 1904 one of the exhibits was "a manure
spreader in operation." [91] The bucksaw for cutting wood was not displaced by the power saw or "buzz saw" until portable gasoline engines
were available. Often a local entrepreneur would do custom work on the
farms of his neighborhood. Specialized devices of great importance to
poultrymen appeared after 1870. In 1875 David C. Voorhees recorded in
his diary that his son William had built a chicken house with self-feeders
"from a model in the American Agriculturist." The incubator and
brooder came in with a flourish in the 1880s and 1890s.[92] Household devices of every kind were constantly being changed and improved. Those
used especially on farms were listed for competition for prizes at the
county fairs. By the 1850s churns, sausage cutters, and washing machines
had evolved considerably. The treadmill churn, operated by a dog, the
patented washing machine, which could be bought for $12 in 1862, and
the clothes wringer, a device of a little later time, proved great laborsavers
for housewives.[93] Of course, as household industries disappeared under the
impact of factory development, many tools once important simply disappeared instead of being improved or replaced by others. Simple examples
are the hatchel and swingle, used in obtaining linen and tow fibers from
flax, and the small spinning wheel, used for spinning those same fibers.

It should be clear that the greatest developments in agricultural machinery were associated with new sources of power. Some devices simply made manpower more efficient, but the significant early ones substituted horse power for manpower, and those of later decades used the steam engine, the internal combustion motor, or, in some cases already, the electric motor. In 1850 it seemed possible that small portable steam engines might replace horses for many tasks. Such machines could be bought for as little as $12 in 1857.[94] But the small steam engine never gained a large following, and when larger steam engines became common later in the century, especially in the form of steam tractors, they were employed most successfully for such specialized jobs as threshing, hulling clover, and filling silos. Attempts to use them for field work were never very successful in New Jersey. The coming of the internal combustion motor eventually proved to be far more important. By the early twentieth century, gasoline engines were being used by a good many farmers for such laborious tasks as threshing, pumping water, grinding feed, and sawing wood.[95] It was perhaps a sign of the times when John Case of Ringoes replaced his steam engine with a gasoline engine in 1904 to operate his threshing machine on his usual custom route.[96] A truly great development of the early 1900s was the harnessing of internal combustion motors to wheels, thus bringing farmers the greatest laborsavers of all, the gasoline tractor and motor truck. This development was clearly on its way by 1917.

In 1839 Jesse Buel, a well-known New York agricultural editor, whose magazine, the *Cultivator,* was much read in New Jersey, wrote, "Our implements are, however, daily improving. . . . A farm may now be worked with half the expense of labor that was required to work it ten years ago." [97] He was probably overoptimistic, but in any case improvements had been coming rapidly and would soon be coming even more rapidly. Bailey, in his *Cyclopedia of American Agriculture,* has estimated that the average farm family of 1850 in the nation was about 50 percent more productive than that of 1800, and that the change of the next half century was "far more." [98] New Jersey agriculture was probably not much below the average. Not all of this increase in productivity was brought about by the new farm machinery, of course, but a substantial part of it was, directly or indirectly. Calculations as to the direct savings in manpower to be credited to specific farm machines seem to be in order. They are, at best, guesses.

The new plows not only did a far better job than the old, but in the aggregate saved at least 50 percent in manpower and animal power. The new harrows were of most importance for being better pulverizers of the soil, but since they were wider they also did their work in less time. Drills and corn planters did a better job of putting the seed into the ground, but only after considerable improvement was their savings in time noticeable. On the other hand, it seems probable that the cultivator in its first stage cut the time of plowing corn in half, and that the wheel cultivator, when it appeared, could be operated even more rapidly. Furthermore, under ordinary conditions, both the skid cultivator and the wheel cultivator probably did a better job than the devices they replaced.

It is estimated that the new mowers of the 1850s reduced by two-thirds the time of cutting a hay crop, and it is probable that later models cut the time at least in half again. A revolving horse rake could bunch the hay on at least an acre in an hour and the sulky rake two or three times as much, probably as much as a man with a hand rake could do in a day. It is harder to estimate the savings for threshers, but it is certain that the gains were very high. Perhaps the greatest gains of all were in the harvesting of small grain. A reaper with a self-rake would cut grain at least five or six times as rapidly as a man with scythe and cradle. In both cases, of course, extra men were required for binding and shocking. The binder, when it came, eliminated the binding, one of the most laborious tasks. Whereas a man with a scythe and cradle needed two helpers in order to harvest less than two acres in a day, a single man with a team and binder could easily cut as much as fifteen acres, and two more men could put the sheaves into shocks. In summary, at a sheer guess, the efficiency of labor was increased at least sixfold for wheat, twofold for corn, sevenfold for oats, fourfold for hay, and twofold for potatoes during the nineteenth century. The new kinds of power in the early twentieth century increased man's efficiency even more rapidly.

The farmer's natural desire to accomplish his work with greater efficiency does not entirely explain the rapid ascendancy of the machine. Many a farmer, faced with the problem of finding farm labor at a time of peak demand, broke a bottleneck by buying a machine or a better machine than he already had. Since small grains shatter a few days after ripening, there is a high premium for speeding the harvest time. Delay in the hay harvest can well result in a considerable loss in the quality of the crop, if not a total loss. By the same token, unchecked growth of weeds in the cornfield will cut down seriously on the yield. Furthermore, the men who owned machines avoided the need of hiring many harvest hands, who in the farmer's opinion had an inflated valuation of their worth. Of considerable consequence was the fact that as markets increased and as farmers became more commercial in outlook, they exerted themselves to plant and sow a greater acreage than previously, without fear of being unable to harvest it. Equally important, the new implements often did a better job than farm hands with poorer tools. The improved plow did not "cut and cover," but really turned over the earth, and the reaper and binder did a cleaner job of harvesting than men with scythes. The wheel cultivator not only did better than the corn plow in cultivating the soil, but if used efficiently it often eliminated days of laborious work with a hoe. Quite aside from questions of productivity and efficiency, it was of some importance that the new machinery eased the backbreaking toil of farming.

There were, of course, some economic and social effects even harder to evaluate, not all of them beneficial in a larger sense. The capital needs of the farmer were increased, and this made it somewhat more difficult to rise from the status of farm hand or renter to that of owner-operator. In any case, the farmer became more dependent on bankers and money-lenders. Again, especially in the post–Civil War period, farmers found themselves in a situation where they must rely more and more on middle-men to market and transport their products and to supply them with an increasingly long list of manufactured goods. It should be clear, of course, that farmers in this period, in New Jersey as elsewhere, were literally forced to adjust to the machine age. Individuals and even neighborhoods might drag their feet for a time, but on the whole there was truly no choice as regards the mechanization of agriculture.

11

Developments in Livestock Husbandry

During the period 1810–1917 New Jersey farmers continued to raise the same breeds of livestock as heretofore, but with considerable changes in emphasis. As elsewhere in the northeastern United States, practices in New Jersey reflected the great alterations in the economy. As the commercialization and specialization of agriculture accelerated, animal husbandry responded. Horses and mules, the source of motive power for the new machinery, increased in numbers, especially heavy draft animals. Cattle also increased in numbers, and were more and more differentiated as to purpose. In the latter part of the period the accent on dairying more than compensated for the decline in beef production. On the other hand, though hogs were greatly improved in quality, their numbers slowly declined. The story was the same for sheep, except that the numerical decline was faster. But the chicken now no longer roosted in the trees. Nicely housed and well cared for, chickens eventually became significant in New Jersey's agricultural economy. As their importance increased, their old designation as "fowls" went out of fashion, and "poultry" became the usual term. For reasons that escape me, no one wanted to be called a chicken farmer.

The greatest single advance in animal husbandry was the adoption of good breeding practices. Like other aspects of the new age, the principles now accepted and applied were not entirely new ones. A few people had been importing blooded livestock from Europe for a long time. But, except to some extent with horses, the effects had not been lasting. Imported sires had temporarily improved the livestock of their neighborhoods, but the effect was soon dissipated, as "common" characteristics again became dominant. When females were also imported, small herds or flocks of purebred animals were sometimes developed. Most of these were eventually dispersed, however, so that their blood lines disappeared, or at least were so adulterated as to have lost most of their value. But there finally developed a general awareness that better animals paid off.

150

As a result, more and more purebred herds of various breeds were built up. Equally important, many farmers acquired purebred sires and through selective breeding built up herds of "grade" animals far superior to their original stock.

The belief that the number of horses on New Jersey farms increased during the early decades of the nineteenth century cannot be supported by statistics. However, it seems safe to assume that the development of horse-powered agricultural machinery caused the average farmer to buy or raise more horses. The first true farm census in 1840 reported approximately 71,000 horses in the state, that of 1860 about 80,000, that of 1880 just under 87,000, and that of 1900 some 94,000. A decline set in by 1910, and by 1920 there were only 73,000.[1] Mechanical horsepower was already on the rise. The numerous stud advertisements in the local newspapers of the first half of the nineteenth century reveal great interest in good animals, but the emphasis was still on fast road horses rather than on draft animals. Stallions with fancy names were quartered at nearly every village, and were advertised as "celebrated running horses," "full blooded horses," "imported horses," or "turf horses." Their pedigrees were played up in detail and lost nothing in reiteration. An occasional stallion was called a "field and road horse," however, and greater interest came to be shown in work horses and "general purpose" horses, doubtless as a result of the need for horses of strength and stamina for the new machines.[2] The county fairs continued to emphasize horse races and racing breeds.[3] But pulling contests and plowing contests also became a common feature, and sometimes, as at the first New Jersey Agricultural Society fair at Trenton in 1840, imported draft horses received special mention.[4]

Stallion advertisements in the county newspapers from the Civil War onward included some for purebred draft animals. But soon a marked decline in the number of stallions offered for hire set in. Many farmers found it more economical to buy horses raised in lands farther west and brought in by drovers. The practice had begun early in the century, and was common enough by the 1830s. Sometimes the customers bought directly from the drovers, as when the Case tannery near Flemington bought two mares from Ohio in 1836.[5] More commonly, buyers competed with one another at auction or vendue. The bidding at an auction of Kentucky mules held at Van Sickle's tavern near High Bridge in 1824 was so spirited that it received notice in a county newspaper.[6] By midcentury the demand for horses was tremendous. Sales grounds, usually the yards of taverns, were to be found in nearly every community. In 1854 John Ten Eyck, who usually preferred raising his own colts, was tempted into buying one of nine "imported" horses on exhibit locally.[7] By the 1870s western horses were also being imported by rail. Newspaper advertisements show that animals were brought from Pennsylvania, Kentucky, Ohio, Indiana, Illinois, Quebec, Michigan, Missouri, Iowa, Nebraska, and points west, as were also "car horses" released by the electrification of city streetcar lines. Midwest and "French" horses from Canada brought the best prices, Indian ponies or "broncos" and western ranch horses the poorest. A good horse in the 1890s would bring more than $200 at auction.[8] Prices advanced spectacularly after 1900 as sources of supply petered out. On the other hand, the cost of raising colts to maturity had mounted even faster. The high price of horses was given as a reason by some farmers for their first purchase of an automobile, tractor, or farm truck when they appeared on the market.

Despite the growing need for good work horses after 1810, the road horse was considered important throughout the period, even by the few purchasers of automobiles for fair-weather driving towards its end. It is true that horse thieves were no longer hanged in the nineteenth century, perhaps because horses were more plentiful or because more public transportation was available. Loss of a prize animal would in most cases merely reduce the owner to riding or driving a slower or less beautiful one. In any case, country people without doubt retained their affection and pride for the trotters and pacers that took them to church on Sunday or to other public events in buggies, carriages, or "pleasure wagons" during the week. When David C. Voorhees of Blawenburg set a "segar" between his teeth on the morning of July 1, 1875, and drove his "span of black horses" to Hopewell so that he could act as judge of oratory at "Miss Bogg's Academy" he felt, quite understandably, that he cut quite a figure. He and Mrs. Voorhees drove the same team to the Somerset County fair, to a local "Sing Song Party," and on all special occasions. He was definitely proud of "the Black Horses," as he designated these trotters, but when a nameless "gray mare," a work horse pure and simple, showed a proud determination never to help pull a plow, he marked her for quick disposal by trade, despite the fact that she liked the task of helping "Ben," a general purpose horse, pull the jagger wagon.[9]

Perhaps it was a carryover from this pride in sleek road horses that made farmers prouder of and caused them to take better care of their buggies and carriages than of their utilitarian farm implements. The owner of a new gig and new harness in 1825 much resented their being stolen, as he proclaimed heatedly in his advertisement about it. The vehicle, which was equipped with the new elliptic springs, had snuff-colored upholstery striped with black, and the new breechen harness was heavily decorated with nickel.[10] One wonders whether some other young man borrowed the turnout for a joy ride. Half a century later we find that to David C. Voorhees his very efficient reaper was only "the machine." But when Grandfather gave young William a spanking new buggy in 1875 it merited special mention, even as to the cost, which was $140.[11] At the Hunterdon County fair in 1878, prizes were offered for the best exhibits of phaetons, buggies, sulkies, sidecar buggies, buggy wagons, phaeton buggies, family carriages, one-seated sleighs, and two-seated sleighs. Considerably more money was paid out for these prizes than was given for agricultural implements.[12]

Well into the twentieth century the rural family was dependent on the horse. Though today it is difficult to picture their way of life, it is clear that most of their new machines either transferred tasks from man to beast or else made the beast's labor more efficient or more productive. All the early stages in the mechanization of farms depended almost entirely on the use of horses and mules. At the mention of lever power or tread power, one must remember that Old Mike was plodding day in and day out at the end of a sweep or on a treadmill, keeping the even pace required by the thresher, huller, sheller, or chopper. A team in the field eventually consisted of three or four horses instead of two, and for hauling produce to market two two-horse teams were sometimes employed in tandem. Hauling or "carting" acquired new significance as the amount of produce for sale increased. The dominance of the Conestoga wagon was gradually shifted to more compact, smoother-running vehicles of various types. These were made mostly by local smiths and wheelwrights until there were factories to take over wagon production. For a wagon with an "Inglish body," James Ten Eyck, Sr., of Somerset County paid a local wheelwright $73 in 1806.[13] In 1868 George W. Moore of Cumberland paid $45 for a lighter wagon, also made at a local shop.[14] In all farm diaries there are constant references to the hauling of hay and grain and produce on the farm itself and to market, to hauling lime and coal and marl from a distance, and to regular weekly trips to the crossroads or village store to market produce and buy farm supplies. In retrospect, it seems clear that the rapid rise of agriculture in the period 1810–1917 was made possible only because horses were used more efficiently.

The typical cattle at the beginning of the period were the nondescript "common" or "native" animals, light in weight and not very productive of milk. In the summer and fall, they were pastured on natural vegetation and sometimes on sowed crops, such as rye, wheat, timothy or clover. But the winter was a time of hardship. Fed little grain, they were expected to "live through" on a ration of indifferent hay, corn fodder, and oat straw. Many farmers did not expect much more from their cattle than a home supply of dairy products and meat. On the other hand, diary entries of James Ten Eyck, Jr., between 1802 and 1824 show that he butchered veal calves for sale nearly as often as hogs. He also had each year some beef animals for sale, one of his main sources of income. A few industrious farmers, strategically located near markets, enlarged their herds and sold considerable amounts of butter, cheese, and beef. Also more farmers began to raise their calves or to buy "feeder" cattle from drovers to fatten for market. An occasional operator produced cheese on a commercial basis, but always found it difficult to secure enough labor.[15] Quite a number of farmers had some butter for sale, and a very few produced it in quantity. In general, however, dairying remained a not too significant sideline for most livestock farmers before 1860 and for many of them even longer. Since there was not much incentive for increasing the supply of milk, little selective breeding was done to improve milk yield before this time.

On the other hand, as a market developed for veal and beef, farmers began to favor heavier cattle. Imported bulls were, therefore, for the most part of beef breeds. Nearly all the important English beef breeds were introduced, including some no longer known, such as the "English bull of Dishley breed" advertised by a farmer in 1828.[16] This breed took its name from Robert Bakewell of Dishley in Leicestershire. But Shorthorns, more commonly known as Durhams, and the smaller Devons received most attention. When Hugh Exton, near present-day High Bridge, imported Shorthorns, beginning in the 1820s, he received much acclaim, and many farmers brought cows to his farm for service.[17] Herefords, though better suited than Shorthorns for rough grazing, were almost unknown in America before 1850. In 1857 the fair at Flemington gave prizes for Herefords for the first time, but most of the exhibits of beef cattle were still Shorthorns and Devons.[18] Purebred beef herds were appearing here and there, and more and more farmers were acquiring purebred sires or "grade" sires with some foreign ancestry. But just as the improvement in breeding of beef cattle became noticeable, the economic situation changed. As western feeder cattle were imported by rail, raising calves for beef ceased to be profitable. As a result, producers of beef gradually turned to dealers for their feeder replacements, buying cattle in the spring, pasturing them during the summer, and, after giving them grain for a time, marketing them in the fall before the cold weather made it possible to ship in western beef.[19] Even this arrangement did not last for long. The introduction of refrigerator cars in the 1880s to bring in western meat the year round hurt beef production in New Jersey so badly that it gradually became a mere sideline to dairying.

As the market for dairy products, particularly butter, grew in importance toward the middle of the nineteenth century, the differentiation between beef and dairy cattle became important. Various imported dairy breeds soon acquired their advocates. The Ayrshire, though today considered a dairy breed, was then thought of as being general purpose, and particularly good for rough grazing land. It was the first nonbeef breed to receive general recognition here. At the fair in Flemington in 1856,

prizes were given for Ayrshires and for "dairy cattle." In 1857 a new category was added for Alderneys, as all Channel Island cattle were then
known, following British practice.[20] A differentiation between Jerseys and
Guernseys was soon made, and other dairy breeds began to appear before
long. The Holstein cow, which gave more but thinner milk, was being
introduced by the early 1870s,[21] but its dominance was to come later as
butter and cheese production were superseded by that of fluid milk for
city markets. A sign of the times was the gradual elimination of prizes
for beef breeds from county fair lists and the adding of one dairy breed
after another. Despite the new emphasis on purebred cattle, animals registered by the new breed associations were not numerous. The most important result of the new development was the improvement of grade
cattle through the use of good purebred sires.

The rise of dairying implies the development of markets for milk and
milk products. The sale of whole milk to local consumers, though not
new, became more important with the increase in the population and
the appearance of village milk wagon routes. Shipment of milk in cans
by rail to nearby cities also began early. But the most important development of the late nineteenth century, as far as markets for New Jersey milk
were concerned, was the appearance of creameries, which took the marketing of butter and cheese out of the home.[22] Since in that day milk
could not be transported very far, individual creameries were small. But
literally dozens of them were started between 1875 and 1915, more than
a score in Hunterdon County alone.[23] Often the capital for starting a
creamery was raised by the farmers themselves. The opening of the creamery in Sergeantsville in 1881 was typical. Some eighty individual farmers
subscribed for shares of stock at $25 each. The creamery opened in April,
and by June it was making 240 pounds of butter each day for city markets, selling ice cream makers 200 quarts of cream, and laying up eighteen
large cheeses in the ripening room. Waste skim milk was returned free
to farmers to feed to their pigs.[24]

The creamery revolutionized the dairy industry, and many farmers discarded their churning equipment and allowed their springhouses to fall
into decay.[25] Not all was rosy, however. Farmers often objected to the
way they were treated by state milk inspectors with their Babcock testers,
stockholders often felt that profits were insufficient, and prices of milk
often dropped to low levels.[26] From time to time a creamery sustained a
loss because a careless or inexperienced workman allowed butter to go
rancid or cheese to become too strong for anything but "decent burial." [27]
An occasional disgruntled cream producer went back to home butter
production, but usually reappeared at the creamery before long, much
to the joy of the local shopkeeper, to whom the handling of butter accepted in trade was a constant nuisance and source of loss.[28] An occasional

community with superior transportation service and many individual farmers near population centers turned from cream to whole-milk production. The market for the latter was growing with the population, and the adoption of the milk bottle about 1880 [29] simplified the problem of delivery to customers. Milk stations for cooling, and later, for pasteurizing milk became the real competitors of the creameries, particularly as their prices did not fluctuate as much as prices at the creameries.[30]

The fate of the creameries was apparent by 1900, and during the next fifteen years most of them discontinued operation, often simply by becoming shipping stations for fluid milk on its way to city markets. A few lingered on into the next period, buying milk from farmers who lived far from fluid milk markets or who did not produce milk clean enough to satisfy the increasingly rigorous standards for whole milk. The switch to a new market by dairy farmers was hailed as a boon, but from the beginning they were at a disadvantage in dealing with the middleman outlets. The feeling that they were being fleeced by distributors began early. In 1899, when farmers were receiving less than two cents a quart and consumers were paying six or more, there was formed the abortive Five States' Milk Producers Association,[31] the first of many attempts to force an improvement in prices paid to farmers.

Everything points to a sizable increase in the numbers of cattle in New Jersey between 1790 and 1840, but the census estimate of 220,000 for the latter year was to prove fairly constant during the next three-quarters of a century, as dairy cattle replaced beef cattle. The figure was somewhat greater in 1860, back to 224,000 in 1880, up to 240,000 in 1900, and again down to 223,000 by 1910.[32] The figures show no great change in distribution by county, decade by decade. The counties with the largest numbers in 1840 were the leaders all the way through to 1910. Sussex, with its rich rolling pastures, had 26,000 cattle in 1840, about the same in 1880, and 33,000 in 1910. The counties with more diversified farming also made small gains through the years. Hunterdon, nearly always second in tally, had 21,000 in 1840, 23,000 in 1880 and again in 1900, and 25,000 in 1910. Burlington, usually a close third, had 17,000 in 1840, 23,000 in 1860 and again in 1880, 29,000 in 1900, and 24,000 in 1910. Mercer, with only 8,000 in 1840, had between 11,000 and 12,000 during most of the time to 1910. The story for Salem County was closely parallel. The gains in these counties made up for the decline in areas being urbanized and in those which were turning to other kinds of farming, in particular the growing of vegetables. Bergen, with 6,400 cattle in 1840, climbed to 9,200 by 1860, then fell by slow degrees to 3,500 in 1910. Atlantic, with 5,000 cattle in 1840, had half that number in 1880 and only 1,400 by 1910.[33]

To estimate the proportion of dairy to beef cattle with any degree of accuracy is not easy, since producers of milk were also producers of beef, by intention during much of the period and by inadvertence thereafter.[34] Especially during the period of general purpose cattle, it was hard to decide whether a cow was a dairy or a beef cow. Only in 1920 would dairy cows be defined by the census authorities as "cows and heifers two years and over kept mainly for milk production." Before then the standards undoubtedly varied somewhat from county to county and decade to decade. In 1850, the first time an attempt was made to count "dairy cattle," a figure of nearly 119,000 was given for the state. By 1880 there were about 152,000. The figure was approximately the same in 1910. If these statistics are to be trusted, three-fifths of the animals in 1850 were of dairy type, and three-fourths by 1880. It is surprising that the proportion of dairy cattle was not much higher by 1910. The explanation is probably that cattle not classed as dairy type were for the most part general purpose or dual purpose. The proportion of dairy cattle to total cattle did not vary greatly in different parts of the state.[35]

The increase in the importance of dairying and the shift from creameries to whole-milk markets caused the dairyman to change the breed of his herd. Rich milk, that is, milk with a high butterfat content, brought a better price per hundredweight than thin milk, but the premium was insufficient to warrant keeping cows of low production no matter how rich their milk. Though selective breeding brought up the amount of milk given by Ayrshires, Jerseys, and Guernseys, farmers were soon trying more productive breeds, among them the Brown Swiss. But it was the Holstein-Friesians which rose in favor, although many herds of grade Holsteins contained a few Guernseys in order to augment the butterfat yield of the herd as a whole. Purebred herds most in the news in the 1880s were Ayrshire, Jersey, and Guernsey, those of the early 1900s primarily Holstein.[36]

As long as a farmer bred his own replacements, he could control the bloodlines of his herd. But before long the wisdom of raising calves came into doubt. The same problem that had arisen earlier with beef cattle now developed with dairy cattle. Farmers in the Middle West, Canada, and upstate New York could raise calves much more economically than farmers in New Jersey. Advertisements in county newspapers show that by 1900 many dairy cattle were being shipped in by rail and sold at auction. Since the prices they fetched ran substantially less than the cost of raising animals on New Jersey farms, many farmers quit raising calves, and others raised only a few of the best ones. From this time on, "York State" and other dairy cattle were brought in by the thousands as dairy herd replacements. The control of bovine tuberculosis was complicated by such large-scale importing of cattle and some farmers therefore continued to raise their own calves rather than risk introducing the disease into their herds. Also those farmers who had registered purebred herds still continued to raise most of their calves, as did some dairymen who had built up herds of high quality grade cattle. However, as time went on the biological quality and health of dairy cows brought into the state improved greatly.

The tremendous increase in milk yield per cow during this period resulted partly from better breeding but also partly from the improvements in care and feeding. Here, especially, did Agricultural Experiment Station testing help the farmer. The greatest change in feeding practices, the introduction of corn ensilage or silage, came late in the period. The underground or pit silo was first developed in Europe and brought to the Middle West by immigrants. There were a few such silos in Pennsylvania in the 1870s, and eventually a few in New Jersey. The idea did not catch on, however, until the American invention of the upright silo. An occasional "patent silo," usually of wood stave construction, was to be seen on New Jersey dairy farms in the 1890s, and the number multiplied after 1900. Tile silos appeared just before World War I. One constructed near Pittstown in 1912 rose forty feet into the air and could hold the corn harvest from seven acres of ground.[37]

The raising of swine remained an important part of the agricultural economy throughout the 1810–1917 period, although there was a considerable decline toward the end. Improvements through selective breeding, already begun on a small scale during the latter years of the previous period, eventually changed the hog to a greater degree than any other farm animal.[38] The common or "lean" hog of an earlier day responded rapidly to selection and to infusions of blood from English purebreds. Owners of swine no longer turned them out in the woods, but fenced them in and put rings in their noses to discourage them from rooting up their pastures and burrowing under their fences. An animal that managed to break out to freedom often wore a wooden yoke thereafter. The "cutting" or castrating of young boars not needed for breeding purposes was a practice somewhat slow in coming, but eventually it became universal, as farmers came to believe that barrows would gain weight faster and produce better meat.[39] The chief purpose in raising hogs on most farms was still to provide a family pork and lard supply,[40] but for many decades, until the rivalry of growers in western lands reduced prices drastically, farmers often had greater or smaller amounts of pork to sell, sometimes on the hoof to drovers, and sometimes as cured pork by the piece or in brine in barrels.[41]

The general demand for fat pork and the greater dependence on corn as a feed led to an overemphasis on size, most marked from about 1820 to the Civil War. Newspaper accounts in nearly every county played up the idea, and gave space to reports about the biggest hogs at butchering time. It was during this period that the famous Jersey Red hog was developed, an animal about whose origin there has been more than one account. The Jersey Reds were tremendous animals of the lard type. Often they weighed more than half a ton, and one monstrosity in Burlington County in 1832 is supposed to have weighed 1,611 pounds. Two decades later a Woodstown hog officially weighing 1,225 pounds was taken to England to exhibit as a freak.[42] Such massive animals were unable to bear their own weight, and had to be held in a standing position at feeding time by use of block and tackle. Such practices, which seem ridiculous to us, did not really pay off, but were resorted to in order to compete for newspaper publicity or prizes at county fairs. The emphasis on fat hogs, however, affected all growers. A comparison of hog weights at butchering time will show the change in viewpoint. In 1805 the Cases at Flemington butchered two sows and eight shoats, judged to be of respectable size. The sows averaged 350 pounds carcass weight, and the young hogs a little over 150 pounds.[43] But the weights reported by the *Hunterdon Gazette* each fall after 1825 contained none so small, and hogs of 500 or 600 pounds were often mentioned.

The usual hog of the first half of the nineteenth century was the "common" hog, which through selection and a considerable admixture of the Jersey Red blood, had become a lard animal.[44] Even such foreign breeds as were introduced, including the Suffolk and Byfield, were also of the lard type.[45] The Berkshire, regarded by experts as one of the best hogs of this type, may well have been one of the ancestors of the Jersey Red. Though Berkshires were exhibited at the first State Agricultural Society fair in 1840,[46] the strain seems to have been lost thereafter. It was introduced from England again at a later time, and in 1875 the American Berkshire Association became the first group in America with registry of purebred swine. Other English breeds included the Yorkshire and the Essex. The Chester White and Poland China, American breeds developed in Ohio, largely from English ancestry, were also introduced into New Jersey. The name of the latter is a misnomer, for it probably had no ancestry from Poland and not much blood of animals from China. The tendency toward somewhat smaller hogs in the latter part of the period led to the crossing of the Jersey Red with a New York strain of similarly obscure origin to create the Duroc-Jersey.[47] The exhibits at the fair at Flemington in 1881 included five Essex hogs, eleven Berkshires, ten Poland Chinas and Magies, fourteen Chester Whites, and six Yorkshires.[48] The Magie was a particular strain of the Poland China breed.

A natural question, perhaps not entirely answerable, is why New Jersey farmers did not turn to bacon-type breeds to a greater extent at this time, rather than merely to a smaller lard type. Tradition and habit played a part, undoubtedly, as did the dominance of corn as a feedstuff. As it was, however, the competition of pork from the Middle West, first as cured

meat, then as whole carcasses brought in refrigerator cars, gradually reduced swine production in New Jersey to lower and lower levels. It has
been estimated that there were over 261,000 hogs in the state in 1840,
some 236,000 in 1860, about 219,000 in 1880, some 175,000 in 1900, and
only 147,000 in 1910. Among the counties, the statistics fluctuated considerably. The greatest decline in general, as would be expected, was in
urban areas and in those that were turning to vegetables and poultry. In
Essex the decline came early, from over 24,000 in 1840 to only 1,200 in
1870. Burlington, with approximately 20,000 in 1840 and 39,000 in 1860,
declined to fewer than 12,000 by 1910. Hunterdon, the most stable, had
something over 26,000 in 1840 and still nearly 21,000 in 1910. A county
that ran counter to the tide was urban Hudson. With a small and declining swine population until 1890, it had approximately 5,500 in 1900 and
22,500 in 1910.[49] The unrestricted feeding of Jersey City garbage explains
this sudden surge.

Not all farmers regretted the decline in the raising of hogs, notorious
from pioneer days to the present as troublemakers. The old expression,
"as independent as a hog on ice," shows something of this attitude. David
C. Voorhees in 1875 observed that the problems involved in moving four
fat young hogs from one pen to another had only "increased his natural
dislike for swine." [50] The objections to swine which developed in residential areas were based largely on the offensive odor of hogpens except
under the most sanitary conditions.

The primary reason for keeping sheep, the need for a supply of wool
for home manufacture, disappeared during the early nineteenth century
with the appearance of cheap factory-made woolens. It is true that surplus
animals had been butchered by farmers, who often sold or traded most
of the meat among their neighbors,[51] but mutton was not really needed
and was disliked by many on the basis of odor. Furthermore, some farmers welcomed the chance to dispense with sheep because they grazed the
grass so short.[52] Nevertheless, the keeping of sheep did not decline seriously until after an attempt had been made to make them pay under
changing conditions. The common or native sheep, descended from stock
from various parts of Europe, were rugged little animals with a short,
rather coarse fleece. English immigrants coming in after the American
Revolution considered them scrubs, and sought successfully to evade English laws against the export of breeding stock. The most common imports after 1810, as for some years before were the Bakewell or New Leicester, sometimes called Dishley sheep, a long-wool mutton breed developed by Robert Bakewell, mentioned previously as a breeder of the
English Midlands.[53] Captain George Farmer of Middlesex County continued to furnish purebred Bakewell rams to breeders in many parts of
the state.[54] Joseph Capner preferred Bakewells to Southdowns, a mutton

breed, and to Spanish Merinos, a long-wool breed, both of which he tried.[55]

For a time, however, it looked as if the Merinos would win out. After 1807 conditions were favorable for American manufactures of woolens and there was a strong demand for fine fleeces by the fifty-six small woolen factories of the state. As a result of the Peninsular War, the Merinos of Spain were available for export. A few large farmers, and especially James Caldwell of Haddonfield, built up large purebred flocks at great expense. The famous flock of former United States Senator John Rutherford of Bergen County, driven each summer across the state to hill pastures in Warren County, became for a time largely Merino. A special state census of 1814 showed 3,800 pure Merinos and 25,800 grade Merinos, together nearly one-seventh of the sheep of New Jersey. Unfortunately, the dumping of English woolens on American markets after 1815 ruined both woolen manufactures and the breeding of Merinos in New Jersey. The fine flocks of James Caldwell and others were sold to dealers who drove them to frontier Ohio.[56] The Bakewells rapidly regained their former favor, along with some other English breeds, among them the Southdowns. These breeds had good fleeces, but whether purebred or crosses, they proved more profitable for mutton than for wool. Until the Panic of 1837, New Jersey farmers, with a fair market for both wool and mutton, found sheep reasonably profitable. The census of 1840 showed 219,000 sheep in the state, not a large decline since 1814. Five northwestern New Jersey counties, Hunterdon with approximately 27,000, Sussex with 24,000, Warren with 20,000, Morris with 19,000, and Somerset with 17,000 accounted for about half the total. The only other counties of sheep-raising importance were Monmouth with 19,000, Salem with 16,000, and Burlington with 15,000. A rapid general decline soon set in, so that by 1860 there were in the state only 135,000 head. In general, the same areas led as before. By 1890 the whole state had only 55,000 sheep, of which more than one-third were in Hunterdon and Warren counties. By 1920 the number had declined to 10,000, more than one-fourth of them in Hunterdon.[57] Once again, a New Jersey staple commodity had been ruined by outside competition.

In this period, for the first time, the raising of poultry gained importance. The obvious reason was, of course, the growth of nearby markets for eggs and meat. The old prejudice against poultry raising as women's work died slowly, and on a majority of farms poultry long remained a sideline, the object of which was to provide a part of the family food supply. But as urban markets grew apace, farm wives found that they could increase their pin money from poultry. Many of them persuaded their husbands to build shelters so that their birds would no longer have to "roost around." In general, partly as a result of articles in farm magazines, they learned to give them better care. Farm and store records, which seldom mentioned poultry before 1800, began to show occasional purchases and sales. Joseph Capner's wife often had a pailful of eggs to sell at the Flemington store,[58] and her neighbors sold on occasion a few dressed fowls, that is chickens, as well as a few ducks and guinea birds.[59] Dr. John Bowne, who liked to try new ventures, had geese to sell at fifty cents each and ducks at sixty cents a pair in 1811 and turkeys at three for two dollars in 1816.[60] With the growth of markets, especially those of New York and Philadelphia, the number of transactions increased and the prices improved. In early December 1856, chickens and geese were worth ten cents a pound at the country stores, and turkeys and ducks twelve cents.[61] Eggs had advanced to two cents and even three cents each, and often were bought and sold by the dozen in wood containers with a little chamber for each egg.[62] By this time, hundreds of farmers, particularly those nearest urban areas, had seen the light. A very few specialized in poultry, and many others made poultry an important sideline. On one day in early 1860 Ralph Voorhees of Somerset County dressed not only a hog and a beef for sale, but also fifty-one chickens and nine turkeys.[63]

Unfortunately, the farm magazines and county fairs had given too much attention to exotic poultry, often spoken of as "show birds." Beginning about 1840, and lasting more than a decade, there was a "hen fever" much like the earlier Merino craze. Apparently the new development made the keeping of poultry more respectable. Be that as it may, the emphasis gradually shifted to "practical fowls." The nondescript birds of most farms, aptly described as "just chickens," were gradually replaced by Brahmas and Cochins from Southeast Asia, fine meat types, by Leghorns of various colors from the Mediterranean, unequaled for egg production, and by various North European breeds, most important of which were the English Dorkings.[64] The Leghorn was not very popular at first because of the prejudice against white eggs and because of its small frame and nervous disposition.

Poultry raisers, seldom professionals up to this time, benefited tremendously from the urban development of the post–Civil War period. Poultry production records at last became news. For example, it was recorded that on one day in September 1870 a store in Flemington sold a consignment of 1,562 chickens to a New York wholesaler, supposedly the largest shipment of poultry ever made to that time from the local railway station.[65] Slowly but surely, the chicken business was spreading through the land. David C. Voorhees of Blawenburg, did not share the disdain for poultry of some of his neighbors, and, as mentioned previously, approved of the efforts of a son to become a scientific poultryman with a "self-feeding chicken house." [66] A new nationwide interest in poultry, and especially in chickens, resulted in the first gathering of the relevant statistics in 1880. It was estimated that there were on June 1 of that year 1,188,492 chickens on New Jersey farms.[67] In the light of future development, this was a modest enough count, but it indicated the new interest. Ownership was fairly widely dispersed, with the southeastern and northwestern parts of the state somewhat low in count and urban Hudson almost without poultry. Since poultry farmers do not need much land for their operations, it is not surprising that many partially urbanized areas shared in the upward trend. But it was the counties with considerable general purpose farming that led. The estimate of nearly 156,000 chickens in Hunterdon and 108,000 in Monmouth indicated the two centers at this time and for coming decades. The total count for the state jumped to nearly 3 million by 1890, fell back to 2 million in 1900, then climbed to approximately 2.6 million by 1910. The statistics show that the gains were fairly proportionate among the counties of the state.[68] The numbers of turkeys, geese, and ducks, surprisingly high with 285,000 in 1880, increased only moderately until 1890, then fell rapidly to less than one-third of the above number by 1900.[69] The decline was undoubtedly a result of the new popularity of the chicken.

The introduction of new breeds was a part of the poultry story. The Barred Plymouth Rock, for several decades the most important chicken in New Jersey, was a dual-purpose fowl developed in New England in the 1860s. A popular belief was that as the result of the crossing of breeds, it was half Cochin, a quarter Dorking, an eighth "Malay," and an eighth "wild India." The proportions are in doubt, but the new bird undoubtedly had Brahma, Cochin, Black Java, and Dominique blood. The last two were themselves of mixed blood, and the Dominique had long been known on American farms. As to Dorking ancestry, it is anyone's guess. The White Plymouth Rock, which also became popular, was a sport of the Barred Plymouth Rock.[70] Two other "American" breeds often mentioned in New Jersey newspapers after 1890 were the Wyandotte, a good egg producer, and the Rhode Island Red, a dual-purpose fowl. The race did not go to any of the new breeds, however, but instead to the Leghorn, despite its faults, and particularly to the White Leghorn. As egg production gradually took precedence over other kinds of poultry specialization, the Leghorn gained public approval, if not affection.[71] The conversion of New York and Philadelphia people to the eating of white eggs had an important bearing on the change.

Technical advances were, of course, basic to the rapid development of the poultry industry. The agricultural press and representatives of the College of Agriculture taught better practices as to care and feeding and the construction of more efficient buildings, feeders, waterers, and nests. The first truly revolutionary advance in poultry raising, however, was the adoption of the incubator. There were incubators before 1877, when the first modern or portable incubator in New Jersey was shown at an exhibit of the New Jersey Poultry Society at Elizabeth, but earlier ones had not proved practical. The 1880s saw a very rapid adoption of the incubator by poultrymen, despite some sympathy for motherless chicks and baseless fears of a taint from the kerosene lamp in the poult's meat.[72] Without the incubator the great expansion of the industry would not have been possible. Its companion, the brooder, appeared at once, and was adopted almost overnight. As a result of these devices, flocks increased in size and markets developed for setting eggs, young pullets, and new-born chicks.[73] Poultry farmers became increasingly numerous. Many of them dropped all pretense of general farming, and even of producing feed. Some of these specialists produced broilers or fryers, but by 1900 egg production was paramount. In 1909 the farms of New Jersey produced an estimated 163,563,624 eggs.[74] The rise of the chicken represented one of the biggest switches in New Jersey agricultural history.

In general, the keeping of livestock was of primary importance to New Jersey farmers during the whole of this long period from 1810 to 1917. The great shifts in emphasis merely reflected market conditions and the rivalry of regions farther west as the stimulus of the great eastern markets spread. The advantages of New Jersey as a source of perishables was increasingly apparent, and this explains in part the rise of dairying and egg production. Natural and probably unavoidable results of the improvement of transportation were the slow decline of swine and beef cattle producers and the more rapid decline of sheep raising. The rise and fall in importance of the horse had, of course, other explanations related to the development of farm machinery and farm power.

The expansion of livestock raising created many problems. Farmers of necessity increased their facilities for housing and storage. More and more, they purchased feedstuffs from outside the state to supplement those produced on New Jersey farms. The change is well illustrated by the practice of two Hunterdon County farmers who lived a half century apart. James H. Blackwell in the fall of 1845 was feeding his cattle, in addition to pasturage, a diet of "corn ears ground," straight corn meal, buckwheat bran, and pumpkins as long as they lasted. In general, he avoided as much as possible any purchases of feed.[75] But Elmer C. Bonnell in the 1890s was a regular buyer of grist, malt, wheat bran, and oil cake meal.[76] As the proportion of their income resulting from raising livestock increased, farmers became more interested and better versed in breeding, care, and feeding. In the case of animal diseases, an awareness of the danger resulted in New Jersey's joining other states in the movement which "extirpated and banished from the United States" two scourges, bovine tuberculosis and hoof-and-mouth disease, the latter a danger to all farm animals.[77] The advances in veterinary science in the latter decades of the nineteenth century provided some cures for the many livestock diseases, old and new, which so often frustrated the efforts of individual farmers to get ahead. Perhaps even more important than the growing number of veterinarians who were on call was the new knowledge of the farmer himself on matters of quarantine, the dangers involved in purchasing new animals, and the treatment of ailing animals. Farmers with livestock were never their own masters. When a farmer like William C. Lippincott reported in his diary that he spent the day "taking care of the stock," one can be sure that he meant it.[78] Likewise, to his successors "care" would have implied a host of additional chores based on new funds of information and experience.

12

Field Crops, Orchards, and Truck Crops

The slow transformation of livestock raising during the period 1810–1917 was matched by a similar change in crop production. Here, too, the modifications were largely a matter of emphasis. Some minor crops all but disappeared, and some new ones were added, but the major field crops remained the same. Again, the tempo of change was gradually accelerated, and particularly after about 1850. Crop husbandry was affected perhaps even more than growing of livestock by the many developments in other aspects of agriculture. The farmer, over this period of more than a century, learned how to restore lost soil fertility and made some progress with the problem of saving the land from the ravages of erosion. The needs of a growing animal population resulted in his expanding some of his field crops. The development of more efficient seeding devices, better tillage implements, and constantly improving machinery for the harvest affected markedly his crop techniques and permitted an expansion of his acreage in crops.

The great improvements in crop varieties therefore need be no surprise, for they were quite in keeping with the general progress of agriculture. Actually, some small improvements in varieties during the previous period had resulted from necessity, or had been the result of the slow percolation of ideas. The general principle of selection had long been known to farmers, and they had used it to some degree, particularly in choosing the better ears of corn for seed. The elimination of less hardy strains of wheat by the onslaught of black-stem rust and the Hessian fly had played some part in the development of stronger strains of that crop. More important, the constant introduction of various European types of field crops, fruits, and vegetables by incoming immigrants had provided a considerable assortment from which to choose, and had led to an admixture of new strains in many neighborhoods. The prejudice against change, so marked in some aspects of agriculture, was perhaps less a handicap for crop husbandry than for other things. Nevertheless, the adjective *com-*

166

mon, which was more usually applied to the livestock that had come down from an earlier day, was at the beginning of this period an aptly descriptive one for many crops as well.

The long course of selection and development which had given the Indians so many varieties of maize had been continued after a fashion by their white successors. But in this period the process was speeded up. Since corn responds so readily to selection, the finding and adoption and sometimes the conscious development of new varieties to fit a particular environment were no more difficult in New Jersey than elsewhere. If the farmer did not like the characteristics of his own crop, he could buy or barter "planting corn" from another farmer, as James Ten Eyck did in the spring of 1795.[1] At the beginning of the period 1810–1917 field corn was tall by today's standards, and the ears were long and slim. Over the decades, the height of the stalk declined and the ear became shorter and fatter. The growing period required was longer at the beginning of the period than at its end. Even as late as 1849 James H. Blackwell considered that June 15 was very late for planting corn. In 1851 several of his fields were caught by an early frost, with a result that they produced only "soft corn," which spoiled easily and had less feeding value than mature corn.[2] Until fairly late, more attention was paid to the development of high-yield varieties than of quick-maturing types.

Down through the years many new names of corn varieties appeared and disappeared. Popular types during the 1840s included Virginia Dent, Red Cob Dent, Monmouth Dent, Red Cob Flint, Red Cob Yellow, and "ordinary white corn." In popular parlance, most new varieties fell into the four varieties indicated, dent, flint, "ordinary yellow," and "ordinary" white corn, the last two being in actuality dent varieties.[3] Sometimes odd kinds gained a following, as Bloody Butcher, Gourd Seed, and Eight-Row Yellow in the 1880s,[4] but their day was usually brief. Scientific testing in the agricultural experiment stations, including that of New Jersey, helped the farmer choose among the many varieties advertised and puffed in the agricultural press. Actual field tests by the farmers themselves under College of Agriculture guidance came into practice at the end of this period.

As with other agricultural totals, those for the acreage and production of corn in New Jersey were of course small in comparison with those of larger states. But for the farmers of New Jersey, corn was a very important crop. There were no yield statistics before 1839, and the estimate for that year was unbelievably low at 4,362,000 bushels. In all likelihood, it was a poor corn year, for the 1849 figure was twice as much. Other indications make it seem likely that the corn crop of the state had been on the increase for several decades. Be that as it may, the crop for 1859 was estimated at 9,724,000 bushels and that for 1879 at 11,151,000. At the turn of the century the state produced just under 11 million bushels, and in

1909 10 million. Ear corn production had been somewhat reduced during the previous years by the ensiling of a small but increasing acreage, which had grown to approximately 18,000 by 1919, the first year with statistics on the subject. Though corn was grown almost everywhere, the centers of largest production during the period were the southwestern and northwestern parts of the state. Burlington and Hunterdon counties produced more than a million bushels each in 1859, and in most years thereafter. In 1879 they were joined by Monmouth and Salem. Hunterdon's neighbors, Warren, Morris, and Mercer, were also high producers throughout the period. The Atlantic coastal areas were in general low, and counties with growing urbanization, Bergen, Essex, and Camden, gradually declined.[5] Average production per acre was comparatively high during the whole period. A careful estimate of average yearly yield between 1897 and 1906 placed New Jersey fifth in the nation with 34.6 bushels per acre, and only 1.4 bushels below the top.[6] None of the above figures include sweet corn, which for our purposes will be considered a vegetable.

Though New Jersey had once been a Bread Colony, the growing of wheat was somewhat hazardous during the early decades of the national period. John Rutherford's remark in 1786 that the New Jersey farmer was "little skilled" in the raising of wheat did not truly get at the root of the matter.[7] The real trouble was that the fertility of the soil had been badly mined during the long period in which wheat was the only cash product of importance. Théophile Cazenove in 1794 had seen this clearly. On the other hand, Charles Chesebrough in the same year reported good yields in northwestern New Jersey, a new area.[8] By 1810 the loss of fertility throughout the state had brought wheat production to new lows. However, during ensuing decades the application of calcined lime in the north and west and of marl in the central part of the state helped improve the situation. The development and wide use of commercial fertilizers brought production to new heights in the second half of the nineteenth century.

It is doubtful that New Jersey in earlier years ever produced as much wheat yearly as it did in 1849, when the crop, according to the census taken in that year, was 1,601,000 bushels. The estimate for 1839, probably a poor year, had been less than half that amount. The total climbed to 2,300,000 bushels in 1869, and was not much below that figure in 1899. A decrease set in soon after that date, however, as wheat lands were converted to other uses. By 1909 production had fallen to 1,489,000 bushels. The most productive counties during much of the period were Hunterdon, Salem, and Burlington, usually in that order. The Hunterdon County production of 340,000 bushels in 1870 was the largest ever reported for a New Jersey county. The decline there during the next two decades was about proportionate to that of the state as a whole, but the county bounced back thereafter, with 284,000 bushels in 1899 and 306,000 in 1909. Though it had been temporarily eclipsed by Salem for a time, it now stood far above all other counties. Its neighbors Warren and Somerset, which had turned from rye to wheat, had an annual production of nearly 200,000 bushels each, and by this time had become second and third in the state. The rapid decline of Burlington County after 1880, and the somewhat slower one of Salem, as wheat land was planted to corn, rye, or vegetables, was a considerable factor in the overall state decline in wheat production. By 1909, near the end of the period, the state wheat crop was largely produced in the part of West Jersey above Trenton. The decline in state acreage, already marked in the 1880s, was more rapid throughout the state than was the decline in production, for average yield per acre climbed during the period from 12 or 14 bushels to approximately 18.[9]

The seemingly low average yields do not tally with the accounts of some of the most progressive farmers, particularly those in districts where wheat grew well. Joseph Capner of Hunterdon grew 15 bushels per acre in the 1790s and considered it a poor yield.[10] In 1794 Cazenove reported yields of 15 or 16 bushels per acre in Morris County, though it is only fair to mention that he also received reports of much lower yields.[11] But by 1833 it was reported that some farmers were getting yields of 30 bushels.[12] In 1841 William P. Emery received the first prize for wheat production given by the Flemington Fair Association for growing 39½ bushels on 1⅕ acres.[13] A decade later, Blackwell thought his average yield of 19.66 bushels "not a bad crop." [14] The increasing yield per acre was not to any large degree the result of the application of the rules of plant breeding, for seed selection was much more difficult with wheat than with corn. Some new varieties did appear at the end of the period as the result of selecting and developing "sports," but the greatest gains came from importing European wheat varieties.[15] Hardiness rather than yield was the usual criterion in choosing varieties. However in 1805–6 one of the Hankinsons ran a test and reported about the same yield per acre from the hardy new Red Chaff wheat as from an older bearded variety.[16] Other new varieties of the early 1800s included Canada and White Bearded. In the 1830s Mediterranean wheat was hailed as "exempt from the fly," and sold at premium prices.[17] The White Flint and Genesee were pushed in the 1840s,[18] and other varieties that had their day were the Blue Stem, Old Ball, Hutchinson, and Australian. The Mediterranean, a soft winter wheat, was probably grown more than all other varieties combined. Farmers learned from practice that late sowing was more important than variety in avoiding the Hessian fly, and the knowledge that eradication of the native barberry would prevent black stem rust in an area became general.

The plebeian crop of rye had long been grown as a food crop in New Jersey, as an alternative to wheat whenever circumstances dictated. A real barrier to rye as a cash crop, however, was that its price never closely approached that of wheat. Normally, therefore, in the colonial period a farmer would plant wheat rather than rye whenever he could, except for a patch of the latter to produce the straw ties for banding his corn fodder shocks and similar purposes. But the situation changed rapidly thereafter. The coming of the Hessian fly during the Revolution helped rye production to some extent, for the invading pest preferred wheat to rye. Rye was not as productive as wheat on good land, but proved its worth in competition with wheat on worn-out lands. Furthermore, it was a surer crop in that its grains would germinate on land where those of wheat would not. At Shipley during the Revolution, James Parker had grown as much wheat as possible each year and only a little rye.[19] Yet in 1794 Cazenove, who crossed the state from Hoboken to Phillipsburg, found many neighborhoods where rye was a staple.[20] The Capners in West Jersey at about the same time reported the importance of rye in the Hunterdon area. A decade later, the prosperous Ten Eycks of Somerset were using rye flour from the local mill for making most of their bread.[21]

During the early nineteenth century, this crop came into its own. If the figures of the 1840 census can be trusted, there was twice as much rye produced in 1839 as wheat, 1,616,000 bushels as against 774,00. The year may well have been a low one for wheat. Whatever the explanation, the situation had changed considerably by 1849. Rye production in the state had fallen to 1,256,000 bushels and wheat had risen to 1,601,000 bushels. In all the important counties for small grains, wheat had outdistanced rye. The largest rye-producing counties were now Sussex with 229,000 bushels and Warren with 224,000. In general, the northwestern part of the state had held to rye, with a decline elsewhere. But a decade later, in 1859, rye, with a state production of 1,439,000 bushels was more than holding its own. Nearly one-third of the gain had been in Burlington County, where rye was grown to a surprising degree during the next decades. The counties of the northwest held up their production fairly well until 1859, but after that time even this area declined. For example, Warren County, presumably under the stimulus of higher wheat prices, made a changeover, and by 1869 it produced only 84,000 bushels of rye.

The production of rye in New Jersey during the next half century remained on the average something above the million-bushel mark yearly. With the coming of commercial fertilizers, better lands were returned to wheat, and rye production until about 1910 was only about half as much as that of wheat. Burlington and Monmouth counties still dominated at the end of the period. In 1909 Burlington produced 212,000 bushels of rye and Monmouth 162,000. A somewhat surprising retention of rye in central New Jersey counties at a time when wheat production was declining there had helped keep up the state total. Rye yields, largely because of the use of commercial fertilizers, were by now from 16 to 18 bushels per acre, nearly twice as much as in 1839, and nearly as much as for wheat. The latter, however, at an average farm price of approximately a dollar per bushel was a full third higher than rye.[22] The spurt of rye growing at this time would prove to be of brief duration. This crop had never had much attention given it by promoters and progressive farmers, probably less than it deserved. Agricultural magazines and county fairs had passed it by, and very little had ever been said about developing better varieties. One wonders whether the same efforts in improving rye as were made so profitably in developing corn and wheat might not have paid off. In general, farmers grew rye where wheat or corn would not do well, only occasionally expanding their acreage when price levels warranted.

Oats, which had been important for both grain and hay from the days of early settlement, were still grown considerably during much of this period. If grown for hay, they were cut before the bottleneck of the wheat and rye harvest. On the other hand, if the crop was grown for its grain, the harvest would come nicely after the wheat and rye crops were in the shock. As a nurse crop for meadow grasses and clovers, oats were preferred to wheat and rye by many farmers. Also oats were almost universally accepted as the best grain for horses. Oats culture before the day of the grain drill was very simple. On April 4, 1851, James H. Blackwell plowed a small field, sowed his oats by broadcasting, and harrowed the ground all in the same day. On the following day he sowed clover seed on the same field and again went over it lightly with a harrow. For the last process he could have used a roller. A grain drill with a small seed attachment would have sown the oats and grass more evenly and in the same operation, but Blackwell, like many farmers, was in this case satisfied with the old methods. He cut part of his oats crop when still green as a hay crop, but most of it he harvested when mature for the grain.[23] Other farm diaries show that many farmers used similar methods and had similar purposes in growing oats. In 1866, the first year with acreage estimates, the state had 236,000 acres of oats, about as much as for wheat and rye together.[24]

There seems to have been little experimentation with varieties of oats until fairly late. The Hunterdon County fair of 1860 had exhibits of black oats, white oats, Poland oats, and one-sided oats, the last considered a great curiosity.[25] During the Civil War, the newly introduced Norway oats recommended by the federal government caused some excitement.[26] For a time this new variety brought premium prices, but it soon fell from public favor. In 1864 James Neilsen, Jr., of New Brunswick, sowed "black oats from Prince Edward's Island." [27] David C. Voorhees of Blawenburg still preferred "prime white oats" in 1875.[28] Varieties of the 1870s included the Waterloo, Schurman, and White Dutch, and in the 1880s a popular variety was the Excelsior.[29] Seed companies soon multiplied the number of varieties from which to choose, and the New Jersey Agricultural Experiment Station gave farmers some aid in choosing varieties.

The oats harvest of the state in 1839 was estimated at a little over 3 million bushels. Two decades later it was 4.5 million and by 1866 reached a high of 6.5 million. A decline then set in which brought the average crop of the 1870s to about 4 million bushels and during the 1880s to approximately 3.6 million. The year 1890 was the last with as much as 100,000 acres sowed and nearly the last with a yield of 2.5 million bushels. During the World War I period the annual average was not far from 2 million bushels. The yield per acre fluctuated to a greater degree from year to year than most crops, but there was not in general any noteworthy gain. The estimate in 1866 was 27.5 bushels and the same in 1916. As with other cereals, oats production was highest in the general farming counties, and lowest in those of the Atlantic coast and the Highlands. The county of greatest production constantly was Hunterdon, with no near rival. Its figure of just under a half million bushels in 1839 rose to 900,-000 in 1869, and then declined to about the 1839 level in the early twentieth century. Its neighbor, Somerset, with over 300,000 bushels in 1839, nearly 750,000 in 1859, and just under 550,000 in 1879, declined rapidly to half the last figure by 1909, as other crops displaced oats. The pattern in nearby Morris and Warren, somewhat lower in production, was almost identical. That of Middlesex, Monmouth, and Bergen, with a still lower production, remained relatively constant. Salem, the second county in 1839 with 300,000 bushels, had less than half that amount by 1879 and one-tenth by the turn of the century.[30]

The story of buckwheat parallels that for oats, except that the decline came earlier and was somewhat more abrupt. The popularity of buckwheat cakes did not abate until late in the period, and perhaps increased for a half century or so with the advent of "New Orleans molasses" on the retail market. Nearly every farmer had at least a patch of buckwheat, and many grew more because buckwheat was considered an excellent feed for swine and poultry. Furthermore, the crop compared favorably with rye and oats in money return, taking into consideration yield per acre and farm price per bushel. Again the fact that buckwheat was not sowed until the summer allowed farmers to fall back on this crop for land that they had been unable to seed to oats or corn because of weather conditions or other causes. The situation in this regard was much the same as for soybeans today.

Buckwheat was an important crop during the latter part of the period before 1810. James Parker grew buckwheat at Shipley during every year of the Revolutionary period.[31] In 1782 a justice of the peace at White-house made a decision in a case which concerned forty bushels of stored buckwheat.[32] A few years later the Capners in Hunterdon were reporting the growing of considerable buckwheat, and in 1793 Isaac Passand wrote that his neighbors used buckwheat as a nurse crop for timothy and clover, though it was sowed in midsummer.[33] The crop remained important in the new period. At farm auctions in the 1820s and 1830s, "buckwheat in the ground" and "buckwheat by the bushel" were common items.[34] Country stores usually kept some of the grain on hand for sale at retail.[35] In 1849 Readington Township of Hunterdon County had 144 of 281 farmers growing buckwheat, though they grew only 45 bushels each on the average.[36] In 1853 George W. Moore of Cumberland County sowed four acres of buckwheat, using a half bushel of seed per acre.[37] James H. Blackwell of Hunterdon, who had a field of buckwheat each year, recorded in his diary on April 5, 1854, "We had a nice little buckwheat shower last night." In 1860 Ralph Voorhees of Somerset plowed for buckwheat in May, sowed in July, and threshed and cleaned the crop in October.[38] David C. Voorhees, a distant kinsman and generally a progressive farmer, still sowed buckwheat by broadcasting it and harrowing it in as late as 1875. However, he had his sons and hired men thresh the crop "with the Machine."[39] Even after production fell off, it was not unusual for many farmers to have a few acres of the crop.

In 1839 New Jersey produced an estimated 856,000 bushels of buckwheat, and this level was maintained until 1869, after which both acreage and yield dropped abruptly. The estimated 50,000 acres of 1868 was reduced to 25,000 in 1869, and the estimated production fell from 852,000 bushels to 354,000. After a few years the number of acres again increased slowly, reaching 36,000 in 1888, only to be followed immediately by decline. For the next two decades the area sowed ranged generally from 10,000 to 15,000 acres. In 1880, a good year, the yield rose to 562,000 bushels. But by 1915 the annual crop average was not much more than 200,000 bushels. In the two decades after the Civil War, wheat acreage gains had paralleled buckwheat losses, a development not explained by price differentials, since wheat fell from two dollars per bushel, farm price, to less than one dollar while buckwheat was declining from ninety cents to sixty cents. Perhaps the explanation lies in the fact that, with the new machinery, wheat was an easier crop to harvest. In neither case was there any apparent gain in average yield per acre before 1885. After this time, when wheat average yields were increasing, buckwheat showed only a slight response to commercial fertilizers. The average yield of 18 bushels per acre in 1869 was bettered only occasionally during the whole period. The early falling from favor of buckwheat is not entirely explainable, though it is clear enough that the modern emphasis on forage crops would in any case eventually have excluded it.

The distribution of buckwheat from its heyday to its latter-day decline has shown some interesting differences from that of the other small grains. In 1839 Sussex County led with 147,000 bushels, Warren was second with 108,000, Hunterdon third with 107,000, and Morris fourth with 89,000. This block of neighboring counties led continuously throughout the period, and in 1899 they were still holding the same order. Sussex had 63,000 bushels, Warren had 54,000, Hunterdon 51,000, and Morris 49,000. The four together had produced more than half the state total in 1839 and had over 70 percent of it in 1899. During the first decade of the twentieth century Hunterdon, the only county which temporarily reversed the general trend, pushed ahead to the state leadership. However, it too eventually dropped buckwheat like a hot cake. It is obvious from the above figures that other portions of the state fell in production more rapidly than the leaders. Essex County, with 40,000 bushels in 1839, fell to less than half that in two decades. Bergen, with 45,000 in 1839, declined a bit more slowly, but just as surely. Somerset, Burlington, Middlesex, and Monmouth, in that order, had yields of about the same as Essex and Bergen in 1839, and declined somewhat more slowly. In all four cases, the post–Civil War years brought them low, and their fall continued thereafter.[40]

Barley had never been a very important grain in New Jersey. It is occasionally mentioned in farm records of the early nineteenth century, and one unidentified farmer has left a record of threshing, winnowing, and hauling to market in Trenton three wagon loads of barley during the winter of 1823–24.[41] The first farm census figures, those for 1839, reported about 12,500 bushels in the whole state, most of it in a belt of central counties, Somerset, Mercer, Middlesex, and Hunterdon, in that order. By 1859 the state acreage had doubled to 25,000 bushels. Sussex, which had little barley previously, led with 5,300 bushels, followed by Monmouth and Hunterdon with 4,300 each. The decline which had already begun in some places, as in Middlesex, soon affected the whole state. By 1869 state production had fallen to 8,300 bushels, nearly half of it grown in Hunterdon. Production everywhere was only minor after this, except for a surprising revival for a time after World War I.[42]

Stray references to broomcorn and to the making of brooms in homes and shops have come down to us from the early part of this period. But only for a few decades in the midnineteenth century was broomcorn a crop of noteworthy importance in New Jersey. These years saw the rise and fall of dozens of small brush and broom shops.[43] The growing of broomcorn became something of a specialty for a few farmers. It is said that a farm in Burlington County in 1840 harvested broomcorn for nearly

5,000 brooms.[44] The crop was easily grown, with a culture similar to that of corn. A by-product was the immature seeds, which were used by the grower as feed for livestock and poultry. Some of the shops, like the one at Flemington, still throve on local trade in the 1870s.[45] But the coming of large-scale machine production of brooms elsewhere eventually drove all the local artisans out of business. Instead of attempting to compete with larger producers in the Middle West, farmers gradually dropped this sideline crop. The census of 1890 reported that only one acre of broomcorn had been grown in New Jersey the previous year.[46]

Sorghum cane, similar in appearance to broomcorn and requiring the same culture, appeared on New Jersey farms under the name of "Chinese sugar cane" in the early 1850s. For the most part, it was grown by individual farmers who wished to provide themselves with a substitute for New Orleans molasses for their breakfast buckwheat cakes. The heavy sirup, which came to be known as sorghum molasses, was not to everybody's taste. John Ten Eyck of North Branch, according to his diary, still bought his molasses, very probably the New Orleans variety, by the barrel in New York in 1855. But there was enough of a sale for surplus gallons of sorghum molasses to encourage some expansion of the crop. George W. Moore of Cumberland County had a "sugar cane" patch each year in the late 1850s and early 1860s. In October 1860 he recorded taking the stalks, stripped of their leaves, to a mill at Bridgeton, and bringing home forty-two gallons of "first-rate" molasses. He paid the mill owner eighteen cents per gallon as toll, rather than give him a share of the molasses. He did not expand his operations, as many farmers did, during the early Civil War period, when New Orleans molasses disappeared from the grocery shelves, and in 1864 quit growing the crop entirely.[47] Partly because New Jersey housewives complained of the baking qualities of sorghum molasses and partly because of its strong taste, the crop declined rapidly. The year 1864 was the last operating year for most sorghum mills in Hunterdon County.[48] In 1869 only a few thousand gallons were reported in the state.[49]

In part because of the continued campaign of Dr. George H. Cook of the New Jersey Agricultural Experiment Station, who envisioned South Jersey as a producer of sugar, "Chinese sugar cane" was not allowed to disappear from the scene just yet, however. In 1881 a state subsidy of a dollar per ton for stripped cane brought to the mill was offered by the state and guaranteed for five years. The resulting development was largely in Cape May County. A sugar refinery was built at Rio Grande, its owners growing cane on the company farm of 2,000 acres and purchasing cane from farmers under contract. The operation was not a success, in part because of inability to extract all the sugar from the cane. In the year of top production, 1884, about 188 tons of sugar and 87,000 gallons of sirup were produced on an investment of a quarter of a million dollars.

The bubble burst in 1885 with the termination of the state subsidy. Local efforts to keep the plant operating soon ended in total failure.[50] By 1889 the production of sorghum cane was again rapidly disappearing from New Jersey.[51]

The importance of flax in the early decades of the period 1810–1917, as in the previous period, was not because of large acreage, but because family plots must produce linen and tow threads for making the home-spun work clothing of the farmers and their families.[52] Then, too, there was still an active market for surplus skeins of thread.[53] Renters, at least in some cases, might give one-third of the flax stalks to their landlords, but might keep the immature seeds for livestock feed or to market at local "oil mills." [54] James Ten Eyck, Sr., of North Branch, though he bought for himself tailored "black clothes" in New Brunswick, grew each year in the 1790s and early 1800s a sizable patch of flax. He and his sons and his slaves retted and broke and swingled the flax stalks, and then he hired Peggy Van Nostrand or some other neighbor woman to spin the fibers into "linsey" and "toe yarn." The resulting skeins were then taken to Peter Sutphin or Abraham Voorhees for weaving, often using cross threads of wool to make "linsey woolsey." Joseph Stull or Robert Little, local tailors, afterwards made the cloth into trousers, "jaccoats," great coats, summer coats, and shirts. Ten Eyck's son, as late as 1824, was pursuing a similar course, though he sometimes bought gingham and other factory cloth from James Jenkins, the peddler.[55] By 1853 the Ten Eyck farm grew no more flax, and it is probable that it had not been grown there for many years.[56] By this time manufactured cotton had replaced home-made linen to such a degree that in only a few households in out-of-the-way places was flax still grown for the making of linen. The local sched-ules for the 1850 census showed only a few individuals in the state still occupying themselves with any kind of household manufactures.[57]

The same local returns showed, however, that flax had assumed a new importance because of the demand for flaxseed or linseed, formerly a by-product, and for flax straw by twine-making establishments. The "oil mills," often operated at local gristmills, increased in numbers for a time and advertised in local papers their wish to purchase flax seed.[58] During the same years cordage mills or twine factories appeared to purchase the flax straw. However, only farmers who lived near the factories could af-ford to bring in the straw, and the price was never very enticing.[59] The Civil War brought better prices for both oil and fiber, and there was a temporary revival of flax growing.[60] The decline during the 1870s was rapid, however, and a small revival in the 1880s as a result of state sub-sidies did not last for long. By 1890 there were only a few acres of flax left in the state.[61] The farmers had only been delayed temporarily in dropping a crop which at best took too much manual labor, and one which they could not produce as cheaply as farmers farther west.

The potato, once a garden crop, had been transferred to the fields, or at least to family truck patches, during the last decades of the previous period. Now the humble tuber became a commercial crop of some importance in areas where it grew best. Its sudden growth of popularity, in the late eighteenth century, common to most of the United States,[62] was probably in part due to the ease of growing and storage. In any case, the potato was a common crop by the 1790s, and a standard item of country trade by the 1820s.[63] In 1824, at a time when variety names were seldom used, the Holcombe store at Mount Airy was selling each spring Foxite seed potatoes.[64] Two decades later this variety was rivaled, at least in West Jersey, by the Mercer, named for the New Jersey county.[65] In 1858 the fair at Flemington gave premiums for the common Mercer, White Mercer, Foxite, Pink Eye, Sandlake, and Scotch varieties, and in 1860 the Peach Blow, Buckeye, and Mexican were added.[66] Potatoes grew well in many kinds of soil. James H. Blackwell, in the red shale belt, grew potatoes commercially in the 1840s, and in 1849 had a yield of over three hundred bushels. Most of the crop was stored in "potato holes," which were opened during the winter. The bad potatoes were sorted out and the good ones were bagged and hauled to market.[67]

At an early time it was found that potatoes did particularly well in areas with limestone soils,[68] which were of limited extent, and in the larger greensand marl belt, where they often replaced oats as a spring crop.[69] At the end of 1860, when George H. Moore of Cumberland County tallied his records for the year, he found that he had sold seventy bushels of the Buckeye variety, thirty-five bushels of Mercers, thirty-five of Peach Blows, and forty of Carters. The price varied from thirty cents to fifty cents according to quality rather than variety. In 1864 he recorded that he used marl, to which a little commercial phosphate had been added, as a fertilizer for his potatoes.[70] Dr. George H. Cook on his field trips as state geologist found farmers using marl and barnyard manure for potatoes in some places and marl and lime in others.[71] William C. Lippincott of Monmouth County, a confirmed user of marl, grew potatoes as a main crop in 1868, and his records show him spending days on end planting potatoes in April, cultivating them in May and June, and sorting them throughout the year for shipping to New York by coastal steamers from Red Bank.[72]

Before 1875 most farmers grew enough potatoes to supply their own families, and some had a surplus for market. In that year David C. Voorhees planted a few rows each of Eureka, Early Rose, Snow Flake, Brownell, and Compton's Surprise. On June 1 he noted the "Notorious

Colorado Bug," which had appeared in New Jersey very recently. By continued picking off of eggs and beetles, and by turning his chickens into the potato patch, he briefly foiled the insect. But on August 16 his farm crew picked 1½ bushels of beetles, at best quite a task.[73] Apparently he had not yet heard of the new insecticide, Paris Green. But on June 30 of the same year John Ten Eyck of North Brook, tired of "picking off bugs," tried this remedy, apparently mixed with flour and applied as a dust.[74] Unfortunately, whether used as a dust or a spray, Paris Green must be applied several times during the season, and particularly after every rain. Larger growers found it difficult to cope with the insect at first, and the appearance of the new insecticide saved the day for them. However, the added chore deterred many farmers henceforth from growing even their own family supply of potatoes and many small commercial producers found other uses for the ground in their truck patches. The larger producers, however, were soon encouraged by several other new developments. Within a short time, potato growing was rapidly mechanized. Better planters, cultivators, and, above all, diggers, made the individual worker more efficient. At the same time, the dissemination of the latest knowledge as to fertilizers and the appearance of more productive varieties brought up acre production markedly. Three of the new varieties, the Irish Cobbler, Redskin, and Crane's Lightning, originated in New Jersey.[75] The estimated average yield per acre in 1914 was 162 bushels, exactly double that of the first five post–Civil War years. Most of this improvement had been since 1900.[76] The emphasis in selection on productivity and keeping qualities may have led to a decline in taste. At least the old-timers thought so. One connoisseur of good food in 1903 wrote nostalgically of "those little kidney-shaped potatoes that were ready to dig early and when cooked with green peas made the most toothsome of vegetable dinners." [77]

In 1839, probably a low year, the state produced a little over two million bushels of potatoes, and double that in 1859. Estimated production varied startlingly from year to year, but on the average did not change greatly until 1902. That year was a magic one, for it brought the state yield to 7.5 million bushels, even though the acreage, a little under 50,000, was scarcely more than in the 1860s when poor prices had led to a decline in acreage. Yields per acre were henceforth always much higher than in the past, presumably because of better use of fertilizers. After 1902 the amount planted rose gradually to nearly 75,000 acres by 1915. Increased average yields on this greater acreage brought up production to 8.4 million bushels by 1907 and to 12 million by 1915.[78]

In the pre–Civil War period, the heavy producing counties were Monmouth, Burlington, Camden, Gloucester, and Salem, in order of rank. Monmouth, always far and away the biggest producer, had 773,000 bushels, with the other four ranging downward from less than half that to just over one-fourth. The same five counties led in 1869, but Camden and Gloucester had reversed their positions. Monmouth now had 1,263,000 bushels and the other four ranged downward from 582,000 to 351,000 bushels. By the turn of the century, Camden and Salem counties had declined somewhat, probably because of increased vegetable growing for the nearby Philadelphia market. Both were now rivaled or surpassed by Cumberland in the south and Middlesex and Mercer in the middle of the state. The next ten years saw a burst of production in both central and southwestern New Jersey. In 1909, Monmouth climbed to nearly 2 million bushels and Salem to 1.3 million, while Gloucester had 876,000, Burlington 747,000, Cumberland 647,000, Mercer 557,000, and Middlesex 476,000. The expansion of potato growing in these areas was not accompanied by one elsewhere. Several general farming counties barely held their own or declined. Sussex County throughout the period had about 100,000 bushels as an average production, and Somerset was nearly as consistent on a somewhat lower plane. Hunterdon with 121,000 bushels in 1839 had declined to just over half that by 1909. Counties that were being urbanized had fallen even more rapidly. Bergen, which had risen from 127,000 bushels in 1839 to 242,000 in 1899, fell abruptly to one-third that amount in a decade. The decline in Essex had occurred even earlier.[79]

Sweet potatoes traditionally grow best in sandy soil, but of course they will not grow in sterile sand. The right combination of fertility and sand are found in southwestern New Jersey, and the sweet potato was grown there from early days as a garden crop. An improvement in markets made it a field crop in some places very early in this period. But even in this area, it could not always compete with other crops. George W. Moore, who lived on a fertile Cumberland farm, scarcely mentioned the crop in his diary between 1853 and 1877. William C. Lippincott of Monmouth grew some sweet potatoes for sale, buying the sprouts from a local nursery. But his diary in 1868 shows that his efforts for the most part went into white potato production. Nevertheless, enough farmers grew "sweets" so that the state had a half million bushels by 1879 and over 3 million by 1909, making this a crop of some importance. It is noteworthy that Gloucester County consistently produced more than half the state crop throughout the period. Burlington, with nearly 300,000 bushels in 1879 and second on the list, produced about that amount yearly thereafter through 1909. Camden with something over 200,000 bushels in 1879 had a similar story. But Cumberland had an erratic record. With 217,000 bushels in 1869, it had fallen to 79,000 in 1889, only to rise rapidly to 412,000 in 1909, third in the state. Salem, too, had an odd story. With 100,000 bushels in 1859, it rose to 400,000 in the later years of the nineteenth century and to 460,000 in 1909, second in rank.[80] The effort put into the growing of sweet potatoes, even in areas where they grew well, depended always on their price levels as compared with the price levels of other crops that liked the same soils.

A colorful field crop of some interest but of no great importance was the pumpkin. The old practice of growing pumpkins in the cornfield was retained until late, though some farmers grew them in separate patches. Field pumpkins, as opposed to "garden pumpkins" for human consumption, were regarded by many as a good supplemental feed for cattle in the fall when pastures were failing. Experience showed that they must be carefully cut up with a spade or a root cutter to avoid choking the animals. Some farmers refused to feed pumpkins because of a belief that the seeds would cause a milk cow to "dry up," but the Blackwell brothers of Hunterdon and George W. Moore of Cumberland fed them for decades with satisfactory results.[81] On September 28, 1853, Moore proudly recorded that one big pumpkin weighed 56 pounds and that fifty-two pumpkins filled a wagon bed. But the crop declined rapidly soon after this time, probably because more and more farmers doubted that pumpkins had much food value. In 1875 David C. Voorhees of Somerset County, a very progressive farmer, grew no field pumpkins, though he had a hundred hills of cheese pumpkins in his truck patch.[82] The various root crops, once thought very important for stock feed, declined in use even faster, and for similar reasons, though so progressive a farmer as James Neilson grew 363 bushels of carrots, beets, and turnips as late as 1863.[83]

A crop which had its brief day of glory during the 1830s was the white mulberry, originally a native of the Orient. The growing of this tree by nurserymen and farmers was one aspect of the "silk craze." Silkworms had been raised by many people as a hobby or pastime, and especially as the result of bounties in the late colonial period. At times, some silk had actually been made into cloth. With the boom of other textile manufactures in the 1820s, the erroneous idea that American silk could be produced profitably from American silkworms became current gospel. But, first, food for silkworms must be available. Almost overnight hundreds of farmers rushed in to raise the white or Chinese mulberry. At first, it was thought necessary to graft it on native American mulberry rootstalks, but it was soon found that the tree could be grown from cuttings. All that was necessary was to plow a furrow down a field, lay in twigs with one or two buds above the ground level, and then plow the furrow shut. The first producers received very fancy prices for their young trees. In the spring of 1830, the current price was thirty cents apiece for small trees, and a dime per foot for larger ones.[84]

The craze lasted for several years. One farmer near Lambertville is on record as having grown several thousand 5-foot trees, and a neighbor who was in the game a little earlier had some 7-foot ones. Within the boundaries of the state there were literally millions of the young trees. The catch, of course, was that "feeding worms" and unwinding silk cocoons were tasks infinitely more laborious than raising trees. Besides, the projected silk factories had not been built. With neither "cocooneries" nor factories to give them markets, the deluded growers of mulberry trees could only reach for their axes, perhaps consoling themselves that others had burned their fingers also. A farm magazine in 1837 reported that the silk mania was "flat on its back," and another stated, "Silk seems to have been tried and exploded." [85] The only permanent result of the craze was that the white mulberry took to the fencerows and abandoned fields and became part of the flora of New Jersey.

With the increase in livestock, forage crops gained importance in the period 1810–1917. Unfortunately, the sources of information are piecemeal and scattered, and there are few statistics as to individual crops until the very end of the period. Hay crops from an earlier day included redtop, orchard grass, burnet, and sainfoin. For a time, redtop had a loyal following in southwestern New Jersey,[86] but because of the difficulty of threshing and the high prices of imported seeds the acreage was undoubtedly rather small. A far more important "cultivated grass" at the beginning of the period was timothy. It was esteemed as a feed for horses, and always had a ready market.[87] Timothy was the easiest of the hay crops to cut with the scythe, sometimes with cradle attached if cut for seed, and to thresh with flail and winnowing sieve. A farmer with surplus seed could easily sell it to a neighbor or through the local store, since there was a strong feeling against importing timothy seed because it might contain new weeds.[88] With the coming of the mowing machine and the horse-tread thresher, the threshing of timothy became easier.[89] This grass remained important as a hay crop as long as farmers owned horses.

Clover, and particularly red clover, was coming into its own at the beginning of the period.[90] Since red clover is a biennial, the requirements for seed were considerable. A diary entry of 1825 with wording, "Cut clover for seed," was a typical one for farm diaries of the day.[91] The cutting of ripened clover with a scythe and the beating out of the seed with a simple "huller" or "machine" was a very laborious task,[92] and it is understandable that the market price was as much as a shilling per pound.[93] But, again, harvesting and threshing were much improved with the coming of the mowing machine and tread power thresher. According to their diaries, John Ten Eyck, who had no mower, hired a neighbor to mow his seed clover in the early 1850s, and James H. Blackwell after he bought a thresher threshed clover seed for his neighbors, charging one-fourth of the seed as toll. In 1874 David C. Voorhees, using the latest machinery, had surplus red clover seed for sale. One transaction was for eighteen bushels at eleven cents per pound.[94] The tendency of farmers to give up the growing of clover seed and to purchase seed from other areas led to the importation of dodder and other unwanted meadow weeds late in the nineteenth century.[95]

Some indication of the gain in importance of forage crops with the increase in livestock is the fact that after the Civil War, when the statistics begin, the acreage of hay crops was almost always greater than that for corn, and often from one-fourth to one-third greater.[96] Total yearly acreage in the 1860s was between 300,000 and 350,000. Yields ranged from approximately a ton per acre to nearly a ton and a half. By the 1880s the average acreage had increased to half a million, with little change in average yield. After that time the areas sowed gradually declined to just under 400,000 in 1900 and to 358,000 in 1915. Only in the later years of the period were the figures broken down into categories. Those for clover and timothy were always the most important. Some complication has arisen, however, from the fact that though both were often grown separately, even more often they were grown together. In 1909 the estimated acreage of timothy and clover, alone or mixed, was 308,000 and the production was 393,000 tons. This was the last census year in which timothy was so important. It is of interest that 33,000 acres of "wild, salt, or prairie grasses" were still being harvested in 1909, though the area was soon to decrease. Far more important for the future was the small figure of 1,386 acres for alfalfa, at last a successful crop and destined to become of primary importance.[97] County returns after 1879 showed a very wide distribution of hay crops, but indicated that yields for counties with considerable urbanization were declining. During the census years from 1879 to 1909, the leading counties for hay, each with an annual acreage not far from 40,000, were Sussex, Hunterdon, and Burlington. Morris and Somerset were in the 35,000-acre range, and Middlesex, Monmouth, and Mercer in that of 30,000 acres.

There were during this period some interesting and quite revolutionary developments in the raising of fruit. Here we find not only local booms which became busts, but widespread general crazes which succeeded for decades before succumbing. There were other frustrations, but the greatest of all was the massive invasion, seemingly from every corner of the globe, of orchard pests, which changed an industry formerly characterized by an easy approach and low overhead almost overnight into a specialized one with exceedingly high costs. Quite suddenly toward the end of the period fruit growing became something for the specialist, who certainly brought up yields and gross returns per acre, but who of necessity invested heavily and risked much. In general, the growing of fruit has always been important in New Jersey. In the early part of this period, farm records and accounts report fruits of all kinds for home use and local markets, and, to a lesser degree, the production of brandy, dried fruit, and other fruit products for more distant markets. It is in a sense a measure of the dignity acquired by "the Orchardist" that in 1817 William Coxe of Burlington County wrote so learnedly about orchard techniques and about his own experiences as a fruit grower that he is considered one of America's best early pomologists.[98] There were few statistics so early, but it is clear that fruit growing was of increasing importance. Census figures indicate an annual fruit crop worth about a half million dollars per year immediately before the Civil War, and a million or more each year on the average for some decades thereafter. Between 1880 and 1900, the figure rose to two and one half millions and by 1909 to four millions.[99]

In the latter decades of the previous period many farmers were expanding their apple orchards to take advantage of the premium prices being paid for New Jersey applejack or brandy. In 1794 Cazenove found the taverns of Essex and Morris counties buzzing with talk about the possible financial returns from apple production, and he reckoned the gross returns from an apple orchard in good years as something over sixty dollars per acre.[100] The boom in the making of applejack proved to be no flash in the pan. By 1810 state production was in the neighborhood of 825,000 gallons, of which about one-third came from Essex County, long famous for its cider and applejack. That county's production of cider was estimated at 200,000 barrels in that year.[101]

In 1817 Coxe characterized the making of good cider as "the most difficult branch of the business of the Orchardist; and that on which the success of his plans most chiefly depends." [102] Thomas F. Gordon in 1834 mentioned that there were 388 distilleries in the state, of which 58 were in Hunterdon, 53 in Warren, and 46 in Monmouth. The coastal areas and South Jersey had few, and northeastern New Jersey had apparently lost its old dominance in cider production.[103] Unfortunately, there were few other reliable statistics until much later. But it is clear that the typical distillery was small, and was often a part-time venture of a farmer or small businessman.

The growing of apples was nearly always a subsidiary activity of general farmers. Even Hugh Exton, owner of Union Farm near Clinton, reputedly the largest farm in the state, and a man who liked to stir with a big spoon, had only some half dozen acres in his apple orchard. His production of 1,500 bushels in 1802 was almost entirely converted into cider.[104] An unidentified smaller farmer near Trenton spent three days in the early spring of 1823 trimming his trees and binding the brush into "faggots" for burning, a rather uncommon practice in this country. In the summer he mowed the hay crop grown among the trees, and in the fall he picked the crop and stored it underground. In late winter 1824 he opened the pits and spent seven days sorting the apples and hauling them to the neighborhood cider press.[105] It would seem that he put quite a bit of time and effort into a not particularly remunerative venture. Many farmers had an even smaller operation. James Ten Eyck, Jr., of North Branch, for example, was interested in having enough "appels for whiskey" for home consumption, but not in commercial production on any sizable scale.[106] Others wanted only enough "eating apples" for their family during the long winter.

The advent of the temperance movement seriously hurt the local market for applejack, and eventually eliminated many small apple growers and many of the small distilleries.[107] By 1860 there were only fifty-six distilleries left in the state, though undoubtedly some of them were larger producers than heretofore. Twelve were in Hunterdon, nine in Warren, eight in Morris, eight in Sussex, six in Somerset, and five in Burlington. None were left in Essex, once the center of the applejack industry.[108] The loss of the southern market during and after the Civil War was a serious blow. The manufacture of applejack did not stop, however, and apparently leveled off to about 150,000 gallons annually in the state for the rest of the century. But by 1914, just before Prohibition, production was only about half that amount.[109]

It should be remembered that the same companies making applejack were also vinegarmakers. It seems probable that the 700 gallons of cider recorded by George W. Moore as being pressed on March 4, 1875, became vinegar rather than applejack, for the date was generally considered too late for the making of good brandy. Of the estimated 29,000 barrels of cider made in 1899, the only year for which there are census figures, over 6,000 barrels became vinegar.[110] The making of vinegar was not prohibited by the Eighteenth Amendment in 1920, of course, but even it would be adversely affected by Prohibition. The story of the rise and fall of applejack in the period after Prohibition will be narrated later.

The apple may have declined somewhat in importance as its use in liquid form fell. But it still remained the most important fruit and gradually staged a comeback as markets grew for table apples. The new situation led to a change in emphasis as to varieties, however. The Harrison, Campfield, Granniwinkle, Poveshon, and many other cider apples disappeared, though the Winesap and several of the Pippins, also good for cider, were retained as good eating apples.[111] New varieties became legion, with increasing emphasis on appearance and keeping qualities. At the fair in Flemington in 1860, one farmer exhibited sixty-one varieties, and a New York nursery was taking orders for thirty-five kinds.[112] In time, Delicious, McIntosh, Winesap, Rome Beauty, Wealthy, and Grime's Golden became dominant, and the taste of the Bellflower, Sweet, and most of the Pippins became a memory.[113]

Before the turn of the century, new pruning practices were reducing apple trees from the tall heavy type to a lower, spreading tree, easier. to pick from and care for. With the appearance of one pest after another, worst of which was the San Jose scale, spraying became a ritual after 1900. As a result, the growing of apples by the end of this period was rapidly becoming a specialty practiced by fewer and fewer men. The number of apple trees of bearing age in the state fell from 1.8 million in 1900, to just over a million in 1910, and the decline in the size of the crop was even more marked. The areas of greatest production at both dates were the Monmouth-Burlington section and the counties of the northwest. The rate of decline was more rapid in the former than in the latter.[114]

The peach had always been a favorite fruit, but its perishability had kept it from becoming important commercially. The drying of peaches was never attempted on a very large scale, perhaps because the task required considerable labor. Peach brandy, a potent beverage, did not gain the popularity of apple brandy or win a market of any size. A British prisoner of war, crossing New Jersey under guard during the American Revolution, persuaded to sample it by a well-wisher at Pluckemin, had called it "a fiery disagreeable spirit." [115] The coming of the railroads made it possible for the first time to transport the fruit considerable distances. The opening up of city markets for the peach ushered in a half-century-long boom for parts of New Jersey. By 1859 the "unnumbered thousands of trees" of West Jersey were supplying peaches for daily consignments from the railroad stations at Trenton, Lambertville, Ringoes, and Flemington.[116] Soon "peach trains" were running during the season on what became the Pennsylvania Railroad, and, after 1875, on the Lehigh Valley. From New York, some peaches were reconsigned for Boston, Albany, and even Montreal.[117] On one day in 1882 the various stations of Hunterdon County shipped out sixty-four cars of peaches.[118] The 1880s were a time of great expansion. Peach growing was widespread throughout the state, but the greatest boom was in a limited area. In 1890, 2 million of the 4.4 million adult peach trees of the state were in Hunterdon County. There were a half million more across the line in Somerset County, and other adjoining counties had also shared in the growth.[119] Peach orcharding and the attendant activities of fruit tree nurseries and basket factories seemed to be permanent additions to the economy.

Even in its heyday peach growing had its detractors. The reader will be surprised to learn that the 4.4 million trees of 1890 produced only ¾ million bushels of peaches.[120] The seeming discrepancy points up one of the weaknesses of the industry, for in most years the crop was curtailed or entirely ruined in many localities by late frosts. Another source of complaint was that years of greatest crops, and particularly those in the early 1890s, brought market gluts and low prices.[121] In 1890 Elmer Bonnell of Clinton had no peaches at all. In 1891 he had a crop, but had to sell at from eighteen cents to forty cents per halfbushel basket. His record of trimming, picking, and peach-basket purchases show that his profit for that year was certainly small, if any. He persisted for some years, but never struck the bonanza that was the hope of all peach growers.[122] Even though overhead costs were low and peaches throve on land not especially valuable for other crops, many farmers had heartbreaks which eventually outweighed their hopes. Owners of orchards which were most often struck by spring frosts as a result of lack of sufficient air drainage were naturally the first to drop out of the game. Even before 1880, there were reports from older peach areas that some farmers were not replanting their old orchards as they were cut down.[123] In the 1880s, perhaps the halcyon days for the industry and certainly a time when the peach craze was advancing very rapidly northward, there were persistent reports that peach acreage was declining even in neighborhoods where orcharding was fairly new. It would seem that the same story was repeated in area after area, one in which the many rushed in and the few persisted. The decline in the count of adult trees in the state during the 1890s by more than a third, to approximately 2¾ millions, was a direct result of low prices during several years of market gluts.[124]

Many thought that the bubble had burst, and it truly had for some older areas of production. But most likely those who continued, especially operators in areas such as Sussex County, where large new orchards were just coming to bearing age, would have benefitted by the rapidly increasing market. In that case, others would soon have rushed in again. As it turned out, repetition of the cycle was prevented by a new disaster in the form of the San Jose scale. The scale, in reality a tiny insect which attacks many kinds of trees, appeared in New Jersey about 1895. The peach tree was as unresisting a victim as had been the orange tree of California, and this time relief did not appear soon enough. The erratic course of the invader was causing some damage by 1898, and considerable by 1903.[125] Sprays with solutions containing oil, lime, salt, or sulphur did little good, and sometimes harm, and the introduction of the right kind of ladybird beetle to feed on the scale came too late to serve most orchards.[126] Some areas escaped damage for a while, and peach production in the state was still 441,000 bushels in 1909. By this time, new but rather expensive sprays were proving of value, and some optimistic growers were planting new orchards. Within a decade, the number of bearing trees in the state would rise above the 1900 level. But by that time the center of production was moving considerably southward to areas where frost damage came less often and where soils once considered of little value for peaches could now be built up by use of fertilizers.[127] The new growers were specialists who, in the nature of the case, must have practical knowledge about insects, chemicals, and soils, and must have the capital or credit to apply their knowledge. Peach growing, still a gamble at best, had become a business.

Pears, although always grown for home consumption and local sale, did not gain much importance until the 1890s, when city markets grew rapidly. The number of bearing trees, only 274,000 in 1890, had increased to 732,000 by 1910, and annual production, by now 791,000 bushels, had multiplied several times. Burlington County had increased its bearing trees five-fold to 175,000 trees and Monmouth County had nearly doubled to 100,000.[128] Had the trend continued, the pear would have soon rivaled the apple. But for various reasons, a decline had already set in. Though the pear was more resistant than most fruit, the appearance of the scale and other orchard pests eventually made it, too, a specialty.

Cherries, though far less important, gained after 1890, and by 1910 the number of trees had trebled to over 100,000. The count would remain at about this point for some years before the inevitable decline caused by mounting costs. Other tree fruits never gained substantial importance in New Jersey.

Commercial strawberry growing gained importance after 1850 as the result of rail connections with the cities. Areas at first particularly afflicted by the "strawberry fever" were in the northeastern and central parts of the state, where picking time brought hordes of pickers from villages and cities and daily strawberry trains to carry the crop to urban markets.[129] By 1875 these areas were rapidly losing ground to South Jersey. Something over 8,000 acres of strawberries were grown in the state in 1909, with Cumberland and Burlington counties leading.

Much less spectacular, though using together a greater acreage in the same general areas as the strawberry were the bush fruits, most important of which were the raspberry, blackberry, currant, and gooseberry. Their area of commercial production, too, moved southward,[130] and their producers were afflicted even more by a growing shortage of pickers in the early twentieth century.

Grapes, which grow well under varying conditions, were to be found on nearly every farm of the state during this period. Nearly every farm diary mentions the crop, yet not a single diarist has been found who grew grapes commercially. Apparently native wine could not compete with applejack in the period before both were hurt by the temperance movement. The estimated wine production of 21,000 gallons in the state in 1859 showed little increase until well toward the end of the century, at which time it stood at 123,000 gallons.[131] The census showed 1.2 million bearing vines in 1899, one-third of which were in Atlantic County, and more than one-third in Cumberland and Salem together. Increase in these and nearby counties, at a time when other areas were declining, brought up the state total by nearly one-half during the next decade, but after that a decline set in.[132] The growing of the traditional small fruits had reached an impasse by the early twentieth century, despite the fact that the world's largest markets were nearby. The bottleneck of production in every case was the harvest, and unfortunately no machines appeared to solve the problem.

A seeming exception was the cranberry, long a New Jersey specialty. Through the work of a number of private experimenters and the New Jersey Agricultural Experiment Station, the plant had been partially domesticated and its yield increased through fertilizing and spraying for insect pests. Since the boggy area in which cranberries thrive is limited, the growers in this and other states, chiefly in New England, were able through organization to control prices and exploit their natural monopoly. When a shortage of handpickers developed, a rake-like device was invented to "scoop" the berries from the vines. Though still a hand operation, picking was thus speeded up.[133] By 1909, New Jersey production, second only to that of Massachusetts, was some 12 million quarts, harvested from something over 9,000 acres. Production declined somewhat thereafter, but not so markedly as for other small fruits.[134] Another wild plant of the same boggy areas as the cranberry was the blueberry. At the very end of the period, it too was being domesticated.

In this period, as heretofore, gardens and truck patches continued to supply farmers and their village neighbors with all of their vegetable needs from spring until fall, and furnished many food items for winter storage. In addition, farmers near to the increasing urban markets or who had good transportation to them, greatly expanded their gardening operations. The coming of the railroads not only gave many more farmers markets for their vegetables, but made it possible to haul carloads of manure to their lands from city stables and stockyards and lime and marl from the areas where they were produced. After the decline in use of these natural fertilizers, it was the railroads that brought in the new fertilizers. The commercial production of vegetables was thus an offshoot of home gardening, and market gardeners found by trial and error those crops that could be transported and sold in city markets at a profit. In the early decades of this period, vegetable crops receiving mention in farm accounts, diaries, correspondence, and periodicals included turnips, cabbage, watermelons, squash, sweet corn, beans, beets, and pie pumpkins. By 1850 these had been joined by rhubarb or "pie plant," asparagus, spinach, muskmelons, peppers, and peas, among others.

When the mythical Burlington County farmer of *Ten Acres Enough* by Edmund Morris began growing vegetables for the Philadelphia market about 1855, he chose sweet corn, cabbage, parsnips, turnips, and pie pumpkins as his specialties and grew smaller quantities of asparagus, peas, beets, and onions.[135] David C. Voorhees of Somerset in 1875 was too far from the New York market to specialize in crops that perished quickly, but he grew, in addition to tomatoes, sweet corn, squash, peppers, kohlrabi, peas, beans, and muskmelons. Being a man who liked peas and potatoes, cooked together, and muskmelon on ice nearly as much as strawberries and ice cream, he raised some of these crops more for his family than for the market. He had, however, 325 hills of watermelons, nearly as many squash and pumpkins, and several acres of Triumph sweet corn, some of which he sold for eating but most of which was marketed as seed through B. K. Bliss and Sons of New York.[136]

In choosing specialties, growers had to consider the time lag between picking and marketing the crop. Edmund Morris, in his account, shows that even in the area just across the Delaware River from Philadelphia, growers must raise only those vegetables which would stand up well during the trip to market. There was little large-scale production even there, and vegetable growing was in most cases an adjunct to general farming. Highly perishable items were grown closer to market. Morris's description would probably have fitted other areas near urban developments at that time and for some time after. An increase in specialization and in the size of operations was apparent, however, in the last decades of the nineteenth century. Most vegetables other than tomatoes were marketed fresh, though canning in glass and "tin," so important in the home in the latter decades of the nineteenth century, gradually became a factory operation as well, usually in the can houses which dotted the state and which had been built primarily for that most important vegetable, the tomato.

Statistics as to the magnitude and distribution of vegetable growing are not as reliable as one would wish, and are often confusing because of changes in basis of estimate and of crops included in the figures. The estimated "value of produce of market gardens" for the state in 1849 was under a half million dollars, surprisingly small. In a decade, the figure more than tripled, and by 1869 was approximately $3 million. For reasons not clear, the total fell to less than $2 million in 1879 for "market garden produce sold" and was only slightly more in 1889. The total of $5 millions in 1899 for miscellaneous vegetables seems a reasonable figure, but that of 1909, $14 million, is thrown askew by including all types of potatoes, valued elsewhere at something like $9 million. Much, though not all, of the gains through the decades was in the south central and southwestern parts of the state. In most years Gloucester and Monmouth counties competed with one another for first place, with Burlington usually third. Two counties which rose rapidly at the end of the period were Cumberland and Salem. A sizable increase in the produce of the northeast reflected the rise of local urban markets there, though these areas could hardly compete with those mentioned above for the New York market. Generally speaking, vegetable production, despite its many problems, including those of employing migratory labor, was definitely on its way to becoming one of the more important segments of the state's agriculture.[137]

The tomato, not truly a vegetable any more than was its nearest competitor, sweet corn, deserves special mention. Known early as the "love apple," it was grown occasionally for decorative purposes. The myth that it was poisonous persisted, though farm children proved again and again that it was not. The traditional story that Colonel Robert G. Johnson in 1820 demonstrated, after making a scathing speech, that the story had no basis by eating tomatoes publicly on the steps of the Salem County courthouse [138] is probably apocryphal, though it seemingly comports with the fiery character of the man who introduced commercial production of tomatoes into his area and with the innate conservatism of the farmers of the time and place. In any case, the tomato, pushed hard by farm periodicals, was rapidly introduced to many parts of New Jersey as a garden vegetable.[139] Edmund Morris, who said of the tomato that it was "a vegetable for whose production the soil of New Jersey is perhaps without rival," reported in the 1860s that tomatoes had been grown for the Philadelphia market for two decades, and that every year a market glut in midseason brought prices to absurd lows. By the time of his writing, commercial canning on a sizable scale was already several years old, and he gave a first-hand description of the operation of one of the early can houses in Burlington County. Of some interest is his comment that tomatoes, once shunned, had by now "a prominent place on every table." [140]

In the 1870s George W. Moore of Cumberland County began growing tomatoes under contract to a local cannery. In 1876 he recorded a "short" crop of less than eight tons per acre, though a neighbor reportedly grew twice as much. The contract price was forty-five cents per hundred-weight.[141] The differentiation among growers between "garden tomatoes" and "field tomatoes" at this time reflects the commercial importance of this relatively new vegetable.[142] Field-grown tomatoes, in season, were transported by rail to the Philadelphia and New York markets in tremendous quantities, and were canned by the millions of cans at dozens of local canneries. Unfortunately, there were no statistics for tomatoes alone until 1919, when 37,000 acres were reported.[143] At a guess, tomato production in most years for a half century had nearly as large a dollar value as that of all other vegetables combined. The love apple had gone far indeed!

4

Modern Agriculture

13

New Approaches

The modern era of New Jersey agriculture from 1917 to the present has been one of constant and sweeping changes for New Jersey agriculture, and to the many frustrations of the past have been added a host of new ones. The New Jersey farmer had long been adept at making the adjustments dictated by economic conditions. By 1917 he had grown accustomed to the obvious fact that agriculture would henceforth have a minor and diminishing place in the economy. He had seen the factory system force the last artisans of the nearby villages from the scene and had himself surrendered his domestic industries, including most of the processing of his own food. And in order to gain and retain a fraction of the new markets for which so many were contending, he had proved his willingness to specialize and to improve his efficiency. As faster and cheaper rail service with other areas had hurt his markets for wheat, potatoes, beef, cattle, pork, and fruits, one after the other, he had increasingly turned to the commercial production of dairy, poultry, and vegetable products. But the wants and needs of his family had increased, and his own costs of production had multiplied. It had become clear that the welfare of agriculture was dependent on the continuation of outlets for cash crops at favorable prices, something which New Jersey farmers had come to take for granted during the last decades of the previous period. The necessary transitions of the new era indeed proved difficult. Those who survived must mechanize and specialize even more than in the past, and must take full advantage of their nearness to markets and the improvements in local transportation.

The golden age prior to 1917 was only a memory during the tough years of the early 1920s, the brief period of easement of the middle 1920s, and the near debacle of the early 1930s. Yet a surprising number of New Jersey farmers survived the vicissitudes of these years and throve during the better period which followed. The estimated number of farms in 1910 had been 33,487.[1] In 1940 there were still over 25,000 farms and in 1950 just under that number. A slight decline had brought that figure to a little less than 23,000 by 1954.[2] But the great and constant danger during these years in each sector of New Jersey agriculture was that rival areas would so cut their costs of production as to overcome the transportation differential. At best, the margin of profit had become a slim one.

The farmer, concerned for both his livelihood and his way of life, was now calling loudly for relief from the mounting taxation of his means of livelihood, for recognition of a special status in his relations with labor, and for government aid through subsidies and regulation. The relief he obtained was not inconsequential, but apparently nothing would have prevented the breaking of the storm that hit New Jersey agriculture after 1956. Far worse than any depression of the past, an unheralded combination of low prices and rising costs led to such an evaporation of profits as to drive a majority of New Jersey farmers from the scene in one short decade. The number of farm units by 1964 had declined to an estimated 10,641. Six years later 8,700 units, operated by some 6,000 farmers, qualified as farms and used approximately 1,000,000 acres, only 40 percent as much as in 1910. The average farm, which had been about 75 acres at the time of World War I, and somewhat smaller during the Great Depression, had grown to 116 acres, as remaining farmers added to their units in the hope of bringing down relative costs.[3] These drastic changes seemingly marked the beginning of a spiral into ultimate oblivion by New Jersey agriculture unless revolutionary alterations so great as to change its very nature could be made.

The agriculture of the 1970s in New Jersey is as far removed from that of the early years of the present century as the farming of those years was from that of the aboriginal Indians. The early decades of the modern period (from 1917 to the present) saw the complete elimination of the horse for power and travel, as the tractor, the truck, and the automobile gave mobility to the internal combustion engine. Somewhat later electricity became an important source of power. During these years a multiplicity of new machines appeared on the scene. Agriculture became so mechanized that the laborious tasks of one decade became child's play in the next. The farmer in the later decades of the era need not be either sunburned or musclebound. The many and varied developments in agriculture during the years reflected a dramatic change in attitudes and responses. One of the words that became most common in the countryside was *scientific*. Many farmers of the period prior to 1917 had learned to apply the lessons of chemistry to soil usage, the lessons of genetics to breeding programs and to the selection of crops, and the lessons of scientific management to working arrangements. General acceptance of these ideas did not come overnight, of course, but a rapidly increasing number of farmers in the new period were open-minded and flexible, and quick to try out suggestions made in the agricultural press and by the experts of the College of Agriculture, the Experiment Station, and the state Department of Agriculture. That some decisions at first were not as yet truly scientific in approach perhaps reflected the fact that their advisers themselves were still feeling their way. In any case, the new farmer was or would rapidly become a believer in scientific feeding, selective breeding, milk testing, artificial insemination, hybridizing, chemical control of parasites, the effective use of the newest machinery, quality control, and, perhaps, above all, the employment of competent technical advice when his own knowledge was inadequate.

In the modern period, government-sponsored and subsidized institutions for the benefit of agriculture finally came into their own. The short-course program of the New Jersey College of Agriculture, initiated in 1906 with state funds, and geographically centered in a building paid for by the state, had proved a great success. The several dozen young farmers who each winter studied down-to-earth problems in their own specialties returned home to become proponents of formal instruction in agriculture. This redounded to the benefit of the already growing college, which by 1914 had sixty-eight students. The Adams Act of 1906, doubling the federal subsidies to the Agricultural Experiment Station, had helped provide teaching personnel for college courses and had permitted new offerings. In 1914 the courses taught were combined to become a new "long course in agriculture." A very fortunate appointment of that year was that of Dr. Jacob G. Lipman, already director of the Experiment Station since 1911, as dean of the college, for he proved as able as an administrator as he had been as a soil scientist on the college faculty. The new era in agricultural instruction corresponded with a rapid expansion at the Experiment Station in many fields hitherto not possible. The College Farm, which had already grown somewhat in size through gift and purchase, increased to 340 acres by 1916. This provided ample space for the conduct of experiments and for the demonstration of improved varieties of crops, fruits, vegetables, and shrubbery, and of better strains of animals and poultry. Hundreds of farmers attended tractor field days in 1917 and succeeding years. In a very real sense, the College Farm became a showplace for New Jersey Agriculture. As a result of long-awaited generosity on the part of the state, beginning in 1912, a new agricultural building was completed in 1914, and both the Experiment Station and the College of Agriculture could now leave their cramped quarters on the Rutgers College campus in downtown New Brunswick.[4]

State legislation in 1912 and 1913 and federal legislation in 1914 (the Smith-Lever Act) brought New Jersey into the parade of states turning to agricultural extension as the newest method of disseminating information to farmers. A Department of Agricultural Extension (later designated as the Extension Service in Agriculture and Home Economics) was created at the College of Agriculture in 1912, with one of its first duties the taking over of the management of Farmers' Institutes from the State Board of Agriculture. Very significant for a few years in bringing lectures and farm demonstrations to the counties, these meetings declined in importance, then ceased altogether, as agricultural extension was fully developed at the county levels. The key men in that development at that time and to this day, were the county demonstrators or county agricultural agents, as they came to be known. The effectiveness of agricultural extension gave both the College of Agriculture and the Agricultural Experiment Station a tremendous shot in the arm. The graduates of the college seldom went back to the farm, but many of them became extension workers on county and state levels, in other states as well as in New Jersey. At the same time, the work of the Experiment Station became widely known within the state for the first time as the result of extension workers advising farmers and disseminating reports in the form of pamphlets and circulars. The pioneer county agricultural agent, Henry W. Gilbertson in Sussex, had requests for more than 1,200 Experiment Station and U.S. Department of Agriculture bulletins during his first year. Extension Service workers, fortunately able to move about rapidly as a result of the revolution in transportation, became a tremendous force in guiding farmers during a period of radical changes.[5]

A number of counties delayed in accepting the new program. Nevertheless, state extension workers held crop demonstrations and other meetings in every county, and often these were a means of stirring up a demand for county extension programs. It was not always easy, however, to persuade a county government to pay its share of personnel and other costs. The strong last-ditch resistance of those opposed to "governmental interference" was well illustrated in Hunterdon County. In 1916 the Ringoes Grange and the Hunterdon County Board of Agriculture went on record as favoring the hiring of a county farm demonstrator. Held up by the period of war, the idea was broached again in 1918, and during the following years the Board of Chosen Freeholders was bombarded by resolutions from the County Board of Agriculture, the various granges, the cow-testing associations, the Lambertville Vigilant Society, and other groups, who often sent committees to present their communications in person. Letters and editorials on both sides of the issue appeared, and the public meetings where the matter was discussed often became heated. In January 1919 a County Board of Agriculture official wrote sadly that the corn exhibit for Agricultural Week at Trenton had "only ten ears from the great agricultural county of Hunterdon." In reply, H. E. Deats, another farm leader, wrote tartly that he hoped that this had been observed by visitors "who are opposed to our having a County Agent." [6] In 1922 a proposition for agricultural extension was decisively defeated by a referendum of the voters of the county, but its proponents only set to work with new zeal, with active aid from state extension workers. The new editor of the *Hunterdon County Democrat,* D. Howard Moreau, gave the project constant and favorable publicity, and other county papers also supported it. Finally, in 1927, the Board of Chosen Freeholders budgeted sufficient funds, and the new county agricultural agent was chosen from a list of candidates by the executive committee of the Hunterdon County Board of Agriculture, which would become the local guide for the program. Henceforth, through succeeding county agricultural agents, guidance and counsel became available to all farmers of the county on a day-to-day basis. A catalogue of the activities of this official, including farm visits, farm meetings attended, pamphlets dispensed, and office calls, would leave the reader either speechless or skeptical. The undoubted hard, practical benefits from the program made Hunterdon before long one of the staunchest supporters of agricultural extension. [7]

A part of agricultural extension that was a success from the start was the 4-H Club program. Through it farm boys and girls were able to learn better agricultural and homemaking methods, as well as practical benefits of working together. The first clubs of the state were promoted by extension workers from New Brunswick soon after the inception of the Extension Service. Those of Sussex County, directly watched by the new county agricultural agent, became the prototype. The drive for food production during World War I gave the added incentive of patriotism to the youthful club members, and by 1918 the program was an integral part of the rural life of the state, with several hundred clubs and several thousand members pursuing livestock, poultry, gardening, and homemaking projects. In 1921 the state Department of Agriculture established the New Jersey Junior Breeder Fund from which loans were to be made to 4-H Club members and vocational agriculture students for the purchase of purebred animals. Gifts from interested persons provided the original capital for this revolving fund. During a half century, more than five thousand boys and girls have borrowed more than a half million dollars to finance livestock projects. Calf clubs of the 1920s in some cases were still going concerns in 1970 with a third generation of dairy farm children as members. Poultry clubs have done well in areas in which poultry farming is important. The leaders of these clubs have taught the boys and girls, and often their elders, the manifold advantages of careful breeding, milk testing, scientific feeding, testing for bovine tuberculosis and brucellosis, hog cholera, pullorum typhoid in poultry, and so forth. Gardening clubs, the membership of which climbed spectacularly during the war periods, have had a sound foundation both in regions of market gardening and in suburban areas. Most 4-H clubs, however, have always been those with a general membership in which club members carry out a project of their own choice. Club work is sometimes under the supervision of an assistant county agricultural agent, but has done best where the county had had a county 4-H Club agent. Homemaking clubs, often in the villages and suburban areas as well as in farm country, have been a sideline of the county home agents, whose chief duties are with adults. The 4-H Club program has been without doubt an effective means of disseminating agricultural knowledge.

The Smith-Hughes Act of 1917, among other things, provided federal aid for vocational training in agriculture in the high schools. As a result, more intensive and formal training in agriculture than the 4-H program could offer has been given to a relatively small number of boys of the state. The impetus given to agriculture by World War I helped those high schools that had begun courses in agriculture to make an impressive start. The boys taking this subject usually became members of the organization known as the Future Farmers of America, with practical projects not unlike those of 4-H Club members. The two movements have sometimes showed a bit of rivalry on a local level, but in the main have got along well, with an occasional boy belonging to both groups. The teaching of vocational agriculture has had solid support in truly rural areas. In 1970 New Jersey had thirty-two agriculture teachers in twenty-seven school systems. Increasing urbanization had made it difficult for teachers of agriculture in many places to attract students and to find agricultural projects for those students who do not live on farms. The fact that a vocational agricultural project in high school does not usually give the educational background for entrance into the College of Agriculture has proved something of a weakness, too. There are no statistics to show how many graduates of vocational agriculture in the high schools have in fact become "future farmers," but probably as large a proportion as of 4-H Club members. Many a city worker can look back to his happy days as a member of an agricultural club of one type or another.

The coming of agricultural extension gave to the College of Agriculture the task of training county and state personnel for the new program, and the Smith-Hughes Act made it necessary to provide training for would-be high school teachers of agriculture as well. In both cases, the college was brought into more direct contact with the grass roots. In reality, public opinion among New Jersey farmers had much to do with ending the anomalous position of instruction in agriculture at Rutgers. In 1918 a "Committee of Farmers" petitioned that the College of Agriculture be reorganized and given its own board of trustees. This was rejected, but public demand persisted. In 1921 the Rutgers Trustees at last created a College of Agriculture as one of the constituent parts of the university. Dean Lipman was now in a position to go directly to the state legislature for funds. A series of appropriations soon permitted the construction of special buildings for horticulture (1919), poultry husbandry (1921), and dairy husbandry (1922). The operations of the College of Agriculture and the Experiment Station became so enmeshed as to almost defy separation. Both entered a period in which their services were deeply needed and fully appreciated by an agricultural population which had been buffeted by repeated vicissitudes.

The College of Agriculture increased its enrollment to 109 undergraduates and about 30 graduate students by 1921. After a period of undergraduate decline, the number accelerated again, so that in 1930 there were 118 undergraduates from eighteen states and several foreign nations. On the eve of World War II there were something over 300 students. After a few years of wartime decline, enrollment figures mounted during the GI Bill period, during which the education of former servicemen was subsidized, declined for a time, then moved upward, at first slowly and then more rapidly. During these years, the curriculum was overhauled, simplified, and modernized to fit the changing times. In September 1970 the enrollment stood at 902 undergraduates, of whom approximately 100 were females, and 354 graduates. Of the 670 undergraduates above freshman level, 250 were majoring in environmental science, a relatively new subject much in accord with the times, 98 in animal science, 93 in agricultural economics, 68 in landscape architecture, 54 in plant science, 49 in agricultural science, 30 in preparation for research, 22 in food science, and 6 in agricultural engineering. Of the graduate students, 72 were in the field of environmental science, 51 in food science, 47 in entomology, 43 in biochemistry, 33 in plant science, 22 in animal science, 19 in soils and crops, 18 in nutrition, 17 in plant pathology, 14 in agricultural economics, 9 in agricultural engineering, and 9 in meteorology. In September 1965 the College of Agriculture became the College of Agriculture and Environmental Science.

The New Jersey Agricultural Experiment Station, still partially financed by the federal government, but to an increasing degree by the state, attained fame through the years far greater than the relative importance of agriculture in this state would indicate. Additional working space was acquired by three purchases of farm land, totaling some 150 acres by 1940, and by the gift of a 1,100-acre dairy farm in Sussex County in 1931 by James Turner as a home for the Experiment Station's outstanding program in the breeding of Holstein cattle. Dozens of articles in scientific and technical journals each year under the signatures of members of the station staff attested to a lively research program. The work included the improvement and development of varieties of crops and breeds of animals, experimentation with plant and animal diseases and parasites, animal feeds, fertilizers, and herbicides. The most spectacular crop developments of the period between the two world wars were the Rutgers tomato in 1934, two hybrid corn varieties in 1935, and Atlantic alfalfa in 1940. The Experiment Station was particularly well known beyond the borders of New Jersey for work in soil microbiology, dairy cattle breeding, poultry pathology, development of peach and apple varieties, mosquito control, and oyster culture. In 1943 came the greatest achievement of all when Dr. Selman A. Waksman and his aides in soil microbiology discovered streptomycin, which has since saved millions of human beings from tuberculosis and other bacterial diseases.

In general, agricultural research suffered during World War II, as scientists were called away from their experiments to help promote the war effort in more practical, or at least more immediate, ways. The lost time was more than made up after the war, however, in part due to liberal state appropriations. Work in the specialties of the earlier period was continued, but the greatest possible efforts now were being made to aid practically the specialized, commercialized, and mechanized agriculture which was developing. As the result of continuous work in hybridization and selection, a regular parade of new plants appeared, including the Jersey Orange sweet potato, the Sparkle and Jersey Belle strawberries, the Queen's tomato, Raritan asparagus, Jersey rhubarb, and the Jerseyred apple. When the M. A. Blake peach was named and put on the market in 1954, it was the fifty-sixth named peach variety developed by the Experiment Station. Today it is one of the three most important varieties of the state. The Holstein cattle blood lines developed at what had become the North Jersey Agricultural Experiment Station became the basis of an artificial breeding program which greatly improved the dairy cattle of the state and of the world. Years of work at the Turkey Research Farm established at Millville in 1939 resulted in a new breed of turkey, the Jersey Buff. A particularly important development has been specialized research in agricultural economics, as Experiment Station and Agricultural Extension specialists have attempted to analyze and guide new developments in New Jersey agriculture. Experiments in practically every sector of agriculture practiced in the state were carried out, including, in addition to those mentioned above, livestock breeding, pasture and hayland development, production of grass ensilage and haylage, feeding, hybrid seed corn development, insecticides, herbicides, fertilizers, animal and plant diseases, and orchard care. Concern for the future of the Agricultural Experiment Station has been shown in recent years by the growing proportion of research subjects that can only indirectly be associated with the agriculture of New Jersey.[8]

The rather anomalous relationship between state government and agriculture was regularized and streamlined by the creation of a State Department of Agriculture in 1916. The State Board of Agriculture, "as general overseer of intimately related services" to agriculture, had been operating under fifteen separate legislative acts. The new law gave these various duties, plus the gathering and publishing of agricultural statistics, to the Department of Agriculture, which functioned under the general supervision of a greatly altered Board of Agriculture. The latter consisted of eight members with staggered terms, selected by a convention of farm organization delegates. In 1944, a change in the law made board appointments subject to approval by the Governor and the upper house of the legislature. The board in turn chose a Secretary of Agriculture. The 1944 law made his appointment subject to the same approval as board members. Every effort was made to have the new setup truly representative of agriculture and to safeguard it from becoming political. By custom at first and by law since 1948, as a special dispensation granted agriculture in the new state constitution, members of the board must be farmers. The term of the Secretary of Agriculture was an indeterminate one, which in practice has resulted in there being only four secretaries in more than a half century. From the beginning, politics had nothing to do with the appointment of department employees, who have grown in numbers from about twenty to more than two hundred. There were originally three bureaus, Animal Industry; Lands, Crops, and Markets; and Statistics and Inspection. The second was renamed the Bureau of Markets in 1917 and the third the Bureau of Plant Industry in 1931. Legislation of 1947, 1948, and 1949 made the department an executive department, changed its bureaus to divisions, added a Division of Administration, and established an Office of Milk Industry to replace the State Milk Control Board. Continuing changes since have brought flexibility in handling the manifold duties of a governmental department concerned with nearly every aspect of the state's agriculture. Creation of a Division of Rural Resources in 1968 brought a total of eight divisions in addition to the Office of the Secretary.

Until 1968 the Division of Administration, in addition to its executive and administrative functions, conducted hearings on violations of state laws and regulations relating to agriculture, gave support to agricultural fairs and shows, administered the New Jersey Junior Breeder Fund, and handled loans to qualified farmers from the State Board of Agriculture Federal Loan Fund. Since that time the hearings have been conducted by an executive assistant to the Secretary of Agriculture, and work with the agricultural fairs and shows and the administration of the Junior Breeder Fund have been in the hands of the Division of Information. The latter furnishes regular reports to the press, radio, and television and itself publishes descriptive booklets and flyers. The Division of

Regulatory Services until recently was called the Division of Agricultural Chemistry. In general, it is concerned with protecting farmers and home-owners in their purchase of feeds, fertilizers, insecticides, fungicides, her-bicides, and other supplies by inspection, analysis, and registration as to conformity with the law. It also has responsibility for inspection and grading of fruits and vegetables, the inspection of eggs, and the testing of milk for butterfat content.

The Division of Animal Health takes measures for the prevention, control, and eradication of the animal and poultry diseases, old and new, which bedevil New Jersey farmers. Since 1968 it has also been responsible for meat and poultry inspection. The Division of Plant Industry en-forces laws and quarantines that are concerned with plant pests, inspects and certifies commercially grown seed and nursery products, uses chemi-cal and biological methods of fighting forest pests, and conducts inspec-tions for new harmful insects. The Division of Markets provides a mul-titude of services in four main areas: market development, services to farm cooperatives, statistical services, and such regulatory activities as administration of federal food programs. The Division of Dairy Industry issues and enforces within the state the orders and regulations of the two federal milk marketing areas that together cover the state and sets minimum retail prices for milk within the state.

The Division of Rural Resources is concerned with the development of rural resources, and contains a State Soil Conservation Committee, which coordinates the programs of the fifteen soil conservation districts of New Jersey. The Office of the Secretary has a Rural Advisory Council which copes with economic and social problems of rural areas and main-tains communications with similar agencies in other states and in the federal government. A committee or team of this group maintains liaison with the county boards of agriculture of the state.[9]

In this new era, the advantages of organization were so important that New Jersey farmers to a greater degree than ever before became joiners of farm organizations, both old and new. The Grange, which after 1870 had absorbed most local farm clubs, took a new lease on life in the twen-tieth century and pushed rapidly forward in numbers and influence. In 1901 approximately 50 local groups and 7 county or Pomona granges had a total membership of only 4,300, but a steady drive increased the number of subordinate granges to 137 by 1914, the number of county groups to 14, and the total Grange membership to 16,720. It should be pointed out, however, that the approximately 4,000 members of the county granges had been counted twice, since they were also members of the local granges. Furthermore, since Grangers are not required to be farmers, a substantial part of the membership by this time were others who expressed "interest" in agriculture. During the next half century, the Grange remained the outstanding farm organization on the social side and one of the most vocal representatives of agriculture on the political. A total adult membership of 15,000 in the 1930s climbed above 20,000 in the 1940s. Again the numbers are somewhat padded because of the overlapping membership of local and county groups. In addition, a juvenile Grange organization, started in 1923, contained several hundred teen-age members in more than a score of local groups.[10]

With the rapid fall in farm production in recent years, and especially because of the elimination of agriculture from some communities, has come a decline in the number of local granges and in total membership. Pioneer Grange No. 1 is a somewhat sad example of what happens as farming declines in a community. Today a bare dozen families are holding together a group to which few new members come to replace the old who leave.[11] Fifteen Pomona granges, representing 17 counties, have persisted, but the number of local granges had fallen to 103 by 1966 and to 95 by 1970. The total net membership, some 9,400 in the latter year, reflected some gains as the result of a sustained membership drive. A recent elimination of inactive groups had brought the number of junior groups to 14, with 325 members. The nonagricultural membership in recent times had far outnumbered the members from farm families.[12] There is every indication that the Grange has in no way declined as a voice in New Jersey agriculture, despite the smaller number of members on its rosters. This, of course, cannot continue for long.

At the ninety-third annual meeting of the State Grange at Atlantic City in 1965, there were delegates from all the Pomona Granges and from sixty-five of the local granges. The State Grange gave tacit approval of some forty points favored by the National Grange, an interesting mixture of ancient conservatism and new liberalism. The gold standard should be brought back when "feasible," the states should retain control of highway beautification, but the federal government should increase farm subsidies and social security payments to widows, should promote sales of agricultural produce abroad and research on farm pests, and should set reasonable minimum wages for agricultural workers. The last, hailed by the State Master as "an historic shift," did not meet the unqualified endorsement of the Atlantic City gathering, which passed a resolution two or three days later that every means possible should be used "to keep to present levels the wages and benefits of migrant laborers." The fifty-seven other resolutions of this group showed a surprisingly wide range. The state was urged to study watershed protection, to curtail deer damages, to protect the birds, including starlings, to push crop variety research, and to legislate a sales tax. The war in Vietnam was approved, the U.S. Post Office was criticized, and the utility companies were told to put their high-tension power lines underground. One general resolution favored "reduction of Federal government control." [13] This state meeting, as had each annual meeting in the past, brought into focus the activities of the county and local groups in their more than a thousand monthly meetings during the previous year. Something of the continuity of the Grange is indicated by the fact that a dozen of the first twenty-five original local groups were functioning more than three-quarters of a century after their founding. These twelve, widely dispersed, were located at Dayton (Middlesex County), Hammonton (Atlantic), Moorestown (Burlington), Swedesboro (Gloucester), Bound Brook (Somerset), Woodstown (Salem), Vineland (Cumberland), Ringoes (Hunterdon), Bridgeton (Cumberland), Greenwich (Cumberland), Hancock's Bridge (Cumberland), and Salem.[14]

A farm group never absorbed by the Grange was the Princeton Agricultural Association, which has maintained for a century its status as a discussion group for farm problems. Its membership, never restricted to farmers, has in the twentieth century, as in earlier times, included an occasional professional man or businessman interested in agriculture. A comparison of topics by speeches at monthly meetings through the years has shown the growing sophistication and wider interests of modern farmers. In recent years, such topics as soil conservation, water needs, the world food situation, and 4-H clubs have shared time with political, cultural, and social subjects. The group, as always through its history, has a larger impact than its membership of some twenty men would seem to indicate.[15] Nevertheless, from a larger view it must be regarded as a pleasing reminder of an earlier day rather than an effective guide in the crosscurrents of modern agriculture.

The County Boards of Agriculture, made possible by a state law of 1887, had gained importance before the beginning of this period as forums for the presenting and debating of agricultural problems and grievances. Their "acknowledged relationship" to the State Board of Agriculture was that of reporting agencies which brought to the latter's attention "current situations" and "attendant problems." With the reorganization and development of the New Jersey State Board of Agriculture in 1916 as an official body governing the State Department of Agriculture, the tie became a closer one, with direct and immediate communication between county and state levels. Delegates of the twenty-one county boards became at that time the nucleus of an annual State Agricultural Convention, to which were later added representatives of the state and county granges and of an increasing number of breed and commodity organizations. With the beginning of formal agricultural extension work as an arm of the College of Agriculture in 1912, and especially after passage of the federal Smith-Lever Act in 1914, county boards of agriculture became sponsoring and advisory groups for the new programs.

As county governments accepted the financial obligation of "matching" federal and state funds for agricultural extension, the boards, through their executive committees, found themselves appraising the work of county agricultural agents, county 4-H Club agents, county home economists, and other personnel of an expanding program. At a later time, they accepted the responsibilities of a somewhat anomolous relationship with soil conservation and other federal programs.

The membership of county boards of agriculture has fluctuated through the years in the various counties, depending upon strength of leadership, energy expended in membership drives, appeal of programs backed by the board, and financial advantages offered by insurance companies and others on a group basis. A substantial and increasing part of the membership in nearly all counties has been nonagricultural. In Hunterdon County in recent years sponsorship of a county medical center has caused membership numbers to soar. In 1970 there were nearly two thousand members there, of whom only four hundred were farmers. County boards of agriculture have not had the social appeal of the Grange, and many a member has never attended even one of the annual meetings. But in the economic and legislative fields the substantial membership of the county boards has provided a strong base of operations for farm leaders in their executive committees, which in the main have been exceedingly active groups.[16]

The story of the growth of the New Jersey contingent of the Farm Bureau Federation, one of the most powerful voices of American agriculture, has been intertwined with that of the county boards of agriculture. After a year or more of maneuvering, an agreement was reached in 1920 by which board of agriculture members became automatically members of the New Jersey Farm Bureau. A State Council (soon Federation) of County Boards of Agriculture was created as a control group. In 1933 the facts of the situation resulted in its becoming officially the Board of Directors of the New Jersey Farm Bureau. For decades, county board and Farm Bureau activities were almost completely merged on the county level. The boards, working through their executive committees, were the local promotional and administering groups for Farm Bureau marketing, insurance, and other programs. Furthermore, through them local farm problems and complaints were channeled upward to become the basis of legislative demands at state and federal levels. At the state level, legislative programs were "developed jointly" with those of the Grange. This arrangement became traditional, and today is secured through a Farm Bureau-Grange Legislative Action Committee.

In 1962, as the result of mounting frictions, there was a drastic change in the relationships of the Farm Bureau and the county boards of agriculture and a complete severance at state level. Early in that year, the

New Jersey Farm Bureau was incorporated with "the purpose of protecting and advancing the interests of farm people through the development
and implementation of sound policies on public issues, legislative action,
education, and commercial services." A board of directors and a presi-
dent and other officers were to be chosen by delegates from the county
units. The problem of what should constitute county units was partially
resolved by confining Farm Bureau membership to farmers and those
with farm ties. The new development, and in particular increases in
Farm Bureau dues at that time and since, has led county boards of agriculture to take one kind of action or another as regards dual membership. Ocean County in 1962 divorced the two groups and set up an entirely independent Farm Bureau unit, and as of 1972 Somerset is in
process of doing the same thing. In several counties, joint membership
is still the rule, a situation which makes it difficult for nonfarmers to be
members of the boards of agriculture. In the other counties, with the exception of the largely urban Hudson and Passaic, which have no Farm
Bureau units, board of agriculture members may or may not be Farm
Bureau members. For example, as of October 1970, the 414 Farm Bureau
members in Hunterdon County were also county board members, but it
was they alone who sent voting delegates to Trenton. Whether the
frankly proclaimed campaign of the New Jersey Farm Bureau leaders to
force complete separation of the two groups, and thus end a situation
peculiar to New Jersey among the states, cannot be foretold at the present
writing. The official count of New Jersey Farm Bureau members as of
October 22, 1970, was distributed among the counties as follows: Burlington 513, Gloucester 498, Hunterdon 414, Monmouth 308, Sussex 287,
Cumberland 273, Warren 253, Salem 248, Morris 226, Mercer 217, Somerset 177, Atlantic 164, Middlesex 114, Bergen 93, Camden 81, Union 62,
Cape May 48, Essex 38, Ocean 33, Passaic 7, Hudson 0.

The New Jersey Farm Bureau is one of the most active and versatile
farm organizations of the state. Its self-stated activities concern state and
national legislation, work with administrative agencies of state government, cooperation with other organized groups, publicity and public
relations, services to members regarding legal problems and taxes, commodity problems, marketing and bargaining, and farm labor. Its motto
in 1970—Save the Farm! Save Open Space!—indicated its concern with
the plight of New Jersey agriculture, and a publication in June of that
year reflected the basic optimism of its leaders that a much-changed but
still very real agricultural sector would survive for decades to come. A
listing of 1969 "efforts and achievements" in still another publication
gave some indication of the group's lines of attack. Among other projects in that year, it backed successfully a campaign for state funds for

special Agricultural Experiment Station projects and helped secure legislation extending the life of the Open Space Policy Commission. In legislative halls and elsewhere it had represented the farmers' point of view regarding minimum wages, migrant labor, farmland assessments, a New Jersey jetport, marketing regulations, and so forth. Through subsidiary organizations the association had provided members and their families with a "complete line of insurance coverage," a hospitalization service plan, a group purchasing program for certain farm supplies, aid in securing seasonal farm labor, and a service program for roadside farm markets. It had sponsored advisory committees for various sectors of New Jersey agriculture, including dairying, horticulture, forest management, horse farming, and natural resources. Its officials had given counsel at conferences on farm programs, had helped publicize agricultural happenings, and had aided and assisted various agricultural groups in times of emergency. The services of the New Jersey Farm Bureau to the agriculturists of the state have been manifold, and its promoters have displayed no false modesty in reciting them.[17] It is in no sense derogatory to add that, in all fairness, other agricultural organizations played a role in all of these issues.

Most of the agricultural fair associations of this period have been lineal descendants of those of the nineteenth century. In a few cases, old organizations have given way to new. Several have fallen by the wayside, for the most part in counties of greatest displacement of agricultural population. In general, the ten organizations still giving farm fairs in 1970 in the counties of Burlington, Cumberland, Hunterdon (the Flemington fair), Mercer (the New Jersey State Fair), Middlesex, Morris, Ocean, Salem, Sussex, and Warren have been able to do so by making an increasingly greater appeal to nonfarmers. In some cases the surrender to carnival attractions, automobile and horse racing, and exhibits entirely unrelated to farming has been less than in others. In 1967 the sponsors of the Burlington fair could still write, "The old-fashioned county farm fair . . . was a place where country folks could gather, exchange ideas, and observe the products of their neighbors, and where city folks could see the results of the toil of their farmer friends. The Burlington County Farm Fair is still holding to this tradition."

All the fairs, ranging in length each year from two or three days in Burlington, Ocean, and Salem counties to a week or more at the Flemington Fair and the New Jersey State Fair, have continued to award a multitude of prizes to individual farmers and to farm organizations. Some, too, have played up rural attractions of an earlier age, from horseshoe pitching to square dancing, but it seems probable that this will prove a losing game in a period when old things have less and less appeal. It is true that fairs of today, even those which play up their Mid-way features, are in some ways reminiscent of those of an earlier time. But "events" at these fairs have a modern application or twist. Pulling contests today are usually, though not always, between tractors rather than teams of horses, and of course they are of as much interest to farm machinery salesmen as to farmers. The most modern of farm machines are on exhibit, too, but their work qualities are shown by short movies rather than field demonstrations. The animals shown in horse shows are usually riding horses, put through their paces by riders in western cos-tume or an approximation thereof. The most important function of the fair was once the competitive exhibiting of purebred livestock, poultry, products of the soil, and domestic arts; and there was then a basis for the hope that good exhibits would educate the ignorant and stimulate the complacent. The old attributes of the fair did not entirely disappear in the new period. But they were no longer important for the disseminat-ing of knowledge, and, understandably enough, the social side became increasingly dominant. The present official sponsorship by the New Jer-sey Department of Agriculture and promotion through a New Jersey Association of Agricultural Fairs will probably insure the retention of county fairs unless or until agriculture disappears from the scene. Should this occur, the farm fairs will be missed, probably most by those who still have a touch of nostalgia for the farms they or their fathers left.

In nine counties that do not have fair associations, the 4-H clubs have gradually taken over. Supported by government subsidies and local dona-tions, 4-H leaders through several decades have made their fairs sub-stitutes for the old county fairs. Centered on competitive exhibits of 4-H teen-agers and the exhibits and demonstrations of their 4-H clubs, these fairs have nevertheless added general interest by having exhibits of other farm and nonfarm organizations, by admitting commercial exhibits, and by promoting diverse kinds of contests and amusements. To give an ex-ample, the Atlantic County 4-H Fair of 1967 had in addition to many categories of 4-H exhibits and events the following attractions: "Farm machinery, automobiles, tractors, commercial farm and homemaking ex-hibits. Livestock show. . . . Fashion revue, Baby parade. Fireman's Day. Chicken Barbecue. Crowning of 4-H Queen. Talent show. Many new features and events." Just as many of the 4-H Club activities have di-verged from agriculture, pure and simple, so have the exhibits and at-tractions at the 4-H fairs. This development, too, has drawn the atten-tion of villagers and suburbanites, who often visit the fairs to see the dog and horse shows, the talent, fashion, and craft shows, the mineralogy and forestry exhibits, projects in entomology, woodworking, mechanics, and electricity, and the archery, photography, and auto-driving skill contests. To be sure, they also see the exhibits of the boys and girls who have livestock, poultry, farm crop, and vegetable projects. A generation or so ago these exhibits were the only ones, and, despite the strong trend in other directions, are still the heart and core of most of the 4-H fairs and certainly their ostensible reason for being. The 4-H fair has filled a gap left by the disappearance of many of the old county fairs. Twenty-one fairs of both types were held in New Jersey in 1972.[18]

14

Cooperation and Regulation

The farm organizations which the period beginning in 1917 inherited from the previous one included some which were dedicated to the bolstering of the farmer's marketing position through cooperation. The idea of trying to break out of their proverbial price bind by joining forces in buying or selling was an old one as far as farmers were concerned. Local granges in the 1870s and 1880s, the Farmers' Alliance movement in the 1890s, the numerous short-lived groups such as the "fruit exchanges" during the heyday of peach production, had all attempted to make their members more efficient commercially and in particular to eliminate or partially control that long-time bogeyman, the middleman.[1]

For some years during the new period it looked as if local granges might again become important as economic agents. Some half dozen Grange stores and buying groups had survived into the twentieth century, and by 1910 two dozen more had been added. Total Grange business, probably less than $100,000 at the turn of the century, grew to several times this amount by 1920. In 1919 there were thirty-four local granges acting as buying and selling organizations. But by 1926 the number had declined to twenty-six. Of these, twenty-three were acting as purchasing units, and eleven sold produce for their members. However, ten of the twenty-six hardly counted, and the total number of farmers using their granges for economic purposes was not more than 850. Total purchases by local granges were about $150,000 in 1926 and total sales of farm products were so small that they were not reported. The decline continuing thereafter brought down the number of granges "in business" to two by the 1950s. The trade of that in Stewartsville in Warren County was already on the decline, indicating a demise which came soon. The Grange store at Moorestown in Burlington County still had a considerable business, but ceased operations a few years later. The granges, set up primarily as social organizations, found it difficult to act in a business capacity day in and day out over a protracted period. Their members, and especially their leaders, were often active in independent cooperative groups.[2]

In general, the farmers' cooperative movement in the new period had a higher batting average than in the previous one. A greater degree of willingness to cooperate and a greater recognition of possible advantages on the part of individual farmers help to explain this. Equally important in this period was the fact that farm leaders showed a gain in business acumen, often the result of hard experience. Furthermore, a changing climate of opinion eroded the attitude of a public which once equated cooperation with socialism, weakened the hostility of competing middlemen, and brought official blessing and government aid at federal, state, and county levels. Last, but not least, have been the advice and guidance of market specialists at the New Jersey Department of Agriculture and the College of Agriculture and of state and county agricultural extension leaders. Cooperation was more important and certainly more effective during and after the Great Depression than ever before. An interesting part of the story has been the interplay of different farm organizations and the participation in the founding and management of cooperatives by farm leaders active in other farm groups. Indicative of the frontal attack on the farmers' problems in buying and selling has been the formation of a New Jersey Council of Farm Cooperatives.

The formation and development of a successful farm supply cooperative, the Farmers' Cooperative Association of New Jersey, known for half a century as FCA, illustrates some of the points made above. In September 1915 a farmers' meeting was called at Trenton by the heads of the new Mercer County Farm Bureau, the Mercer County Fruit Growers' Association, and the Mercer County Potato Growers' Association. The members of the second and third groups joined the new Farmers' Cooperative Association en masse, and a newly appointed manager was soon installed at a telephone, purchasing supplies for individual members on order. Starting with a working capital of a few hundred dollars, the cooperative did a business of more than $100,000 the first year, most of it in purchases of seed, fertilizers, insecticides, and general farm supplies. By 1934 the directors felt justified in taking the plunge of acquiring buildings for a store and for grinding local grain and mixing feed. It was tough sledding for a few years during the Depression, but with the aid of GLF, a giant farm cooperative, the organization survived. By 1940 things were going so well that more equipment was purchased and by 1944 all mortgages were paid off. In the meantime, a branch store had been opened at New Brunswick, and soon a new one was started at Hightstown. A fourth store with grinding and mixing equipment would be opened at Hopewell in 1948. By the 1940s an increasing part of the

FCA business was the handling of local grain, something over a million dollars' worth per year.

In 1952 the FCA became a stock cooperative, managed by 1,000 farmer-owners of common stock and financed by the owners of 240,000 shares of preferred stock, which paid a guaranteed 4 percent per year. Profits not used for expansion went as patronage refunds to customers. By 1965 the organization could report that in a half century it had returned more than $1.5 million to purchasers out of a total business of $90 million. In expanding its operations, FCA's ties with GLF and with its successor organization, Agway, have become increasingly close. Within a perimeter quite far out from its four outlets, FCA has become a supplier of most farm supplies and services. A farmer-dreamer of the nineteenth century would have considered this cooperative almost ideal. A natural question is how it will adjust as agriculture continues to decline in its area. A noticeable appeal to suburbanites in recent years by handling garden, lawn, and landscape materials perhaps indicates the direction it will take.[3]

Other cooperatives concerned primarily with farm supplies multiplied in numbers during the first decade of this period. Farmers of the twentieth century used an increasing variety and amount of supplies of many kinds, and the old belief that middlemen's profits were high had some basis in fact, especially during the time of increasing demands during World War I.[4] It was a propitious time for the formation of buyers' cooperatives, and by 1924 the number had grown to twenty-seven, well distributed among the counties of the state. A number of these were business ventures by poultrymen's and fruit grower's associations, but most were farmer-owned cooperatives in the ordinary sense. The total business in 1926 was approximately $2.5 million. Nearly three-fourths of this was done by twelve cooperative supply stores, and the remainder was for the most part the result of "car door" arrangements made by eleven buying clubs.[5]

A survey of New Jersey farm cooperatives in 1926 showed that some were losing money, that some were making fair profits, and that all were plagued by problems of capital formation and maintenance of a sufficiently large volume of sales. Only one other besides FCA passed profits back to farmers in the form of patronage refunds, generally speaking a better device for gaining the trade of large operators than that of declaring dividends.[6] In retrospect, therefore, it seems understandable that many of these organizations fell by the wayside during the days of adversity which soon came. Of the two dozen local farm supply cooperatives of the 1920s other than the Granges, only FCA and one other, the Belle Mead Farmers' Co-Operative Association in Somerset County, were still in operation in 1970. However, new groups had appeared, except in areas most completely urbanized. In the 1930s new buying cooperatives developed, oftentimes with some of the old faces. Founded on better business practices, aided partially as to financing by the benevolence of the federal government, and benefitting through the growth of GLF, which acted as a reliable and sympathetic wholesaler, the eighteen new buying cooperatives, as well as the two older ones, have done rather well. The recrudescence of cooperative purchasing has not been as spectacular as that of cooperative marketing, and it is impossible to assign its proper fraction of the yearly cooperative business of approximately one hundred million dollars annually. Nevertheless, it seems that cooperative buying has become at last a permanent part of the agricultural picture in New Jersey.[7] Ironically enough, as farming declines the cooperative stores rely to an increasing degree on purchases by suburbanites and nonfarm rural dwellers.

A truly great success story in farm cooperation in the larger area of which New Jersey is a part was the rise of GLF. The alphabetical designation of this organization was the result of an effort to shorten the name with which it was christened in 1920, that of Cooperative Grange League Federation, Inc. The official name did honor to the three sponsoring groups, the New York State Grange, the New York Farm Bureau, and the Dairymen's League. All three had been acting as buyers of supplies for their members, a function subordinate in each case to the main purpose of the organization. The formation of GLF was an almost spontaneous thing, and its success from the start was the result of advice, aid, and assistance from the parent groups. Except for Dairymen's League members in northwestern New Jersey, the farmers of this state had no part in the original forming of GLF, and growth in New Jersey was somewhat slow at first. By 1926, however, GLF had more than $2 million of "car door" business annually in New Jersey, more than $250,000 in sales through farm cooperatives, and about $8,000 in sales through local "buyer-agents." Three business principles of GLF perhaps explain its rapid expansion even during the Depression: (1) "one man, one vote"; (2) net earnings, except as used to hire capital, to be returned to cooperators as patronage refunds; and (3) flexibility which permitted working with other cooperatives and with retail farm supply dealers.[8]

An early example of GLF penetration in New Jersey was furnished in Hunterdon County. In 1921 a countywide supply cooperative was founded there with the blessing of the Hunterdon County Board of Agriculture. This group established a retail store in Flemington, which soon found it advantageous to use the then new GLF as a wholesaler. The relationship became so close that in 1928 GLF absorbed the Hunterdon County Farmers' Cooperative Association. The members of the latter became GLF members and its store became a GLF "service store," one of the first in New Jersey. Soon thereafter another was established at Clinton.[9] Flexibility of approach shown in Hunterdon was also being applied elsewhere in New Jersey. As GLF became one of the biggest manufacturers and suppliers of "open formula" mixed feeds for live-stock and poultry, a wholesaler on a large scale for seeds, fertilizers, in-secticides, foodstuffs, and farm supplies generally, and a considerable purchaser of farm grain and other produce, it used a number of new or almost new devices on the retail level. Local cooperatives became GLF retailers, and in a few cases, as with FCA, were aided enough through extension of credit so as to survive hard times. Service stores, which had proved practicable elsewhere, were established in New Jersey only after 1926, but their number soon grew, particularly in areas where local sup-ply cooperatives were having a hard time. In 1925 the practice, one new to cooperatives, was begun of selling to established private dealers, who became known as "agent buyers." Resented by some farmers at first as a compromise with the enemy, this new policy caught on very soon.[10] Through one device or another, GLF outlets became available in many farming communities of the state.

Increasing demand led to the building of a GLF feed mill at Borden-town in 1948 and a seed "plant" at the same place soon thereafter. Next to appear in New Jersey was a modern fertilizer plant at Yardsville, with mill-to-farm service. In recent years several bulk plants were established to furnish farmers, and to an increasing degree nonfarmers, with gaso-line, diesel fuel, heating oils, and other petroleum products. Already the largest supply cooperative in the United States, GLF expanded in 1964 by merging with Eastern States Farmers' Exchange, another regional cooperative of northern New York and New England, to form Agway, Inc.[11] The merger had no marked effect in New Jersey except as to labels and signboards, and this change, too, came almost without protest. GLF stores at Bridgeton, Clinton, Flemington, Englishtown, Little Falls, Somerville, and Washington became almost overnight Agway Coopera-tives. It seems a mark of the times that nearly all businesses which con-tinue must expand, and the regional cooperatives of the farmers have proven no exceptions. In New Jersey this development has been the means of bringing the savings made through mass purchasing and mass production to the individual farmer. These savings are now generally recognized as of more consequence than those which can be made in the retail field. The creation of such a mammoth complex as Agway would have been deemed impossible a few decades ago. Its development, which has come rather late to aid materially the small New Jersey portion of its membership, is indicative of how farmers have imbibed business prin-ciples.

Cooperation in the field of selling farm products in this period ran into even greater problems and complications than those in the field of buying.[12] Methods of attack included the formation of bargaining agencies, the creation of cooperatives actually handling farm produce as middlemen, and various combinations of the two. In general, marketing cooperatives have tended to specialize in one farm product or a number of related products. Regional rivalry has often been a factor in the formation of these cooperatives. Every improvement in transportation and every adoption of more efficient techniques elsewhere have reacted strongly on the farmers of New Jersey, an area of high production costs. Throughout the nation governmental action has been more effective in coping with market gluts than have the activities of cooperatives. However, only a relatively few New Jersey products have been much affected by federal legislation. It is understandable, then, that farmers here, having already tasted some of the benefits of cooperation, would turn to it for help in marketing. Cooperatives have not always been able to get effectively at the basic root of the trouble, but there can be no doubt that they have helped to some degree. And in one case, that of milk, they have played a part in bringing the state and federal governments into the picture.

Dairying, the most important single sector of New Jersey agriculture during most of this period, seemed a natural field for cooperative selling. There were, however, many serious difficulties. Ultimate markets were widely dispersed, and the largest ones were quite distant and were shared with producers of other states. For the most part, therefore, farm cooperatives must deal with a multitude of retailers. As to weapons, it was a great handicap that any withholding from the market of milk, which is highly perishable, would be, except under the best conditions, more ruinous to the farmers involved than to their customers. Despite these handicaps, milk cooperatives came to stay. Their story in New Jersey has had a triple plot. One narrative has concerned the dairy farmers of the northwestern part of the state, who were in and would remain in the New York City milkshed. The second has been that of the dairy farmers of the southwestern part, who sold and still sell to milk dealers of Philadelphia. The third narrative, with many subplots, has concerned the large central belt of the state, the farmers of which have produced a fair but diminishing part of the milk consumed in New Jersey's own booming urban areas. At the beginning of the period, that is, just after World War I, some milk was still being sold to condenseries and creameries, but their prices were consistently below those paid by dealers in fluid milk. They were, therefore, of little importance in providing an alternative market, and were, in fact, disappearing in New Jersey. Many areas in New York and Pennsylvania still converted milk into condensed and evaporated milk and into butter and cheese, but the New Jersey dairy industry could not afford to do so except in the case of troublesome seasonal surpluses. For the New Jersey dairy farmer in this era the only market of importance has been that for fluid milk.

The farmers of northern New Jersey and neighboring areas in New York had been involved since the 1880s in attempts to control prices of milk destined for New York City. However, the loosely organized bargaining agencies of the farmers were no match for the tight dealers' organization, the New York Milk Exchange. Failure of a five-day strike in 1898 presaged the inability of farmers to find relief through "unions" and "exchanges" during the next decade.[13] The first successful bargaining agency was the Dairymen's League, Inc., organized in 1907 by Grange leaders of New York and northwestern New Jersey. By 1910 the organization was functioning, but it was not until the favorable period of World War I that its weight was strongly felt. In 1916 after a two-week strike by the 15,000 league members, dealers buying from them were forced to pay $2.05 per hundredweight, a considerable increase in price. Within a year the organization included the producers of four-fifths of the milk of the milkshed. Some indication of the heartening effect of this development is shown in a letter of November 1917 in which a Hunterdon County dairy farmer wrote, "We had standing room only at the last meeting of the Dairymen's League." After American entry into World War I, milk strikes were averted through arbitration by the Federal Food Administration, which was resented by some farm leaders as being too pro-consumer. After the war, the lines were soon drawn between the league and the exchange, culminating in a victorious eighteen-day strike which nearly doubled the 1916 price. But the league, officials and members alike, considered it a very expensive victory, and one not likely to be repeated.[14]

Since March 1918 farm dairy leaders had been working out details of a new corporation, the Dairymen's League Cooperative Association. Conforming with a New York law of that year, the new organization would supplant the old league as a bargaining agency and would also acquire facilities for handling and selling milk for local cooperatives. In making contracts, the league would sell milk for its membership according to use, thus for the first time applying a classified price plan that would pool or blend the price to members, so that all producers of milk of like quality would receive the same price. The new league was fully organized and in business by May 1, 1921. For the several hundred dairy farmers of northwestern New Jersey who were concerned, as well as for many times as many in southeastern New York, the league's aggressive bargaining and its willingness to acquire milk plants and retail outlets brought a measure of stability to its members for a decade. After 1926 it was undoubtedly aided by an upturn of the economy and a rising demand for milk. In the early 1930s, however, an increase in production coincided with a declining demand, as unemployment in the cities increased. The league was able for a time to hold up the price of fluid milk, but the increasing sale at lower prices of surplus milk for manufacturing purposes brought down its blended price to a level where independent dealers with no such load to bear paid higher prices to selected farmers than the league could pay and sold milk retail at lower prices than could dealers buying from the league. A consequence was that the league membership, once three-fourths of all "eligible producers" in the New York City milkshed, fell gradually to one-third. A final effort to unify all milk producers of the milkshed under the league was made under the auspices of the New York Farm Bureau Federation in 1932, but failed. After this the farm leaders of the milkshed turned to government action for price support.[15]

The story for the Philadelphia milkshed was in many ways similar, though for reasons not clear there was less shouting and near violence. The dominant organization in this area, the Interstate Milk Producers' Association, also had its historic origins in the past. Sometime before 1890 a group of producer cooperatives had a central organization for sales and for operation of a plant to convert surpluses into saleable products. Twice reorganized and renamed, it became by 1900 the collective bargaining association for a group of local cooperatives too small to affect prices seriously. After the outbreak of World War I, the desperation of dairymen in a time of rapidly mounting costs brought a great increase in membership and improvement in the bargaining weight of the organization. Another reorganization in 1915, this time as a stock corporation, brought to it greater flexibility and more appeal to dairymen.[16]

In 1919 Interstate was able to initiate a basic-surplus plan by which dealers paid a pooled price, graduated on a quality basis, for fluid milk, but a smaller price for amounts produced above an individual "base" during spring months, when there was a surplus. Unlike the New York milkshed, this area was not troubled with year-round surpluses until 1926. In 1927, however, it was necessary to extend the base-surplus device for the whole year. During these years of relative prosperity, when Interstate was a successful bargaining agency, its membership included most of the dairy farmers of southwestern New Jersey. Since the dozen or so Philadelphia firms which dealt with the organization also delivered milk in New Jersey cities from Trenton to Atlantic City, the effect of the activities of Interstate were pervasive on the New Jersey side of the river. Unfortunately, the coming of the Great Depression brought the same insuperable difficulties in collective bargaining as in the New York milkshed. By early 1933, noncooperating dealers paying flat rates could pay

better prices to selected farmers than could those under the control of
Interstate, and could sell at cut-rate prices. As a result, there was an
almost immediate outcry, which brought milk control legislation by the
individual states, then by the federal government.[17]

Milk control legislation was passed by New York and New Jersey in
1933 and by Pennsylvania in 1934. The New Jersey law setting up a Milk
Control Board was devised by William B. Duryee, Secretary of the State
Department of Agriculture, who became its chairman during its initial
three and a half years. After that, the ties between the groups remained
close, and in 1949 the Milk Control Board was absorbed by the department. The Dairymen's League and Interstate, because of their numerical
weight and closeness to the situation, still had an important part in
determining the price paid to producers in their respective areas. In the
central part of New Jersey there soon appeared a new bargaining cooperative, the United Producers' Cooperative Association of New Jersey,
with offices in Trenton and functions similar to the Dairymen's League
and Interstate. As its influence grew, it rapidly pulled in most New
Jersey milk producers who did not belong to the league or Interstate,
and by actual count a majority of all the state's dairymen. In the nature
of the case, and especially since its membership was entirely within the
state, it became the most influential spokesman for the New Jersey industry. Whereas the acceptance of the permanency of milk control led
to the establishment of federal milk districts for the New York City area
of New York and the Philadelphia area of Pennsylvania in 1937, United
became a strong opponent of extension of federal milk orders into New
Jersey. Since New Jersey minimum retail prices were higher than those
of nearby states, New Jersey members of the league and Interstate received a "nearby differential" somewhat above the New York and Philadelphia prices. The arrangement worked fairly well for some years, and
was continued for nearly two decades. The situation was not one which
could last indefinitely, however, for out-of-state milk at cut-rate prices
appeared in New Jersey in larger and larger quantities.

In 1957 a federal New York-New Jersey Marketing Order extended
the New York federal milk district to include northern New Jersey.
Though many farmers received a somewhat reduced price, marketwide
pooling under federal orders put a stop to displacement of New Jersey
milk by out-of-state milk. In addition, New Jersey producers, led by
United, presented so ably the situation of New Jersey dairymen that a
differential in price was allowed which at least partially compensated
for the price squeeze in which they found themselves. Loss of this differential as a result of a court case at the end of 1966 became a grievance
for United members. Most dairymen of New Jersey had remained with

United, truly regarded as most representative of the state's dairy industry. In the early 1960s, United became more than a bargaining agency,
as it began and rapidly expanded a "procurement program" by which it
purchased and assembled the milk of members and sold it to dealers.
By the late 1960s, the loyalty of United members began to seem a little
pathetic under existing conditions. The base price of 1946 had increased
very little in two decades, and gains thereafter were too late and too small
to remedy the situation for either United or its members. Due to constantly rising costs, more than half of the United members went out of
business by 1970. In late 1971 United ceased operations. The Dairymen's
League absorbed nearly half of the approximately 350 producers still
on the United rolls at its demise. The others who continued in dairying
have joined Dairylea Cooperative and other groups selling milk within
New Jersey.

The New Jersey members of the Dairymen's League, at that time some
two or three hundred in number in a territory constituting the tail of
an enormous dog, welcomed the extension of the federal district in 1957.
In general, league members of the state, their numbers somewhat augmented and the area under their influence expanded, have remaind loyal
to their organization, which as the most important "operating cooperative" in the New York milkshed has had much influence in determining
milk prices for producers and consumers in that area.

Increase in size of the Philadelphia federal milk district waited until
late 1963. At that time, the area delineated by the Delaware Valley Milk
Marketing Order included eight South Jersey counties which had a significant dairying industry. Because of the inclusion of dairying districts
in northern Delaware and an extension of the district lines to include a
much larger area to the north and west of Philadelphia in Pennsylvania,
the amount of milk brought under the pooling arrangement was so great
as to bring down prices. The effect was a disastrous one for many of the
451 New Jersey dairymen placed under the Philadelphia order, and
within three years nearly two hundred dropped out of the Philadelphia
market. A score or so joined the more than two hundred South Jerseymen
who were already selling in the New York-New Jersey market, and some
of the others found local markets. But most of them, on the verge of
failure already, simply quit dairy farming. It was hoped by some that
changes in pricing practices which began in 1969 might save their market
for those still selling to Philadelphia, but it was evident that membership
in Interstate had not proved a firm anchor once bureaucratic pricing
policies were changed so that they no longer favored the high-cost New
Jersey corner of the Philadelphia milkshed.[18]

Inspired in part by hopes that they might again become effective in collective bargaining, the various state laws for milk control had encouraged the continuance of dairy cooperatives. When the federal government came into the picture, it too encouraged the formation and continuance of cooperative dairy associations. When it eventually became clear that regulation had bred greater regulation, the functions of the cooperatives were changed to fit the situation. They still represented their members, and to some extent nonmembers, in negotiations with handlers within the framework of state and federal regulations. In practice they became the strongest proponents of milk orders, and at the same time assumed the task of representing the whole dairy industry in dealing with the governments concerned. Lest cooperative members be placed in an unfair position as compared to nonmembers because of the costs of the services performed by their cooperatives, federal milk orders at first provided for "cooperative payments" from market equalization pools.[19] But such payments, already discontinued elsewhere earlier, were dropped in the New York-New Jersey marketing area in 1968. It is clear that, for the dairy industry of the area of which New Jersey is a part, cooperation and government control of prices have become inextricably involved. It would be difficult to imagine a situation involving one without the other, or, for that matter, a situation without both. At best, it would seem that the combination of the two approaches of cooperation and government regulation has postponed for a time the day when dairy barns and silos become a rarity on the New Jersey scene. But it is doubted that even the considerable increase in farm milk prices which began in 1970 can long delay the trend in that direction unless truly drastic steps are taken to cut costs and increase income for dairymen.

The story of cooperative selling in other fields has not been quite so complicated. During the three decades of enormous development of the poultry industry, cooperative selling of eggs and other poultry products, which had never been of great importance until that time, appeared suddenly and expanded rapidly, only to be deflated by the ruinous decline of the poultry industry after 1955. A survey of New Jersey cooperatives in 1926 mentioned only four that sold eggs. Two of them, in Hunterdon and Middlesex counties, were small informal retailing groups. A third was a pool for selling hatching eggs by breeders of Jersey Black Giant chickens. The fourth and most important, one that was still operating four decades later, was the Quality Egg Club at Vineland. Acting as a go-between for its 175 members and selected New York dealers anxious to have a quality product, it was the first cooperative bargaining association in the poultry field in New Jersey.[20] Another type of cooperative, the auction market, attempted to bring dealers to bid against one another. The first of these was the Flemington Auction Market Cooperative Association, sponsored by the Hunterdon County Poultry Association, advised by the New Jersey Department of Agriculture, and blessed by the Hunterdon County Board of Agriculture. Its first auction, held in a Flemington basement, sold only sixty cases of eggs of thirty dozens each, yet within five years it passed the million-dollar mark of gross annual sales.

The success of the Flemington Auction Market resulted in its being copied at Mount Holly and Vineland in 1931, at Hightstown in 1932, at Paterson in 1933, and at Hackettstown in 1941. At all of these there were auctions of livestock or vegetables, but their chief reason for existence, with the possible exception of the one at Hackettstown, was to maintain egg prices. At the height of their operations in the mid-1950s, the Flemington and Vineland auction markets together were selling a million cases of eggs annually, while the other four totaled nearly one-third of a million. Total membership of the six groups was more than four thousand. During the same period, the Quality Egg Club, always relatively small, was emulated by several other cooperative bargaining associations in the poultry field. Three of these were started at Toms River in 1933, 1941, and 1957, three at Lakewood in 1941, 1947, and 1950, two at Vineland in 1952 and 1957, and one at South Vineland in 1950. The total amount sold yearly in their heyday was somewhat greater than that of the auction markets, and total membership was some fifteen hundred. It was estimated that in 1955 the cooperative auction markets were selling 18 percent of New Jersey's eggs and the cooperative bargaining associations 24 percent. The decline which set in soon thereafter was a sudden one. By 1967 the auction at Mount Holly had closed and that at Hightstown had turned to fruit and vegetables. The auctions at Hackettstown and Flemington now acted only as assembly points and price-setters for poultrymen delivering eggs and for dealers wishing to purchase. With the great decrease in egg production, most of the others closed their doors or greatly curtailed or changed their operations.[21]

Cooperative selling of fruits and vegetables has a long history in New Jersey, but its important period is the recent one. The first fruit cooperative in the United States was founded at Hammonton in Atlantic County in 1869, and for three full decades it marketed the fruits, berries, and sweet potatoes of its members. Like all such cooperatives before 1900, its functions were the assembling, packing, and sending to market the products of its members.[22] Never a large operation, the Hammonton Fruit Union sold $46,000 worth of fruit in 1886 for its 233 members and operated a store which handled supplies. A patronage dividend of 5 percent was paid to its members in that year. One of its greatest services was its distribution, using boys on bicycles, of its *Daily Bulletin* with market information. The success story came to an end in 1897, partly because of "mismanagement and too much credit," and partly because of the loss of a $20,000 lawsuit brought by an injured clerk.[23]

In the twentieth century it seemed to many that efficient marketing cooperatives could perform such valuable services for members as the applying of standard grading, arranging transportation, keeping abreast of market news, finding reliable commission merchants, and making savings on selling costs. Numerous marketing cooperatives, often aided and advised by the Bureau of Markets, had been attempted by 1928, but the rate of survival was low. Some examples will illustrate. A potato-growing group started at Robbinsville in 1917 lasted only two years because of lack of patronage. Another at Hightstown and Freehold lost heavily in 1922 as a result of poor grading and overpaying its members. It closed disastrously and a successor cooperative in the same area only broke even in 1923. Thereupon, the group concluded that cooperation wasn't worth the bother. A sweet potato cooperative in Ocean County in 1922 disbanded for similar reasons. A successful venture, however, was the cranberry cooperative, an older group which was reorganized in 1919. With an article so scarce, for natural reasons, it could hardly go wrong. One of the great disappointments was that of the canhouse tomato growers, who tried to organize a cooperative bargaining association. In the face of the adamant attitude of the canners, disloyalty of members, and underselling by Maryland growers, the attempt failed completely.[24]

Auction markets for fruits and vegetables, though known to some degree elsewhere earlier, first came to New Jersey in 1928. The one established at Cedarville in that year sold over $150,000 worth of strawberries, peas, beans, lima beans, onions, and peppers in its initial effort, saving its members an estimated $30,000. Within five years it was doing over $500,000 worth of business annually. A similar market at Rosenhayn sold approximately $100,000 worth of peppers, beans, and berries for its members each year during its early years. Other cooperative markets at Landisville, Williamstown, and Beverly got off to a slower start in 1929, running into the usual problems of attracting buyers and coping with competition.[25] By 1936 fourteen cooperative auction markets for fruits and vegetables had been started, of which nine were still operating at the end of that year. All of them except those at Beverly and Hightstown were in the southern one-fifth of the state, in the intensive vegetable and berry area. Whereas the two original auction markets for fruits and vegetables had sold 160,000 packages in 1928, the nine sold over 3 million in 1936. In the latter year, approximately half of the cucumbers of the state, one-third of the peppers and lima beans, and one-fifth of the cantaloupes, string beans, green peas, and strawberries were sold cooperatively at auction.[26]

Cooperative auctioning remained an important marketing device during the next two decades, for a time with mounting sales totals, and three cooperative auction markets for fruits and vegetables were still functioning in their original form in 1970 at Beverly, Camden, and Trenton. But sale by auction is a time-consuming device for both buyer and seller, and the drift away from it is understandable. Gradually at first, and more rapidly after 1955, cooperative groups found other methods of selling, usually by consignment to city dealers, either with or without agreed prices. The other important services of cooperatives, including advertising, promotion, grading, processing, packaging, storage (sometimes refrigerated), and shipping were retained to a greater or lesser degree. Including the three auction market groups and the two specialized cooperatives for cranberries and blueberries, there were eighteen functioning fruit and vegetable cooperatives in New Jersey in 1965. Their sales for the previous crop year had reached the impressive total of 22½ million dollars. This was, of course, only a relatively small part of total fruit and vegetable production. But it is fairly obvious that the cooperatives have helped the growers who need it most, and that their total effect on the market has been a beneficial one.[27]

Cooperation has in recent years extended into the field of farm banking, with Farm Credit Service offices at Bridgeton, Flemington, Freehold, Newton, and Moorestown and Production Credit Associations at Moorestown, Blairstown, and Bridgeton. The Garden State Service Cooperative Association at Trenton and the Glassboro Service Association have become large recruiters of Puerto Rican and, more recently, of Mexican-American labor for their members. In addition a number of cooperatives provide members with various services not already mentioned. In a sense, too, the associations representing various sectors of agriculture are cooperative ventures for particular purposes. In 1970 there were about forty groups representing New Jersey farmers of specific types. A half dozen groups were concerned with breeds of cattle and nine with horses. There were one or more associations representing peach orchardists, small fruit growers, florists, horticulturists, potato growers, sweet potato growers, poultrymen, nurserymen, vegetable growers, cranberry growers, beekeepers, raisers of rabbits, flower gardeners, growers of Christmas trees, and cultivators of lawn sod. In times past, New Jersey farmers shunned all ties with their fellows. This was no longer the case in the middle decades of the twentieth century.

The subsidization and regulation of portions of American agriculture by the federal government since 1933 have had very uneven and haphazard results in New Jersey. The programs here have had no direct effect on such specialized branches of farming as orcharding and vegetable growing, unless potatoes, for which there was a program for a time, be regarded as a vegetable. New Jersey dairymen, except as they benefitted directly from regulation of milk price levels and indirectly from programs for butter and cheese, have been affected adversely by federal programs, rather than otherwise, at least in the short run. Nearly all New Jersey dairymen are net purchasers of feedstuffs; any policy that raises feed prices can hardly be regarded by them as helpful. Poultrymen, except for the relatively few who have raised their own grain, have been even more adversely affected. The diminishing number of truly general farmers have been the greatest recipients of federal subsidies. At the bottom of the Great Depression, AAA (Agricultural Adjustment Administration) payments brought a welcome infusion of cash, but not in amounts as great as usually imagined. Even in 1935, after the program recovered from a slow start, the federal government pumped only one-third of a million dollars into New Jersey agriculture, including soil conservation payments. Other cash farm income in that year totaled $72 million. In 1939, when federal payments totaled nearly $1.5 million dollars, their proportion of agricultural income was only 1.5 percent.[28] During World War II, government measures in net effect probably curbed rather than helped the profits of a suddenly prosperous agriculture.

Government subsidies immediately after the war benefitted farmers of the state on an even more unequal basis than before, and the amounts were not large in total. In 1950, when total cash farm income was over $293 million, government payments were less than $1 million. During the next decade, government payments trebled, while total farm income did not vary greatly from year to year. Due largely to the federal feed grain and wheat programs, subsidies in the 1960s were somewhat larger, but still only a minor fraction of farm income. Total government payments between 1962 and 1968 varied between $4.1 million and $4.8 million annually. In 1966, the highest year to that time, something less than 1.7 percent of farm receipts originated with the federal government.[29]

An interesting aspect of the feed grain and wheat programs has been the making of government payments for keeping idle some land that would have been idle anyway. In most cases the recipient has been a farmer, often an older man staying with his land to the last, but undoubtedly in some cases a person with no close agricultural ties who hopes for land developments more profitable than agriculture. Inadvertently the programs helped landowners keep open space, something few people would decry. Changes in the feed grain program of 1971, requiring that even the smallest owners must have part of their acreage planted in order to qualify for government payments, saved the federal government a small outlay, presumably needed for better purposes, but worked a hardship for a group already hurt by mounting property taxation and inflation costs.[30]

New Jersey farmers at the present time differ considerably as to their opinion of the philosophy behind government "intervention" and as to their assessment of the net results. From a short-time point of view, and possibly from a longer, many of them believe that they have been hurt by policies which have kept up the price level of feed grains. There is, however, general, though not total, approval of the work of the Soil Conservation Service. In many parts of the state its projects for erosion control, improved pastures, stock ponds, and so forth, have brought tangible benefits. It should be remembered, however, that payments toward approved projects are contingent upon similar or larger payments on the part of the farmer "cooperator." In general, the net effects of federal programs in New Jersey have been much less important than those of developments closer home.

Local taxes, municipal and county, have always been a subject of complaint by New Jersey farmers. In the modern period there has been considerable justification for their arguments that they, far more than any other economic group, have had their means of livelihood taxed. In a state in which horse-and-buggy-day boundaries have persisted and in which until recently broad-based taxes on a statewide basis have been avoided as a plague, real estate taxes have varied greatly from area to area. Furthermore, the custom of giving farm property low valuations for tax purposes persisted later in some areas than in others. The tax burden on farmers, therefore, has not been uniform, but the general tendency to increase it everywhere as population increased and as demand for public services grew became alarming. An attempted remedy, which might logically have come decades earlier, was the Farmland Assessment Act of 1964. According to this legislation, plots of land five acres or larger in size with gross sales of $500 per year might qualify as functioning farms and, in such cases, be assessed for tax purposes at a "value which such land has for agricultural or horticultural use." However, in case of change in land use, "roll back taxes" might be assessed for current and two previous years.

This act had been made possible by an amendment to the state constitution. Devised by representatives of the Department of Agriculture, the College of Agriculture, and other spokesmen for the farmers, the Farmland Assessment Amendment had been referred to the voters of the state in September 1963, after a stirring campaign in its behalf in which agricultural interests were joined by conservationists, by urban and suburban organizations, and by most of the newspapers of the state. The compelling aim of the chief sponsors of this legislation was to "revitalize"

New Jersey agriculture. But the appeal to the urban voters was that such legislation would encourage the keeping of speculative land, so often a blight on the landscape, in farms until needed for actual building. In rural and suburban areas, taxpayers were hopeful that small farmers, now able to qualify for lower taxes, would stay in business and thus delay the building of small houses on small lots, the owners of which almost never pay their way as far as public services are concerned. The referendum figures in the election showed some interesting results. A million voters subscribed to the idea, while 419,000 were opposed. The affirmative vote in the state was thus nearly 71 percent. Only two counties, Hudson and Passaic, had fewer than 65 percent, and none had over 80 percent. Most of the people of the state had thus wholeheartedly endorsed a plan which promised them more "green acres and open spaces" for the time being. Attempts since 1965 to change the law, and especially to increase the amount of farm produce necessary to qualify, have not gained much backing thus far, though sometimes it has been rather noisy. Naturally the chief objectors have been nonfarmers of rural and suburban municipalities.[31] The New Jersey Farm Bureau believes that its lobbying prevented introduction into the state legislature in 1969 of a bill that would have required an income limitation for those benefitting from the law.[32]

The 1964 legislation provided for a State Farmland Evaluation Advisory Committee to determine "fair" values of farmland in various parts of the state, based on "productive capabilities." In practice this group had suggested assessments for "cropland harvested," "cropland pastured," "permanent pasture," and "woodland" in five soil-group categories for each county. The valuations suggested for the very best croplands in 1967 varied from $312 per acre in Hunterdon and Cape May counties to $720 in the four northeastern counties. The range meant, of course, that in practice some consideration had been given to location. But no land in typical farm areas was valued as high as $500, and poorer croplands were significantly lower. Permanent pastures and woodlands were in all cases given quite low valuations. In practice this legislation has encouraged the leasing of speculative land to actual farmers at reasonable rentals and the creation and preservation of tiny farms operated and often owned by persons making part of their living at occupations other than farming. The easing of their tax burden has also made it possible for some farmer-owners to continue their operations or at least hold the line until they can benefit as a result of spiraling land values.

The alacrity with which farmers have made application for tax adjustment under the Farmland Assessment Act in areas where population pressure has increased taxation markedly is an indication that the legislation has answered a need. More than three-fourths of the farmers in

Monmouth, Middlesex, Mercer, and Hunterdon counties had applied by 1968, about half in Somerset, Morris, and Warren, and more than a third in Burlington. Since that time the proportion has increased in these areas. A lag in Sussex County in the extreme northwest, in Ocean County on the coast, and in the block of six counties in South Jersey, has been indicative that the tax burden in these areas has been less, but even here there has been a recent increase in applications.[33]

15

Mechanization and Automation

The appearance and rapid adoption of agricultural machinery in the nineteenth century had been hailed as an important break with the past. There was considerable justification for this point of view. As we have seen, many of the new devices and machines used man's strength more efficiently and the more important ones literally substituted horse power for man power. And toward the end of the century there were harbingers of the coming of mechanical power, which would be one of the most outstanding factors in the agricultural revolution after 1917. The earlier uses first of the steam engine and later of the internal combustion motor were of importance, but it was only with the development of the tractor that the supremacy of the horse was endangered. Steam tractors were already a part of the rural scene by the 1890s, though their use was limited, and by 1910 gasoline tractors were being exhibited at county fairs and were being tried out hesitantly by an occasional farmer. After the outbreak of World War I, the scarcity of farm labor and the shortage of good horses at any price caused a rapid increase of tractor sales. A Hunterdon County auctioneer reported selling a carload of western horses at an average price of $250 in 1915.[1] For the cost of two or three of these "plugs" a farmer could buy a tractor. It should be noted that by this time the word *tractor* in popular parlance meant the type powered by an internal combustion motor. After our entry into the war, the changeover came more rapidly than anyone could have foretold.[2]

The tractor of that day was a clumsy thing by present standards, with heavy steel wheels in front and heavier ones with large cleats behind. Such a machine required much room to turn, resulting in wastefully large turnrows at the ends of fields, and it was helpless in mud and slush. But it moved rapidly in comparison to a team of horses, it required no periods of rest, and consumed fuel only when working. It was a great labor saver on the hardest tasks, but of course no one dreamed that it would ever more than supplement the horse. Like all new contraptions, tractors

228

broke down at inconvenient times in early years, but in due course they became considerably more reliable. A great step forward was the adoption of rubber tires, tentatively by 1930 and universally by 1940. The creation of smaller tractors in the 1930s was a boon for the truck farmer and market gardener, and later enabled many a small farmer to hang on in the face of the trend toward larger farms. The tractor of 1940 had most of the characteristics of that of today, although it was not nearly as "sophisticated." During the next decade, widespread adoption first of the power takeoff and then of hydraulic controls made the tractor a marvel of versatility for farmers who still remembered the farm horse, by then a rare animal indeed. Every year brought new and improved models, until eventually tractors came in such a variety of sizes and shapes that a type was available for almost any imaginable farm task. A substantial number of today's tractors, invariably the larger ones, use diesel fuel instead of gasoline. During these decades of change, pulling contests at county fairs were more and more often between tractors rather than between teams of horses. A poor performer was still called a "dog," however.

The farm family of the old day had been dependent on sleek road horses to keep it in touch with civilization. The early years of the twentieth century brought tremendous changes, as first main roads and then lesser ones were surfaced, in part at the farmer's expense. The farmer who purchased one of the many "devil machines" on the market by this time found himself suddenly much closer to the rest of mankind. This development was indeed heady fare, and it is little wonder that a substantial part of the farm population was soon on wheels. There was resistance, of course, but many a farmer, at first bitter at his neighbor for scaring his horses, found himself with a new viewpoint once he drove his own automobile. In any case, almost no farm families remained in the horse and buggy age beyond one generation. The automobile thus became a part of the life of the farmer as he became more peripatetic. But a greater, or at least a more direct, contributor to his livelihood was the farm truck. Just as his tractor replaced his work horses in the field, the truck took the place of teams and wagons on the road. The pickup truck, known before World War I, became increasingly common on farms in the 1920s. In general, the types of trucks used by others fitted the needs of the farmer well enough. As the truck was further developed, it appeared on farms in many forms. Only in the case of the bulk-milk tank truck has a special type been developed for farm use.

A newer kind of farm power was electricity, important also in lighting up the farmer's world at night. In this case, demand developed far more rapidly than supply, for only a few farmers had access to electricity from power companies at the beginning of the period. Very few larger farms had home electric plants even before World War I, and quite a number

added them soon thereafter, particularly dairy farms needing power for
the newly invented milking machines. Eventually electric power companies, prodded by the federal government, realized the potentialities of the
new market. As a result, rural electrification has been one of the most
spectacular developments in New Jersey farm country during the last four
decades. For many farmers, the electric motor has become almost indispensable, and all sectors of agriculture share in the need for cheap, effective light. On many a New Jersey farm the failure of electric current is
more to be dreaded than a hailstorm.

The general adoption of the internal combustion motor and electricity
went hand in hand with tremendous changes in farm plant. Nowhere has
urban, or perhaps I should say suburban, influence been more marked
than in the building of country homes. As the twentieth century farm
wife became truly a modern woman, new architectural forms, including
the ranch house and the split-level, were brought to the countryside, thus
sacrificing living space for convenience. Just as marked has been the adoption of modern facilities and gadgets, many of them made possible only
by the coming of electricity to the farm. Working buildings on the farm
were also gradually transformed. In the new buildings, structural steel,
sheet metal, concrete cinder blocks, and asphalt became important materials, with plastics beginning to break into the field after 1960. As with
the farmhouse, efficient space utilization was important. The requirements for feed storage had become much less as the result of the baling
of hay. The barrack, the last mark of Dutch influence, largely disappeared
by the 1930s, and the tremendous hay mows built in the nineteenth century were only partly filled. New hay sheds, built of poles and sheet metal,
and only one or two stories in height, were far more efficient.

With modern facilities and improved efficiency, more cattle and hogs
could be taken care of in less space than formerly, and the same was true
to an even greater degree for poultry. Garages rapidly replaced horse
barns and wagon sheds, but the new machinery required additional space
for storage. Silos, the unmistakable sign of a dairy farm, were often built
in clusters and were sometimes of that startling blue color which indicates
a lining of glass and a fantastic cost. On the other hand, a windmill became a rare sight indeed. Buildings constructed in the days of general
farming for such special purposes as the do-it-yourself processing of meats,
fruits, vegetables, and feed grains, disappeared or were remodeled. In
their places came several entirely new buildings. On dairy farms appeared
loafing barns, "milking parlors," and feeding shelters. Vegetable and
potato farmers built unpretentious sheds for sorting and storage. Especially after 1930, long tiers of poultry houses marked the great expansion
of a new industry. Never beautiful, many of them have become, with the
decline of egg production, unlovely ruins awaiting the bulldozer. The

typical farmstead of today presents an odd mixture of the old and the new. Only in rare instances has the process of evolution improved it as to beauty. In all fairness, however, it should be said that the greatest despoilers of rural beauty have been the electric power companies, with their thousands of miles of poles with wires, accentuated here and there by an unsightly transformer.

The equipment of the farmstead has undergone an almost complete transformation during this period. The elaborate array of goods and gear of the early 1900s in part disappeared, and in part was augmented by the tools and equipment which went with the new power revolution. The twentieth century farmer was not a jack-of-all-trades in the earlier sense of the expression, but was forced by circumstances to be a handyman and something of a mechanic. The new equipment which gradually filled the buildings of the modern farm would have astonished the farmer of an earlier day, and perhaps would have driven him to despair. The use of electricity brought wiring, motors, and lights. Water systems used piping, tanks, and drinking devices of various kinds to furnish livestock or poultry with a constant supply of water. The new dairy buildings acquired armaments of laborsaving devices for efficient handling of livestock, feed, and manure, and the poultry plant gradually became almost as elaborate. The farmstead in truth became a small factory where improvements in techniques led to a constant replacement of obsolescent equipment. As for fencing the land, barbed and woven wire still ruled, but the flexible and efficient electric fence became common on livestock farms for temporary fencing. Steel posts largely replaced those of Osage orange, though some farmers used posts of lighter wood chemically treated to delay rotting. The farmer of today has become a true pragmatist as regards his profession. His working equipment has become more and more costly, as it has replaced labor that is even more expensive. He uses his capital and credit to the limit, and asks in return that his gadgets be really functional. No one is more impatient of built-in obsolescence so far as working equipment is concerned than the farmer. But like most other people, he seems willing to tolerate this modern blight in his automobile and household equipment, apparently applying here the same fatalism with which he regards the weather.

At the beginning of the present century, the farmer of New Jersey, using from half a dozen to a dozen horses, was able, by putting in long hours, to plant, tend, and harvest a sizable acreage of each of the main crops of his area. His investment in machinery was high compared with that in the past, and constant replacement had brought up his overhead costs considerably. But any operational figures of that period eventually seemed quite small in retrospect. Once he had acquired a tractor and the equipment that went with it, both the farmer's level of capital outlay and his scale of annual expenses mounted rapidly. To his machinery costs were added those entailed by modernizing his farm plant. The money costs of these changes, which put New Jersey farmers deeply into debt for the first time in history, was justified on the grounds of saving labor, speeding up performance, and expanding operations. The new machines of any given date were marvels of efficiency, and when they wore out they were replaced with new machines still more efficient. From time to time, inventions made one piece of equipment or another obsolete before it was worn out. For example, the farmer who bought for the first time a tractor with power takeoff and hydraulic controls must purchase entirely new machines for many operations in order to utilize the new inventions. To the modern New Jersey farmer after 1940 his economic life doubtless seemed a merry-go-round. It was certain, however, that he could not get off it and still remain a farmer.

We have seen how the speeding up of operations even earlier sometimes led to breaks with tradition and to the upsetting of ancient myths. The evolution of new farm equipment in the modern period went hand in hand with drastic changes in techniques, some of them small but many others of real consequence. These statements are particularly applicable to the culture of corn. The delay between the plowing of the land and the putting in of the corn crop was once a considerable one, the theory being that it was good to give the soil a chance to settle. But in recent decades the time allowed has become shorter and shorter, until now many a farmer applies a new rule, "Plow and plant." The old belief that corn ground must be well pulverized before being planted has also been disproved, and as of the present time the soil between the rows is often left rough until the new crop is cultivated. Not only is labor thus saved, but the germination of weed seeds is retarded in the middles. Several implements once used in preparing corn ground are no longer necessary, but the rule of the disc harrow, usually pulled in tandem, is now complete. Hydraulic controls on the tractor make it possible to carry a pair of disc harrows from field to field behind the tractor without disconnecting. The corn planter has evolved into a beautiful piece of equipment, planting four or more rows at once and at the same time applying a "side dressing" of fertilizer to each row. Supplemental equipment may drop a "band" of "preemergent herbicide" dust near the rows or broadcast a spray that will retard the germination of weed seeds or kill the newly sprouted weeds.

Even before the general use of the multirow planters the check system had been discarded in favor of "drilled" rows. Since it was no longer possible to cultivate the corn crossways of the field, and thus eliminate the weeds that appeared in the rows between the stalks, improved cultivators were developed. As rubber tires came into general use for tractors in the late 1930s, their use in the fields of growing corn became practical. The practice of having the cultivator mounted on the tractor itself eventually became almost universal. However, with the rapid introduction of herbicides during the past two decades weeds became a minor problem. The furor that has developed regarding the possible harmful side effects of these poisons has not yet worried the average farmer very much. A recent development is that of having tanks of liquid nitrogen and other "booster" fertilizers for application at cultivation time. With better cultivation and the use of herbicides, it has become unnecessary for the farmer to cultivate the crop more than once or twice during the growing season. (It is interesting to note that this operation is still commonly called "plowing corn.")

The handpicking or husking of corn became a lost art in the 1930s and 1940s as mechanical pickers were perfected and widely adopted. More recently, the field sheller is eliminating the picker on many farms. Especially interesting have been the changes in the ensiling of corn. As a result of increasing mechanization, the once laborious task has become one which can be taken in stride. In the early decades of this century, gangs of men cut the stalks and piled them for collection by wagon crews. A combined cutter and blower at the silo converted the fodder into ensilage and blew it up into the silo. The corn binder, adopted rather slowly in New Jersey, eventually eliminated all hand cutting, and it in turn gave way to the field chopper, which cuts up the ensilage in the field and drops it into a wagon or truck for transportation to a blower at the silo. In truth, the high-quality cattle feed thus manufactured has never been touched by human hands. The use of the field chopper has made it possible to chop into ensilage other crops than corn, including alfalfa and soy beans.

The changes in the techniques for growing and handling small grains and grasses (as all hay crops are still called) have been less spectacular, but still considerable in the aggregate. In order to save time and to use machinery most effectively, the delay between plowing and sowing again in this case has been largely eliminated. Since the soil must be well tilled, the versatile disc harrow, refined versions of the spike-toothed and spring-toothed harrows, and various new types of pulverizers have come into full play. The grain drill has been gradually beautified through the decades and, more significantly, has been perfected for its triple function of sowing the grain to one desired depth, sowing the grass seed to another, and applying one or more kinds of fertilizer. For harvesting the grain, the header or combine, long known in the drier areas of the West, made an appearance here in the 1920s and was soon manufactured in small enough and flexible enough versions to use in New Jersey fields. This development has made antiques of both the grain binder and the thresher.

The latest combine promoted by machinery manufacturers is self-propelled, rather than being dependent on a tractor for power. With some adjustment, it can be used for husking and shelling corn in the field as well as for threshing small grains and soybeans.

In the making of hay, there have also been many changes. A long cutting bar mounted on the tractor itself nearly eliminated the mower by 1940, and the side delivery rake eventually made the sulky rake and sweep rake of 1900 as obsolete as the broadax. During the late nineteenth century the hay baler had been taken to the fields, but the farmer had to wait until the 1930s for the "pickup baler," which scooped up the hay directly from the windrow. By 1940 the baler was entirely automatic in action. The first portable balers had used baling wire for tying, but by 1960 most of them were using twine. The ejector, patented in 1947 and still not accepted by a majority of the farmers by 1972, tosses the bales into a wagon pulled behind the baler. At the storage building, a motor-driven conveyor carries the bales to the place where they are wanted. As yet someone must still pull the loaded wagons from the field to the barn with a tractor, and must place the bales on the conveyor and stack them in place by hand.

The growing of vegetables and small fruits, less often referred to as "truck farming" than was once the case, has been traditionally considered the most laborious kind of farming. The development of small tractors and specialized tillage implements, already common by the 1930s, did something to reduce the work involved in planting and cultivating these crops, but harvesting still remained for the most part a hand operation. Mechanization of harvesting came only gradually and piecemeal, the most spectacular developments being recent ones. In the case of the digging of potatoes, the earliest improvement was the use of better diggers for the unearthing and spreading of the potatoes, which were then picked up by hand. During the past four decades, the victory has been made almost complete with the appearance and improvement of mechanical potato harvesters. The most recent one is often referred to as a "potato combine." This machine digs up the potatoes in the rows, along with a considerable quantity of earth, and elevates them by conveyor belt to a series of rollers where they are separated from the loose soil and vines. The potatoes are then carried by conveyors past workers who ride on the machine and who inspect and sort the potatoes before they are carried away and dropped into boxes. This method of harvesting results in less crop injury than any previous method, including digging by hand. These machines are also being used, though to a lesser extent, for digging the delicate-skinned sweet potato. Devices somewhat similar in nature have come into use for harvesting onions and some of the root crops.

A problem here is that whatever is said in 1972 about some of the newest mechanical marvels will soon be outdated. A number of new harvesting machines are already a success, while others are in various stages of experimentation. Since about 1963 New Jersey's cranberry crop has been for the most part "water harvested," making a collector's item of the old cranberry scoop. The harvest in this case is a spectacular one. Mechanical beaters are pushed through the flooded bogs, knocking the cranberries into the water. By one development they are then floated to a particular part of the bog for rescue by men with rakes; by another they are pushed onto conveyor belts which have their ends in the water. The berries are trucked immediately to drying sheds, where they remain briefly before being sorted and "processed," that is, put into containers for market. Since 1967 robot pickers have been tried out for the harvesting of blueberries, and it now seems that they are a complete success. Machines for shaking peaches, apples, cherries, and plums, though still not entirely perfected, came into practical use in 1971. Pea and bean harvesters have been generally adopted. Tomato harvesters, modeled after those of California, were being tested in 1969 and 1970, but 1971 was the first year in which they were much used. In all probability they will largely replace handpickers by the time a truly one-crop tomato variety for New Jersey has been developed. Several of the new experimental machines for other crops are quite selective, thus obviating the need for new varieties. For example, a cucumber picker takes only "pickles" of the right length, and one type of asparagus harvester measures all stalks with its electric eye, then cuts only those of sufficient height. In 1971 for the first time, a considerable portion of the asparagus crop was harvested by machine. Hard to imagine until seen is a new machine which measures electrically the firmness of lettuce heads and harvests only those ready to go to market. It is increasingly obvious that many fruits and vegetables will remain in New Jersey only if their culture and harvest is mechanized.

A word should be said about home gardeners, who are more numerous than most readers realize. They, too, want machines for their heaviest work. In fact, the mechanization of home gardening has made this hobby a rather costly one, in part because ownership of a garden tractor has become as much a status symbol in some parts of Suburbia as that of a riding rotary lawn mower. The day may well soon arrive when the sight of a pudgy amateur gardener or groundsman putting one or the other of these machines through its gyrations from a seat safely above the dirt no longer seems a little ludicrous. In any case, he already refers to his operations as "farming." The garden tractor comes in many forms, and the tillage and other implements for use with it are truly multitudinous. The rotary lawn mower, a fairly new development, is a cousin of the farmer's "bush hog," an implement which, when pulled and powered by a tractor, makes short work of brush and briars and even of small trees.

A full catalogue of the new machines that have been accepted by the farmers of New Jersey would make a formidable list. Some of the devices, such as the milking machines of the dairymen, the spraying equipment of the orchardists, the automatic feeders and waterers and conveyor-belt egg collectors of the poultrymen, and the many machines of the vegetable grower are highly specialized. Many others, including electric pumps, manure and litter spreaders, and equipment for overhead irrigation, are more generally useful. There is every indication that the number of kinds of equipment will multiply as the trend toward specialization continues. This is particularly true for types of agriculture which have nothing to do with field crops or livestock. As farmers get farther and farther away from traditional farming, they rapidly evolve new methods and adopt new devices strange indeed to those who have changed less. Yet, despite their differences in practices and outlook, New Jersey farmers generally have been forced by circumstances to plow back their profits into plant and equipment and in most cases to borrow heavily in order to keep up with their neighbors here and their competitors elsewhere.[3]

Increasing mechanization has gone hand in hand with marked changes in agricultural labor. The decline in size of farm families and the increasing emphasis on education of farm youth led to a greater dependence on hired labor. For obvious reasons, the workers in greatest demand, both regular and seasonal hands, have been those skillful with machines and with a talent for keeping them running. On the other hand, the newer branches of agriculture, and in particular vegetable growing and poultry raising, could utilize many workers with little or no background in agriculture and even without much knowledge of the English language. In the nature of the case, these were mostly seasonal workers, and New Jersey, for the first time on a considerable scale, became an annual importer of itinerant labor and thereby acquired all the economic and social problems attendant upon such a development. As happened in every area with a similar situation, both the wages paid to seasonal workers and the conditions under which they lived caused first a public outcry and then belated legislation bringing minimum wages and state supervision.

It was estimated that the farm labor cost in New Jersey in 1919 was $18 million, nearly triple that of 1899 and double that of 1909, and about the same as what it would be during the Depression years. The leading counties were Burlington and Monmouth, with about $2.5 million each. Salem and Gloucester followed with approximately half as much, and Cumberland farmers paid out nearly $1 million. The figures indicate that already vegetable growing had pushed ahead of other sectors of agriculture in the hiring of labor. Morris, Middlesex, Mercer, Hunterdon, Bergen, Somerset, and Warren, all counties with considerable dairying, poultry raising, and general farming, ranged downward from $750,000 to $500,000 each. A survey in 1929 showed that farmers of the state hired laborers for 5,636,000 days. The three leading counties, all vegetable growers, were Burlington with 940,000 days, Cumberland with 520,000, and Monmouth with 495,000.[4] In 1955 the year-round average number of hired workers on New Jersey farms was 24,000 compared with 34,000 family workers. The years of rapid agricultural change which followed brought the average of hired workers down to 19,000 and the number of family workers to 10,000 by 1969.[5] Average farm labor wages by the month climbed from $180 in 1960 to $225 in 1966. Average hourly rates rose in the same years from $1.16 to $1.38.[6] By legislation of 1965 and 1966, farm workers in New Jersey over eighteen years of age must be paid minimum hourly wages of $1.25 in 1967, $1.40 in 1968, and $1.50 after January 1, 1969, including a fair value for food and lodgings, if furnished.[7] A bill to increase the state minimum wage to $2.00 per hour and to remove all agricultural differentials was defeated in 1969, but a bill of similar tenor became law in 1972.[8] Traditionally, many of the seasonal agricultural workers "migrate" into New Jersey by automobile annually, but the proportion brought in from Puerto Rico under contract and returned after the growing season was on the increase until very recently. In 1971, however, the 8,000 Puerto Ricans of previous years declined to 6,400, while the number of Mexican-Americans from the Southwest, brought in with similar wage guarantees and fringe benefits, rose rapidly to nearly 9,000.[9]

The drastic decline in the number of agricultural laborers in the 1960s is in part due to the decline of some sectors of agriculture, and in particular poultry raising, but a more important cause, especially as regards the production of fruit and vegetables, has been the development of machines. Farmers near the breaking point as to operating profits simply cannot afford the additions to their labor bill brought by wage increases. Their alternative to quitting, if they can raise the capital, is to mechanize still further, hoping that the costly machinery will pay for itself by eliminating field hands. It has been predicted that soon most of the few farm laborers remaining will be skilled workers with considerable mechanical ability.[10]

16

Modern Livestock Developments

The displacement of the farm workhorse, the faithful servant of New Jersey agriculture for more than two centuries, came with surprising rapidity. There were nearly 100,000 horses and mules in the state in 1900, and still three-fourths that many in 1920.[1] During these years the place of Dobbin seemed secure enough, though most farmers purchased their replacements rather than raising them. In fact, the annual outlay of New Jersey farmers for western, Canadian, and other horses from areas where they were still raised was a much-regretted drain on farm income. To some extent it explains the eagerness with which farmers purchased tractors, automobiles, and trucks when they became sufficiently reliable and reasonably priced. The rapid replacement began in the early 1920s, and by 1940 the few thousand horses of the state were entirely supplemental to machines. It must be remembered that at the same time there was an almost complete outmoding of all the harness, vehicles, machinery, and other paraphernalia that went with the use of horses. A very few working animals were retained here and there for various reasons. As late as 1961 there were nearly 500 workhorses and nearly 300 mules in the state, most of them used in South Jersey for asparagus growing. Even here work animals are gradually being replaced by machines today.

There have always been, of course, establishments where race horses were kept and trained, and where, quite often, racing animals were bred. The old reason given for encouraging racing was the "improvement of the breed." A new reason has been that the state of New Jersey, highly elated to find something to tax without recriminations on the part of those taxed, since 1940 has treated "betting on the horses" as no longer a sin but a public benefaction. Most of New Jersey's nearly 15,000 Thoroughbreds, quarter horses, and standard breeds are to be found in the central part of the state. A fairly recent development has been the increase in the number of horses throughout the state kept because of nostalgia, for prestige reasons, because of the hobby of riding, and be-

cause horses make excellent, though expensive, pets. In 1971 it was estimated that more than 11,000 families owned horses or ponies, and that
the state had more than 35,000 "equines," double the number of a decade
previous.[2] The horse has thus regained something of a place in New Jersey, though in an entirely different relationship to its agriculture. Some
landowners attempting to find tax relief under the Farmland Assessment
Act of 1964 are turning to the raising of horses as an acceptable agricultural pursuit.

The most important farm animal in this period, as in earlier ones,
has been the cow. The dominance gained by dairy cattle in the latter
part of the 1810–1917 period has persisted throughout the modern period
to the present. There were still 15,000 animals characterized as beef cattle
in 1910, but the number fell to fewer than 1,000 by 1940. An interesting
development since World War II has been a slow increase in the number
of "cows other than milk cows" in census reports. According to the Federal Census of Agriculture for 1964, New Jersey farmers reporting such
cattle numbered 677. State estimates of the total number of beef cattle
climbed from 14,000 in 1961 to 22,000 in 1969. A recent factor has been
the change in policy in taxing farmland. In general, whether raised as
a sideline to other agriculture or as a hobby by "city farmers," beef cattle
have not really been profitable here since the invention of refrigerated
transportation. Though a few dairymen have turned to beef cattle, no
important increase is predicted. It is noticeable that most of the beef
animals at the present time are to be found in very small herds. Nevertheless, what had seemed a vanishing type of agriculture is now apparently staging a revival in a small way.

Many of the characteristics of dairying in the latter part of the previous
period persisted for a time in this one. However, rapid changes were
soon on the way. The milking machine, which appeared about 1920,
spread as rapidly as rural electrification would permit, and with it came
water systems and other equipment dependent on electric motors. At the
same time, the drive to replace labor brought new devices for the handling of feed, bedding, and manure and the erection of new buildings
or the remodeling of old ones, with efficiency always the aim in mind.
Farmers who relied heavily on their monthly milk checks for an income
were soon rapidly modifying their crop practices so as to produce on their
farms as much of their feed as possible. More and more silos were built,
and a larger and larger part of the corn crop was ensiled. After about
1940 an increasing amount of alfalfa and other "grass" ensilage, often
designated today as "haylage," was also made each year. Alfalfa, already
becoming the most important hay crop in the 1920s, was gradually improved and made more productive. A relatively new development was

that of the "improved" pasture, carefully fertilized and seeded to a number of forage plants far more productive for grazing than bluegrass. Despite these changes, the typical dairyman was a large purchaser of "milled" feed, as he increased his herd size and, to an even greater extent, his daily production of milk.

Lest the last sentence seem an enigma, let me point out that in this period the dairyman greatly improved the quality of his herd by better breeding practices or by the purchase of adult animals with high production records or of young animals with high-producing ancestors. The importance of owning better cows shows up markedly in the statistics. The average cow of 1945 in New Jersey produced an estimated 6,740 pounds of milk per year. By 1956 this had increased to 7,850. In 1969 the average was 10,493 pounds. New Jersey cows had thus increased their productivity by one-half in two decades, and their record was fourth highest in the nation. No longer the "Bossy" of tradition, the cow of this period was rated entirely on her statistical record. Because of the high and increasing cost of raising calves, most farmers purchased their replacements from the large imports of out-of-state animals brought into New Jersey each year. The estimated number of such imported animals for 1950 was 16,520 and for 1960 some 21,000. Such a situation did not encourage the building up of purebred herds, and in 1940 fewer than 2 percent of the herds of the state were made up entirely of registered dairy animals. This reflected no scorn of good breeding. Nearly all the animals purchased by farmers were of one of the dairy breeds, either purebred or "grade" animals. For those farmers raising their own replacements, artificial insemination proved a great boon. In 1938, the first cooperative association for artificial insemination of cattle in the United States was formed at Clinton, and soon every dairy section of the state had a similar group. The use of superior sires from the state Holstein herd and to a lesser extent from private herds played a very important part in improving hundreds of herds both as to quantity of milk and as to its butterfat content.[3]

Traditionally, the American customer has always wanted rich milk, and with the coming of the Babcock tester it had become possible for dealers in milk to buy on the basis of butterfat content. Long before 1900 it had been generally agreed that fluid milk sold at retail should have a fat content of 3.5 percent, even if, as was often the case, fat separated from other milk must be added. A farmer of that time, as of today, must produce milk up to the standard or else be assessed penalties. As an emergency measure he might sacrifice those cows giving thin milk or he might buy a few cows giving milk with a high test and thus bring up the average of his herd. A better solution for the long run has been to raise or buy cows that combined high production with at least standard test. The dominant dairy breed, the Holstein-Friesian or Holstein, has been more noted for the first of these characteristics than the second. But selective breeding has proven an answer to the dilemma, and through the years the Holsteins have been gradually improved in fat production. Some farmers have remained loyal to the Guernseys and Jerseys, with their creamier milk, and thus have been able to obtain premium prices for lesser quantities of milk. Most farmers, however, have stayed with or have turned to the Holsteins.

To guide farmers in improving their herds, both as to average production and as to butterfat content, cow testing associations, soon called dairy herd improvement associations, were formed. Members, for a fee, had all animals of their herd tested periodically for quantity and quality of production. Animals deficient in either could be replaced. Before the widespread use of artificial insemination, many farmers considered the ownership of a good sire, sometimes cooperatively, the best way of bringing up herd quality. After 1938 the practicality of the new artificial breeding program was recognized at once, and before long the bull pen had disappeared from the average farm. The owners of purebred herds for a time chose to keep their own bulls, since in that way they had better control of their breeding programs. However, as the availability of semen from "proved sires" increased, they too in many instances turned to artificial insemination. For farmers buying their replacements, the quality of sire used makes little difference, inasmuch as they dispose of calves as soon as possible for veal. But they too have found it advantageous from the point of cost to have their cows bred artificially. In buying their cows, dairy farmers often "buy by test," the price of a given cow depending on the quantity and quality of the milk given in the past.

The general acceptance of fat content as an important standard is not very logical, and is hardly in accord with consumer trends. There are strong indications that 3.5 percent butterfat for milk is higher than is best for health. In time, enough of the public may buy 2 percent milk or fat-free milk to upset the old tradition. Though it will not happen soon, there is a possibility that breeding programs some day may select sires and dams according to tests for "milk solids" rather than fat content.

There were in 1910 an estimated 154,000 dairy cows in New Jersey, not counting younger animals. Of these, some 60,000 were to be found in the northwestern block of counties, Sussex, Hunterdon, Warren, and Morris in order of magnitude. Another large fraction of the whole, some 45,000, were in the southwest, where Burlington and Salem counties led. The greater part of the remainder were in the counties at the narrow waist of the state. There were some fluctuations in the intervening years, notably a decline about 1930, but the state total in 1940 was still nearly 140,000 adult dairy cows. The dominance of the northwestern counties was even more marked by this time. Sussex had increased from 22,000 to 26,000, Hunterdon had remained at 17,000, Warren had increased from 11,000 to 16,000. Morris, however, had declined from 9,000 to 6,000. The changes in southwestern and central New Jersey were ones of slow decline, except for Burlington County, which still had 16,000 cows. After 1940 the general story was one of a gradual increase to 1954, when the count was roughly the same as that of 1910, but there has been a rapid decline since. Milk production in the state in 1909 and again in 1919 was in the neighborhood of 60 million gallons. By 1929 it was over 90 million, by 1945 some 120 million, and by 1954 approximately 160 million.

Of the 119,000 dairy cows in 1954 (171,000 total dairy animals), about two-thirds were in the northwest. Sussex County led the state as heretofore, with nearly 25,000 cows, Hunterdon was second with nearly 20,000, and Warren was third with approximately 18,000. The fourth and fifth counties of the state were Burlington and Salem, which held firm with nearly 15,000 and 12,000 respectively. On January 1, 1970, the farmers of New Jersey owned approximately 80,000 dairy cows and 30,000 younger dairy animals. The five leading counties were Sussex with about 21,500 dairy animals of all ages, Warren with 20,000, Hunterdon with 18,000, Salem with 12,700, and Burlington with 11,700. Fifteen years of steady decline had brought down the count in the dairy herds of the state by more than one-third. The milk production of the state fell during those years from about 160 million gallons in 1954 to just over 90 million in 1970.

Throughout this period the only market of any consequence for New Jersey dairy farmers was that for fluid milk. Nevertheless, it is of interest to note in the 1930s the expiration of those last few creameries which, until then, had given an outlet to the declining number of farmers who could not or would not qualify for sale of fluid milk. The increasingly difficult and expensive requirements for the fluid markets led some marginal dairymen, particularly small ones, into dropping out of milk production altogether. But a far more potent factor in eliminating dairy farmers was the price squeeze to which the industry was subjected from time to time. As we have seen, the spread between farm price and city price was already a sore point for dairymen at the beginning of the period. In the early years of the century the lucky farmer netted two cents per quart at a time when city customers were complaining that dealers had advanced their prices above the traditional nickel per quart. Attempts to cut the middleman's profit first through local cooperation and later through cooperative associations were not as yet very fruitful. However, mounting farm costs after 1915 were so unendurable that dairymen fought desperately, and with some success, for better prices. As already chronicled, there followed a decade and a half during which farm milk prices were favorable. This was due perhaps as much to the great increase in consumption as to the united cooperative front which the farmers presented.

The decline in consumption during the Great Depression, regrettable for many reasons, brought a reversal, however. Soon the cooperatives completely lost control of the price structure. The helplessness of the dairy farmer with his high and rather inflexible costs brought state action in setting minimum milk prices. The resulting stability lasted through the World War II period. But the advantageous situation was not to last for very long. With the mounting milk production of the hill country of New York and Pennsylvania, the best that the dairymen of New Jersey and other high-cost areas were able to secure for themselves during nearly two decades, despite both state and federal help, was a plateau of prices. The farmer during most of this period received an average price of about ten cents a quart, and only about twelve cents in 1968. Rises in prices since that time, as consumption has finally caught up with production, have eased the situation markedly for those dairymen who have weathered the storm. But in New Jersey no new dairymen are appearing, and those who left the industry are not returning. During the years since 1945 the dollar price of tractors, milking equipment, silos, other buildings, mill feed, and labor have advanced by from 75 percent to more than 100 percent. Since 1950 many a dairyman has been netting fewer dollars profit than his best hand receives as wages. Under the circumstances, the individual farmer often concludes that he is subsidizing the dealers, the consumers, or his labor force, and perhaps all three. The time comes sooner or later when he reluctantly decides to give up what for him has been a way of life.

In 1930 there were approximately 5,000 farmers designated in the census as "dairy farmers" and some 2,000 "general farmers," who together owned 85,000 dairy cows and heifers. Other farmers who kept small dairy herds as a sideline held 20,000 more. An overall survey in 1940 reported 17,624 dairy herds, averaging 11.7 animals each, in the state. After World War II, an at first slow and then rapid decline set in both for those farmers specializing in dairying and for those keeping dairy cattle as a sideline. By 1954 there were still 3,648 farms classed as "dairy farms," and there were of course some other farms with a few cows. But the census of 1964 reported only 3,500 dairy herds of all sizes in the state. At the present writing the number is under 2,000 and still shrinking despite the better milk prices of the moment.

To account for the fact that a sector of agriculture once considered fundamentally sound has come close to the end of its rope is not simple, for undoubtedly the market is larger than ever before. That too much

milk has been produced most of the time for two decades is obvious, but
in this case the New Jersey farmer is not at fault. It is true that the remaining dairymen of the state have more than doubled their productivity
per laborer during the past dozen years, and that they have increased
the size of their individual operations. Nevertheless, New Jersey's milk
production has diminished. The crux of the matter is that New Jersey
has not been able to hold its fraction of the market in the face of competition by farmers in lower-cost areas who are becoming rapidly just as
efficient as dairymen here. The belated, though most welcome, tax relief
afforded by recent legislation may, hopefully, delay the decline. But the
situation is such that Farmer X, with fifty cows, has more than $100,000
of capital invested in cattle alone, yet gets in a year a smaller net return
than he would receive if he worked for someone else. Farmer X may grit
his teeth and hold on, at least until a real estate developer comes along,
but his son will not be a dairyman. The average age of dairy farmers in
New Jersey in 1964 was fifty-three, and there were very few young ones.
It is understandable, therefore, that more than half of New Jersey's dairy
farmers have quit their operations in ten years.[4] The very real danger that
imitation milk will take over part of the market in the near future is
already causing quite a furor in dairying circles.[5] Doubtless this new problem will bedevil Farmer X's competitors in other states. But it is quite
probable that Farmer X will no longer be a dairyman when this threat
becomes a serious one. Only a crash program of imaginative legislation
might possibly save him.

A continuing decline had brought the growing of sheep to a place of
little importance by the beginning of this period. In 1910 there were
some 30,000 sheep and 14,000 spring lambs in New Jersey, more than two-
thirds of them in the counties of the northwest, led by Hunterdon and
Warren. Most of these sheep were dual-purpose animals, kept for both
wool and meat production. The word *mutton* was falling into disuse by
this time, as city-dwellers and suburbanites developed a taste for *lamb,*
of whatever age. The growing market did not help the New Jersey
farmer, however, for his mounting costs, especially after 1914, usually
made it uneconomical to raise sheep, even as a minor sideline. By 1920
there were not more than 12,000 mature sheep in the state and by 1940
not many more than half that number. A slight revival, based on good
lamb prices, brought temporary gains during World War II, but most
of the animals were sold off in 1945. A slow recovery thereafter brought
the number in 1950 to 15,000, where it remained for a decade. But by
the time of the 1964 census it had fallen to 10,000. An estimate for the
state in early 1970 was 7,700, over two-fifths of which were in Hunterdon

and Warren. It would seem that sheep should be profitable for the small farmer in areas of rough pastures and relatively cheap land. However, this is apparently not the case. A well-subsidized State Fat Lamb Show and Sale has stirred some interest among 4-H and Future Farmers clubs.

The raising of swine had once been a mainstay of New Jersey agriculture, and in 1900, despite the ravages of cholera, which had hit the aristocratic Berkshires and the plebeian Jersey Reds alike, there were still an estimated 175,000 hogs in the state. By 1910 this number had declined to about 150,000 and by 1920 to about 140,000. During these decades, production was fairly widespread. Hudson County, with its garbage-fed hogs, led the state in 1910 with 22,000 hogs, but declined to less than half that number by 1920. Hunterdon, Burlington, and Monmouth, in that order, were the most important producers of hogs during these decades. Though cholera and other diseases were rapidly being eliminated by inoculation and sanitation programs, the general malaise of agriculture immediately after World War I affected swine production in New Jersey badly. Numbers declined by half within a few years, but by 1930 had recovered somewhat, standing at 95,000 at that time. By 1940 there were 124,000 hogs. A part of the rise was accounted for by a revival of garbage feeding in Hudson County, and its initiation elsewhere, but much more important was the increase in a truly farm county, Hunterdon, which had 37,000 hogs in 1930 and 57,000 in 1940.

The abnormal demands of the World War II period brought up production in a steep upward spiral, so that at the war's end there were nearly 250,000 hogs in the state. The increase this time was almost entirely the result of garbage feeding, by now mostly in the central and southern parts of the state. For a short time after the war, numbers declined, but soon they increased again, reaching a high of 258,000 in 1951. The long-expected decline set in soon thereafter, and by 1965 there had been a fall of one-half. Of the 121,000 hogs estimated in the state on December 1, 1969, nearly three-fifths were in Gloucester County, which had 70,500. Burlington County was second with 15,200 head, Monmouth third with 8,800, and Ocean fourth with 7,300. In contrast, the farm hog population of Hunterdon County was by then only 6,000. Four-fifths of the swine in the state are now fed on garbage, steam-cooked under state inspection, and New Jersey leads the country in production of garbage-fed hogs. Recent figures do not indicate that the decline in numbers will be reversed. The feeder of swine who can secure garbage seemingly has everything on his side. But he is being hurt by the rising costs of labor, and even more by the mounting opposition of ever-nearer neighbors. Whether local ordinances banning hogs, or for that matter poultry or horses, as a nuisance are fair depends on the point of view.

The raising of poultry, already of considerable importance in New Jersey in the latter part of the nineteenth century, grew by leaps and bounds in the twentieth. This development, made in response to a great increase in market demand, had been possible as a result of laborsaving inventions. It would be hard to imagine any considerable development of the poultry industry without the incubator and the brooder, which had long since replaced the hen for hatching and mothering baby chicks. Now, as efficiency became the watchword of the day, new equipment came rapidly into general use, including trap nests, automatic fountains and feeders, and even devices to bring the eggs directly from the nest to the casing bench, already sorted as to weight. That abomination, the individual cage or "battery," which makes a crippled recluse of every hen, was not widely adopted here until fairly recently, probably more because of initial cost than kindness. At the present time, however, it seems to be coming in rapidly, as remaining poultrymen find their profit margins more and more narrow. Techniques for cleaning eggs, for electronic candling or inspection, for building poultry houses, for providing litter, and for taking care of the manure have been constantly improving. The modern poultryman in New Jersey has been quick to try suggestions of the New Jersey and other Experiment Stations, and there are times when he is ahead of them.[6]

The keeping of poultry was already becoming specialized and divided as to function before this period began, and the process continued rapidly. Some poultrymen operated hatcheries to the exclusion of other poultry operations, others fattened friers and broilers for market, and still others, in this case a majority, concentrated on the production of eggs. Other sidelines also developed, including the production of hatching eggs, incubation of eggs for laboratory use, and the raising of pullets for sale at laying age. The once-startling development of sending baby chicks by mail became a big business. In 1923 the post office at Frenchtown, one of the many hatchery centers of the state, mailed out more than $3\frac{1}{2}$ million chicks.[7] Kerr Hatcheries of that area pioneered a little later in two important developments, chick sexing and artificial insemination of poultry.[8] The first, and possibly second, of these techniques came from Japan. Chick sexing, that is, sorting by sex, was important to egg producers because it enabled them to purchase only female chicks. Since Leghorn chicks are generally considered nearly worthless for meat production, by far the greater part of the unfortunate cockerels are hustled off to the gas chambers. Artificial insemination has resulted in a further decline in the numbers of those noble birds whose clarion call at dawn once inspired poets and awoke farmers and villagers to the tasks of the day.

As will be shown in some detail later, poultry raising in general and egg production in particular gained phenomenally during this period, and especially after 1940. By 1956 a full third of total farm cash receipts of the state came from poultry products. The underlying reason for this development, was, of course, the fantastic growth of urban markets. Balanced feeding, the use of lights to lengthen the poultry working day, and selective breeding all played a part in the increased production, but the most important factor was simply an increase in the number of chickens. With new equipment, flocks could be doubled or tripled in size. The rule of the White Leghorn became almost absolute because of its high egg productivity. Some of the best layers of this breed averaged nearly an egg a day the year round in egg-laying contests, and the average for many flocks became higher than two hundred eggs per year. In fact, the seemingly optimistic estimate by the New Jersey Department of Agriculture in 1966 was exactly two hundred eggs per laying hen in the state. Proponents of the New Hampshire Reds, the Rhode Island Reds, and the Plymouth Rocks have not quite given up as to egg production to this day, though they have to sell their brown eggs on a market where white ones are preferred. It is these breeds, and various crosses among them, which dominate poultry meat production. New Jersey never reached a prominent place among the states in this field, but there was a rather remarkable growth between 1940 and 1956. In the meantime, New Jersey chick hatchery production, with its wide markets, increased by more than 150 percent. Egg production, far and away the most important part of the poultry industry, had gained so phenomenally that New Jersey, one of the smallest states, was fifth in the nation by the mid-1950s. Monmouth County for several years produced more eggs than any other county in the United States.

A report early in 1958, which failed to note the downturn that had already set in, indicated that egg production in New Jersey had doubled in twelve years, "due to favorable prices that brought many new poultry farms into existence." If the story for poultry in New Jersey could stop on that note, I would be quite happy about it. Unfortunately, the bubble burst at the very time when appearances were most rosy. The first segment of the industry to be affected was poultry meat production. The unheralded and steep decline was almost entirely explainable on the basis of relative cost of production. This development, shared by nearby states, helped bring down hatchery statistics, which would soon plummet farther as the result of the steady decline in egg production. When their profits turned to losses, the new egg producers left the industry nearly as rapidly as they had entered it. More serious was the fact that the change in conditions made it difficult for even the long-established producer of eggs to stay in the black. The debacle, in this case fully as much as with dairying, was the result of lower production costs elsewhere. The competition that had ruined the price for meat chickens came from lower-cost areas not far distant. As for eggs, more distant competitors, some of them west of the Mississippi and others south of the Mason-Dixon Line, brought prices down sufficiently in 1958 so that many marginal producers began dropping out of the game. Most of them had small flocks, and quite a number were on newly cleared farms in the Barrens. From then until the present, the situation became progressively worse. The statistical summary which follows might well be called "The Rise and Fall of the Little White Hen," but the story is too serious to be facetious about it. For many poultrymen, the price squeeze has meant unemployment and serious financial loss; for many others, who still held on, it has meant a decline in living standards and the loss of educational opportunities for their children.

In 1919 somewhat more than 20,000 New Jersey farmers reported that they had raised approximately 3½ million chickens during the previous year, and in June 1920 they owned about 2½ million that were kept as layers. Poultry raising was still quite widespread, being heaviest in counties as far apart as Cumberland, Hunterdon, Monmouth, and Burlington (named in order of rank), and light only in counties with considerable urbanization. A decade later poultry farmers grew approximately 8 million birds and kept half of them for egg production. The distribution had not changed markedly, except that Atlantic County had passed Burlington, and Gloucester had nearly done so. In 1939 10 million chickens were grown in the state, and in 1940 there were 5.4 million in laying flocks. The counties of Cumberland, Hunterdon, and Monmouth had each gone considerably over the million mark as to layers. The same three counties had the most hens and pullets in 1940, Hunterdon leading with 720,000. A new center of importance was indicated by the high figures for Ocean and Atlantic counties. In 1940 there were about 19,000 farmers in New Jersey reporting poultry, no great change in several decades. However, there had been a very great increase in the average production.

Poultry farming is a sector of the economy which can be expanded greatly in a single season. Generally favorable prices during World War II and thereafter led to a phenomenal increase in poultry numbers. In 1950 the state produced 7½ million meat chickens and in 1956 more than 10½ million. The gross sales return for meat chickens, less than $1 million in 1940, was $11 million in 1956. During the same years, the hatcheries increased their output from 18 million baby chicks to 46 million. At the beginning of 1950 there were 13 million birds kept for laying, and in 1956 nearly a million more. The great increase in poultry raising had been in the central and southern parts of the state. Monmouth County led with 3.2 million layers, followed by Ocean with just over 2.5 million and Cumberland with just under that number. Hunterdon County, center of the northern poultry area, had increased also, but only to 1.8 million in 1950, a number which had declined to 1.6 million by 1956. Total egg production for the state rose from 1.1 billion eggs in 1945 to 2.7 billion in 1956. Interestingly enough, the expansion in poultry numbers had not led to a net increase in the number of poultry farms. New poultry establishments due to "colonies" of refugees from city life, like that on Davidson Avenue in Franklin Township of Somerset County and those on the edge of the Barrens in Monmouth and Ocean counties, had not made up for the decline in areas near growing population centers. In 1950 there were about 17,000 farmers reporting poultry, and the figure continued to decline slowly despite the poultry boom.

The period of rapid decline after 1956 affected every branch of poultry farming. The federal agricultural census of 1964 showed fewer than 3,000 farms with poultry in the state. There were about 300 in the most productive county, Monmouth, and about 400 in Hunterdon, which ranked second in production. Ocean, Cumberland, and Atlantic ranked third, fourth, and fifth in importance. A state survey in 1968 found 2,313 poultry growers, only 735 of them significant.[9] In 1966 poultry farmers sold 2 million meat chickens and in 1969 fewer than 1 million. A burst of heavy pullet production in 1970 brought the figure to 1.8 million. Baby chick production fell below 4 million by 1968 and to considerably less than 2 million in 1970. There were $7\frac{1}{2}$ million layers in the state in 1965, but under 4 million by 1970, fewer than any year since 1937. In 1970 state egg production was 779 million. Of these, Monmouth County produced 124 million, a large recent decline, Hunterdon 160 million, Cumberland 140 million, Salem 85 million, and Ocean and Atlantic under 65 million each, both considerable declines. Despite adoption of the newest equipment and some recent improvement in prices, nearly all areas have shown a steep and continuing decline. New Jersey poultrymen have made valiant attempts to fight back, but with little success. Though a New Jersey Poultry Products Promotion Council, set up by state legislation and financed by the poultrymen themselves, has used the Madison Avenue approach in attempting to increase sales, prices received have remained generally depressed in terms of production costs. No practicable method of federal or state aid has as yet been suggested, and it does not seem likely that any will be devised. The market for all poultry products is, of course, increasing rapidly. Nevertheless, the possibility of making money from production of meat chickens in New Jersey, even as a sideline, seems small. But with increasing efficiency here and mounting costs in Iowa and Minnesota and Georgia, some egg producers with 25,000 or more layers seem to be holding the line. The latest talk is of skyscrapers housing a million or more layers.

In part because chickens stole the spotlight, the story for other poultry in this period in New Jersey has not been of great importance. In the spring of 1920 there were an estimated 131,000 turkeys, geese, and ducks on New Jersey farms, much fewer than half the number of 1890. The most important counties were Cumberland, Hunterdon, Burlington, and Monmouth. Developments during the next two decades were clearly in the direction of raising more of these kinds of poultry, but of keeping fewer and fewer adult birds on the farms. This meant, of course, that nearly all hatching was done in the chick hatcheries, using eggs shipped in from other areas. In 1940 some 129,000 turkeys, 34,000 geese, and 437,-000 ducks were grown on New Jersey farms, a total of 600,000. A closer look at the statistics shows a strong trend toward regional specialization. Nearly 90 percent of the ducks were grown in the two counties of Atlantic and Cumberland and more than 90 percent of the geese in Morris County. The raising of turkeys was more widespread. In a decade turkey production had quadrupled in the state, and in most of the important counties nearly so. Burlington led with 16,000 turkeys and Hunterdon and Monmouth followed with 14,000 each. Since 1940 the raising of geese has become of minor importance, and that of ducks, despite ups and downs, of no great consequence. The story for turkeys is quite different, however. By the mid-1940s some 350,000 were being raised and by 1952 more than 384,000. A slow decline for three or four years was followed by a swift one, bringing the total down to 156,000 by 1962. Then came another surprising reversal, due entirely to the demands of the "turkey roll" industry for heavy birds. The number of turkeys raised in 1964 increased to 250,000, in 1965 to 500,000, and in 1966 to 610,000. Then came unpredictable bad luck. A geographical shift by the processors of prepared turkey meat caused a drastic cut in the contracts for turkeys. Production slumped to 488,000 in 1967, to 349,000 in 1968, and to 111,000 in 1969. An increase in light breed numbers and a decline in heavies resulted in a 1970 figure only slightly lower than that of 1969.[10]

The producers of poultry products have been affected in recent years by a development known, for reasons not clear, as integration. In essence, a feed manufacturer or dealer subsidizes the production of eggs or broilers or turkeys to the extent of the feed bill, and contracts to buy the product at an agreed price. This arrangement keeps down the farmer's capital outlay and eliminates much of the market risk for him. His vaunted independence of action is gone, but he may be able to stay in business when he would fail otherwise. Such contracts seem more likely, in the long run, to help the owner or owners of an egg or broiler or turkey "factory" than the farmer with a family-size farm, who has, until recently, been the dominant figure in poultry raising in New Jersey.

17

Crops in the Modern Era

The production of field, orchard, and vegetable crops in New Jersey during the past half century has undergone even more sweeping changes than those concerned with livestock raising.[1] Here, too, the farmer has discarded crops ruthlessly on the basis of monetary returns. But thus far he has retained more from the past than at first meets the eye. In a recent article about the agricultural economy of New Jersey, there is no mention by name of the traditional crops of corn, wheat, rye, and oats or, for that matter, the newer ones of soybeans and alfalfa. However, potatoes, tomatoes, asparagus, eggplant, and green peppers are given specific treatment. This no doubt intentional slight reflects the spectacular increase in the growing of vegetables in this state, but distorts the total picture somewhat. Since most grain and hay crops in New Jersey in recent times have been fed to livestock, they defy the statistician; when a farmer feeds his own crops to his own livestock, the crops have no gross monetary return of their own. But inasmuch as the category of livestock and livestock products is still one of the largest in value among farm products, the crops used largely for livestock feed must not be considered insignificant. The average returns on these crops have declined, and some crops have slipped more than others, but their yearly total net value has held up fairly well. Orcharding, too, has declined in acreage, but very little even yet in value of gross product.

These remarks in no way detract from the rise in vegetable growing, which indeed has been spectacular. In fact, during recent years vegetable sales have provided about one-fourth of the cash receipts for the farmers of the state. These crops have been an answer to the cry for intensive farming. The same is true for greenhouse and nursery products, which together bring in about one-sixth of gross agricultural income, a considerable increase in their proportion in recent years. It is clear that New Jersey agriculture, in adapting to new conditions, has radically changed its emphasis. Some parts of the industry once minor or subsidiary

251

have become very important, and in some areas dominant. Furthermore, unless conditions change sharply, nontraditional sectors seem likely to withstand longest the buffeting that all of New Jersey agriculture is receiving.

Because of new machinery and new techniques, the growing of corn no longer requires the long hours of labor which were once necessary. Corn is a tough crop, singularly resistant to the various diseases and insects that attack it, even corn blight, which struck in especially virulent form in 1970. Corn is quite responsive, too, to large applications of fertilizer. It is true that in New Jersey lack of sufficient rain during the growing season sometimes curtails the yield seriously or, at best, causes a larger acreage to be ensiled. Supplemental irrigation has been little used for field corn in New Jersey. The hybrid corn of today has been bred out of close resemblance to the plant grown among deadened trees by the Indians, but it gives a tremendously greater return for the work expended on it. Despite the rapid decline in the cultivation of the crop recently, corn will doubtless remain of importance in New Jersey as long as livestock are grown.

In 1919 some 18,000 New Jersey farmers grew 234,000 acres of corn, of which 18,000 acres went into silos. The most important areas were the northwestern and southwestern counties, with one-third of the state production each. Most of the rest was produced in the counties of the narrow waist of the state. Hunterdon County, with 30,000 acres, was the leader, with Burlington not far behind. The corn crop of the state was 8.8 million bushels, something over 37 bushels per acre. Two decades later some 14,000 farmers grew 175,000 acres of corn, with distribution and acreage yield about the same. But by this time, as ensilage had become the most important feed for dairy cows, nearly a quarter of the acreage was ensiled. A considerable factor in the decline in plantings was the expansion of other forage crops, again largely for feeding of cattle. A further decline brought down the number of farmers reporting corn to 10,400 by 1950, and the acreage to 160,000, of which two-fifths was cut for ensilage. As a result of the fairly widespread general planting of hybrid corn by this time, average yields per acre of corn grown for grain had increased to something over 40 bushels per acre, actually still surprisingly low, for by 1965, a rather dry year, average yield would increase to 68 bushels, and by 1969, a good year, to 81 bushels.

The statistics for 1965 showed 71,000 acres of corn grown for grain, yielding 4.8 million bushels, and 53,000 acres more grown for ensilage. Increase in productivity in fifteen years had more than made up for the one-fifth decline in acreage. The value of the corn grown for grain was estimated at $86 per acre and that for ensilage at $92, considerably more than any other grain crop. The four northwestern counties, with 26,000 acres for grain and 34,000 for ensilage, grew nearly half of the corn in New Jersey. Warren County had nearly 20,000 acres, followed closely by next-door Hunterdon. The largest producers in the rest of the state, where grain acreage considerably outranked that for ensilage, were Burlington with nearly 17,000 acres and Salem with 14,000. Since 1965 there has been a decline in corn plantings, bringing down the total to 102,000 acres by 1970. Most of the decline was in acres ensiled, which had fallen to 33,000, with 3,000 planted for green chop. The area grown for grain, still 65,000 acres, produced a crop of just over 5 million bushels, slightly more than that of 1965. The decline in corn acreage since 1965 has been fairly evenly distributed among the counties. The 3,400 farmers growing corn in 1964, about one-third the number of 1950, had declined further by 1972.

The wheat crop harvested in 1909 was only 84,000 acres, the lowest on record to that time except for 1902. The yield of less than 1.5 million bushels showed a decline of one-fourth since the turn of the century. During World War I acreage climbed to 110,000 in 1918, but a steady decline thereafter brought the figure to half that amount in 1941. With the use of better varieties and the application of more and better fertilizers, the decline in total yields was less than that of acreage, the harvest of 1941 being 1.2 million bushels. The demands of World War II brought up sowings somewhat, and the trend continued during the next decade, in part under the stimulus of favorable prices but even more because of the demands of a booming poultry industry. For seven years in a row, more than 100,000 acres were harvested each year, and the average crop was more than 2 million bushels. With the decline in poultry, a predictable contraction began in the late 1950s, which by 1962 brought acreage harvested down to 35,000. The amount increased somewhat during the next several years, but in 1970 fell to 32,000, the lowest acreage in a century. Yields in the 1960s varied from just under a million bushels in 1963, a poor crop year, to almost 2 million in 1967, an excellent one, with an average yield of 39 bushels per acre. Something over 10,000 acres were sowed each year that were not harvested the next summer, usually because of winterkilling or pasturage. Federal statistics showed that about 5,000 farmers in New Jersey grew wheat in the 1920s and 1930s, and over 4,000 in the 1940s. But by 1959 there were fewer than 2,500, and in 1964 they numbered only 1,754.

Distribution of wheat growing throughout the state in the modern period changed little before 1940. Hunterdon County led with over 300,-000 bushels in 1919 and just under that in 1939. Warren, Somerset, and Salem ranked next, in that order, with just under 200,000 each in 1919 and about 125,000 each in 1939. Figures since that time have shown some surprising changes, however, with gains for central New Jersey, an area with slightly higher acre yields than the northwest and with fewer dairy cattle to feed. The leading counties in 1969 were Mercer with 287,000 bushels and Monmouth with 239,000. Hunterdon had declined to 173,000 bushels. It may be that, as dairying declines in the block of counties of which it is a part, farmers there, too, will turn to grains, particularly wheat, as an alternative. But even if the average yield per acre can be brought up still more, there seems little likelihood that the farmers of New Jersey will find wheat growing profitable in the long run.

The story for rye, wheat's companion grain, is complicated by the fact that the considerable acreage always used for spring pasturage for cattle has increased markedly with the rise of dairying. There is a wealth of statistics concerning "rye for grain," but none for rye for pasture. However, state figures since 1945 do indicate rye acreage planted and acreage harvested. Rye production in New Jersey had seldom been more than half as much as that of wheat in any given year in the latter half of the nineteenth century. But for reasons not clear rye held up better for a time in the twentieth century. In fact, a small annual increase in acreage and a slight improvement in yield brought the amount harvested for grain to 100,000 acres in 1910 and the bushels harvested to 1.5 million. This record was almost equaled again in 1915 and in 1918. About one-fifth of the state's yield was from Burlington County and another fifth from Monmouth, and there was considerable production by adjoining counties in each case. A third area of importance was that of Hunterdon and its neighbors. The rapid decline in acreage harvested, which was halved by 1925, halved again by 1935, and again by 1945, brought yearly production, despite a considerable improvement in acreage yield, to 250,-000 bushels per year. In the 1960s, the average yield annually was about 200,000 bushels. Interestingly enough, the decline in rye grain harvest since 1918 was shared about equally by each of the chief areas of production. The chief importance of rye for several decades has been for pasturage. In 1945 as many acres of rye were not harvested as were harvested. Soon the amount not harvested was a much larger proportion of the crop. In the 1960s, approximately 100,000 acres were sowed each year and only 10,000 acres harvested. The future of rye in New Jersey is in some doubt, though at present it has as many acres as corn. Since the dollar return per acre harvested has been for a decade only about one-half as much as for wheat and only a little more than one-fourth as much as for corn, there is little incentive to grow rye for grain where wheat or corn will grow. On the other hand, rye for pasture will undoubtedly decline with the fall in the number of dairy cattle.

The gradual decline in the production of oats in the last decades of the nineteenth century was temporarily arrested by 1910. The state figures for production of that year was over 2.5 million bushels from 83,000 acres harvested. These figures were not equaled again until 1918, when over 3 million bushels were produced on a slightly greater acreage. A gradual decline thereafter brought acreage harvested in 1940 to 43,000 acres and production to 1.4 million bushels. Besides this, some 6,000 acres were "cut and fed unthreshed." Consistently during this period, one-third of the threshed oats of the state was produced by farmers of Hunterdon County and another third by those of its neighbors, Warren and Somerset. This area, until recently always "oats country," made good use of its oats crop as feed for its teeming cattle population. Even more important, perhaps, was the fact that oats are an excellent nurse crop for starting clovers, alfalfa, and improved pastures. The oats crop continued important until the mid-1950s, and of some consequence to the present. In 1942 about 52,000 acres were sowed, of which 42,000 were threshed. In 1955 the figures were 45,000 and 35,000. By that time most of the acreage not grown for grain was cut for ensilage or for green chop. After 1955 the rivalry of other crops caused oats acreage to decline rapidly. In 1962 only 25,000 acres were sowed. The 16,000 acres that were threshed produced 672,000 bushels. By 1969 the acreage figures were 16,000 sowed and 10,000 threshed, and production of grain was 400,000 bushels. In the latter year, nine-tenths of the grain production was in the five northwestern counties. In 1970 the estimated crop was the same as that of 1969, but was grown on 2,000 fewer acres.

The small revival of buckwheat production of the early years of the twentieth century did not continue. The crop of 1919 was only 110,000 bushels, nearly one-third of it in Hunterdon. By 1940 only about 500 acres were grown in the entire state. Since that time the crop has not been statistically important.

A surprising development of recent decades has been the increasing acreage of barley, never of much importance heretofore. But the 150 acres grown in 1909 had increased to 900 by 1919 and to 4,200 by 1939. Production in 1939 was 116,000 bushels, with Burlington and Hunterdon counties far in the lead. By 1945 there were 9,000 acres of barley in the state, of which 8,000 were harvested for grain and 1,000 acres pastured or cut for cattle feed. In 1956 some 30,000 acres were grown for grain and 5,000 acres for other purposes. Inasmuch as on-farm return per acre was not much more than a dollar per bushel, down by one-third in a decade, and average production was still under 40 bushels per acre, one must reach a bit to find a full explanation for the increase. Barley is a hardy crop, an excellent nurse crop for grasses, and fairly good as green chop, and New Jersey produces grain considered excellent for brewing and for poultry feed. At any rate, the expansion continued to 1961, when 25,000 acres were grown for grain and 20,000 for other purposes. The figures in 1969 were 20,000 and 22,000. An average yield of 55 bushels per acre returned a crop of 1.11 million bushels, a yield surpassed only in 1966. Leading counties for grain production of barley were Salem with 5,100 acres, Burlington with 5,000 acres, and Cumberland with 2,400. With advances in both acre yields and prices, it seems probable that harvested barley will continue to crowd other grains for acreage, at least in areas near breweries and in nondairying areas. The federal census of 1964 showed more than a thousand New Jersey farmers growing barley for grain. Farmers of a century ago would have found this development hard to envision.

A newcomer among New Jersey field crops is the soybean. In the 1920s some progressive farmers were experimenting with the "soja bean," an import from China, and a crop especially recommended because it is a legume. Some farmers plowed under the crop as green manure, a few produced soybean hay, and even more at first planted climbing types in rows of corn intended for the silo. In 1924 some 450 farmers were growing soybeans for feed purposes. By 1929 nearly 2,600 acres of soybeans were grown solely for feed purposes, and nearly 500 acres with corn or other crops. By this time, bush types were predominating, and the agricultural experiment stations and seed growers were developing bush varieties with higher bean production. Recommended strongly by agricultural extension workers, popularized by farm magazines, and promoted by seed growers, the new crop had reached a position of some importance by 1939. In that year some 2,500 farmers grew nearly 30,000 acres of soybeans, by far the greater part without companion crops. Three counties quite distant from one another led in acreage, Burlington with 5,700 acres, Hunterdon with 3,200 acres, and Salem with 2,900. The soybean had proved to be a reliable and versatile crop. Its bean production, when harvested, averaged about 20 bushels per acre, seemingly not very high, but still giving a return comparable to wheat. But for a decade more the soybean was grown largely as a forage crop, and especially for ensilage.

In 1945 only 11,000 acres of the 36,000 grown were harvested for the beans. The situation changed rapidly thereafter, although bean prices tended to fall rather than rise. By 1949 half the crop was threshed, and in 1956 about 45,000 of the 51,000 planted. Production in the latter year for the first time passed the million-bushel level. A substantial fall in prices in the late 1950s brought down acreage threshed at the expense of acreage ensiled, but a recovery by 1962 caused 85 percent of the crop to be threshed, with a resulting yield of 631,000 bushels. Soybean plantings fell in the mid-1960s, but forged ahead beginning in 1968, when 45,000 acres (out of 48,000 planted) again brought a million-bushel year. With an additional thousand acres in 1969, the harvest was nearly 1.3 million bushels. The yield of 28 bushels per acre, worth $66, made soybeans for grain more remunerative than wheat. Though the crop grows well in other parts of the state, three counties of central New Jersey produced three-fourths of the crop. In 1969 Monmouth County harvested 285,600 bushels from 12,000 acres, Mercer 259,200 from 10,800 acres, and Burlington 200,000 from 8,400 acres. State acreage in 1970 rose to 50,000 acres. The production of the northwest has been particularly low, though that area still grows some beans for ensilage. As dairying declines, it is probable that farmers there, too, will grow more crops with a commercial market, including soybeans.

The most important single hay crop in the nineteenth century, timothy fell after 1920 with the drastic decline in horse numbers. Nevertheless, it continued to be grown to some extent for dairy cattle, usually in combination with red, white, or alsike clover. In 1929 some 212,000 acres of the 229,000 acres of hay in the state were "timothy or clover, alone or mixed." The situation changed rapidly thereafter, largely as a result of the successful introduction of alfalfa, the subject of experimentation at the New Jersey Agricultural Experiment Station as early as 1887. It was already widely known in 1900 that inoculation of the seed or soil with *Bacillus radicicola* would make the growing of alfalfa possible, but it took more than three decades for the crop to catch on. Eventually, however, New Jersey dairy farmers found it far superior to other hay crops as to quality and production. An acreage of 15,000 in 1919 increased to 53,000 in 1939. The production of 102,000 tons of alfalfa in the latter year compared favorably with 133,000 tons of clover (sometimes still mixed with timothy) and approximately 50,000 tons of other hay, including soybeans, redtop, orchard grass, various mixtures, and some "natural hay."

In 1920 the production of all hay in New Jersey was estimated at 674,-000 tons. The rapid decline in the horse population was perhaps the most important factor in bringing down the figures for a time, but the great upsurge in dairying soon increased demand again. Production in 1945 was approximately half a million tons. At the turn of the century, New Jersey still exported hay for the horses of New York and Philadelphia. By the 1940s her dairy farmers must import hay, particularly in years of spring drought.

In 1949 there were 78,000 acres of alfalfa grown in New Jersey and 117,000 acres of clover and timothy hay, which by this time was for the most part pure clover. Other hay crops, including soybeans, totaled 44,-000 acres. Since alfalfa yielded an average of $2\frac{1}{4}$ tons per acre, and other hay crops $1\frac{1}{2}$ tons, it was obviously advantageous to grow alfalfa where quality and depth of soil permitted. After another decade, in 1959, the acreage of alfalfa was 97,000 acres. That year the crop averaged $2\frac{3}{4}$ tons of hay per acre, making it next to corn the most remunerative field crop in the state. Other hay crops had 105,000 acres. However, the reduction in cattle numbers after this time gradually brought a decline in hay crops. In 1969 alfalfa acreage was down to 60,000, yielding an all-time high to date of more than 3 tons per acre, and that of other hay to 76,000 acres, yielding about 2 tons per acre. Northwestern New Jersey, always the great producer of hay, in 1969 produced two-thirds of the state crop. Warren County led the state for alfalfa with 20,800 acres. Hunterdon predominated for clover and timothy hay with 28,400 acres. Figures for 1970 show no material change in the picture, except that alfalfa gained 2,000 more acres at the expense of other hay crops.

In the second half of the nineteenth century, the potato had proved very successful in areas with congenial soils, and particularly in the greensand marl belt and in smaller areas of limestone soils. Production at the turn of the century was about what it had been for three decades, something over 4 million bushels per year on an acreage of from 40,000 to 50,000. The story in the twentieth century became much more erratic. A sudden spurt in production brought the yield to 8 million bushels by 1910, and to over 10 million by 1920. The changeover from long, slender varieties, such as the American Giant, to more productive round varieties, such as the Irish Cobbler, the Green Mountain, and the Rural New Yorker, probably helped boost the yield per acre, and certainly it was increased by the application of more fertilizer. But the most important factor was an increase in acreage brought on by good prices, almost all of it in the greensand marl belt. Nearly 73,000 acres were grown in the state in 1909, and nearly 83,000 in 1919. Monmouth County, by far the greatest potato producer as long as there have been records, had nearly 15,000 acres in 1909 and 25,000 in 1919. Its production increased from 1.9 million bushels in 1909 to 4.2 million in 1919. Salem County, where acreage had been increased markedly, had 1.3 million bushels in 1909 and 1 million in 1919. By the latter year it had lost second place to Mercer, with 1.2 million bushels. These three counties produced 60 percent of the state's potatoes in 1919. Except for Cumberland and Middlesex counties, where there had been a burst of production, the yield of other areas had slowly declined, even in Burlington, which had ranked fourth with a million bushels in 1909. The potato, once a crop grown in most soils, had become definitely a specialty of specific areas.

A tremendous fall in average farm price of potatoes from $1.42 per bushel in 1921 to 72¢ in 1922 brought production down by more than half by 1923. Acreage was cut to 37,000 by 1929, but by 1940 had leveled off at just over 50,000 acres. However, a considerable improvement in average acre yield had made possible crops of 10 million bushels in most years. The 12,000 potato farmers of the state in 1924 had declined to 6,000 by that time. An increase in prices led to a large expansion during World War II. Acreage in 1945 was 69,000 and production 12.4 million bushels. In 1946 acreage was less, but production considerably more. The boost proved a temporary one, however, and by 1956 acreage planted fell to 17,000. The decline in production had been much less spectacular, of course. The best areas had been kept in use, and through liberal use of fertilizer, and of water by overhead irrigation, growers had increased the acre yield enormously. In 1956 a yield of 350 bushels per acre brought a crop of nearly 6 million bushels. Potato farmers that year had a price bonanza, and grossed $500 per acre return, the highest on record. About 1,500 farmers were still growing potatoes at that time. The greatest relative changes since have been the decline in the southwest and the rise of Middlesex County to second position. Total acreage had fallen to 13,000 by 1969. The trend toward regional specialization had seemingly reached a final conclusion. Monmouth County had 3,300 acres of potatoes, Middlesex 2,500, Mercer 1,900, Cumberland 1,850, and Salem 1,850. The small potato farmers of the remainder of the state had nearly dropped out of the race, and the total number of producers had declined to under 400. Production, however, was nearly 5.5 million bushels, or more than 400 bushels per acre. Because of competition from warmer areas, New Jersey has long since given up raising early and midseason potatoes. It is also obviously unprofitable to raise potatoes here except on the very best land. Until land values and taxes become too high, potato production in New Jersey may well remain on its present plateau.

Sweet potatoes, which have always thrived in the sandy soils of South Jersey, had a rise in production in the early years of the twentieth century similar to that of potatoes. The yield in 1909, for the most part of the Yellow Jersey variety, was over 3 million bushels, with nearly half in Gloucester County and almost all the remainder in nearby counties. But because of the diseases that struck soon thereafter, production fell to considerably less than 2 million bushels by 1920. By the mid-1930s, largely as a result of the development of disease-resistant strains, annual production had again risen to over 2 million bushels. At that time, nearly 5,000 farmers were growing sweet potatoes, probably the most in New Jersey history. In 1939 Gloucester County, with 681,000 bushels, Atlantic with 521,000, and Cumberland with 506,000 had together over two-thirds of state production. By that time, the average of 20,000 acres grown in the state at the turn of the century had declined to about 15,000, where it remained until the mid-1950s. Total yield increased slightly from 2.4 million bushels in 1946 to 2.5 million in 1956. About 1,600 farmers by then accounted for the crop. A decline in acreage after that time struck first in Cumberland and Gloucester counties, then in Atlantic. State acreage had declined to 12,000 by 1961, to 11,000 by 1963, to 9,000 by 1965, and to 7,200 by 1966. Because of drought and disease, total yield decreased even faster, and in 1966 under 1 million bushels were grown by fewer than 500 farmers. The decline thereafter was precipitate. In 1970 the "sweet" crop acreage in New Jersey had declined to 3,300, most of it in Atlantic County with 850 acres, Gloucester with 650, and Cumberland with 450. The state yield was under a quarter of a million hundredweight, the lowest report on record until that time.

New Jersey was once famous for the quantity and quality of its fruit, and, despite a considerable decline in acreage, still deserves that fame. Apples and peaches have always been very important, and have held their own as well as they have as the result of better methods and better varieties. An important handicap has been the mounting cost of pest control, which has grown to more than $50 per acre of orchard per year. The 2 million bearing apple trees of 1899 had declined by half in 1910. Apple orchards then were scattered throughout the state, with Monmouth and Burlington leading. The decline, in part due to scale and other pests, was reversed soon after, markedly so in the northwest, once a leading area. By 1925, the number of bearing trees of the state had increased to nearly 1.5 million, and remained at nearly that figure for a decade. In 1935 about 10,000 orchardists grew apples, actually a considerable fall in numbers during a decade. The steady decline that set in at this time brought the number of trees down by half by 1950, and further attrition reduced it to under one-half million by 1965. That only the larger orchardists remained by this time is obvious from the figures, for the 7,000 apple growers of 1950 had declined to under 1,000 by 1965. At the turn of the century, production was estimated at over 4.5 million bushels for the state. Two decades later it was 2.7 million, and in 1939 approximately 3.2 million. The last period of marked decline in yield was the period of World War II, when labor was difficult to obtain. Production in 1945 was approximately 1.6 million bushels, but nearly 3 million in 1946. Due largely to the greater productivity of individual apple trees, production in the best years has remained not greatly below that level, despite a considerable decline in acreage. In 1969 the best recent year, 2.7 million bushels were produced. One-fourth of the crop was grown in Gloucester County, and one-sixth in Monmouth. Third and fourth places were held by Burlington and Cumberland. Nearly all nonurban areas still have apples. For some decades the leading variety has been Rome, with over one-fourth of the crop in 1970. It was followed closely by Red Delicious and Stayman. Others grown in substantial amounts were Golden Delicious, McIntosh, Jerseyred (a New Jersey Experiment Station development), Starr, Winesap, and Jonathan, in order of importance.

Just as there was no indication in the twentieth century that the area of greatest apple production had once been northeastern New Jersey, so the dominance of South Jersey in peach production eventually left the orchardists of Hunterdon and adjacent counties with only traditions of their halcyon days. The revival of the peach industry in the traditional peach areas after the almost complete destruction by the San Jose scale was a slow and expensive one. Nevertheless, some growers made the attempt. In 1910 there were 300,000 peach trees in Hunterdon County. This seems a pitiful number as compared with over 2 million trees in 1890, but it was, nevertheless, a quarter of the state total and as many as the total for competing counties Monmouth, Burlington, Cumberland, and Atlantic. Unfortunately, Hunterdon was seldom as lucky as regards frosts as counties farther south. In 1920 both Monmouth and Burlington, with nearly 60,000 bushels each, topped Hunterdon's 50,000 bushels. The state production of 441,000 bushels in that year was more than half that of the old days. Peach pests were now under control, and another peach boom was soon on its way. In 1920 Burlington County, center of the boom, had 640,000 trees, Atlantic was second with 418,000, and Cumberland, Gloucester, Camden, and Hunterdon followed with about one-quarter million trees each. The state had all told nearly 3 million trees.

State production in 1924, a good year, was nearly 3 million bushels, probably an all-time high, and Burlington County's 963,000 bushels may have been a county record to that time. But the old tale of boom and bust must again be related. Low prices, the result of market glut, was already causing many a farmer to reach for the ax. The rapid decline that soon set in brought the state peach tree count down to just over 1 million by 1940. Nearly one-fourth of them were in Burlington, while Atlantic ranked second with 200,000 trees and Gloucester third with over 150,000. Peach production in 1939, just over 1 million bushels, was about in the same proportion. It is worth noting that the rate of decline was least in the latter two counties. An interesting survey in 1937 showed that whereas the old Elberta, Hale, Golden Jubilee, and Belle of Georgia were still leading, a New Jersey Experiment Station variety, N.J. 87, Golden East, with 11.4 percent of the count, ranked fifth in number of trees in the state. Experiment Station numbers 94, 66, 70, 73, 71, and 82 held respectively the tenth, twelfth, eighteenth, twenty-second, and twenty-sixth positions. Some of these numbered varieties later proved their excellence and were honored with names.

A partial recovery brought state peach production to an average of over 1.5 million bushels yearly between 1945 and 1950, and somewhat higher during the next five years. A crop of 2.1 million bushels in 1956 was topped by 2.8 million in 1960, the record year in recent times, and 2.5 million in 1965. The chief deterrent during most years of the 1960s, as with apples, was the yearly drought, which cut production in half for several years. Many peach orchardists put in overhead irrigation systems during these years. The crops of 1968 and 1969 were about 2 million bushels each year, and that of 1970 three-fourths as much. After 1962 the victory of South Jersey was almost complete. Gloucester County's production in that year was over four times that of Burlington, which had slipped slowly to fourth place. In 1965 Gloucester's 1.1-million-bushel production set an all-time county record, but its crop was nearly as large in 1969, when that county had over half the state crop. During the 1960s, Atlantic and Camden counties vied for second place, with Cumberland and Burlington not far behind.

Despite generally high prices, all has not been rosy for the New Jersey peach orchardist in recent years. His production costs, including those for irrigation, have mounted steeply. Many trees, after years of drought, died, especially in 1965. In that year, despite an average price of $3.75 per bushel, some 70,000 bushels of peaches were unharvested "for economic reasons." Then in 1966 a late cold spring, in the words of the state report, "was climaxed by an extensive freeze early in May." For some orchardists, the blow was a fatal one. It seems probable, however, that peach production in deepest South Jersey will continue, at least for the near future. The Gloucester County tryout of a peach harvester in 1971 indicates an effort to mechanize further to cut labor costs.[2] Peach orcharding has tended to become the specialty of a few. There were more than 5,000 peach orchardists in New Jersey in 1930. The number in 1968 was about 500.

The story of other orchard fruits is less important. Pears, once of some significance, declined rapidly after 1920. The half million trees at that time, most of them in Burlington, Camden, and Cumberland counties, had declined to 50,000 by 1940 and to 8,000 by 1964. Production in 1909 was nearly one-half million bushels, but in 1930, the last year with a significant figure, it had declined to one-fourth as much. The 5,500 pear orchards of that year had declined to 240 by 1964, with a production in that year of only 12,400 bushels. Cherries also declined rapidly in the same period. The 134,000 trees of the state in 1920, more than one-third of them in Burlington County, had declined to 50,000 by 1940, when one-half were in Burlington. State production by this time was 13,000 bushels annually, one-third of that of 1910. In 1964 some 7,000 trees produced some 6,000 bushels. The number of farmers with cherry trees had declined from 3,400 in 1930 to 150 in 1954. The very similar development for plums, but at a still lower level, does not seem worth recording, and the same is true for several of the bush fruits, most of which, regrettably, can hardly be found on the market today.

Grapes, which have caught the imagination of many in New Jersey from colonial days to the present, have never been a great success here. In 1910 Atlantic County, with over 800,000 grapevines in commercial production had half those of the state. Cumberland County was second, with less than half as many, and Camden a poor third. The state in 1909 produced 3,250 tons of grapes. By 1934 production had fallen to 2,750 tons. At the latter date, Atlantic led in production, followed closely by Burlington, which had come up to second place. The decline thereafter was abrupt, with half the five thousand growers dropping out by 1948 and state production falling to 1,400 tons. The one exception was Monmouth, where new vineyards had been planted as the result of favorable markets for wine grapes. State production remained on a plateau for several years thereafter, with a little more than half the crop being processed for wine. But a decline for market grapes in the late 1950s brought the total crop below 1,000 tons annually. However, with some 300,000 vines in the state in 1964 and an improving market for wine grapes, it seemed that grapes might regain some importance. In 1965 the total crop was 1,350 tons. Processed grapes by this time were five times as many as market grapes. After a number of poor years, production rose to 1,400 tons in 1970. The remaining two hundred commercial growers were again enlarging their vineyards, and a minor resurgence seemed under way. An undoubted factor was the success of a new picker for wine grapes.

The strawberry was the most important of the small fruits at the beginning of the modern period. The 8,700 acres of 1899 had expanded to 9,700 by 1909. Strawberries are a crop which can be wonderfully productive under favorable treatment, and the upsurge in production from 13 million quarts to 19 million had been out of proportion to the acreage. Interestingly enough, Cumberland and Atlantic counties, with nearly half the state production in 1897, had declined, while some areas near cities had expanded considerably, and particularly parts of Burlington, Camden, and Salem counties. The traditions of the wonderfully succulent and amazingly cheap strawberries of the Paterson area apparently reflect very local conditions; for Passaic and Bergen counties, already rapidly declining, had together only 2,000 acres in 1909. Because of overproduction, market prices in general had declined despite the growth of the market. Soon a bigger problem was the shortage of labor. During World War I, state acreage fell to 5,000 acres and berries actually picked declined by more than half. After something of a revival in the mid-1920s, the decline continued, so that by 1930 fewer than 4,000 acres were harvested. Cumberland County was again far in the lead, followed in order by Atlantic, Burlington, and Camden. In 1940 there were about 3,300 acres of strawberries in the state. A considerable decline was followed by an increase, so that the acreage of 1951 equaled that of 1940.

The acreage of strawberries in 1956 and again in 1965 was 2,500. A steady decline thereafter resulted in a figure of only 1,700 acres in 1970. Use of better varieties and more and better fertilizers in recent decades has brought up acre yields considerably. As a result, the approximately 7-million-pound average per year of the 1940s increased to 13 million in the early 1960s, despite a decline in acreage. Since 1965, however, the state yield has fallen with acreage. The crop of 1969 was only 7.9 million pounds and that of 1970 only 6.8 million. Strawberries today are produced by specialists in a limited but very productive area in South Jersey. The 3,000 commercial strawberry growers of 1929 fell to 2,200 by 1939, to 1,900 by 1949, to 900 by 1959, and to fewer than 500 by 1969. The greatest single problem of the growers is that of securing enough pickers at harvest time. It is extremely doubtful that an effective and economical machine to pick strawberries will be invented in the near future.

The cranberry, never truly domesticated, but given considerable care in its native bogs, continued to be of importance in this period. In 1909 some 9,000 acres were harvested by booted pickers, perhaps the most in New Jersey history until that time. Considerably more than half the total was in Burlington County. Atlantic County, with 1,200 acres, was still developing new bogs, but would soon reach its maximum. Ocean, on the other hand, with 800 acres, had declined by half in a decade, but would soon revive. The decline in all areas during World War I brought acreage harvested to less than 7,000 in 1919. An increase in demand, with better prices, stimulated the development of more bogs, bringing acreage to 11,000 in the 1920s. Of this nearly 6,000 acres were in Burlington County, nearly 2,000 in Atlantic, some 1,400 in Ocean, and a few hundred acres each in six other counties. Acreage held up during the Great Depression, but fell rapidly to 5,000 in 1940. Due to high prices, there was a revival just after World War II, but the boom quickly subsided. The 7,000 acres of 1950 had declined to 4,000 by 1959. Since then the amount has seldom been more than 3,000 acres. The attrition in acreage, common to all the cranberry counties, was partly the result of encroachment for other land usage, including the raising of blueberries, but was caused particularly by the abandonment of noneconomic bogs as labor became scarce and wages increased.

Yet as techniques improved, acre yields so increased that the total crop often became larger as the area used became smaller. The largest harvest in the 1920s was in 1926, when there were 210,000 barrels of 96 pounds each. In 1937, a banner year, 175,000 barrels were produced. In 1953 the state crop was 112,000 barrels, of which 79,000 came from Burlington County, 27,000 from Ocean, and 16,000 from Atlantic. In the five years 1965–69, average annual harvest was over 150,000 barrels, and the crop of 177,000 barrels in 1970 was the largest crop since 1926. Shortage of handpickers in some years was once a deterring factor, but during recent years a larger and larger part of the crop has been "water harvested." The "wet-pick" method not only eliminates much hand labor but also avoids the large loss in harvesting by handpicking. The decline in the number of cranberry growers from 146 in 1954 to 64 in 1965 in part reflects the cost of tooling up for the new kind of harvesting. The chances of more than a moderate increase in cranberry production in New Jersey seem slim. Both Massachusetts and Wisconsin get a higher yield per acre, and presumably both would increase acreage considerably if the market should warrant it. As it is, both states produce several times as much as New Jersey. Washington and Oregon have a higher yield per acre than New Jersey, though with smaller acreage.

Before 1910 the highbush blueberry grew wild in the fringes of cranberry bogs. Experiments here and in other states had failed to domesticate it. But in 1911 Elizabeth C. White, daughter of a leading cranberry grower in Burlington County, read about the experiments of F. V. Coville in a bulletin of the United States Department of Agriculture. An agreement was worked out by which "Whitesbog" at New Lisbon was used for Department of Agriculture field trials. Here were developed several successful varieties, some brought in from outside, but most found by "Piney" neighbors as the result of bounties paid by Miss White.[3] Decades of work at Whitesbog and other places led to the complete domestication and hybridization of the blueberry and its development as a field crop. By 1940 there were 650 acres in production in New Jersey and by 1946 some 2,100 acres. By the time of Miss White's death in 1954 the acreage had reached the 5,000 mark, with 2,800 of this amount in Burlington County and 1,600 in Atlantic. The state harvest of that year was 1.6 million trays of 12 pints each.

Ten years later, in 1964, New Jersey had 8,300 acres and was by far the most important state for blueberry culture. The value of the crop in that year was $5.5 million, two and one-half times the value of the cranberry crop. Blueberry acreage was for the most part split between Burlington County with 3,900 acres and Atlantic with 3,700. By 1969 acreage for the state had fallen to approximately 8,000, but the 2 million trays harvested brought more than $6 million. The 1970 crop fell by one-fourth and its sales value by one-sixth. By 1969 Atlantic County had secured first place with 3,900 acres harvested compared with 3,250 for Burlington in that year. With a harvest return of nearly twice that of Burlington, Atlantic has definitely become the center of blueberry production. In 1969 there were something under 500 commercial blueberry producers in the state. It seems probable that these specialists will be saved from the bogey of labor shortage by mechanical pickers. The picker for large-bush varieties will soon be supplemented by a newly developed small-bush harvester.[4] It is reckoned that fifty man-hours are required to pick an acre of blueberries by hand. If the new mechanical monsters can entirely replace handpickers, blueberry production in New Jersey may well increase. This possibility at once raises two haunting questions. First, will some other ideal areas for raising blueberries be found, and, second, can the American appetite for blueberries be greatly increased?

Edmund Morris, the author of *Ten Acres Enough,* describing a tomato "canhouse" of about 1860, made the remark, "Few vegetables have gained so rapid and wide-spread a popularity as this." But not even he could have foretold the enormous expansion of tomato growing in the future. The tomato, once maligned by many as poisonous, was already in 1910 one of New Jersey's most important crops. But its most spectacular development came after World War I. In 1919, the first year with statistics for tomatoes as apart from other vegetables, there were 37,000 acres in the state. Gloucester County had 8,000 acres, Salem 7,600, Cumberland 6,200, and Burlington 6,000. Ten years later, some 8,000 farmers grew 42,000 acres, and the crop was estimated as worth nearly $6 million, about equal to that of the corn crop, which was grown on four times the acreage. It is little wonder that the tomato aroused enthusiasm. But by 1939, tomato acreage was down to 37,000. In a time of depressed prices, the crop was valued at $3.5 million. Demand for canned tomatoes during World War II, however, brought an expansion. In 1945 total state figures for tomato acreage were 55,000. Nearly four-fifths of the crop was grown under contract to canning companies, the remainder as market tomatoes. The crop in that year was valued at $10 million. This was twice the valuation of all vegetables, including tomatoes, in 1900.

One of the most startling developments in tomato growing in recent years has been the great increase in crop yield per acre. In the early 1940s, the average was 9 or 10 tons per acre, but in 1962 it was 20.5 and in 1970 it was 19.3. On the other hand, there has been a constant dwindling in acreage. Using state census figures, the area devoted to tomatoes for processing fell from 43,000 acres in 1945 to 25,000 in 1955 to 19,000 in 1965. At the same time, market tomato acreage fell from 11,500 acres in 1945 to 8,000 in 1955 to 7,500 in 1965. In 1970 market tomatoes were grown on 6,700 acres and canning tomatoes on 14,500, in both cases a considerable decline from previous years. The counties with the greatest production have been consistently the same for half a century. Their acreage figures in 1969 were as follows: Gloucester 5,800, Salem 5,400, Cumberland 3,950, and Burlington 2,500. The tomato has been consistently the New Jersey crop with the largest gross returns; in recent times more than 10 percent of the value of all crops produced in the state and 30 per cent of the valuation of all vegetables. But not everything is bright for tomato growers. Problems at present are legion, headed perhaps by that of labor supply, but they are no worse than they have been for some time and perhaps no worse than in rival areas. However, in an industry of high costs and intense industrial competition, there is always the danger that processors can drive better bargains elsewhere. Increasing mechanization, particularly with a new harvester coming rapidly into use, may help counter labor advantages of other areas. A technique first tried commercially in 1970 was direct seeding, thus obviating plant and labor costs.[5] Greenhouse production of market tomatoes is receiving some attention, but it is doubted that New Jersey can successfully compete with states farther south.

The phenomenal increase in other vegetable growing in recent times has resulted in this sector of agriculture becoming one of the most important in New Jersey. At its beginning, however, it was not obvious that a branch of agriculture so laborious and so financially hazardous would be a great success. Factors in the change have been continued mechanization, a great increase in nearby markets, the appearance of large-scale producers, and the increasing possibility of contracts with processors. In 1909 all vegetables, including tomatoes, utilized only 86,000 acres in New Jersey. But by 1919 it was clear that a change was already on the way. Vegetable acreage, no longer counting that of tomatoes, was nearly 60,-000, in that year. The three highest counties by far were Gloucester and Burlington, each with about 10,000 acres of vegetables, and Cumberland with 7,000. In 1929 state acreage, still centering in the same areas, was approximately 90,000 and in 1939 nearly 100,000. A listing of the more important vegetables, with amounts grown, in the latter year, will indicate the diversity: sweet corn 20,000 acres, asparagus 15,000, green lima beans 13,000, carrots 12,000, snap (green) beans 11,000, peppers 6,600, green peas 4,200, cabbage 3,800, spinach 3,500, melons 3,300, cucumbers 2,500, onions 2,400, lettuce 1,700, beets 1,300, celery 1,300, eggplant 1,300, squash 1,100, broccoli 1,000, pumpkins 900, cauliflower 700, rhubarb 300. There had been a significant increase in acreage during the decade for asparagus, green lima beans, peppers, cabbage, carrots, beets, and eggplant and a significant decline for sweet corn, snap beans, cabbage, spinach, melons, cucumbers, and celery.

The outstanding vegetable in 1939 for value was asparagus, nearly half of which was grown in Cumberland County. Sweet corn, with two-fifths in Burlington and the rest scattered throughout the state, was second in value. Snap beans, also a specialty of the two counties just mentioned, were third in rank, and lima beans, nearly half of them grown in Cumberland, were fourth. Peppers, spinach, cabbage, celery, lettuce, and onions came next in descending order. With the notable exceptions of lima beans, carrots, peppers, eggplant, and beets, the number of producers had declined for most vegetables, and in some cases by a large fraction. Vegetable farmers were increasing the size of their operations, and at the same time were showing a tendency to specialize. Nevertheless, the period of the 1940s was still one of considerable diversity and one of fluctuations in operations. All told, some fifty truck crops were grown com-

mercially in the state. In nearly every case, by far the greater part of the
production was in the counties from Burlington south, though muck
areas of limited extent in North Jersey deserve mention.

Statistics for 1949 showed that asparagus had retained its first-place
position and increased its lead. A crop of 24,000 acres nearly equally
divided between asparagus for market and asparagus for processing was
grown in that year. More than two-thirds was grown in Cumberland and
Salem counties. Lettuce, with a total of 4,600 acres, was now second in
value. Half of this crop was grown in Cumberland County. Sweet corn
was now third, though the crop required 19,000 acres. It was still grown
widely, with considerable amounts as far north as Hunterdon, but the
great leader was Burlington County, with one-third of the crop. Peppers,
with 7,400 acres, were fourth in value, and snap beans, with now only
6,200 acres, were fifth. Next in rank came cabbage with 6,000 acres, and
spinach with 3,200 acres. Lima beans had by now fallen to an acreage
under 3,000 (possibly indicating a change in taste), whereas onions had
risen to 1,800, muskmelons (universally called cantaloupes by this time)
to 1,700, and eggplant to 1,400. Cucumbers, carrots, celery, and beets were
still of some consequence.

In the 1950s, the development was one chiefly of expansion. The four
leading vegetable crops of 1959 were still the same as those of 1939. Asparagus had pushed ahead greatly as a fresh-market crop, while nearly
maintaining its place as to processing. With an acreage of 31,500, larger
than that of tomatoes, the crop was worth more than twice that of sweet
corn, which had regained second place, despite a decline from 19,000 to
14,000 acres. Lettuce, now third in value, still had 4,800 acres. An acreage
of 8,300 in peppers, a slight increase, returned a crop fourth in value.
Cabbage, despite a decline to 4,100 acres, was fifth, snap beans, with a
slight increase in acreage, were sixth, and onions, also with a slight increase, seventh. A surprising, and temporary entry into the million-dollar
class was broccoli, with 3,300 acres. Lima beans had continued to decline
in importance, with their money return considerably exceeded by comparative newcomers, escarole and eggplant. The state Department of
Agriculture, in its annual survey of the nineteen or twenty most important fresh-market vegetable crops and nine processed crops, also included
in its statistics, in order of value of crop, cucumbers with 1,900 acres,
carrots with 1,100, celery with 450, and cantaloupes with 1,700.

During the 1960s there was a slow decline in acreage and total product.
The 1970 crop of commercial vegetables other than tomatoes totaled just
over 80,000 acres, fairly evenly divided between fresh-market vegetables
and vegetables grown for processing. If tomatoes are included, the gross
return from vegetables in 1970 was approximately $55 million. Changes
in emphasis among vegetable crops since 1959 have not been substantial.

Asparagus declined in acreage nearly one-third, to 19,800 acres by 1970, about three-fourths grown for processing. Receipts were the lowest in years, but asparagus was still by far the most important vegetable other than tomatoes in New Jersey. Recent market changes have led to wide adoption of the planting pattern of Delaware growers, in which roots and crowns or, in many cases, seeds are placed in double rows to facilitate harvest by machine.[6] Next in order of value were peppers with 8,000 acres, cabbage with 3,500 acres, sweet corn with 11,500 acres, lettuce with 2,700 acres, and snap beans with 5,700 acres. Other crops of importance were, in order of value, onions, escarole, eggplant, cucumbers, and spinach. The carrot crop was worth $656,000.

Vegetable growing suffered from the severe decline of New Jersey agriculture in the 1960s, but until very recently less than other sectors. Increasingly localized in the extreme southern part of the state, vegetable growers seem at present safer than most farmers from the intrusion of Megalopolis. But already suburban and exurban developments have begun to appear in their area. And already they are being troubled by problems that assailed farmers of other parts of the state earlier, including a rise in taxes and other overhead costs. Vegetable farming is particularly vulnerable as regards labor. A farm leader recently made what it is hoped is an overpessimistic statement: "If our producers are forced too far too quickly in terms of labor costs and further reductions in farm labor force, we stand in real danger of forcing the fruit and vegetable industry out of New Jersey."[7] Another observer reports that vegetable growers are applying a new maxim: "If it cannot be grown and harvested mechanically, it will not be grown."[8] Because of mounting pressures, farmers will increasingly concentrate on vegetables for which mechanization is a paying proposition, to the exclusion of those for which it is not.

The importance of horticultural specialties has kept pace with the rapid urbanization of New Jersey, and some have benefitted especially from the development of suburban areas. A survey in 1954 showed sales of nursery products totaling $6.5 million, of flowers totaling $14.5 million, and of allied specialties bringing something over $1 million. The federal census of 1964 showed a total of $28 million received by about 1,600 farmers for "nursery and greenhouse products, flowers, vegetable seeds and plants, and bulbs grown for sale." Of this amount, nearly $11 million was received by 854 nurseries and $16 million by 920 greenhouse operators for flowers. State figures for 1970 show 1,022 certified nurseries in the state, utilizing 11,028 acres of land. A small but increasing business is that of growing vegetables under glass or transparent plastic.

Epilogue
New Jersey Agriculture in Decline

In 1945 Willard H. Allen, long a prominent farm leader and at that time state Secretary of Agriculture, wrote ebulliently as to the future of New Jersey agriculture. He pointed out that since 1930 the downward trend in the number of farms had been reversed and that rural population was at an all-time high, double that of a century earlier. He cited figures to show that gross farm income in 1940 was double that of 1900, that New Jersey farm acres paid the highest gross return in the nation, and that the average sales of crop and livestock products per farm were third highest. The yield of milk per cow, of eggs per hen, and of crops per acre had increased markedly. Mr. Allen's optimism for the future was based on the "scientific direction and efficient operation of New Jersey farmers," their "excellent market outlets," and "the Garden State's successful diversification of farming projects." [1]

Mr. Allen's enthusiasm at the time is understandable. New Jersey farmers had adjusted to the new mechanization, had weathered the Great Depression, and had fought successfully for a part of the huge urban markets nearby. The devouring maw of city, suburban, and exurban development was already taking sizable bites from New Jersey farmland, but signs that the movement would accelerate rapidly in the near future were easily overlooked. Even less optimistic observers than Mr. Allen did not foresee that an increasing number of New Jersey farmers would in the near future be presented with two alternatives, both distasteful. They might persist in trying to make a living in one of the highest cost areas in the nation. Or they might, as the result of selling at a temptingly high price, give up the way of life to which they were accustomed or move to a farming area in which they would be strangers.

During the decade of war and peacetime adjustment which followed Mr. Allen's prognostication, a slow decline in rural population and in

270

LAND IN FARMS, 1860-1970

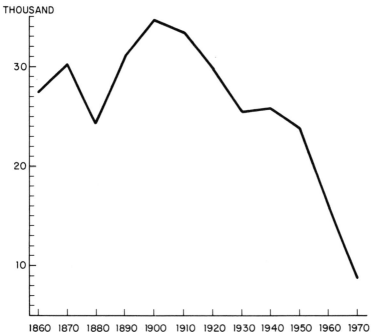

NUMBER OF FARMS, 1860-1970

Based upon New Jersey Department of Agriculture, *Statistical Handbook of New Jersey Agriculture* (Trenton, 1929) and *New Jersey Agricultural Statistics: 1945-56* and annuals 1957-70.

farmland acreage presaged ultimate trouble for New Jersey agriculture. But in a period of relative prosperity such portents received little attention. After 1950, however, the decline increased and, beginning about 1957, accelerated by mounting costs and new price squeezes, became calamitous. In 1950 there had been 24,838 farms in the state, a thousand less than in 1940. The number declined to 22,686 by 1954, then fell off steeply to 15,459 in 1959 and to 10,641 in 1964. By 1971 the number was estimated, perhaps a bit optimistically, at 8,400. The number of farm families was approximately one-fourth less. By all indications the decline was still continuing.

Actually, farmers had been selling their holdings at a pace faster than farmland had been removed from cultivation, and remaining farms had as a result increased considerably in size. The average farm in 1951 was 67 acres, little changed in two decades, but by 1960 it had climbed to 95 acres, by 1965 to 110 acres, and by 1972 to perhaps 120 acres. Nevertheless, the decrease in total farm acreage had been startling. In 1940 there had been 1.9 million acres of farmland, about a million less than at the turn of the century. In 1950 there were some 1.7 million acres, in 1960 some 1.5 million, and in 1972 just under 1 million acres. Farmland, once more than half the acreage of the state, had fallen to just over one-fifth. The "urban and built up areas" of the state occupied over 1.4 million acres.[2]

There are, of course, other methods of measuring agricultural developments. Agricultural experts continually point out in well-reasoned speeches, research papers, and articles that agriculture in New Jersey is still of importance. From a dollar standpoint, the value of New Jersey farm products, estimated at $261,600,000 in 1971, declined only 6.5 percent in the previous five years.[3] The proponents of the view that those farmers who are left are more flexible and business-minded than the farmers of any other period in New Jersey history are probably correct, as are those who state that man-hour return in some sectors of agriculture is continuing to improve. There are those who point out, quite fairly, that some portions of the state have thus far been to one side of the great flow of suburban development. Unfortunately, none of these approaches in any way detracts from the fact that New Jersey agriculture, of both traditional and newer types, is faced by overwhelming forces. The economic decline, even in depreciated dollars, is fairly obvious, and the social impact of the disappearance of two-thirds of the farm population in two decades is truly momentous. The very rapidity with which the situation has changed shows the perilous position of what remains of New Jersey agriculture.

Unless something drastic and immediate is done, even the highly mechanized, intensive agriculture often envisioned will be confined to a smaller and smaller part of the state. As the agricultural and woodland

areas are taken over for housing developments, factories, highways, air-
fields, and badly needed municipal, county, and state parks, agriculture
will be increasingly cramped. As the bulldozers advance, the true lands-
man, willy-nilly, can only flee to farming areas outside New Jersey, his
sole consolation being the money he has acquired from the sale of Jersey
land. But under the circumstances, and particularly since there are now
so few young farmers, most farmers will become part of the urban throng,
will retire to uneasy leisure in a village or in Suburbia, or will find themselves lured to Florida or southern California. An observer in Hunterdon
County, the one county of the state with half its land still in farms,
doubts that more than "a handful of farmers [are] actually making
enough of a net profit from their farming operations to warrant continuance of farming." [4] Unless means of halting or substantially slowing the
process are found, soon only small islands of traditional farming will
remain. The operators of greenhouses, nurseries, and turf farms may well
be the last to go, but like the smile of the Cheshire cat, they too are
likely to disappear in time.

It is predicted by demographers that New Jersey will enter the twenty-
first century with some 20 million people. It already has the greatest
population density among the states, more than 900 people per square
mile in 1970. A trebling or quadrupling of the population in three decades undoubtedly will mean continued and intensified pressure on the
land, even if some revolutionary change in housing is successfully devised
and widely adopted. In particular, suburban and exurban development,
if unchecked, will continue to eliminate more forest and farmland. As an
observer in 1970 put it: "They [the farmers] do not have to farm in New
Jersey. They can sell their land at a good price, move to another state,
and continue their farming operations." [5] Whether the farmer sells, or
simply steps off the treadmill, the results for New Jersey are the loss of
another farm and another farm family. The farm population, less than 1
percent of the total of the state, cannot, of course, by its own efforts do
very much to prevent ultimate takeover of the last million acres of farmland for nonagricultural uses. It remains to be seen whether general public concern and official policy, both aroused belatedly, can do more. The
problem is not a future danger but a calamity which has already arrived.

News of the acceleration of the rate of decline of state farm population
and cropland came as a surprise to the general public, among whom responses of apathy or fatalism were all too prevalent. Unfortunately, the
friends of agriculture were also caught off balance, and it took some
time for them to agree on a course of action and to marshal support for
it. The Farmland Assessment Amendment of 1963 and the implementing
legislation of 1964 constituted a solid achievement by giving farmers—and
other landowners—tax relief. But it was soon obvious that much more

sweeping measures would be necessary if any substantial part of New Jersey agriculture were to be saved. A conference jointly sponsored by the New Jersey Department of Agriculture and the New Jersey Department of Conservation and Economic Development in December 1966 brought the problem into open consideration, and numerous later meetings at local and state levels discussed it from every angle.

Not all discussants have been sympathetic. One farm leader in 1967, observing the progress of "urban sprawldom," was shocked to find that some of his counterparts in other sectors of the state's economy suggested openly that agriculture was no longer "important to the economy of the state and should be forced out." [6] As the debate has come into the open, it is clear that an effective program will meet considerable resistance. Many individuals who gain financially from the largely unregulated, unplanned expansion of residential and business areas are naturally opposed to any change in the existing disorder. Many others resist automatically any suggestions for planning and for the governmental controls entailed. The suburbanite majorities in areas undergoing change are often unsympathetic to proposals for any tax or other sort of break for their farmer neighbors. Perhaps the greatest menaces to constructive action are the general apathy, disinterest, and lack of knowledge of a substantial number of voters.

On the other hand, many thinking nonfarmers who wish to preserve open space have shown willingness to give aid to any program aimed at preserving the state's agriculture. Farm leaders, as in the case of the Farmland Assessment Amendment referendum in 1963, have wisely stressed arguments with urban appeal, including the need for open space, the availability of locally grown food, the esthetic and health values of country visits, and the ecological need for preserving some areas with uncontaminated land, water, and air. A publication of the New Jersey Farm Bureau at the end of 1970 ably marshaled these arguments, analyzed the problems involved, and suggested possible remedies based in part on experimental legislation and suggested programs in other rapidly urbanizing states. It stated the conviction that "through proper planning we can retain enough good land for the continuation and expansion of agricultural production, and also make room for the growth in population the experts tell us will take place in our state." [7] Newspaper items from time to time indicate a generally favorable attitude on the part of the press. The general tenor is indicated by an editorial in an influential local newspaper, the *Hunterdon County Democrat,* in May 1970, which urged citizens to "work actively to keep farming a going thing, this precious, low-cost way of preserving green acres." [8] Many prominent individuals, official and otherwise, have been favorable from the start or have later expressed approval. An effective program, if one can be devised, will undoubtedly have many endorsers.

On September 13, 1971, Secretary of Agriculture Phillip Alampi appointed twenty-one "representatives of agriculture and related industries" to a Blueprint Commission on the Future of New Jersey Agriculture. Under orders from Governor William T. Cahill, this group is to prepare a plan that will assure "the permanence of New Jersey agriculture." If its recommendations meet the approval of the governor, the state legislature will be asked for appropriate legislation. If, then, members of the legislature and the general public they represent show the ability and desire to comprehend, a willingness to act quickly, and a persisting concern for the future, a program could emerge that would preserve a substantial portion of both traditional and newer forms of agriculture.[9] Such a program of necessity must be flexible, imaginative, generous, and blessed with astute leadership now and in the future, generation after generation. It is a big order, but should it prove successful there may eventually be more chapters to add to the history of agriculture in New Jersey.

Notes

CHAPTER 1

1. New Jersey Department of Agriculture, *Statistical Handbook of New Jersey Agriculture* (Trenton, 1929), p. 7; Kemble Widmer, *The Geology and Geography of New Jersey* (Princeton, 1964), pp. 151–52.

2. Erwin R. Biel gives an excellent treatment of the climate of New Jersey in Salomon J. Flink and others, *The Economy of New Jersey* (New Brunswick, 1958), pp. 53–98. See also David Ludlum, *Early American Winters, 1604–1820* (Boston, 1966), and *Early American Hurricanes, 1492–1870* (Boston, 1963).

3. Capner Collection, 1750–1846, MSS, Hunterdon County Historical Society, Flemington.

4. Johann D. Schoepf, *Travels in the Confederation, 1783–1784,* trans. A. J. Morrison (Philadelphia, 1911), I, 21.

5. The chief sources for the geographical and geological information given in this chapter have been Widmer, passim; Lynwood L. Lee, *Survey of New Jersey* (1965), typescript, Rutgers University Library; and Granville A. Quackenbush, *Our New Jersey Land* (New Brunswick, 1955). A wealth of information is to be found in the dozens of publications on these subjects by the state of New Jersey. For the probable effects of the Tocks Island Dam, see Elizabeth M. C. Menzies, *Before the Waters: The Upper Delaware Valley* (New Brunswick, 1966).

6. Robert Juet, *Robert Juet's Journal, The Voyage of the "Half Moon"* (Newark, 1959), p. 29.

7. "David De Vries's Notes," in Albert Cook Myers, ed., *Narratives of Early Pennsylvania, West New Jersey, and Delaware, 1630–1707* (New York, 1912), p. 25.

8. Jasper Danckaerts, *Journal of Jasper Danckaerts, 1679–1680,* trans. and ed. H. C. Murphy (New York, 1913), p. 91.

9. Peter Kalm, *The America of 1750: Peter Kalm's Travels in North America,* trans. and ed. Adolph B. Benson (New York, 1937), I, 79 ff., 174 ff., 219, 224, 262, et passim.

10. A. L. Patrick and others, *Soil Survey of the Belvidere Area, New Jersey* (Washington, D.C., 1920).

11. New Jersey Department of Agriculture, *New Jersey Farm Facts* (flyer, Trenton, March 1971).

12. Danckaerts, p. 95.

13. [Jacob Magill], "Traditions of Our Ancestors," *Hunterdon Republican* (Flemington), Apr. 21, 1870.

14. Kalm, I, 93–324, 631–48; Thomas Budd, *Good Order Established in New Jersey in America* (New York, 1865; first published in 1685), p. 34; A. L. Patrick and others, *Soil Survey of the Bernardsville Area, New Jersey* (Washington, D.C., 1923), pp. 420–68; and various letters of the Capner Collection.

15. The chief sources for this short sketch of wildlife in New Jersey were Kalm, passim; Budd, passim; early accounts in William Starr Myers, *The Story of New Jersey*, vol. I (New York, 1945); Albert Cook Myers, ed., *Narratives of Early Pennsylvania, West New Jersey, and Delaware, 1630–1707*, passim; Thomas Anburey, *Travels Through the Interior Parts of America* (London, 1791), II, 157–61; John Rutherford, "Notes on the State of New Jersey" (1788), New Jersey Historical Society, *Proceedings*, 2d ser., I (1867), 79–89; various unpublished store records, particularly those of Janeway and Broughton (full names unknown), who were located somewhere on the lower Raritan, probably at Raritan Landing, at least from 1735 to 1747, Rutgers University Library; and the letters of the Capner Collection.

16. Kalm, I, 111, 259–70; Gabriel Thomas, *An Historical and Geographical Account of the Province and the Country of Pennsilvania and of West-New-Jersey in America* (New York, 1848; first published in London, 1698); Samuel Smith, *A History of the Colony of Nova-Caesaria, or New Jersey* (Trenton, 1877; originally published at Burlington, 1765); John Reading, "Journal of John Reading" (1715–16), New Jersey Historical Society (Newark), *Proceedings*, 3d ser., XVIII (1915), 35–46, 90–110, 128–33; Max Schrabisch, *Archaeology of Warren and Hunterdon Counties*, Bulletin 18, Geological Series, Reports of the Department of Conservation and Development, State of New Jersey (Trenton, 1917), passim; F. G. Speck and C. M. Story, "Notes on Indian Life in Bergen County," Bergen County Historical Society (Ridgewood), *Papers and Proceedings*, III (1906–7), 20–23; "Journal of New Netherlands," New York (State), *Documentary History of the State of New York* (New York, 1933–37), IV, 3–4, 79–80; William Nelson, *Indians of New Jersey* (Paterson, 1894), passim; G. K. Holmes, "Aboriginal Agriculture—The American Indians," in L. H. Bailey, ed., *Cyclopedia of American Agriculture* (New York, 1909), IV, 24–38.

CHAPTER 2

1. J. Franklin Jameson, ed., *Narratives of New Netherland, 1609–1664* (New York, 1909), passim; Adrian C. Leiby, *The Early Dutch and Swedish Settlers of New Jersey* (Princeton, 1964), pp. 1–23, 34–58, 65–75; John R. Brodhead, *History of the State of New York* (New York, 1853), pp. 202–3, 288–89, 347–433, 578–613, 642–43, 662, 737–50; Edwin P. Tanner, *The Province of New Jersey, 1664–1738* (New York, 1908), pp. 25, 28, 31, 70, 83, 86; John E. Pomfret, *The Province of East New Jersey, 1607–1702* (Princeton, 1962), pp. 3–17; Charles H. Winfield, *History of the County of Hudson, New Jersey* (New York, 1874), pp. 17–105, 125–30; Kalm, I, 16, 266–68, 272–74, 307–8; II, 640, 644–45, 710–13, 726; New York (State), *Documents Relating to the Dutch and Swedish Settlers on the Delaware River*, Vol. XII of *Documents Relative to the Colonial History of New-York* (Albany, 1877), passim.

2. Anburey, II, 160.

3. Israel Acrelius, *A History of New Sweden,* trans. from the Swedish by William M. Reynolds (Philadelphia, 1874; originally published in 1757), pp. 314–50; Amandus Johnson, *The Swedish Settlements on the Delaware,* 2 vols. (Philadelphia, 1911); John E. Pomfret, *The Province of West New Jersey, 1609–1702* (Princeton, 1956), pp. 3–64; Carl R. Woodward, *Agriculture in New Jersey* (New York, 1930), pp. 9–10; John H. Wuorinen, *The Finns on the Delaware* (New York, 1938), passim; Albert Cook Myers, ed., *Narratives of Early Pennsylvania, West New Jersey, and Delaware, 1630–1707,* pp. 83–176; C. A. Weslager, *The English on the Delaware, 1610–1682* (New Brunswick, 1967), pp. 54–71.

4. Pomfret, *East New Jersey,* passim; William A. Whitehead, *East Jersey under the Proprietary Governments* (Newark, 1875), pp. 35–226; Tanner, pp. 1–80, 125–38; Danckaerts, pp. 93–95; John Brush, "The History of Piscataway Township," unpublished typescript, 1966, Rutgers University Library; letter of Richard Hartshorne, in Mariam V. Studley, ed., *Historic New Jersey Through Visitors' Eyes* (Princeton, 1964), pp. 9–11.

5. Pomfret, *West New Jersey;* Tanner, pp. 97–138; Hubert G. Schmidt, *Rural Hunterdon; An Agricultural History* (New Brunswick, 1946), pp. 97–138.

6. Hubert G. Schmidt, "Germans in Colonial New Jersey," *American-German Review,* June–July 1958, pp. 4–7, and *Rural Hunterdon,* pp. 33–35; J. C. Honeyman, "Zion, St. Paul's and other Lutheran Churches in Central New Jersey," New Jersey Historical Society, *Proceedings,* n.s., vols. IX (1924), 255–73; X (1925), 41–56, 294–306, 395–410; XI (1926), 57–70, 191–99, 378–96, 532–42; XII (1927), 67–78, 214–24, 326–36, 462–71; XIII (1928), 209–23, 330–48, 443–46; XIV (1929), 55–69, 336–51, 466–75; XV (1930), 95–109, 250–62, 392–401, 503–8; XVI (1931), 34–51, 180–86, 441–51; T. F. Chambers, *The Early Germans of New Jersey* (Dover, N.J., 1895), passim; A. B. Faust, *The German Element in the United States,* 2 vols. (New York, 1909); Rutherford, pp. 78–89.

7. Pomfret, *East New Jersey* and *West New Jersey,* passim; Schmidt, *Rural Hunterdon,* pp. 29–31, 36–41.

8. Théophile Cazenove, *Cazenove Journal, 1794* (Haverford, Pa., 1922), p. 17.

9. Schmidt, *Rural Hunterdon,* pp. 32, 35, 46; Adrian C. Leiby, in collaboration with Albert T. Klyberg, Jr., and Emorie A. Leiby, *The Huguenot Settlement of Schraalenburgh* (Rahway, 1964), passim.

10. J. Hector St. John de Crèvecoeur, *Letters of an American Farmer* (New York, 1957; first published in 1782), pp. 35–82.

CHAPTER 3

1. New Jersey, *Archives of the State of New Jersey,* 1st ser., XXIII, XXX, XXXII, passim; Henry C. Mercer, "Tools of the Nation Maker," Bucks County (Pennsylvania) Historical Society, *A Collection of Papers Read Before the Bucks County Historical Society,* II (1909), 486–87; III (1909), 469, 473.

2. Thomas Capner, Flemington, to Samuel Coltman, Leicester, England, Nov. 17, 1787, Capner Collection.

3. C. A. Weslager, *The Log Cabin in America* (New Brunswick, 1969), pp. 149–202; Henry C. Mercer, "Origin of Log Houses in the United States," Bucks County (Pennsylvania) Historical Society, *A Collection of Papers Read Before the Bucks County Historical Society,* V (1926), 563–83.

4. G. H. Larison, "The Mode of Life in Our Early Settlements," ibid, I (1909), 461–63.

5. G. H. Larison, "Last Primitive Houses Near Howell's Ferry," MS, n.d., pp. 1–8, Hunterdon County Historical Society; E. T. Bush in *Hunterdon County Democrat,* July 17, 1930.

6. N. R. Ewain, *Early Brickmaking in the Colonies* (Camden, 1938), pp. 1–3, 8.

7. Schoepf, I, 37.

8. John Hall, Flemington, to Mr. and Mrs. James Choyce, Austrey, England, 1786, Capner Collection.

9. Kalm, I, 118.

10. Adriaen van der Donck, "A Description of New Netherlands," trans. Jeremiah Johnson, *Collections of the New-York Historical Society,* 2d ser., I (1841), 129–242; van der Donck, "The Representation of New Netherland," trans. Henry C. Murphy, ibid., 2d ser., II (1849), 261–338; Danckaerts, p. 83; Carl W. Woodward, *Agriculture in New Jersey,* pp. 7–9; Pomfret, *East New Jersey,* pp. 3–17; Bidwell and Falconer, pp. 16–17; Harry B. Weiss, *The History of Applejack or Apple Brandy in New Jersey* (Trenton, 1954), pp. 32–33.

11. Kalm, I, 266–74, II, 710–35; van der Donck, *"A Description of New Netherland,"* passim; Leiby, *The Early Dutch and Swedish Settlers of New Jersey,* pp. 24–33; Pomfret, *West New Jersey,* pp. 16–34, 38–39; Albert Cook Myers, ed., *Narratives of Early Pennsylvania, West New Jersey, and Delaware, 1630–1707,* pp. 83–176; Woodward, *Agriculture in New Jersey,* pp. 9–10.

12. Cited in Weslager, *The English on the Delaware,* pp. 156–57.

13. Danckaerts, p. 98.

14. Kalm, I, 272; II, 710–35.

15. *A Further Account of New Jersey in an Abstract of Letters Lately Writ from Thence by Several Inhabitants There Resident* (London, 1676), passim; *A Brief Account of the Province of East-New-Jarsey in America, Published by the Scots Proprietors Having Interest There* (Edinburgh, 1683), passim; Bidwell and Falconer, pp. 9–17.

16. Letter of Ester Huckens, 1675, in Studley, pp. 11–12; *An Abstract or Abbreviation of Some Few of the Many (Later and Former) Testimonys from the Inhabitants of New Jersey . . .* (London, 1681), passim; Thomas, passim.

17. *A Brief Account of the Province of East-New-Jarsey . . . ,* passim; George Scot, *The Model of the Government of the Province of East-New-Jersey in America* (Edinburgh, 1685), pp. 146–272. See also Harry B. Weiss and Grace Weiss, *The Early Promotional Literature of New Jersey* (Trenton, 1964).

18. Rutherford, p. 88.

19. Lyman Carrier, *The Beginnings of Agriculture in America* (New York, 1923), pp. 269–71.

20. R. R. Honeyman, "More Local History—New Germantown," *Our Home,* I (1873), 120.

21. Schoepf, pp. 103–10.

22. "Andrew Johnston's Journal," *Somerset County Historical Quarterly,* III (1914), 23.

23. Chambers, pp. 127–28.

24. See van der Donck, Kalm, Scot, and Danckaerts.

25. Aarom Leaming and Jacob Spicer, compilers, *The Grants, Concessions and*

Original Constitutions of the Provinces of New Jersey, the Acts Passed during the Proprietary Government and Other Material Transactions before the Surrender Thereof to Queen Anne (Philadelphia, circa 1751), pp. 86–87, 112–14, 262.

26. Inventories in *Archives of the State of New Jersey,* 1st ser., XXIII, XXX, XXXII; Mercer, "Tools of the Nation Maker"; Larison, "The Mode of Life in Our Early Settlements"; Janeway and Broughton, general store, Raritan Landing, daybook, 1735–45, ledger, 1738–47; letters of Capner Collection, passim; *Federal and New Jersey Gazette* (Trenton), Feb. 4, 25, 1799; *Hunterdon Gazette* (Flemington), Jan. 27, 1830, Aug. 28, 1838; Magill in *Hunterdon Republican,* July 21, 1870; Woodward, *Agriculture in New Jersey,* passim; Bidwell and Falconer, passim. See also Kalm, passim.

CHAPTER 4

1. *American Husbandry,* ed. by H. J. Carman (New York, 1939; originally published in London, 1775), p. 106.

2. Cazenove, p. 12.

3. C. F. Volney, *A View of the Soil and Climate of the United States of America,* trans. C. B. Brown (Philadelphia, 1804), p. 6.

4. Mrs. Mary Capner, Flemington, to Mr. and Mrs. Hugh Exton, Ashby de la Zouche, England, 1788, Capner Collection.

5. Kalm, I, 317.

6. *American Husbandry,* pp. 105–6.

7. "Charles Read's Notes on Agriculture," in Carl Raymond Woodward, *Ploughs and Politicks* (New Brunswick, 1941), pp. 235–53.

8. Ibid.

9. Job Roberts, *The Pennsylvania Farmer* (Philadelphia, 1804), pp. 11, 134–36.

10. Inventories of estates in New Jersey, *Archives of the State of New Jersey,* 1st ser., XXIII, XXX, XXXII; Janeway and Broughton, general store, Raritan Landing, accounts, 1735–47; unidentified general store, Whitehouse, accounts, 1771–72; unidentified general store, Amwell, accounts, 1798–99; Kalm, passim; Woodward, *Agriculture in New Jersey,* passim.

11. Rutherford, p. 85; Cazenove, passim; inventories of estates in New Jersey, *Archives of the State of New Jersey,* 1st ser., XXIII, XXX, XXXII.

12. Quoted in James P. Snell, compiler, *History of Hunterdon and Somerset Counties, New Jersey* (Philadelphia, 1881), pp. 185–86.

13. Probate records, Office of Secretary of State, Trenton.

14. Rutherford, pp. 79–89.

15. "Book of Estrays," in Hopewell, New Jersey, *Town Records of Hopewell, New Jersey* (New York, 1931).

16. C. W. Opdyke, *The Op Dyck Genealogy* (Albany, 1889), pp. 224–33, 259–78, 339–49, 351–94, 411–34.

17. H. O. Rockefeller, ed., *Transactions of the Rockefeller Family Association for the Five Years, 1905–1909, with Genealogy* (New York, 1910), pp. 242–46.

18. Letter to Mrs. Hugh Exton, Feb. 7, 1791, Capner Collection.

19. *Archives of the State of New Jersey,* 1st ser., XXIII, XXX, XXXII, passim.

20. William Bailey, "More Local History—White House," *Our Home,* I (1873), 385–89; *New York Journal,* Apr. 20, 1775, reprinted in *Hunterdon County Democrat,* Feb. 14, 1924.

21. Newspaper extracts in New Jersey, *Archives of the State of New Jersey*, 1st ser., XI, XII, XIX, XX, XXIV, XXV, XXVI, XXVII, XXVIII, XXIX, XXXI; 2d ser., I, II, III, IV, V.

22. Johann Karl Büttner, *Narrative of Johann Carl Buettner in the American Revolution* (New York, n.d., originally published in Germany in 1828).

23. Ezekial Cole, Justice of the Peace, Readington Township, Hunterdon County, dockets, 1790–1804; *Federal and New Jersey Gazette*, Trenton, Aug. 26, 1800.

24. Capner Collection, passim.

25. T. F. Gordon, *A Gazetteer of the State of New Jersey* (Trenton, 1834), p. 29.

26. Henry Schofield Cooley, *A Study of Slavery in New Jersey* (Baltimore, 1896), pp. 9–31; A. Q. Keasbey, "Slavery in New Jersey," New Jersey Historical Society, *Proceedings*, IV (1901), 90–96, V (1902), 79–86, passim; U.S. Census of 1830, pp. 6–7, 58–59.

27. Cooley, pp. 45–58; newspaper extracts in New Jersey, *Archives of the State of New Jersey*, 1st ser., XI, XII, XIX, XX, XXIV, XXVII, XXVIII, XXIX, XXXI, 2d ser., I, II, III, IV, V, passim; Capner Collection, passim; Dr. John Bowne accounts, 1801–34, Hunterdon County Historical Society, passim; Hankinson family commonplace book, 1747–1842, Rutgers University Library; John Lambert, mill accounts, 1774, Rutgers University Library, passim; Hubert G. Schmidt, *Slavery and Attitudes on Slavery in Hunterdon County, New Jersey* (Somerville, 1941), passim; Brush, pp. 17–18.

28. *New Jersey Gazette,* Mar. 21, 1781.

CHAPTER 5

1. New Jersey, *Archives of the State of New Jersey*, 1st ser., XXIII, XXX, XXXII, passim.

2. Letter to Hugh Exton, Nov. 2, 1795, Capner Collection.

3. *New Jersey Wills*, passim.

4. Mary Choyce to Mr. and Mrs. James Choyce, May 1, 1793, Capner Collection.

5. Capner Collection, passim; Case tannery account books, 1783–1851, passim; Atkinson and Johnson general store, daybook, 1793–94. The reader interested in the technical side of New Jersey agriculture during this period should visit the Mercer Agricultural Museum at Doylestown, Pennsylvania. The collection of tools and implements there was originally gathered from both sides of the Delaware River.

6. Thomas Capner to John, Samuel, and Rowland Coleman, Leicester, England, Nov. 17, 1787, Capner Collection.

7. Samuel Alison, compiler, *Acts of the General Assembly of the Province of New Jersey, 1702–1776* (Burlington, 1776), p. 91.

8. *Pennsylvania Packet,* Jan. 8, 1776, in New Jersey, *Archives of the State of New Jersey*, 2d ser., I, 13–14.

9. Alison, p. 94.

10. Swain, pp. 332–33; Cross, p. 429; Case tannery, Ledger C, circa 1817; *Federal and New Jersey Gazette,* Feb. 4, 25, 1799; *Hunterdon Gazette,* Jan. 27, 1830,

Aug. 27, 1838, June 1, 1842; Isaac Passand to John Hall, London, Jan. 17, 1793, Capner Collection. See also, Bidwell and Falconer, p. 121.

11. Alison, p. 95.

12. "Charles Chesebrough Journal (1794)," *American Historical Review,* Oct. 1931, p. 69.

13. George H. Larison, "Last Primitive Houses Near Howell's Ferry."

14. C. W. Larison, *The Ancient Village of Amwell* (Flemington, 1916), pp. 4–7; John Blane, "About Pattenburgh," *Our Home,* I (1873), p. 189; Bailey, IV, 385–89; Isaac Passand to John Hall, Jan. 17, 1793, Capner Collection; "An Ancient Homestead and Its Inhabitants," *Home Visitor,* Mar. 4, 1896; Kalm, I, 117.

15. Kalm, I, 118–19.

16. Inventories in New Jersey, *Archives of the State of New Jersey,* 1st ser., XXIII, XXX, XXXII, passim; Newspaper extracts in New Jersey, *Archives of the State of New Jersey,* 1st ser., XI, XII, XIX, XX, XXIV, XXV, XXVI, XXVII, XXVIII, XXIX, XXXI, 2d ser., I, II, III, IV, V, passim.

17. There is a particularly good description of a barrack by Mrs. Mary Capner in a letter to Mrs. Hugh Exton, Nov. 13, 1787. See Schmidt, *Rural Hunterdon,* p. 95.

18. *American Husbandry,* p. 106. See also Kalm, I, 162.

19. Capner Collection, passim.

20. *Federal and New Jersey Gazette,* Feb. 4, 25, Mar. 18, 1788; Mrs. Mary Capner to Mrs. Hugh Exton, May 18, 1788, Capner Collection.

21. Carrier, pp. 269–73; Bidwell and Falconer, p. 233; Isaac Passand to John Hall, Jan. 17, 1793, Capner Collection.

22. Roberts, pp. 107, 118–31.

23. Case tannery accounts; Capner Collection, passim; Hankinson family commonplace book, entries in 1809–17; Büttner, passim; Charles Read, in Woodward, *Ploughs and Politicks,* pp. 266–78, 281; Kalm, I, 75, 183–84, 264–65; Cazenove, passim; Bidwell and Falconer, pp. 20, 103–04, 126; New Jersey, *Archives of the State of New Jersey,* 1st ser., XXIII, XXX, XXXII, passim.

CHAPTER 6

1. Kalm, I, 115, 164; H. W. Gross, "Horse Hopples," in Bucks County (Pennsylvania) Historical Society, *A Collection of Papers Read Before the Bucks County Historical Society,* V, 187; Anburey, II, 252; *Town Records of Hopewell, New Jersey,* passim.

2. Kalm, I, 236.

3. Letters of Mrs. Mary Capner, Capner Collection.

4. Budd, p. 38.

5. Chesebrough journal, p. 69.

6. New Jersey, *Archives of the State of New Jersey,* 1st ser., XI, 280–81.

7. *Pennsylvania Gazette,* Dec. 25, 1750, New Jersey, *Archives of the State of New Jersey,* 1st ser., XII, 696.

8. *Pennsylvania Gazette,* June 13, 1751, and *Pennsylvania Journal,* May 30, 1754, New Jersey, *Archives of the State of New Jersey,* 1st ser., XIX, 76–77, 367.

9. *New York Gazette or Weekly Post Boy,* Oct. 22, 1753, *Archives of the State of New Jersey,* 1st ser., XIX, 309.

10. Alison, pp. 13, 93.

11. *New Jersey Gazette*, Trenton, Apr. 24, 1782, New Jersey, *Archives of the State of New Jersey*, 2d ser., V, 422.

12. *Pennsylvania Gazette*, Apr. 1, 1756, New Jersey, *Archives of the State of New Jersey*, 1st ser., XX, 15.

13. "John Lambert's Almanack or Account Book, 1774," interlined in a copy of *Aitken's American Register and Calendar for the Year, 1774.*

14. James Parker farm diary, 1778–83, Shipley (near Pittstown), Rutgers University Library; Cazenove, pp. 3, 4, 9, 12; Capner Collection, passim.

15. Kalm, I, 236–78, 306. See also Carrier, pp. 254–55.

16. "Book of Estrays" in Hopewell, New Jersey, *Town Records of Hopewell, New Jersey.*

17. Parker farm diary, June 5, 1778.

18. Case tannery accounts; letters of Capner Collection; New Jersey, *Archives of the State of New Jersey*, 1st ser., XXIII, XXX, XXXII, passim.

19. Mary Choyce to Mr. and Mrs. James Choyce, Austrey, England, May 31, 1795, Capner Collection.

20. Büttner, pp. 29, 33; Chesebrough journal, p. 69.

21. Janeway and Broughton, daybook, 1735–45, ledger, 1738–47; Parker farm diary, entries of 1778; Atkinson and Johnson, general store, Flemington, daybook, 1793–94; Rutherford, pp. 79–89; Case Tannery accounts; Cazenove, p. 4; New Jersey, *Archives of the State of New Jersey*, 1st ser., XXIII, XXX, XXXII, passim.

22. Parker farm diary; "Book of Estrays," in Hopewell, New Jersey, *Town Records of Hopewell, New Jersey*; New Jersey, *Archives of the State of New Jersey*, 1st ser., XXIII, XXX, XXXII, passim.

23. New Jersey, *Archives of the State of New Jersey*, 1st ser., XXXV, 497.

24. Büttner, pp. 32–33.

25. Mrs. Mary Capner to Mrs. Hugh Exton, Dec. 22, 1787, Capner Collection.

26. Parker farm diary, May 23 and June 13, 1778.

27. Ibid., June 7, 1778.

28. Mrs. Mary Capner to Mrs. Hugh Exton, Dec. 22, 1787, Capner Collection.

29. Capner Collection, passim.

30. Woodward, *Agriculture in New Jersey*, p. 27.

31. Farm account book, Joseph Capner, 1804, Capner Collection.

32. Dr. John Bowne accounts, passim.

33. Parker farm diary.

34. Rutherford, p. 76.

35. Woodward, *Agriculture in New Jersey*, p. 45.

36. Samuel Coltman to Thomas Capner, Feb. 7, 1788, Capner Collection.

CHAPTER 7

1. Budd, pp. 33–34; Thomas, p. 21.

2. Inventories of John Reading (1717), Vincent Roberts (1721), Philip Edington (1727), John Comfort (1728), John Howell (1733), probate records, Office of Secretary of State, Trenton, 11J, 27J, 32J, 39J, 90J.

3. Kalm, I, 89, 179, 335; *American Husbandry*, pp. 98–99; Bidwell and Falconer, pp. 10–11, 89–90, 168; Woodward, *Agriculture in New Jersey*, pp. 14–15. See also C. S. Plumb, *Indian Corn Culture* (Chicago, 1908), chap. III, and Paul Weatherwax, *The Story of the Maize Plant* (Chicago, 1923), chaps. XVII and XXIV.

4. *American Husbandry*, pp. 98–99; Charles Read in Woodward, *Ploughs and Politicks*, pp. 278–80, 284–85; Kalm, I, 89, 179; Capner Collection, passim; Bidwell and Falconer, pp. 92, 240.

5. Parker farm diary, entries from May to November 1778.

6. Kalm, I, 75; Schoepf, I, 44. See Carrier, p. 14.

7. Rutherford, p. 87.

8. John Hall to Hugh Exton, June 17, 1795, Capner Collection.

9. Kalm in 1749 reported the wheat harvest as being in early July, but James Parker in 1778 began mowing only on July 18.

10. Inventories, New Jersey, *Archives of the State of New Jersey*, 1st ser., XXIII, XXX, XXXII, passim; Parker farm diary; H. C. Mercer, "Ancient Methods of Threshing in Bucks County," in Bucks County (Pennsylvania) Historical Society, *A Collection of Papers Read Before the Bucks County Historical Society*, V, 315–19; Case tannery account books, 1783–1851, passim; Hankinson commonplace book entries of 1809–17; Büttner, passim; Charles Read in Woodward, *Ploughs and Politicks*, p. 281; Kalm, I, 75, 183–84; Bidwell and Falconer, p. 126.

11. New Jersey, *Archives of the State of New Jersey*, 1st ser., XXIII, XXX, XXXII, passim.

12. Parker farm diary, Aug. 25, 1778; Chesebrough journal, p. 69.

13. See Cazenove, pp. 4, 14–15.

14. *American Husbandry*, p. 99; Capner Collection, passim.

15. See Parker farm diary, passim.

16. John L. Stillwell, *Old Readington* (Somerville, 1935), p. 43.

17. New Jersey, *Archives of the State of New Jersey*, 1st ser., XXIII, XXX, XXXII, passim. Capner Collection, passim.

18. Kalm, I, 176, 183–84.

19. Parker farm diary, June 3, July 21, 1778.

20. Isaac Passand to John Hall, Jan. 17, 1793, Capner Collection.

21. Atkinson and Johnson general store, Flemington, daybook, 1793–94; Peter Brunner, justice of the peace dockets, 1780–88, entry of Sept. 18, 1782; Chesebrough journal, p. 69.

22. New Jersey, *Archives of the State of New Jersey*, 1st ser., XXIII, XXX, XXXII, passim; Capner Collection, passim; Parker farm diary, passim.

23. New Jersey, *Archives of the State of New Jersey*, 1st ser., XXIII, XXX, XXXII, passim; Charles Read in Woodward, *Ploughs and Politicks*, p. 283.

24. Kalm, I, 185; Burnaby, p. 58.

25. See G. L. Beer, *British Colonial Policy, 1754–65* (New York, 1907), pp. 217–18; Samuel Alison, compiler, *Acts of the General Assembly, 1772–1776*, pp. 281, 313.

26. Unidentified general store, ledger, 1771–72; Atkinson and Johnson general store, daybook, 1793–94; unidentified general store, Amwell Township, Hunter-

don County, daybook, 1798–99; Case tannery records, passim; "John Lambert's Almanack or Account Book," passim.

27. See J. W. Lequear, "Flax Culture and Manufacture," (MS 1889), Hunterdon County Historical Society.

28. Ibid. See also Hubert G. Schmidt, *Flax Culture in Hunterdon County, New Jersey* (Flemington, 1939).

29. Parker farm diary, July 25, 1778.

30. Kalm, I, 181. See also A. W. Sampson, *Native American Forage Plants* (New York, 1924).

31. Charles Read in Woodward, *Ploughs and Politicks*, pp. 254–55; Mrs. Mary Capner to Mrs. Hugh Exton, Dec. 22, 1787, May 18, 1786, Capner Collection; Roberts, pp. 147–51.

32. See Bidwell and Falconer, pp. 20–21, 103–4.

33. New Jersey, *Archives of the State of New Jersey*, 1st ser., XXIV, passim.

34. Bidwell and Falconer, p. 104.

35. Parker farm diary, entries of July, 1778.

36. Case tannery, ledger, 1783–91, p. 114.

37. John Hall, Flemington, to Mr. and Mrs. James Choyce, Austrey, England, Apr. 30, 1793, and to Hugh Exton, Ashby de la Zouch, England, June 17, 1795, Capner Collection.

38. Charles Read in Woodward, *Ploughs and Politicks*, pp. 268, 276, 287, 303, 310; Büttner, pp. 13–14; Kalm, I, 264–65; Bidwell and Falconer, pp. 20, 103–4, 126; Capner Collection, passim; inventories in New Jersey, *Archives*, 1st ser., XXIII, XXX, XXXII, passim.

39. Rutherford, p. 84; Cazenove, p. 16.

40. Bidwell and Falconer, pp. 97–98; Bailey, II, 520.

41. Kalm, I, 336; Acrelius, p. 150.

42. Capner Collection, passim.

43. Parker farm diary, May 27, 1778.

44. Kalm, I, 336.

45. Kalm, passim; *American Husbandry*, pp. 100; Parker farm diary, July 3, 20, Aug. 5, 7, 1778, et passim; Capner Collection, passim.

46. Kalm, I, 193–94; *American Husbandry*, pp. 100–03. Parker grew turnips as a commercial crop in 1778.

47. Thomas, p. 25. See also Scot, passim, and Budd, pp. 33–34.

48. Kalm, I, 97, 118–20, 324, II, 659.

49. Letter to Samuel Coltman, Leicester, England, Nov. 17, 1787, Capner Collection.

50. Cazenove, p. 12.

51. Woodward, *Agriculture in New Jersey*, p. 20.

52. Mary Choyce to Mr. and Mrs. James Choyce, 1793, Capner Collection.

53. L. B. Strawn, "Applebutter Making as Practiced by Our Ancestors," in Bucks County (Pennsylvania) Historical Society, *A Collection of Papers Read Before the Bucks County Historical Society*, IV, 331; J. K. Blackfan, "Our Household Industries," ibid., V, 422.

54. Parker farm diary, Nov. 24, 1778.

55. Crèvecoeur, pp. 102–3.

56. Bidwell and Falconer, pp. 99–100.

57. Letter of James Mudie, Mar. 9, 1675, quoted in Scot, p. 244.

58. Weiss, *The History of Applejack or Apple Brandy in New Jersey*, pp. 35–36.

59. Ibid., pp. 18, 97–98, 131–36; Chesebrough journal, p. 69.

60. Kalm, II. 616–17; Cazenove, p. 12. See also Woodward, "New Jersey Cider," *New Jersey Agriculture*, Jan. 1927, pp. 14–15.

61. Woodward, "An Early New Brunswick Orchard," *New Jersey Agriculture*, Oct. 1929, p. 14.

62. Thomas Capner to Samuel Coltman, Sept. 17, 1787, Capner Collection.

63. Cazenove, p. 11.

64. Rutherford, p. 81.

CHAPTER 8

1. Jedidiah Morse, *The American Universal Geography* (Boston, 1796), II, 521–22.

2. Morse, *The American Universal Geography* (Boston, 1819), p. 430.

3. Woodward, "New Jersey's Contributions to the Development of the Plow," *New Jersey Agriculture*, Dec. 1927, p. 12.

4. See Woodward, *Agriculture in New Jersey*, pp. 88–90.

5. Woodward, *The Development of Agriculture in New Jersey, 1640–1880* (New Brunswick, 1927), pp. 103–49; Richard F. Hixson, *Isaac Collins; A Quaker Printer in 18th Century America* (New Brunswick, 1968), pp. 57–58. See also Harry J. Carman, ed., *Jesse Buel, Agricultural Reformer* (New York, 1947).

6. Weiss and others, *The History of the New Jersey Agricultural Society* (Trenton, 1949), p. 9, and Weiss, *History of the New Jersey Board of Agriculture* (Trenton, 1949), p. 7.

7. Bidwell and Falconer, pp. 187–88.

8. Woodward, *Agriculture in New Jersey*, pp. 57–62.

9. Weiss and others, *The History of the New Jersey Agricultural Society*, pp. 9–11.

10. Woodward, *Agriculture in New Jersey*, pp. 57–62, and "County Fairs in the Nineteenth Century," *New Jersey Agriculture*, Oct. 15, 1929.

11. Weiss, *History of the New Jersey Board of Agriculture*, pp. 5–9.

12. George W. Moore farm diary, 1853–57, Rutgers University Library.

13. John Ten Eyck farm diary, 1853–77, Rutgers University Library.

14. Ralph Voorhees farm diary, 1860, Rutgers University Library, entry of Oct. 4, 1860.

15. James Neilson, Jr., farm diary, 1862–70, Rutgers University Library, passim.

16. William Campbell Lippincott farm diary, 1868, Rutgers University Library, passim.

17. Moore diary, passim.

18. David C. Voorhees farm diary, 1875, Rutgers University Library, entries of early October.

19. Weiss and others, *The History of the New Jersey Agricultural Society*, pp. 13–49; Woodward, *Agriculture in New Jersey*, pp. 62–63.

20. See Woodward, *The Development of Agriculture in New Jersey,* pp. 178, 180.

21. George A. Hough, *A Brief History of the Princeton Agricultural Association* (1949), pp. 1–5.

22. David C. Voorhees diary, Apr. 15, 1875.

23. Ibid., Sept. 9, 1875.

24. Ibid., Dec. 16, 1875.

25. *Hunterdon County Democrat,* Jan. 16, 30, 1872, Jan. 14, 1873.

26. Woodward, *The Development of Agriculture in New Jersey,* pp. 179–80, 246–47.

27. *Proceedings of the Thirty-Fourth Annual Session of the State Grange in New Jersey . . .* (Flemington, 1906), pp. 21–27, 37.

28. Weiss, *History of the New Jersey Board of Agriculture,* passim.

29. Woodward, *The Development of Agriculture in New Jersey,* pp. 152–65.

30. Ibid., pp. 253–70, 274; Woodward and Ingrid Nelson Waller, *New Jersey's Agricultural Experiment Station* (New Brunswick, 1932), p. 25; William H. S. Demarest, *A History of Rutgers College, 1766–1924* (New Brunswick, 1924), pp. 405–12; Richard P. McCormick, *Rutgers, A Bicentennial History* (New Brunswick, 1966), pp. 87–91, 93.

31. Woodward, *The Development of Agriculture in New Jersey,* pp. 270–72; Woodward and Waller, pp. 50–52; McCormick, pp. 118–26.

32. Woodward, *The Development of Agriculture in New Jersey,* pp. 272–74; Woodward and Waller, pp. 83–84; McCormick, p. 174.

33. Woodward and Waller, pp. 22–34, 49–50.

34. Ibid., pp. 64–65; Demarest, pp. 405–12, 463–66, 511; McCormick, pp. 118–26, 146–47.

CHAPTER 9

1. Dimity T. Pitt, and Lewis P. Hoagland, compilers, *New Jersey Agriculture: Historical Facts and Figures* (Trenton, 1943), pp. 79–97; U.S. Census, 1850, pp. 146–47. The census definition of a farm varied somewhat between 1850 and 1910, particularly as to minimum acreage. However, the changes were not significant, and by 1910 the definition was nearly the same as in 1850. See U.S. Census, 1910, Agriculture, pp. 22–25.

2. Chesebrough journal, pp. 65–88.

3. James Ten Eyck, Jr., farm diary, 1802–24, Rutgers University Library, entries of May and June 1807.

4. *Federal and New-Jersey Gazette* (Trenton), Dec. 17, 1798, Feb. 4, 24, Mar. 18, 1799; *Hunterdon Gazette,* Aug. 11, 1825, June 14, 1826, Nov. 14, 21, 1827, et passim; C. W. Larison, *A Sketch of the Fisher Family,* pp. 83–84.

5. Stillwell, p. 17.

6. *Hunterdon Gazette,* Sept. 17, 1828.

7. C. W. Larison, *A Sketch of the Fisher Family,* pp. 83–84.

8. Moriscot Farm (Somerset County) workbook, 1903, John B. Thompson Collection, Rutgers University Library, entry of May 25, 1903.

9. Cazenove, pp. 3, 7.

10. Letter to John Hall, Jan. 17, 1793, Capner Collection.

11. See farm advertisements in *Federalist and New-Jersey Gazette*, Dec. 17, 1798, Feb. 4, 25, 1799, et passim; broadside notice of public sale, Henry Waterhouse, 1807, Hunterdon County Historical Society.

12. James Ten Eyck, Sr., farm diary, 1787–1809, Rutgers University Library, passim.

13. James Ten Eyck, Jr., diary, passim.

14. John Ten Eyck diary, passim.

15. Lippincott diary, passim.

16. David C. Voorhees diary, passim.

17. Dr. John Bowne accounts, daybook, 1807, ledgers, 1801–34, passim; Moore diary, passim.

18. Case tannery, Flemington, accounts, 1783–1851, Hunterdon County Historical Society, daybook entries of Feb. 23, 1791, Feb. 21, 1798, et passim, ledgers and bark books, passim.

19. Ralph Voorhees diary, passim.

20. *Hunterdon Gazette*, Mar. 26, 1828, Feb. 3, 1831.

21. Ibid., Aug. 8, 1825, Feb. 23, 1826, et passim; E. T. Bush in *Hunterdon County Democrat*, Apr. 21, 1932.

22. E. T. Bush in *Hunterdon County Democrat*, Mar. 13, 1920; letter, Joseph Thompson to John B. Thompson, Aug. 8, 1870, Thompson Collection, Rutgers University Library.

23. Thomas Capner to John, Samuel, and Rowland Coltman, Nov. 17, 1787, Capner Collection.

24. *Hunterdon County Democrat*, May 10, 1904.

25. Information given by Fred Totten, Ringoes.

26. See Bidwell and Falconer, p. 121.

27. David C. Voorhees diary.

28. [Jacob Magill], "Traditions of Our Ancestors," *Hunterdon Republican*, July 21, 1870.

29. Numerous letters of Capner Collection; see also Roberts, pp. 82–92.

30. Stillwell, p. 26; *Hunterdon County Democrat*, Mar. 3, 1869, Sept. 9, 1873.

31. Lippincott diary, passim.

32. Moriscot Farm workbook, entries of June, 1903.

33. James H. Blackwell farm diary, 1842–66, Hunterdon County Historical Society, entries of Oct. 10, 1850, June 18, 1851.

34. John Ten Eyck diary, June 29, 1870.

35. Weiss, *History of the New Jersey Board of Agriculture*, p. 22.

36. *Hunterdon County Democrat*, May 30, 1882, July 10, 1883, July 1, 1884, Mar. 2, 1886.

37. Elmer E. Bonnell, Clinton, farm diary, 1878–95, in possession of Miss Ella M. Haver, R.D. 1, Annandale, N.J., Nov. 1, 1878, Dec. 10, 14, 22, 1883, Mar. 31, 1887, Jan. 18, 30, 1888.

38. Rental agreement between H. E. Deats and Henry Butcher, 1898, H. E. Deats Collection, Hunterdon County Historical Society.

39. Moriscot Farm workbook, entries of May 1903.

40. *New Jersey Wills*, Office of the Secretary of State, Trenton, passim; Mercer, "Tools of the Nation Maker," in Bucks County (Pennsylvania) Historical

Society, *A Collection of Papers Read Before the Bucks County Historical Society*, II, 480–89, III, 469–81.

41. Mrs. Mary Capner to Mrs. Hugh Exton, Nov. 17, 1887, Capner Collection; Joseph Thompson to Rev. C. S. Conkling, Feb. 2, 1876, quoted in "Mementoes for the One Hundred and Seventy-Fifth Anniversary of the Reformed Church of Readington, N.J.," Thompson Collection.

42. James Ten Eyck, Sr., diary.

43. Hiram Deats machine shop accounts, Clinton, H. E. Deats Collection, Hunterdon County Historical Society, daybook, 1834–40, passim.

44. *Hunterdon County Democrat*, Oct. 11, 1843.

45. David C. Voorhees diary, passim.

46. Blackwell diary, passim; Neilson diary, passim.

47. Case tannery accounts, Ledger B and Ledger 1808–12, passim, and daybook entry of Apr. 10, 1798; Bowne accounts, Ledger B, p. 17, et passim; Lippincott diary, passim.

48. See G. H. Sanford, *The Story of Agriculture in the United States* (New York, 1916), pp. 293–94; also Bidwell and Falconer, pp. 232–33.

49. Moore diary, passim; David C. Voorhees diary, passim.

50. Blackwell diary, passim; Bonnell diary, passim.

51. Neilson diary, Nov. 11–20, 1863, et passim.

52. Case tannery accounts, daybook entry of Mar. 30, 1798, et passim.

53. Blackwell diary, May 7, 1852, et passim; John Ten Eyck diary, passim.

54. Roberts, pp. 12, 131–32; *Hunterdon Gazette*, Oct. 1, 1856.

55. *Hunterdon County Democrat*, Jan. 13, 1888; see also Bonnell diary, May 6, 1882.

56. James Ten Eyck, Sr., diary, scattered entries of 1809; Bergen Brokaw accounts, 1812–51, Hunterdon County Historical Society, daybook entries of 1825.

57. Carrier, pp. 269–71; Bidwell and Falconer, p. 133.

58. John Hall to Isaac Passand, Jan. 17, 1793, Capner Collection; Case tannery accounts, daybook entries of Jan. 31, Apr. 15, May 8, 1798.

59. Roberts, pp. 107, 118–31.

60. Cazenove, pp. 35–36.

61. Bowne Accounts, Ledger B, pp. 4–31; Case tannery accounts, daybook entries of spring, 1816.

62. Samuel Holcombe general store accounts, Mount Airy, Hunterdon County Historical Society, daybook entry of June 28, 1824.

63. Blackwell diary, May 6, 1858, et passim.

64. *Hunterdon County Democrat*, Feb. 16, 1875.

65. Bonnell diary, May 16, 17, 1881, Apr. 27, 1887, et passim.

66. Woodward and Waller, p. 153.

67. E. T. Bush in *Hunterdon County Democrat*, Apr. 21, 1932.

68. Charles Read in Woodward, *Ploughs and Politicks*, pp. 145–52, 284, 286.

69. Parker diary, June 12, 1778.

70. Rutherford, pp. 78–89.

71. John Hall to Isaac Passand, circa 1792, Capner Collection; Cazenove, pp. 12–13.

72. Isaac Passand to John Hall, Jan. 17, 1793, Capner Collection.

73. Parker diary, June 16, Aug. 25, 1786, et passim.

74. Elmer Robertson, *The Centre Bridge* (Flemington, 1928), p. 8; E. T. Bush in *Hunterdon County Democrat,* Apr. 21, 1932.

75. Broadside notice of public sale, Emley Papers, Rutgers University Library.

76. Robertson, p. 8.

77. *Hunterdon Gazette,* Aug. 8, Oct. 24, 1837, et passim.

78. Ibid., Jan. 4, 1843.

79. W. S. Ely, "Lime Burning Industry, Its Rise and Decay in Bucks," in Bucks County (Pennsylvania) Historical Society, *A Collection of Papers Read Before the Bucks County Historical Society,* IV, 72–73.

80. Wheaton J. Lane, *From Indian Trail to Iron Horse* (Princeton, 1939), pp. 223–45, 261–76; Charles J. Schillon, "An Economic History of the Delaware Division Canal," unpublished paper, 1968.

81. George H. Cook, field notebooks, 1855–69, George H. Cook Collection, Rutgers University Library, Notebook No. 9, p. 24.

82. *Hunterdon Republican,* Oct. 26, 1860.

83. Jesse Buel, "Notes on New Jersey Farming," *The Cultivator,* 1839, quoted in *Hunterdon Gazette,* Sept. 17, 1839; George H. Cook, *Geology of New Jersey* (Newark, 1868), pp. 393–95, 407–8. See also the Cook field notebooks, passim.

84. Woodward, *Ploughs and Politicks,* pp. 245, 248–49.

85. Blackwell diary, passim; Bonnell diary, Mar. 23, Apr. 26, Nov. 29, 31, 1887, et passim; E. T. Bush in *Hunterdon County Democrat,* Apr. 21, 1932; Moriscot Farm workbook, May 15–16, 1903.

86. Cook field notebooks, passim.

87. Quoted in *Hunterdon Gazette,* Sept. 17, 1839.

88. Cook, *Geology of New Jersey,* p. 408.

89. Widmer, pp. 103–4; Cook, *Geology of New Jersey,* p. 261.

90. See articles by Alex L. Moreau in the *Freehold Transcript,* Mar. 29, Apr. 12, 1929.

91. Thomas F. Gordon, *Gazeteer of the State of New Jersey* (Trenton, 1834), p. 5.

92. Cook, *Geology of New Jersey,* p. 442, and passim.

93. Lippincott diary, passim.

94. Woodward, *Agriculture in New Jersey,* pp. 55–56. See also Cook, *Geology of New Jersey,* passim.

95. Blackwell diary, entry of Apr. 19, 1855.

96. *Hunterdon Republican,* July 7, 1870.

97. David C. Voorhees diary, Apr. 27, 1875, et passim.

98. Cook field notebooks, passim.

99. Ibid., Notebook No. 2, p. 28.

100. Cook, *Geology of New Jersey,* p. 264.

101. Cook field notebooks, passim; see also articles signed "A. A. Y." in *Annual Report of the New Jersey State Agricultural Society, 1873,* pp. 127–32.

102. *Geology of New Jersey,* p. 458.

103. Quoted in Annual Report of the *New Jersey Agricultural Society, 1873,* p. 131.

104. *Freehold Transcript,* Apr. 12, 1929.

105. "Marl in Salem County, New Jersey," *Almanac and Year Book* (Woodstown, 1913), pp. 37–39.

106. A. W. Blair, "The Experimental Value of Greensand Marl," Circular 61, *New Jersey Agricultural Experiment Station* (New Brunswick, 1916).

107. *Hunterdon Gazette,* July 28, 1847, et passim; *Hunterdon Republican,* Mar. 22, 1854, Oct. 15, 1856, Dec. 30, 1857, July 27, 1859; *Lambertville Press,* Aug. 4, 1859.

108. John Ten Eyck diary, entries of spring 1854.

109. Moore diaries, entries of spring 1868.

110. Woodward, *Agriculture in New Jersey,* p. 56; Bidwell and Falconer, p. 234.

111. Bidwell and Falconer, p. 319.

112. Woodward, *Agriculture in New Jersey,* p. 56.

113. Moore diary, passim.

114. Woodward and Waller, pp. 126–27.

115. Moriscot Farm workbook, entries of spring 1903.

CHAPTER 10

1. Local schedules, Census of 1850, Bethlehem Township, New Jersey State Library, Trenton.

2. Stillwell, pp. 2–3.

3. *Hunterdon County Democrat,* May 15, 1883.

4. Bonnell diary, July 15, 1891.

5. Thomas Lauderdale, farm accounts, 1886–98, Hunterdon County Historical Society, passim.

6. Crevecœur, *Sketches of 18th Century America,* p. 146.

7. Capner Collection, passim.

8. See Bidwell and Falconer, p. 215.

9. *Ringos,* I, 169.

10. Woodward, *Agriculture in New Jersey,* pp. 89–90; Bidwell and Falconer, pp. 209–10.

11. John Ten Eyck diary, entries of June 1854.

12. Letters patent issued to John Deats, Apr. 26, 1828, Hunterdon County Historical Society.

13. Woodward, *Agriculture in New Jersey,* p. 90.

14. Ibid.

15. Ibid.

16. Hiram Deats machine shop, Quakertown, daybooks, 1831–40; Deats, Case and Co., machine shop and foundry, Pittstown, daybrook, 1869–74, Hunterdon County Historical Society.

17. Blackwell diary, entries of 1858.

18. Bidwell and Falconer, p. 282.

19. Ibid., p. 210.

20. See Sanford, p. 250.

21. *Hunterdon County Democrat,* Aug. 3, 1880; Bonnell diary, Dec. 28, 1883.

22. Moriscot Farm workbook, p. 23.

23. James H. Blackwell vendue list, Blackwell Papers, Hunterdon County Historical Society; Neilson diary, passim.

24. Woodward, *Agriculture in New Jersey,* p. 90.

25. Unsigned article in *Hunterdon County Democrat,* Feb. 24, 1924; interviews at various times with the late H. E. Deats.

26. Moriscot Farm workbook, passim.

27. Bidwell and Falconer, p. 300.

28. *Hunterdon Republican,* Mar. 25, 1857.

29. Tunis Ten Eyck, farm diary, 1877–93, Rutgers University Library, passim.

30. *Hunterdon County Democrat,* Apr. 16, 1895, May 18, 1909.

31. David C. Voorhees diary, May 19, 20, 1875.

32. *Hunterdon County Democrat,* Apr. 17, 1900, Aug. 30, 1904.

33. Bidwell and Falconer, pp. 299–300.

34. Moriscot Farm workbook, Apr. 2, 11, 1903.

35. Stillwell, p. 30.

36. *Hunterdon Gazette,* passim.

37. Woodward, *Agriculture in New Jersey,* pp. 90–91, and "Tillage Implements Invented by Jerseymen, *New Jersey Agriculture,* June 1929, p. 14; see also Bidwell and Falconer, pp. 210, 302.

38. Woodward, "More Tillage Implements," *New Jersey Agriculture,* August 1929, p. 14.

39. *Hunterdon County Democrat,* Aug. 19, 1873, June 15, 1875.

40. Lippincott diary, June 3, 4, 1868.

41. David C. Voorhees diary, entries of June and July 1875.

42. Woodward, "Jerseymen Who Helped Build the Harvester," *New Jersey Agriculture,* December 1928, p. 14.

43. Blackwell diary, June 7–Aug. 19, 1954, et passim.

44. Ralph Voorhees diary, Junc 15–July 31, 1860.

45. Woodward, "Jerseymen Who Helped Build the Harvester," *New Jersey Agriculture,* December 1928, pp. 14–15.

46. *Hunterdon Republican,* July 14, 1958.

47. "A Header Invented by a Jerseyman," *New Jersey Agriculture,* August 1930, p. 16.

48. David C. Voorhees diary, July 6–Aug. 6, 1875.

49. *Hunterdon County Democrat,* July 31, 1883.

50. Bonnell diary, May 15–July 16, 1884, et passim.

51. John Ten Eyck diary, passim.

52. Tunis Ten Eyck diary, passim.

53. *Hunterdon County Democrat,* July 31, 1894, Mar. 7, 1899.

54. Stillwell; Blackwell diary, July 18, 1855; E. T. Bush in *Hunterdon County Democrat,* Feb. 23, 1933; see also Bidwell and Falconer, pp. 213–14, 296.

55. Stillwell, pp. 29–30.

56. *Hunterdon Republican,* Mar. 30, 1860; *Hunterdon County Democrat,* May 3, 1881; records of the Hunterdon County Agricultural Society, 1878, Hunterdon County Historical Society.

57. *Hunterdon Republican,* Oct. 6, 1870.

58. Neilson diary.

59. David C. Voorhees diary, July 7–9, 1875.

60. *Hunterdon County Democrat,* June 26, 1894, et passim; interviews with H. E. Deats.

61. *Hunterdon Gazette,* Oct. 1, 1856.

62. Neilson diary, Dec. 5, 1863.

63. F. K. Swain, "Passing Events," in Bucks County (Pennsylvania) Historical Society, *A Collection of Papers Read Before the Bucks County Historical Society,* V, 327.

64. Sanford, p. 255; *Hunterdon County Democrat,* Sept. 3, 1895.

65. *New Jersey Journal,* Oct. 15, 1788.

66. Bidwell and Falconer, p. 215.

67. *Hunterdon Gazette,* Aug. 4, 1830.

68. Ibid., July 18, 1838, Feb. 9, 1839, Nov. 2, 1842.

69. Blackwell diary, passim.

70. Moore diary, July 19, Aug. 20, 22, Sept. 27, Oct. 25, 1853.

71. John Ten Eyck diary, passim.

72. Bonnell diary, Dec. 13, 22, 1888.

73. Neilson diary, Feb. 22, 1875.

74. David C. Voorhees diary, Feb. 22, 1875.

75. *Hunterdon County Democrat,* Nov. 11, 1892, et passim.

76. Ibid., Sept. 27, 1904, Nov. 14, 1905, July 26, 1916.

77. Ralph Voorhees diary, Jan. 5–10, 1860.

78. David C. Voorhees diary, Mar. 2, Apr. 12, 1875.

79. Moore diary, Sept. 27, 1853; John Ten Eyck diary, entries of March 1854 and September 1860; "Reminiscences of Shuster's Hollow," clipping from unidentified newspaper, 1892, Hunterdon County Historical Society.

80. John Ten Eyck diary, passim; Ralph Voorhees diary, passim.

81. *Hunterdon Gazette,* Jan. 27, 1841; *Hunterdon Republican,* July 22, 1857; records of Hunterdon County Agricultural Society, passim.

82. *Hunterdon Republican,* July 22, 1857.

83. Ibid., July 22, 1857, Mar. 30, 1860; *Hunterdon County Democrat,* Oct. 13, 1874, Feb. 21, 1888.

84. *Hunterdon County Democrat,* Aug. 17, 1897, Sept. 20, 1898, Feb. 28, 1908, Aug. 23, 1916, Feb. 21, 1924.

85. Ibid., Aug. 30, 1904, May 15, 1906.

86. "Jno. Hall's Book," Capner Collection, passim.

87. *Hunterdon Gazette,* July 18, 1828.

88. John Ten Eyck diary, entries from December 1853, to February 1854.

89. *Hunterdon Gazette,* June 18, 1828, Oct. 1, 1856; records of Hunterdon County Agricultural Society, passim.

90. See Sanford, p. 256.

91. *Hunterdon County Democrat,* Aug. 30, 1904.

92. Ibid., Apr. 12, 1887, Feb. 21, 1888, June 3, 1890.

93. *Hunterdon Gazette,* Oct. 1, 1856; *Hunterdon Republican,* Oct. 8, 1858; *Hunterdon County Democrat,* Feb. 10, 1864; records of Hunterdon County Agricultural Society.

94. *Hunterdon Republican,* July 22, 1857.

95. Sanford, pp. 258–59; Swain, p. 328; *Hunterdon County Democrat,* July 31, 1900.

96. *Hunterdon County Democrat,* Aug. 30, 1904.

97. Jesse Buel, *The Farmer's Companion* (Boston, 1839).

98. III, 194.

CHAPTER 11

1. Pitt and Hoagland, pp. 370–71.

2. See Woodward, *Agriculture in New Jersey,* p. 76; for excellent illustrations of stud advertisements, see *Hunterdon Gazette,* Mar. 31, 1825, Mar. 1827, Mar. 31, 1847.

3. Hunterdon County Agricultural Society records, passim.

4. *Hunterdon Gazette,* Nov. 25, 1840.

5. Receipt, Case tannery records.

6. *Hunterdon Democrat,* Sept. 14, 1842.

7. John Ten Eyck diary, entries of May 1854.

8. *Hunterdon County Democrat,* passim.

9. David C. Voorhees diary.

10. *Hunterdon Gazette,* June 14, 1825.

11. David C. Voorhees diary, June 16, 1875, et passim.

12. Hunterdon County Agricultural Society records, accounts of 1878.

13. James Ten Eyck, Sr., diary, June 30, 1806.

14. Moore diary, May 4, 1868.

15. Letters and accounts of Joseph Capner, James Choyce, and Hugh Exton, 1785–1825, Capner Collection.

16. *Hunterdon Gazette,* May 14, 1828.

17. Ibid., Apr. 14, Oct. 27, 1830, July 13, 1831, Mar. 12, 1832, Nov. 25, 1840.

18. *Hunterdon Republican,* July 15, Sept. 27, 1857.

19. See John Ten Eyck diary, Aug. 6, 1870, et passim.

20. Hunterdon County Agricultural Society records, 1856, 1857; for use of the term *Alderney,* see Plumb, *Types and Breeds of Farm Animals,* p. 325.

21. *Hunterdon County Democrat,* Apr. 5, 1871.

22. See Sanford, pp. 277–78.

23. *Hunterdon County Democrat,* Jan. 18, 25, May 16, July 26, Aug. 2, 16, 23, 1881, June 16, Sept. 14, 1886, Nov. 8, 1887, Oct. 9, 1888, Dec. 6, 1891, Feb. 16, Apr. 19, Dec. 13, 1892, Apr. 4, July 18, Sept. 5, 1893, Mar. 6, Apr. 10, 1894, Jan. 22, Oct. 15, Nov. 12, 1895, Apr. 28, 1896, Apr. 12, May 2, Aug. 23, 1898, et passim.

24. Ibid., Jan. 18, Apr. 19, June 28, July 22, 1881.

25. See Swain, pp. 413–17.

26. *Hunterdon County Democrat,* June 24, 1884, Nov. 8, 1887, July 16, 1895.

27. Bush, ibid., Nov. 24, 1932.

28. See Lewis Runkle, "A Chapter on Butter," ibid., Mar. 4, 1890.

29. Ibid., July 5, 1881.

30. Ibid., Dec. 2, 1902, Dec. 15, 1908, June 14, 1910.

31. Ibid., Mar. 21, Apr. 11, 1899.

32. Pitt and Hoagland, pp. 342–43.

33. Ibid.

34. See Lippincott diary, accounts at end of year 1868, and David C. Voorhees diary, Aug. 25–26, 1875, et passim.

35. Ibid., p. 346.

36. *Hunterdon County Democrat,* June 11, 1882, Apr. 25, July 3, 1883, Sept. 2, 1890, Jan. 7, 1902, Jan. 30, 1906, July 8, 1913, Mar. 21, 1917.

37. *Hunterdon County Democrat,* Sept. 28, 1912.

38. See Bailey, III, 646–47.

39. John Hall to Hugh Exton, July 5, 1795, Capner Collection.

40. See Bidwell and Falconer, p. 111.

41. Farm diaries of James Ten Eyck, Jr., John Ten Eyck, Ralph Voorhees, and David C. Voorhees, passim.

42. Woodward, *Agriculture in New Jersey,* pp. 9, 73.

43. Case tannery records, daybook, 1805–12, back cover.

44. See Woodward, *Agriculture in New Jersey,* pp. 74–75, and "The Jersey Red Hog," *New Jersey Agriculture,* April 1929, p. 14.

45. Hunterdon County Agricultural Society records, passim.

46. *Hunterdon Gazette,* Nov. 25, 1840.

47. Bailey, III, 659–81.

48. Hunterdon County Agricultural Society records, 1881.

49. Pitt and Hoagland, p. 380.

50. David C. Voorhees diary, Dec. 22, 1875.

51. Carrier, p. 160; Mrs. Mary Capner to Mrs. Hugh Exton, Dec. 22, 1787, Capner Collection, James Ten Eyck, Jr., diary, passim.

52. Isaac Passand to John Hall, Jan. 17, 1793, Capner Collection.

53. Bailey, III, 616–17.

54. Woodward, *Agriculture in New Jersey,* p. 76.

55. Mrs. Mary Capner to Mrs. Hugh Exton, Feb. 7, May 27, 1791, June 3, 1793 and John Hall to Thomas Capner, c. 1805, Capner Collection.

56. Woodward, *Agriculture in New Jersey,* pp. 77–79. "Sheep at $1000 a Head," *New Jersey Agriculture,* October 1928, pp. 14–15.

57. Pitt and Hoagland, pp. 382–83.

58. Joseph Capner accounts, Capner Collection.

59. Various letters, 1787–1803, Capner Collection.

60. Dr. John Bowne accounts, Ledger C.

61. *Hunterdon Republican,* Dec. 10, 1856.

62. Holcombe store daybooks, Jan. 22, Feb. 2, 1856.

63. Ralph Voorhees diary, Jan. 16, 1860.

64. Bailey, III, 563–69; *Hunterdon County Democrat,* passim.

65. *Hunterdon County Democrat,* Sept. 28, 1870.

66. David C. Voorhees diary, Mar. 18, 1875, et passim.

67. Pitt and Hoagland, p. 420.

68. Ibid.

69. Ibid., p. 459.

70. Bailey, III, 563–64.

71. *Hunterdon County Democrat,* Jan. 16, 1912, Jan. 13, Sept. 20, 1914, Feb. 21, May 9, Nov. 14, 1917.

72. Bailey, III, 543; *Hunterdon County Democrat,* Apr. 12, 1887.

73. *Hunterdon County Democrat,* Aug. 27, 1895, Mar. 18, 1902, Jan. 16, 1906.
74. Pitt and Hoagland, p. 433.
75. Blackwell diary, Oct. 20, 1845, et passim.
76. Bonnell diary, Mar. 17, 31, Apr. 19, May 12, 1890.
77. Bailey, III, 123.
78. Diary entries of Mar. 21, 22, 1868.

CHAPTER 12

1. James Ten Eyck, Sr., diary.
2. Blackwell diary, June 9, 1849, Nov. 8, 1851.
3. Bailey, II, 398–402; Weatherwax, pp. 182–207.
4. *Ringos,* I, 148.
5. Pitt and Hoagland, pp. 210–11.
6. Bailey, II, 404.
7. Rutherford, p. 87.
8. Cazenove, pp. 14–15; Chesebrough journal.
9. Pitt and Hoagland, pp. 214–17.
10. John Hall to Mary Capner, Nov. 5, 1792 and to Hugh Exton, June 17, 1795, Capner Collection.
11. Cazenove, pp. 4, 14.
12. Report of the Hunterdon County Agricultural Society to the New Jersey Agricultural Society, printed in *Hunterdon County Democrat,* Mar. 13, 1883.
13. *Hunterdon Gazette,* Nov. 3, 1841.
14. Blackwell diary, Feb. 3, 1852.
15. Bailey, II, 666.
16. Hankinson commonplace book, entries of 1805–6.
17. *Hunterdon County Democrat,* Aug. 15, 29, 1838, et passim.
18. Blackwell diary, Sept. 6, 9, 1848.
19. Parker diary, passim.
20. Cazenove, passim.
21. James Ten Eyck, Sr., diary, passim.
22. Pitt and Hoagland, pp. 222–23.
23. Blackwell diary, passim.
24. Pitt and Hoagland, p. 221.
25. *Hunterdon Republican,* Oct. 5, 1960.
26. *Hunterdon County Democrat,* August 4, 18, 25, Sept. 1, 1864.
27. Neilson diary, Apr. 9, 1864.
28. David C. Voorhees diary, Feb. 25, 1875.
29. Hunterdon County Agricultural Society records, 1878, 1882.
30. Pitt and Hoagland, pp. 218–81.
31. Parker diary, passim.
32. Brunner dockets, Sept. 18, 1782.
33. Isaac Passand to John Hall, Jan. 17, 1793, Capner Collection.
34. *Hunterdon Gazette,* Dec. 11, 1825, Aug. 31, 1831, et passim.
35. Atkinson and Johnson accounts, daybook, passim; unidentified general store, daybook, 1848–49, passim; Holcombe store accounts, 1824–32, 1868–71, passim.

36. Local schedules, census of 1850.

37. Moore diary, July 19, 1853.

38. Ralph Voorhees diary, July 5, Oct. 5, 1875.

39. David C. Voorhees diary, May 21, July 19, Oct. 17, 18, 1860.

40. Pitt and Hoagland, pp. 226–27.

41. Unidentified farm diary, Capner Collection.

42. Pitt and Hoagland, p. 230.

43. Stillwell, pp. 28–29; Lequear, "Some Recollections of Lambertville," *Lambertville Record,* 1891; Blackwell diary, Oct. 19, 1849.

44. Woodward, *Agriculture in New Jersey,* p. 71.

45. *Hunterdon County Democrat,* May 13, 1879.

46. United States Census, 1890, *Agriculture,* p. 482.

47. Moore diary, passim.

48. *Hunterdon County Democrat,* Oct. 19, 1864, et passim.

49. United States Census, 1870, III, 207.

50. Woodward, *Agriculture in New Jersey,* pp. 125–26; Woodward and Waller, pp. 45–47; Louis T. Stevens, *The History of Cape May County, New Jersey* (1897), pp. 382–83.

51. United States Census, 1890, *Agriculture,* p. 413.

52. See Lequear, "Flax Culture and Manufacture," (MS, 1889); also Hubert G. Schmidt, *Flax Culture in Hunterdon County,* 1942.

53. Atkinson and Johnson accounts, daybook, 1793–94, passim; Holcombe store, daybook, 1824–32, passim.

54. Rental agreement between Rebeckah Compton and William Birch, MS, 1811. Hunterdon County Historical Society.

55. Diaries of John Ten Eyck, Sr., and John Ten Eyck, Jr., passim.

56. James Ten Eyck diary, passim.

57. Local schedules, census of 1850; United States Census, 1850, p. 149.

58. Grier Sheetz and others, "Flax Seed Mills," in Bucks County (Pennsylvania) Historical Society, *A Collection of Papers Read Before the Bucks County Historical Society,* IV, 725–28; unsigned article, *Hunterdon Republican,* January 1870.

59. *Hunterdon Gazette,* Apr. 21, 1831, et passim.

60. United States Census, 1870, III, 207, 339.

61. United States Census, 1880, *Agriculture,* p. 235; United States Census of 1890, *Agriculture,* p. 400.

62. Bidwell and Falconer, p. 98.

63. Capner Collection, passim; Berkaw mill daybook, 1812–51, Rutgers University Library, passim.

64. Holcombe store accounts, daybook, May 24, 1824.

65. Blackwell diary, passim.

66. *Hunterdon Republican,* Oct. 6, 1858, Oct. 9, 1860.

67. Blackwell diary, passim.

68. See *Hunterdon County Democrat,* Sept. 4, 1906, Oct. 25, 1934.

69. Woodward, *Agriculture in New Jersey,* pp. 114–15.

70. Moore diary, Dec. 8, 1860, May 24, 25, 1864.

71. Cook field notebooks, passim.

72. Lippincott diary, passim.

73. David C. Voorhees diary, passim.

74. John Ten Eyck diary, June 30, 1875, et passim.

75. Woodward, *Agriculture in New Jersey*, p. 115.

76. Pitt and Hoagland, p. 283.

77. *Hunterdon County Democrat*, Mar. 24, 1903.

78. Pitt and Hoagland, pp. 279–84.

79. Ibid.

80. Ibid., pp. 284–86.

81. Blackwell diary, passim; Moore diary, passim.

82. David C. Voorhees diary, May 22, 1875, et passim.

83. Neilson diary, Nov. 21, 1863.

84. *Hunterdon Gazette*, passim; Woodward, "When Silk Was Grown on New Jersey Farms," *New Jersey Agriculture*, August 1927, pp. 14–15.

85. Albert Lowther Demaree, *The American Agricultural Press, 1819–1860* (New York, 1941), p. 61.

86. Woodward, *Agriculture in New Jersey*, p. 113.

87. Atkinson store accounts, 1820–29, passim; Bowne accounts, passim; Roberts, pp. 46–47, 147.

88. *Hunterdon Gazette*, Jan. 27, 1830, Aug. 27, 1845.

89. Blackwell diary, Aug. 22, 1850; Ralph Voorhees diary, Aug. 7, 1870.

90. John Hall to Mr. and Mrs. James Choyce, Apr. 30, 1793, and Mary Choyce to Mr. and Mrs. James Choyce, May 31, 1795, Capner Collection.

91. Unidentified diary, Aug. 1, 1825, Capner Collection.

92. Roberts, pp. 46–47; James Ten Eyck, Jr., diary, Sept. 7, 1808.

93. Case tannery accounts, ledger 1783–91, p. 114.

94. David C. Voorhees diary, Feb. 2, 1875.

95. *Hunterdon County Democrat*, July 14, 1908.

96. Pitt and Hoagland, pp. 213, 238.

97. Ibid., pp. 235–50.

98. William A. Coxe, *A View of the Cultivation of Fruit Trees and the Management of Orchards and Cider, . . .* (Philadelphia, 1817).

99. Pitt and Hoagland, p. 336.

100. Cazenove, pp. 4, 11–12.

101. Coxe, p. 93; Morse, edition of 1819, I, 430.

102. Coxe, p. 58.

103. Thomas F. Gordon, *A Gazeteer of the State of New Jersey* (Philadelphia, 1834), p. 37.

104. Peter Haward diary, Capner Collection.

105. Unidentified farm diary, ibid.

106. James Ten Eyck, Jr., diary, passim.

107. Weiss, *History of Applejack*, pp. 94, 132.

108. Census of 1860, *Manufactures*, pp. 329–47.

109. Weiss, *History of Applejack*, p. 77.

110. Pitt and Hoagland, p. 304.

111. Coxe, pp. 59–60, 94, 133–34, 142–44, 147–48, 153–54; *Hunterdon Gazette*, passim.

112. *Hunterdon Republican*, Oct. 5, 1860.

113. *Hunterdon County Democrat,* Nov. 21, 1882. See also E. T. Bush, ibid., Mar. 19, 1931.

114. Pitt and Hoagland, pp. 295–96.

115. Thomas Hughes, *A Journal by Thomas Hughes* (Cambridge, England, 1947), p. 61.

116. *Lambertville Press,* Mar. 24, Sept. 8, 29, 1859.

117. *Hunterdon Republican,* Aug. 11, 1870.

118. *Hunterdon County Democrat,* Sept. 12, 1882.

119. Pitt and Hoagland, p. 305.

120. Ibid., p. 306.

121. *Hunterdon County Democrat,* Sept. 22–29, 1891, Sept. 27, 1892, Aug. 15, 1893.

122. Bonnell diary, passim.

123. Ibid., Oct. 13, 1878.

124. *Hunterdon County Democrat,* May 24, 1892, et passim; Pitt and Hoagland, p. 305.

125. Ibid., Aug. 2, 1898, Sept. 29, 1903.

126. Ibid., June 12, 1900, Apr. 28, 1903, Aug. 30, 1904, Dec. 4, 1906, Feb. 21, July 21, 1911, et passim.

127. Pitt and Hoagland, pp. 204, 306.

128. Ibid., 310–11.

129. See Edmund Morris, *Ten Acres Enough* (New York, 1868), passim.

130. Pitt and Hoagland, pp. 312–34.

131. Ibid., p. 325; United States Census, 1860, *Agriculture,* p. 98.

132. Pitt and Hoagland, p. 324.

133. Woodward, *Agriculture in New Jersey,* pp. 120–22.

134. Pitt and Hoagland, pp. 326–27.

135. Morris, pp. 67–70.

136. David C. Voorhees diary, passim.

137. Pitt and Hoagland, pp. 267–87.

138. Joseph S. Sickler, *Old Homes of Salem County* (Salem, 1949), pp. 40–42.

139. See *Hunterdon Gazette,* Sept. 1, 1847.

140. Morris, pp. 118–22, 156–57.

141. Moore diary, entries of 1876, passim.

142. David C. Voorhees, July 18, 1875.

143. Pitt and Hoagland, p. 277.

CHAPTER 13

1. Pitt and Hoagland, p. 71. Changing the definition of the word *farm* from census year to census year did not materially affect the statistics.

2. United States Census of Agriculture, 1964, New Jersey, p. 7.

3. Ibid.; *New Jersey Agricultural Statistics,* yearly volumes, 1957–71; New Jersey Farm Bureau and College of Agriculture and Environmental Science, Rutgers University, *1970 Yearbook of New Jersey Agriculture,* p. 10.

4. Woodward and Waller, passim.

5. Ibid. For an interesting discussion of how agricultural extension has adapted itself to suburbia in Bergen County, see *New York Times,* Feb. 26, 1972, news section, p. 100.

6. E. T. Bush to H. E. Deats, Jan. 23, 1919, and H. E. Deats to E. T. Bush, Jan. 24, 1919, H. E. Deats Collection, Hunterdon County Historical Society, Flemington.

7. See Schmidt, *Rural Hunterdon*, pp. 293–94.

8. Demarest, pp. 511, 518, 524, 541–42; McCormick, pp. 146–47, 153, 157, 215, 243, 259, 268, 270, 277, 279; Schmidt, *Rural Hunterdon*, pp. 293–94; Ingrid Nelson Waller, *Where There Is Vision: The New Jersey Agricultural Experiment Station, 1880–1955*, passim; Woodward and Waller, pp. 99–100, 495–511; enrollment figures from Office of Director of Resident Instruction, College of Agriculture and Environmental Science, Rutgers University.

9. Harry B. Weiss, *The New Jersey Department of Agriculture, 1916–1949* (Trenton, 1950), passim; New Jersey Department of Agriculture, *Fertile Furrow . . . 50 Miles Long, The Grassroots Government of New Jersey Agriculture* (Trenton, 1966), pp. 9–11, and *Duties and Functions of the New Jersey Department of Agriculture* (Trenton, 1967), passim, and *Highlights of the 1968–69 Annual Report* (Trenton, 1969), passim; information given by Robert D. McMillen, Director of the Division of Information, New Jersey Department of Agriculture.

10. Weiss, *The New Jersey State Grange*, pp. 17–34.

11. Patricia Roberts, "Grange, Like Farmer, Is Fading from Scene," *Home News* (New Brunswick), Dec. 22, 1971.

12. New Jersey State Grange, *Roster of State, Pomona, and Subordinate Granges of the State Grange, 1966;* information given by William A. Schlechtweg, Sr., Master of the New Jersey State Grange, Freehold.

13. New Jersey State Grange, Journal of Proceedings, *New Jersey State Grange Ninety-third Annual Session, 1965,* sections 1, 2, 6.

14. Weiss, *The New Jersey State Grange*, p. 18.

15. *A Century of the Princeton Agricultural Association, 1867–1967* (New Brunswick, 1967).

16. New Jersey Department of Agriculture, *Yearbook, July 1, 1965–June 30, 1966,* p. 3, and Section AC; Frank App, *County Boards of Agriculture* (Trenton, 1964), pp. 1–3 et passim; information given by William G. McIntyre, Senior Agricultural Agent, Hunterdon County.

17. New Jersey Farm Bureau and College of Agriculture and Environmental Science, Rutgers University, *1970 Yearbook of New Jersey Agriculture* (Trenton, 1970), passim; New Jersey Farm Bureau, *By Laws Adopted March 1, 1962, Amended November 16, 1969* (Trenton, 1969, flyer), *Safeguard Your Investment with a Farm Bureau Membership in 1970* (Trenton, 1970), and *A Farm Bureau for the Seventies* (Trenton, 1970), pp. 1–4; William C. Spargo, *My 57 Years in Farm Bureau* (Trenton, 1967); information given by Clarence H. Fields, Executive Director of the New Jersey Farm Bureau.

18. New Jersey Department of Agriculture, *New Jersey Agricultural Fairs, 1967* (Trenton, 1967); information given by Robert D. McMillen, Director of the Division of Information, New Jersey Department of Agriculture.

CHAPTER 14

1. Woodward, *Agriculture in New Jersey,* p. 100; Schmidt, *Rural Hunterdon,* pp. 133, 155–56, 159, 288–90, 296.

302 AGRICULTURE IN NEW JERSEY

2. Charles B. Howe, *Farmers' Cooperation in New Jersey, 1926* (New Brunswick, 1928), pp. 4, 22–24, 94; New Jersey State Grange, *The New Jersey State Grange, Patrons of Husbandry, 1873–1954* (Trenton, 1955), pp. 50–52, 56–58.

3. Farmers' Cooperative Association of New Jersey, *Farmers' Cooperative Association of New Jersey, Inc., 1915–1965* (Trenton, 1965), pp. 3–18.

4. United States Department of Agriculture, *Farmer Cooperatives in the United States* (Washington, 1965), p. 256.

5. Howe, pp. 4, 14–15, 95.

6. Ibid., pp. 15–22.

7. Morris S. Fabian, *Directory of Farmer Cooperatives in New Jersey* (New Brunswick, 1966). See also New Jersey Farm Bureau and College of Agriculture and Environmental Science, *1970 Yearbook of New Jersey Agriculture*, pp. 77–120.

8. Howe, pp. 30–34; Grange-League-Federation, *Farmers Together, the Story of G.L.F.* (n.p., 1959), passim.

9. Information given by Dwight M. Babbitt, former Hunterdon County Agricultural Agent.

10. Howe, pp. 34–52.

11. See *New York Times,* Jan. 7, 1968.

12. United States Department of Agriculture, *Farmer Cooperatives in the United States,* pp. 257, 265; Farmers' Cooperative Association of New Jersey, *Farmers' Cooperative Association of New Jersey, Inc.,* p. 15.

13. Ernest C. Strobeck, *The Development of Cooperative Milk Marketing in the New York Milkshed* (Syracuse, New York, 1957), pp. 3–9.

14. Ibid., pp. 2–16; Howe, pp. 40–41; H. E. Deats, Flemington, to E. T. Bush, Stockton, November 21, 1917, H. E. Deats Collection, Hunterdon County Historical Society, Flemington.

15. Howe, pp. 40–51; Strobeck, pp. 16–34; Leland Spencer, *Cooperative Organization of Producers in the New York Milkshed* (Ithaca, New York, 1953), pp. 9–10; Leland Spencer and S. Kent Christiansen, *Milk Control Programs of the Northeastern States* (Ithaca, New York, 1954), pp. 12–17.

16. Howe, pp. 51–60.

17. Ibid.; Spencer, pp. 9–10.

18. Weiss, *The New Jersey Department of Agriculture, 1916–1949,* passim; Spencer, pp. 12–15; Spencer and Christiansen, pp. 17–21; William S. Park, *Should the Nearby Formula Under Order 2 Be Changed?* (Typescript, New Brunswick, 1965) and *Market Wide vs. Handler Pooling Under the Delaware Valley Milk Marketing Order* (Typescript, New Brunswick, 1967); interviews with William S. Park, College of Agriculture and Environmental Science, Rutgers University; Amos Kirby, "U. M. P. Breakup," *American Agriculturist and Rural New Yorker,* December, 1971.

19. Park, *Relationship Between Members and Non-Members of Cooperatives in Fluid Milk Markets* (Typescript, New Brunswick, 1966), pp. 1–5, 13, 23.

20. Howe, pp. 34–35, 68–69.

21. Alan A. Meredith, *Marketing Eggs in New Jersey* (New Brunswick, 1957), pp. 1–6, 18–20; interview with Alan A. Meredith, College of Agriculture and Environmental Science, Rutgers University; Fabian, passim.

22. United States Department of Agriculture, *Farmer Cooperatives in the United States,* pp. 128, 134.

23. Chastina Gardner, *Beginnings of Cooperative Fruit and Vegetable Marketing* (Washington, 1928), pp. 1–2.

24. Howe, pp. 34–40, 60–68.

25. Warren D. Oley, *Marketing New Jersey Fruits and Vegetables* (Trenton, 1930), pp. 25–27 and *Producers' Auction Markets in New Jersey* (Trenton, 1932), pp. 19–22.

26. Edwin W. Cooke, *Operation of Small-Lot Country Fruit and Vegetable Auctions* (Washington, 1936), pp. 9–10, 24.

27. United States Department of Agriculture, *Statistics of Farmer Cooperatives, 1964–65* (Washington, 1967), pp. 4, 18; Fabian, passim.

28. Pitt and Hoagland, pp. 511–13.

29. New Jersey Department of Agriculture, *New Jersey Agricultural Statistics, 1969,* p. 47.

30. *Hunterdon County Democrat,* Feb. 24, 1971.

31. Ibid., Aug. 15, 1968.

32. New Jersey Farm Bureau, *Safeguard Your Future with a Farm Bureau Membership in 1970,* p. 3.

33. "Farmland Assessment Act," Chapter 48, *Laws of 1964, State of New Jersey; Fourth Report of the State Farmland Evaluation Advisory Committee* (Trenton, 1967); John M. Hunter, "Farmland Assessment," *American Agriculturist and Rural New Yorker,* February 1971; interviews with John M. Hunter, Specialist in Agricultural Policy, College of Agriculture and Environmental Science, Rutgers University, and William G. McIntyre, Hunterdon County Senior Agricultural Agent.

CHAPTER 15

1. *Hunterdon County Democrat,* Dec. 30, 1915.

2. Schmidt, *Rural Hunterdon,* p. 149.

3. Sources used in this chapter were too numerous and diversified to chronicle fully. Files of county newspapers and of farm magazines were useful. An invaluable feature for recent developments found in the latter has been the monthly page or pages by Amos Kirby, New Jersey editor of *The American Agriculturist and Rural New Yorker.* Several publications of the New Jersey Department of Agriculture were used, and in particular the annual report, *New Jersey Agricultural Statistics.* A very useful chapter on the new machines is printed in New Jersey Farm Bureau and College of Agriculture and Environmental Science, Rutgers University, *1967 Yearbook of New Jersey Agriculture.*

4. Pitt and Hoagland, pp. 502–3.

5. New Jersey Department of Agriculture, *New Jersey Agricultural Statistics, 1969,* p. 57.

6. United States Census of Agriculture, 1964.

7. New Jersey Farm Bureau and College of Agriculture and Environmental Science, Rutgers University, *1967 Yearbook of New Jersey Agriculture,* p. 24.

8. New Jersey Farm Bureau, *Safeguard Your Investment with a Farm Bureau Membership in 1970,* p. 3.

9. Amos Kirby in *The American Agriculturist and Rural New Yorker,* December 1971 and March 1972.

10. New Jersey Farm Bureau and College of Agriculture and Environmental Science, Rutgers University, *1967 Yearbook of New Jersey Agriculture,* p. 26.

CHAPTER 16

1. Except where otherwise stated, statistics in this chapter are taken from the summary by Pitt and Hoagland, from United States census figures, or from New Jersey Department of Agriculture series, *New Jersey Agricultural Statistics.*

2. New Jersey Department of Agriculture, *New Jersey Equine Survey* (Trenton, 1961), p. 4 et passim; *New Jersey Equine Industry News* (Trenton), vol. 3, no. 4 (Winter, 1971), p. 1.

3. Waller, p. 78.

4. Information given by Dr. William L. Park, College of Agriculture and Environmental Science, Rutgers University; *New York Times,* Mar. 29, 1968.

5. Gordon Conklin, "Stainless Steel Cows," *American Agriculturist,* January 1968, p. 6.

6. See Schmidt, *Rural Hunterdon,* pp. 158–59.

7. *Hunterdon County Democrat,* Sept. 20, 1923.

8. Ibid., Dec. 13, 1934, Oct. 14, 1937.

9. New Jersey Department of Agriculture, *1968 Commercial Egg and Poultry Survey in New Jersey* (Trenton, 1969), pp. 4–5.

10. See note 1, this chapter.

CHAPTER 17

1. Unless otherwise indicated, statistics and comparisons in this chapter are taken from or computed from reports given in Pitt and Hoagland, in United States censuses, and in the New Jersey Department of Agriculture series, *New Jersey Agricultural Statistics.*

2. Amos Kirby, "Changes in Farming," *American Agriculturist and Rural New Yorker,* November 1971, p. 18.

3. Carl W. Woodward, "The Tame Blueberry," MS, Carl W. Woodward Papers, Rutgers University Library, New Brunswick.

4. *American Agriculturist and Rural New Yorker,* March 1972, p. 24.

5. Amos Kirby, "Vegetable Innovations," ibid., June 1971, p. 10.

6. Ibid.

7. Arthur W. West in New Jersey Farm Bureau and College of Agriculture and Environmental Science, Rutgers University, *1967 Yearbook of New Jersey Agriculture,* p. 26.

8. Amos Kirby, "Changes in Farming," *American Agriculturist and Rural New Yorker,* November 1971, p. 18.

EPILOGUE

1. Willard H. Allen, "Agriculture in the State of New Jersey," Myers, II, 351–425.

2. New Jersey Department of Agriculture, *New Jersey Agricultural Statistics: 1945–1956* (a single volume); 1957–72 (annuals), passim.

3. New Jersey Department of Agriculture, flyer A1403 (Trenton, 1972).

4. *Hunterdon County Democrat,* Jan. 18, Feb. 22, 1973.

5. New Jersey Farm Bureau and College of Agriculture and Environmental Science, Rutgers University, *1970 Yearbook of New Jersey Agriculture,* p. 5.

6. Arthur H. West in New Jersey Farm Bureau and College of Agriculture and Environmental Science, Rutgers University, *1967 Yearbook of New Jersey Agriculture,* p. 26.

7. New Jersey Farm Bureau and College of Agriculture and Environmental Science, Rutgers University, *1970 Yearbook of New Jersey Agriculture,* pp. 2–28.

8. *Hunterdon County Democrat,* May 7, 1970, p. 22.

9. New Jersey Department of Agriculture, news release, Sept. 13, 1971; Phillip Alampi, New Jersey Secretary of Agriculture, to Hubert G. Schmidt, May 25, 1972.

Bibliography

PRIMARY SOURCES

I. Manuscripts and Typescripts

Anderson and Welles, general store, New Hampton. Daybooks, 1865–68, 2 vols. Rutgers University Library, New Brunswick.

Atkinson and Johnson, general store, Flemington. Daybook, 1793–94. Hunterdon County Historical Society, Flemington.

Atkinson, Asher, general store, Flemington. Daybook, 1820–29. Hunterdon County Historical Society, Flemington.

Berkaw, Bergun, mill, Readington. Daybook, 1812–51. Rutgers University Library, New Brunswick.

Blackwell Collection. Correspondence, personal papers, and accounts of Blackwell family, 1820–70. Hunterdon County Historical Society, Flemington.

Blackwell, James H., Blackwell's Mills (Flemington Junction). Farm diary, 1843–66. Hunterdon County Historical Society, Flemington.

Bonnell, Elmer E., Clinton. Farm diary, 1878–95. In possession of Miss Ella M. Haver, R.D. 1, Annandale, New Jersey.

Bonnell Papers. Correspondence and personal papers of Elmer E. Bonnell, Clinton, 1849–1902. In possession of Miss Ella M. Haver, R.D. 1, Annandale, New Jersey.

Bowne, Dr. John, Bowne Station. Daybook, 1814–18; ledgers, 1801–34. Personal, farm, and medical accounts. Hunterdon County Historical Society, Flemington.

Brunner, Peter, Readington. Justice of the peace docket, 1780–88. Rutgers University Library, New Brunswick.

Burrough, James, Hopewell. Farm account book, 1833–50. Rutgers University Library, New Brunswick.

Bush, E. T., "Croton and Vicinity." Personal recollections, 1896. Hunterdon County Historical Society, Flemington.

Capner, J., and Capner, J. Q., general store, Flemington. Daybooks, 1834–39. Hunterdon County Historical Society, Flemington.

Capner, John H., Flemington. Personal accounts and daybook, 1840. Hunterdon County Historical Society, Flemington.

Capner, Thomas, estate, Flemington. Cash book, 1832. Hunterdon County Historical Society, Flemington.

Capner Collection. Correspondence, personal papers and accounts of Capner family, relatives, and friends, England and United States, 1750–1846. Hunterdon County Historical Society.

Case Tannery, Flemington. Daybooks, ledgers, hide books, bark books, and other tannery, farm, and personal accounts, 1783–1851. Hunterdon County Historical Society, Flemington.

Choyce, Richard, Flemington. Records of fulling and weaving shop and farm, interspersed with narrative, circa 1810. Hunterdon County Historical Society, Flemington.

Cole, Ezekial, Readington. Justice of the peace dockets, 1790–1804. Rutgers University Library, New Brunswick.

Compton, Rebecca, and William Birch, Hunterdon County. Rental agreement, 1811. Hunterdon County Historical Society, Flemington.

Cook, George H., New Brunswick. Geology field notebooks, 1855–69. Rutgers University Library, New Brunswick.

Deats, Case and Company, machine shop and foundry, Pittstown. Daybook, 1869–74. Hunterdon County Historical Society, Flemington.

Deats Collection. Correspondence, personal papers, and accounts of Deats family, 1832–1940, Stockton, Quakertown, Pittstown, and Flemington. Hunterdon County Historical Society, Flemington.

Deats, H. E., Flemington. Farm account books, 1910–30. Hunterdon County Historical Society, Flemington.

Deats, Hiram, machine shop and foundry, Quakertown. Daybooks, 1831–40. Hunterdon County Historical Society, Flemington.

Delaware Valley Farmers' and Mechanics' Agricultural Society. Account book, 1877–81. Hunterdon County Historical Society, Flemington.

Distillery, Tewksbury Township, Hunterdon County. Ledger, 1825–27. Hunterdon County Historical Society, Flemington.

Emley Papers. Accounts, surveyor's records, agent's accounts, and personal papers of John Emley, Kingwood, 1750–70. Rutgers University Library, New Brunswick.

Fabian, Morris S., Directory of Farm Cooperatives in New Jersey. New Brunswick, 1966. College of Agriculture and Environmental Science, Rutgers University, New Brunswick.

Flemington Vigilant Society. Minute books, 1822–83. Hunterdon County Historical Society, Flemington.

General store, Amwell Township, Hunterdon County. Daybook, 1798–99. Hunterdon County Historical Society, Flemington.

General store, Annandale. Daybook, 1880–83. Rutgers University Library, New Brunswick.

General store, Clinton. Daybook, 1865. Hunterdon County Historical Society, Flemington.

General store, Jacksonville (Lebanon). Daybooks, 1829–32. Hunterdon County Historical Society, Flemington.

General store, New Germantown (Oldwick). Daybook, 1815–21. Rutgers University Library, New Brunswick.

General store or stores, Flemington. Daybook, 1793–94, 1855–56. Hunterdon County Historical Society, Flemington.

General store, Whitehouse. Ledger, 1771–72. Hunterdon County Historical Society, Flemington.

Hall, John. "Jno. Halls Book, 1779." This diary is the work of two men, John Hall and his nephew, John Hall Capner. The first part was written by John Hall in England, the second after a gap of several years by his nephew following their emigration. It has irregular entries to 1807. Hunterdon County Historical Society, Flemington.

Hankinson family commonplace book, 1787–1842. Rutgers University Library, New Brunswick.

Haward, Peter, Flemington. Excerpts from diary, May 14–Nov. 11, 1804. Hunterdon County Historical Society, Flemington.

Holcombe, Samuel, general store, Mount Airy. Daybooks, 1824–32, 1868–71. Hunterdon County Historical Society, Flemington.

Hunterdon County Agricultural Society. Minutes, 1856–77; premium awards, 1878–84. Hunterdon County Historical Society, Flemington.

Hunterdon County Board of Agriculture. Minutes, 1915–70. Hunterdon County Board of Agriculture, Flemington.

Janeway and Broughton general store, Raritan Landing. Daybook, 1735–47. Rutgers University Library, New Brunswick.

Lambert, John. "John Lambert's Almanack or Account Book, 1774." Personal observations and mill and store records, entered in a copy of *Aitken's General American Register and Calendar for the Year, 1774.* Hunterdon County Historical Society, Flemington.

Larison, George H. "Last Primitive Houses Near Howell's Ferry." Personal recollections, circa 1890. Hunterdon County Historical Society, Flemington.

Lauderdale, Thomas, Mount Airy. Farm account books, 1876–95. Hunterdon County Historical Society, Flemington.

Lauderdale, William, Jr., Mount Airy. Farm account books, 1911–51. Hunterdon County Historical Society, Flemington.

Lequear, J. W. "Flax Culture and Manufacture." Hunterdon County Historical Society, Flemington.

Lippincott, William C., Little Silver. Farm diary, 1868. Rutgers University Library, New Brunswick.

Moore, George W., Cumberland County. Farm diary, 1853–77. Rutgers University Library, New Brunswick.

Moore, John, Hunterdon County. Memorandum book, 1800–34. Hunterdon County Historical Society, Flemington.

Moriscot Farm, North Branch. Workbook, 1903. Rutgers University Library, New Brunswick.

"Mowing and Harvesting." Account book of unidentified farmer, 1827. Hunterdon County Historical Society, Flemington.

Neilson, James, Jr., New Brunswick. Farm diary, 1862–70. Rutgers University Library, New Brunswick.

Parker, James, Shipley (near Pittstown). Farm diary, 1778–83. Rutgers University Library, New Brunswick.

Race Papers. Correspondence and papers of Dr. Henry Race, Pittstown, 1820–60. Hunterdon County Historical Society, Flemington.

Readington Reformed Church. "Mementoes for the One Hundred and Seventy-Fifth Anniversary." Scrapbook, 1894. Rutgers University Library, New Brunswick.

Shoemaker located in turn at Cherryville, Raritan, and Rowland's Mills. Daybooks, 1854–98. Hunterdon County Historical Society, Flemington.

Smith and Bowman, general store, Jacksonville (Lebanon). Ledger, 1832–33. Rutgers University Library, New Brunswick.

Smith, W. R., general store, Jacksonville (Lebanon). Daybooks, 1828–29. Rutgers University Library, New Brunswick.

Ten Eyck, James, Jr., North Branch. Farm diary, 1802–24. Rutgers University Library, New Brunswick.

Ten Eyck, James, Sr., North Branch. Farm diary, 1787–1809. Rutgers University Library, New Brunswick.

Ten Eyck, John, North Branch. Farm diary, 1853–77. Rutgers University Library, New Brunswick.

Ten Eyck, Tunis, North Branch. Farm diary, 1877–93. Rutgers University Library, New Brunswick.

Thompson, Aaron J., Three Bridges. Diary, 1902–21. Rutgers University Library, New Brunswick.

Thompson, John Bodine, Readington. Correspondence and diary, 1843–52, 1857–59. Rutgers University Library, New Brunswick.

Voorhees, David C., Blawenburg. Farm diary, 1875. Rutgers University Library, New Brunswick.

Voorhees, Peter A., Somerset County. Farm diary, 1847–83. Rutgers University Library, New Brunswick.

Voorhees, Ralph, Somerset County. Farm diary, 1860. Rutgers University, New Brunswick.

II. Books and Pamphlets

Abstract or An Abbreviation of Some Few of the Many (Later and Former) Testimonys from the Inhabitants of New Jersey . . . , An. London, 1681.

Acrelius, Israel. *A History of New Sweden.* Trans. by W. M. Reynolds. Philadelphia, 1874; first published in Stockholm, 1759.

Aitken's General American Register and Calendar, for the Year 1774. Philadelphia, 1774.

American Husbandry. Ed. by H. J. Carman. New York, 1939; first published in London, 1775.

Anburey, Thomas. *Travels Through the Interior Parts of America.* 2 vols. London, 1791.

Barnum, H. L. *The American Farrier.* Philadelphia, 1832.

Brachen, Henry. *Farriery Improved*. London, 1785.

Brief Account of the Province of East-New-Jarsey in America Published by the Scots Proprietors Having Interest There, A. Edinburgh, 1683.

Bucks County (Pennsylvania) Historical Society. Easton, Pa. *A Collection of Papers Read Before the Bucks County Historical Society.* I (1908), II (1909), III (1909), IV (1917), V (1926), VI (1932), VII (1937), VIII (1940).

Budd, Thomas. *Good Order Established in New Jersey in America*. New York, 1865; first published in London in 1685.

Buel, Jesse. *The Farmers Companion*. Boston, 1839.

Burnaby, Andrew. *Travels Through the Middle Settlements in North America*. London, 1775.

Büttner, Johann Karl. *Narratives of Johann Carl Buettner in the American Revolution*. New York, 1915; first published in Kamenz, Germany, 1828.

Cazenove, Théophile. *Cazenove Journal, 1794*. Trans. and ed. by R. W. Kelsey. Haverford, Pa., 1922.

Conway, M. D. *The Life of Thomas Paine*. 3 vols. New York, 1892. Contains long quotations from the diary of John Hall, now lost.

Cook, George H. *Geology of New Jersey*. Newark, 1868.

Cox, William A. *A View of the Cultivation of Fruit Trees and the Management of Orchards and Cider . . . .* Philadelphia, 1817.

Crèvecœur, J. Hector St. John de. *Letters of an American Farmer . . .* London, 1782.

——. *Sketches of Eighteenth Century America . . .* Ed. by H. L. Bourdin and others. New Haven, 1925.

Danckaerts, Jasper. *Journal of Jasper Danckaerts, 1679–1680*. Trans. by Henry C. Murphy for original printing, Brooklyn, 1876. Ed. by Bartlett Burleigh James and J. Franklin Jameson. New York, 1913; reprinted, 1959.

Demaree, Albert Lowther. *The American Agricultural Press, 1819–1860*. New York, 1941.

Furman, Moore. *Letters of Moore Furman*. New York, 1912.

Further Account of the Province of East-New-Jersey in an Abstract of Letters Lately Writ from Thence by Several Inhabitants There Resident. London, 1676.

Gordon, Thomas F. *A Gazeteer of the State of New Jersey*. Trenton, 1834.

Hughes, Thomas. *A Journal by Thomas Hughes, 1778–79*. Cambridge, England, 1947.

Jameson, J. Franklin, ed. *Narratives of New Netherland, 1609–1664*. New York, 1909.

Juet, Robert. *Robert Juet's Journal, The Voyage of the "Half Moon."* Newark, 1959.

Kalm, Peter. *The America of 1750; Travels in North America*. Ed. by A. B. Benson. New York, 1937; first English version, London, 1770.

Messler, Abraham. *Forty Years at Raritan; Eight Memorial Sermons with Notes for a History of the Dutch Reformed Churches in Somerset County, New Jersey*. New York, 1873.

Moreau, D. H., ed. *Traditions of Hunterdon*. Flemington, 1957. Moreau attributed probable authorship to John W. Lequear, as did I in my book *Rural Hunterdon* in 1946. Later research has proved that the author of the columns in the *Hunterdon Republican* reprinted in this book was Jacob McGill.

[Morris, Edmund]. *Ten Acres Enough: A Practical Experience Showing How a Very Small Farm May Be Made to Keep a Very Large Family*. New York, 1864.

Morse, Jedidiah. *The American Universal Geography*. 2 vols. Boston, 1796. Revised ed., 1 vol., Boston, 1819.

Myers, Albert Cook, ed. *Narratives of Early Pennsylvania, West New Jersey, and Delaware, 1630–1707*. New York, 1912.

New Jersey Department of Agriculture. *Duties and Functions of the New Jersey Department of Agriculture*. Trenton, 1967.

———. *New Jersey Agriculture Fairs, 1967*. Trenton, 1967.

Roberts, Job. *The Pennsylvania Farmer*. Philadelphia, 1804.

Schoepf, J. D. *Travels in the Confederation, 1783–1784*. Trans. by A. J. Morrison. Philadelphia, 1911.

Scot, George. *The Model of the Government of the Province of East-New-Jersey in America*. Edinburgh, 1685.

Stillwell, J. L. *Old Readington, 1867–1876*. Somerville, 1935.

Studley, Miriam V., ed. *Historic New Jersey Through Visitors' Eyes*. Princeton, 1964.

Thomas, Gabriel. *An Historical and Geographical Account of the Province and Country of Pensilvania and of West-New-Jersey in America*. New York, 1848; first published in London, 1698.

Volney, F. *A View of the Soil and Climate of the United States of America*. Trans. by C. B. Brown. Philadelphia, 1804.

Woodward, Carl R. *Ploughs and Politicks: Charles Read of New Jersey and His Notes on Agriculture, 1715–1774*. New Brunswick, 1941.

III. Documents

Allison, Samuel, compiler. *Acts of the General Assembly of the Province of New Jersey, 1702–1776*. Burlington, 1776.

Elmer, L. Q. C. *A Digest of the Laws of New Jersey*. Bridgeton, 1838.

Hopewell, New Jersey. *Town Records of Hopewell, New Jersey*. New York, 1931. Records of Hopewell Township, 1721–99, and of Hopewell Baptist Church, 1749–1849.

Hunterdon County Clerk, Flemington. Deed record books.

Leaming, Aaron, and Spicer, Jacob, compilers. *The Grants, Concessions, and Original Constitutions of the Provinces of New Jersey, the Acts Passed during the Proprietary Government and Other Material Transactions before the Surrender Thereof to Queen Anne*. Philadelphia, circa 1751.

Nevill, Samuel, compiler. *The Acts of the General Assembly of the Province of New Jersey*. Philadelphia, 1752, and Woodbridge, 1761. 2 vols.

New Jersey. *Annual Statements of the Several Banks of the State of New Jersey*. Trenton, 1849.

———. *Archives of the State of New Jersey*. Newark, Paterson, Somerville, and Trenton, 1880–1944.

———. *Business Review of the Counties of Hunterdon, Morris and Somerset, New Jersey*. Philadelphia, 1891.

———. Census of 1850, local schedules. New Jersey State Library.

———. *State of New Jersey. Census of 1915*. Union Hill, 1916.

———. *State of New Jersey. Compendium of Censuses, 1726–1905, Together with the Tabulated Returns of 1905, and the Federal Census of 1910*. Trenton, 1910.

New Jersey Department of Agriculture. Annual reports, 1916–71.

———. *New Jersey Agricultural Statistics: 1945–1956;* and annuals, 1957–71.

———. *New Jersey Equine Survey*. Trenton, 1961.

———. *1968 Commercial Egg and Poultry Survey in New Jersey*. Trenton, 1969.

———. *Statistical Handbook of New Jersey Agriculture*. Trenton, 1929.

———. *Tabulated Returns of 1905, and the Federal Census of 1910*. Trenton, 1910.

New Jersey Secretary of State. Deed record books. Deeds and probate records, including wills, inventories, records of vendues, reports of executors, and so forth.

New Jersey State Grange. *Journal of Proceedings, Ninety-Third Annual Session, 1965*.

———. *Proceedings of the Thirty-Fourth Annual Session of the State Grange in New Jersey*. Flemington, 1906.

———. *Roster of State, Pomona, and Subordinate Granges of the State Grange, 1966*. Annual publication, place not given.

New Jersey Statutes, 1776–1970. Commonly called "Session Laws."

New-York Historical Society. *Collections*. 2d ser., I (Albany, 1841); II (Albany, 1849).

New York (State). *Documents Relative to the Colonial History of New-York*. Vol. XII, *Documents Relating to the Dutch and Swedish Settlers on the Delaware River*. Albany, 1877.

———. *Documentary History of the State of New-York*. 3 vols. Albany, 1849–1850.

Paterson, William, compiler, *Laws of the State of New Jersey*. Newark, 1800.

Pitt, Dimitry T., and Hoagland, Lewis P., compilers. *New Jersey Agriculture: Historical Facts and Figures*. Trenton, 1943.

United States Census, 1790–1970. Various reports.

IV. Periodicals

American Agriculturist. Ithaca, New York, 1939–72.

American Historical Review. No. 37 (October 1931), pp. 65–88.

Daily True American. New Brunswick, 1860–88. Rutgers University Library, New Brunswick.

Democrat. Flemington, 1866–67. Hunterdon County Historical Society, Flemington and Hall of Records, Flemington.

Democrat-Advertiser. Flemington, 1881–1926. Incomplete files. Hunterdon County Historical Society, Flemington.

Federalist and New Jersey Gazette. Trenton, 1796–1802. New Jersey State Library, Trenton.

Freehold Transcript. Clippings, 1929. Rutgers University Library, New Brunswick.

Home Visitor. Flemington, 1885–1902. Only occasional copies and clippings available. Hunterdon County Historical Society, Flemington.

Hunterdon County Democrat. Flemington, 1867–1972. Hunterdon County Historical Society, Flemington.

Hunterdon Democrat. Flemington, 1838–66. Hunterdon County Historical Society, Flemington.

Hunterdon Gazette. Flemington, 1825–67. Hunterdon County Historical Society, Flemington.

Hunterdon Independent. Frenchtown, 1878–90. Clippings, 1893–97. Hunterdon County Historical Society, Flemington.

Hunterdon Republican. Flemington, 1856–1944. Incomplete files, Hunterdon County Historical Society, Flemington.

Jerseyman. Hightstown and Flemington, 1891–1905. Hunterdon County Historical Society, Flemington.

Lambertville Press. Lambertville, 1858–61. Hunterdon County Historical Society, Flemington.

Lambertville Record. Clipping, 1891. Hunterdon County Historical Society, Flemington.

Milford Leader. Clippings. Dec. 2, 1897–Feb. 10, 1898. Hunterdon County Historical Society, Flemington.

New Jersey Agriculture. New Brunswick, 1925–72. Rutgers University Library, New Brunswick.

New Jersey Medical Society, *Journal,* Trenton, Vol. XXXIV (1937).

New York Times. New York, 1932–72.

Our Home. Somerville, I (1873). Only one volume was published.

Papers and Proceedings. 1902–23. Bergen County Historical Society, Hackensack.

Proceedings. 1847–1972. New Jersey Historical Society, Newark.

Ringos (A Monthly Magazine Devoted to the History of Ringos—Past and Present—and to the Current News of the Village and Vicinity). Vol. I, Ringoes, 1889–90.

Somerset County Historical Quarterly. 8 vols. Somerville, 1912–19.

SECONDARY MATERIALS

I. Pamphlets, Typescripts, and Articles

"Account of the Minisink Indians." Rutgers University Library, New Brunswick, n.d.

App, Frank. *County Boards of Agriculture.* Trenton, 1964.

Blair, A. W. *The Agricultural Value of Greensand Marl.* Circular 61, New Jersey Agricultural Experiment Station. New Brunswick, 1966.

Brush, John. "The History of Piscataway Township." Rutgers University Library, New Brunswick, 1966.

Century of the Princeton Agricultural Association, 1867–1967, A. New Brunswick, 1967.

Clement, John, ed. *Notes and Memoranda Relating to the West New Jersey Society of West New Jersey.* Camden, 1880.

Cooke, Edwin W. *Operation of Small-Lot Country Fruit and Vegetable Auctions.* Washington, 1936.

Cooperative Grange League Federation. *Farmers Together: The Story of G.L.F.* N.p., 1959.

Ewain, N. R. *Early Brickmaking in the Colonies.* Camden, 1938.

Gardner, Chastina. Beginnings of Cooperative Fruit and Vegetable Marketing. Washington, 1928.

Hammond, D. S. *Early Land Ownership in North Hunterdon County.* Hunterdon County Historical Society, Flemington, n.d.

Hough, George A. *A Brief History of the Princeton Agricultural Association.* Trenton, 1949.

Howe, Charles B. *Farmers' Cooperation in New Jersey, 1926.* New Brunswick, 1928.

Larison, C. W. *The Ancient Village of Amwell.* Flemington, 1916.

Lee, Lynwood L. "Survey of New Jersey." 1965. Rutgers University Library, New Brunswick.

Meredith, Alan A. *Marketing Eggs in New Jersey.* New Brunswick, 1957.

New Jersey Department of Agriculture. *Fertile Furrow . . . 50 Miles Long: The Grassroots Government of New Jersey Agriculture.* Trenton, 1966.

———. *Garden State Agricultural Trends.* Trenton, 1971.

———. *Highlights of the 1968–69 Annual Report.* Trenton, 1969.

———. *Idle Farms in Hunterdon County, New Jersey.* Trenton, 1932.

———. *New Jersey Farm Facts.* Trenton, 1971.

New Jersey Farm Bureau. *Safeguard Your Investment with a Farm Bureau Membership in 1970.* Trenton, 1970.

New Jersey: Its Cities, Towns and Railroads, Together with Descriptions of New Jersey Real Estate Offered for Sale by A. D. Mellick, Jr. and Bro., No. 6 Pine Street, New York. New York, 1873.

Oley, Warren D. *Marketing New Jersey Fruits and Vegetables.* Trenton, 1930.

———. *Producers' Auction Markets in New Jersey.* Trenton, 1932.

Park, William L. "Market Wide vs. Handler Pooling under the Delaware Valley Milk Marketing Order." Library, College of Agriculture and Environmental Science, Rutgers University, New Brunswick, 1967.

———. "Relationship Between Members and Non-Members of Cooperatives in Fluid Milk Markets." Library, College of Agriculture and Environmental Science, Rutgers University, New Brunswick, 1966.

———. "Should the Nearby Formula under Order 2 Be Changed?" Library, College of Agriculture and Environmental Science, Rutgers University, New Brunswick, 1965.

Patrick, A. L., and others. *Soil Survey of the Belvidere Area, New Jersey.* Washington, D.C., 1920.

———. *Soil Survey of the Bernardsville Area, New Jersey.* Washington, D.C., 1923.

Quackenbush, Granville A. *Our New Jersey Land.* New Brunswick, 1955.

Robertson, Elmer. *The Centre Bridge.* Flemington, 1928.

Schillon, Charles J. "An Economic History of the Delaware Division Canal." 1969. Rutgers University Library, New Brunswick.

Schmidt, Hubert G. *Flax Culture in Hunterdon County, New Jersey*. Flemington, 1939.

———. "Germans in Colonial New Jersey. *American-German Review*. June–July 1958. pp. 4–7.

———. *Slavery and Attitudes on Slavery in Hunterdon County, New Jersey*. Somerville, 1941.

Sim, R. J. *Some Vanishing Phases of Rural Life in New Jersey*. New Jersey Department of Agriculture, Circular 327, Trenton, 1945.

Sinclair, Jesse. "Early Settlers of Holland Township." Flemington, n.d. Hunterdon County Historical Society, Flemington.

Spargo, William C. *My 57 Years in Farm Bureau*. Trenton, 1967.

Spencer, Leland. *Cooperative Organization of Producers in the New York Milkshed*. Ithaca, N.Y., 1953.

Spencer, Leland, and Christensen, S. Kent. *Milk Control Programs of the Northeastern States*. Ithaca, N.Y., 1958.

Stamets, Cora W. "History of Ringoes Grange." 1933. Hunterdon County Historical Society, Flemington.

State Farmland Evaluation Advisory Committee. *Fourth Report of the State Farmland Advisory Committee*. Trenton, 1967.

Strobeck, Ernest C. *The Development of Cooperative Milk Marketing in the New Jersey Milkshed*. Syracuse, N.Y., 1954.

Vail, M. C. *History of Land Titles in the Vicinity of Quakertown*, New Jersey. Flemington, 1915.

Vassar, T. E. *Three-Fourths of a Century Reviewed*. Flemington, 1873.

II. Books

Anderson, J. A. *Navigation of the Upper Delaware*. Trenton, 1913.

Bailey, L. H., ed. *Cyclopedia of American Agriculture*. 4 vols. New York, 1909.

Barber, J. W., and Howe, Henry. *Historical Collections of the State of New Jersey . . . with Geographical Descriptions of Every Township in the State*. New York, 1844.

Beer, G. L. *British Colonial Policy, 1754–1765*. New York, 1907.

Bidwell, P. W., and Falconer, J. I. *History of Agriculture in the Northern United States, 1620–1860*. Washington, 1925.

Bittinger, L. F. *The Germans in Colonial Times*. Philadelphia, 1901.

Blane, John. *History of the District Medical Society for the County of Hunterdon from Its Organization in 1821 to the Annual Meeting in 1871; Together with the Medical History of the County (As Its Boundaries Now Exist), from Its First Settlement to the Present Time, 1872*. Newark, 1872.

Blowe, Daniel. *A Geographical, Historical, Commercial, and Agricultural View of the United States, Forming a Complete Emigrant's Directory Through Every Part of the Republic*. London, 1820.

Boer, L. P. de, ed. *The Sutphen Family*. New York, 1926.

Bond, B. W., Jr. *The Quit-Rent System in the American Colonies*. New Haven, 1910.

Boyer, C. S. *Early Forges and Furnaces in New Jersey*. Philadelphia, 1931.

Brodhead, John R. *History of the State of New York*. New York, 1853.

Burtt-Davy, Joseph. *Maize*. London, 1914.

Carman, Harry J., ed. *Jesse Buel, Agricultural Reformer*. New York, 1947.

Carrier, Lyman. *The Beginnings of Agriculture in America*. New York, 1923.

Casson, H. N. *Romance of the Reaper*. New York, 1902.

Chambers, T. F. *The Early Germans of New Jersey*. Dover, New Jersey, 1895.

Chastellux, François Jean. *Travels in North America in the Years 1780, 1781, and 1782*. Trans. by G. Grieve. London, 1787.

Clayton, W. Woodford. *History of Union and Middlesex Counties . . . New Jersey*. Philadelphia, 1882.

Clement, John. *Historical Sketches Relating to Early Settlements in West New Jersey*. N.p., n.d.

Converse, C. S. *History of the United First Presbyterian Church* of Amwell, N.J. Trenton, 1881.

Cooley, H. S. *Slavery in New Jersey*. Baltimore, 1896.

Curtler, W. H. R. *A Short History of English Agriculture*. Oxford, 1909.

Cushing, Thomas, and Sheppard, Charles E. *History of the Counties of Gloucester, Salem, and Cumberland Counties, New Jersey . . .* Philadelphia, 1886.

Demaree, Albert Lowther. *The American Agricultural Press*. New York, 1941.

Demarest, William H. S. *A History of Rutgers College, 1766–1924*. New Brunswick, 1924.

Ege, Ralph. *Pioneers of Old Hopewell*. Hopewell, 1908.

Ellis, Franklin. *History of Monmouth County, New Jersey*. Philadelphia, 1885.

Fargo, C. B. *The Story of the Delaware Valley*. Frenchtown, 1936.

Faust, A. B. *The German Element in the United States*. 2 vols. New York, 1909.

Flink, Salomon V., and others. *The Economy of New Jersey*. New Brunswick, 1958.

Gilbert, A. W. *The Potato*. New York, 1917.

[Halsey, E. D.] *History of Morris County, New Jersey*. New York, 1882.

Hixson, Richard F. *Isaac Collins, A Quaker Printer in 18th Century America*. New Brunswick, 1968.

Hunt, T. F. *Cereals in America*. New York, 1914.

Johnson, Amandus. *The Swedish Settlements on the Delaware*. 2 vols. Philadelphia, 1911.

Kaempffert, Waldemar, ed. *Popular History of American Invention*. 2 vols. New York, 1924.

Kemmerer, D. L. *Path to Freedom*. Princeton, 1940.

Kugler, J. B. *History of the First English Presbyterian Church in Amwell*. Somerville, 1912.

Kuhlmann, C. B. *Development of the Flour Milling Industry in the United States*. New York, 1929.

Kull, I. S., ed. *New Jersey: A History*. 6 vols. New York, 1930–32.

Lane, W. J. *From Indian Trail to Iron Horse*. Princeton, 1939.

Larison, C. W. *A Sketch of the Fisher Family of Old Amwell Township in Hunterdon County, New Jersey*. Ringoes, N.J., 1890.

Lee, F. B. *New Jersey as a Colony and as a State*. 4 vols. New York, 1903.

Leiby, Adrian C. *The Early Dutch and Swedish Settlers of New Jersey*. Princeton, 1964.

Leiby, Adrian C.; Klybert, Albert T.; and Leiby, Emorie A. *The Huguenot Settlement of Schraalenburgh*. Rahway, 1964.

Ludlum, David M. *Early American Hurricanes, 1492–1870*. Boston, 1963.

———. *Early American Winters, 1604–1820*. Boston, 1966.

Madeira, C. C., Jr. *The Delaware and Raritan Canal*. East Orange, 1941.

McCormick, Richard P. *New Jersey from Colony to State, 1609–1789*. Princeton, 1964.

———. *Rutgers: A Bicentennial History*. New Brunswick, 1966.

Mellick, A. D., Jr. *Story of an Old Farm*. Somerville, 1889.

Miles, Manly. *Silos, Ensilage and Silage*. New York, 1889.

Mott, G. S. *History of the Presbyterian Church in Flemington, N.J., with Sketches of Local Matters for Two Hundred Years*. New York, 1894.

Myers, William Starr, ed. and author in part. *The Story of New Jersey*. 5 vols. New York, 1945.

Nelson, William. *Indians of New Jersey*. Paterson, 1894.

New Jersey Department of Agriculture. *Commercial Egg and Poultry Survey in New Jersey*. Trenton, 1968.

New Jersey Farm Bureau in cooperation with the College of Agriculture and Environmental Science, Rutgers University. *Yearbooks of New Jersey Agriculture*. Trenton, 1967–70.

Opdyke, C. W. *The Op Dyke Genealogy*. Albany, 1889.

Osgood, H. L. *The American Colonies in the Eighteenth Century*. New York, 1924.

Pocket Farrier or Farmers' Receipt Book. Boston, 1840.

Pomfret, John E. *The Province of East New Jersey, 1607–1702*. Princeton, 1962.

———. *The Province of West New Jersey, 1607–1702*. Princeton, 1956.

Plumb, C. S. *Indian Corn Culture*. Chicago, 1908.

———. *Types and Breeds of Farm Animals*. Boston, 1920.

Prevost, Severo Mallet, compiler. *Historical Notes and Biographical Eketches Regarding the American Branch of the Mallet Family, 1794–1930*. New York, 1930.

Prothero, R. E. *English Farming Past and Present*. New York, 1927.

Prowell, George R. *The History of Camden County, New Jersey*. Philadelphia, 1886.

Quintance, H. W. *Influence of Farm Machinery on Production and Labor*. New York, 1904.

Rockefeller, H. O., ed. *Transactions of the Rockefeller Family Association for the Five Years, 1905–1909, with Genealogy*. New York, 1910.

Salter, Edwin. *History of Monmouth and Ocean Counties, . . . New Jersey*. Bayonne, 1890.

Sampson, A. W. *Native American Forage Plants*. New York, 1924.

Sanford, A. H. *The Story of Agriculture in the United States*. New York, 1916.

Schmidt, Hubert G. *Rural Hunterdon: An Agricultural History*. New Brunswick, 1946.

Schrabisch, Max. *Archaeology of Warren and Hunterdon Counties*. Trenton, 1917.

Schuyler, Hamilton. *A History of St. Michael's Church, 1719–1894*. Princeton, 1920.

Shaw, Thomas. *Soiling Crops and the Silo*. New York, 1904.

Shaw, William H. *History of Essex and Hudson Counties, New Jersey*. Philadelphia, 1884.

Sickler, Joseph S. *Old Homes of Salem County*. Salem, 1949.

Smith, Samuel. *History of the Colony of Nova-Caesaria or New-Jersey*. Ed. by W. S. Sharp. Trenton, 1877; originally published at Burlington, 1765.

Snell, James P. *History of Hunterdon and Somerset Counties, New Jersey* . . . Philadelphia, 1881.

Snell, James P., compiler. *History of Sussex and Warren Counties, New Jersey* . . . Philadelphia, 1881.

Stevens, Louis T. *The History of Cape May County, New Jersey*. Philadelphia, 1897.

Tanner, E. P. *The Province of New Jersey, 1664–1738*. New York, 1908.

Thompson, H. P. *History of the Reformed Church at Readington, N.J., 1719–1881*. New York, 1882.

United States Department of Agriculture. *Farmers' Cooperatives in the United States*. Washington, circa 1965.

Van Horn, J. H., compiler. *Historic Somerset*. New Brunswick, 1965.

Van Syckle, Emogene. *The Old York Road and Its Stage Coach Days*. Flemington, 1936.

Varlo, Charles. *A New System of Husbandry*. Philadelphia, 1785.

Waller, Ingrid Nelson. *Where There Is Vision: The New Jersey Agricultural Experiment Station*. New Brunswick, 1956.

Weatherwax, Paul. *Indian Corn Culture*. Chicago, 1923. Revised and reprinted as *Indian Corn in Old America*. New York, 1954.

Weiss, Harry B. *History of Applejack, or Apple Brandy, in New Jersey*. Trenton, 1954.

———. *History of the New Jersey Board of Agriculture*. Trenton, 1949.

———. *The New Jersey Department of Agriculture, 1916–1949*. Trenton, 1950.

———. *The New Jersey State Grange, Patrons of Husbandry, 1873–1954*. Trenton, 1955.

Weiss, Harry B., and Weiss, Grace M. *Early Brickmaking in New Jersey*. Trenton, 1966.

———. *The Early Promotional Literature of New Jersey*. Trenton, 1964.

Weiss, Harry B., and others. *The History of the New Jersey Agricultural Society*. Trenton, 1947.

Weslager, C. A. *The English on the Delaware*. New Brunswick, 1967.

———. *The Log Cabin in America from Pioneer Days to the Present*. New Brunswick, 1969.

Whitehead, William. *East New Jersey under the Proprietary Governments*. Newark, 1875.

Whitman, C. A. *Flax Culture*. Boston, 1888.

Widmer, Kemble. *The Geology and Geography of New Jersey*. Princeton, 1964.

Winfield, Charles H. *History of the County of Hudson, New Jersey*. New York, 1874.

Woodward, Carl R. *Agriculture in New Jersey*. New York, 1930.

———. *The Development of Agriculture in New Jersey, 1640–1880*. New Brunswick, 1927.

Woodward, Carl R., and Waller, Ingrid Nelson. *New Jersey's Agricultural Experiment Station, 1880–1930*. New Brunswick, 1932.

Woodward, E. M., and Hageman, John F. *History of Burlington and Mercer Counties, New Jersey* . . . Philadelphia, 1883.

Wuorinen, J. H. *The Finns on the Delaware, 1638–1655*. New York, 1938.

Index

Acrelius, Israel 28, 98

Adams Act 117, 195

Agricultural Adjustment Administration 224

Agricultural Experiment Station, *see* New Jersey Agricultural Experiment Station

agricultural extension programs 113, 114, 115, 117, 171, 195–98, 200, 204–05, 211

agricultural fairs, *see* fairs and exhibits

agricultural societies, *see* farm organizations

agriculture, courses in 113–17 passim, 195, 197, 198–99; *see also* agricultural extension programs; College of Agriculture

Agway, Inc. 212

Ahismus 25, 26

Alampi, Phillip 275

alfalfa 182, 200, 233, 239, 255, 257, 258

Allen, Willard H. 270

American Agriculturist 107

American Farmer 107

American Husbandry 60, 61–62, 75, 98, 126

Appalachian Valley and Ridge Province 7, 17–18, 19

applejack (apple whiskey, apple brandy, "Jersey lightning") 56, 65, 100, 121, 183, 184, 187; *see also* brandy

apples 45, 46, 47, 48, 51, 55–56, 99, 100, 101, 184–85, 200, 235, 260, 261; *see also* applejack; cider

apricots 99

artificial insemination, *see* livestock

ash, wood 24, 54, 63, 124–25

asparagus 98, 235, 238, 251, 267, 268, 269

Assunpink Creek 9

Atlantic County: agriculture and livestock 119, 156, 187, 206, 248, 249, 250, 259–65 passim

soil 10

automobiles 152, 194, 229, 231

Bailey, L. H.: *Cyclopedia of American Agriculture* 147

Bakewell, Robert 154, 160

barley 47, 50, 65, 89, 94, 174, 255–56

barns 74, 92, 93, 119–20, 230

barracks 44, 75, 92, 96, 97, 120, 230

Beans (Beanes), Captain 87

beans 23, 24, 45, 46, 50–51, 89, 98, 222, 235, 268, 269; *see also* lima beans; soybeans

beer and brewing 26, 47, 255, 256

bees and beekeeping 87–88, 94, 223

beets 45, 98, 145, 267, 268

Belcher, Jonathan 81

Belle Mead Farmers' Co-Operative Association 212

Belvidere 99, 111

ABOUT THE AUTHOR

Hubert G. Schmidt is professor of history at the Newark campus of Rutgers University. He is the author of *Rural Hunterdon: An Agricultural History* and of three books on the economy of Germany during Allied occupation. He is also the editor of *The Old Farm* by Andrew D. Mellick, Jr., and *George Washington's Map Maker: A Biography of Robert Erskine* by Albert H. Heusser.